BILL CLINTON ON STUMP, STATE, AND STAGE

BILL CLINTON ON STUMP, STATE, AND STAGE

The Rhetorical Road to the White House

STEPHEN A. SMITH, EDITOR

The University of Arkansas Press
Fayetteville   1994

Copyright © 1994 by The Board of Trustees of the
University of Arkansas

All rights reserved
Manufactured in the United States of America

98   97   96   95   94   5   4   3   2   1

Designed by Gail Carter

⊖ The paper used in this publication meets the
minimum requirements of the American National
Standard for Permanence of Paper for Printed
Library Materials Z39.48-1984.

Library of Congress Cataloging-in-Publication Data
Bill Clinton on stump, state, and stage: the rhetorical
road to the White House / Stephen A. Smith, editor.
      p.   cm.
   ISBN 1-55728-365-6.—ISBN 1-55728-372-9 (pbk.)
   1. Presidents—United States—Election—1992.
2. Clinton, Bill, 1946–   —Oratory. 3. Rhetoric—
Political aspects—United States—History—20th century. 5. United States—Politics and government—
1989–1993.   I. Smith, Stephen A., 1949–   .
E884.B54   1994
324.973'0928—dc20   94-17161
                                           CIP

To William Jefferson Clinton and "the people"...
and to the Republic, for which they stand.

CONTENTS

List of Contributors   ix

Introduction:
  The Rhetorical Invention of Bill Clinton   I
      Stephen A. Smith

Bill Clinton's Campaigns for Governor of Arkansas:
  Prelude to a Presidency   13
      Diana B. Carlin and Charles C. Howard

Rhetoric and Ritual in the Arkansas Inaugural Addresses   23
      Glenn C. Getz

Bill Clinton's Stump Speaking:
  Persuasion through Identification   52
      John T. Llewellyn

The Jeremiadic Logic of Bill Clinton's Policy Speeches   73
      Craig Allen Smith

The Stylistic Persona of Bill Clinton:
  From Arkansas and Aristotelian Attica   101
      Ronald H. Carpenter

The Voice of Concern and Concern for the Voice   133
      Tony M. Lentz

Dodging Charges and Charges of Dodging:
  Bill Clinton's Defense on the Character Issue   150
      Greta R. Marlow

De/reconstructing Hillary:
  From the Retro Ashes of the Donna Reed Fantasy
  to a '90s View of Women and Politics   163
      Sandra Goodall

Imagining the Image: Reinventing the Clintons   187
    Irving J. Rein

The New York Convention:
Bill Clinton and "A Place Called Hope"   201
    Larry D. Smith

The Intertextuality of "The Man from Hope":
Bill Clinton as Person, as Persona, as Star?   223
    Thomas Rosteck

Presidential Debate as Political Ritual:
Clinton vs. Bush vs. Perot   249
    Dale A. Herbeck

Riding the Roller Coaster:
Bill Clinton and the News Media   273
    Philip Seib

Easy Access to Sloppy Truths:
The '92 Presidential Media Campaign   292
    Rita Kirk Whillock

The First E-Mail Election:
Electronic Networking and the Clinton Campaign   315
    Thomas W. Benson

Clinton Goes to Town Hall   341
    Janette Kenner Muir

Living in the Rock n Roll Campaign, or Mystery,
Media, and the American Public Imagination:
An Intertextual Quest   365
    H. L. Goodall Jr.

CONTRIBUTORS

Thomas W. Benson is a professor of speech communication at the Pennsylvania State University. He is a former editor of the *Quarterly Journal of Speech*.

Diana B. Carlin is an associate professor of communication studies at the University of Kansas where she teaches courses in political communication and speech writing. Carlin has published extensively in the area of political debates and coordinated a major focus group research project on the 1992 debates. Carlin's articles have appeared in *Argumentation and Advocacy*, *Political Communication and Persuasion*, and *Political Communication*.

Ronald H. Carpenter, University of Florida, publishes about stylistics in *Style*, *Language and Style*, *Communication Monographs*, and the *Quarterly Journal of Speech*. Carpenter conducts writing workshop-seminars and is the recipient of an SCA Golden Anniversary Monograph Prize for Outstanding Scholarship.

Glenn C. Getz, Ph.D. candidate, communication studies, University of Iowa, has published in rhetorical, ritual, and television studies. A former SCA Student Section Chair, Getz founded a computer network for communication students.

H. L. Goodall Jr. is a professor of speech and communication studies at Clemson University, specializing in organizational and cultural studies. He is also a senior partner to GENESIS COMMUNICATION, an organizational and media relations consulting firm.

Sandra Goodall serves, in virtual cyberspace, at the Center of Excellence on behalf of PowerCerv, a Tampa-based software firm. In empirical and mediated space, she serves as political director for GENESIS COMMUNICATION.

Dale A. Herbeck is an associate professor of communication and director of forensics at Boston College, Chestnut Hill, Massachusetts. Dr. Herbeck has authored dozens of articles on various aspects of debate theory and practice, presented over fifty papers at communication conferences, and written numerous debate handbooks and guides. He is presently serving a two-year term as president of the American Forensic Association, a national organization of forensic educators.

Charles Howard is an assistant professor of speech at Tarleton State University. He has published on political communication and has been active in several political campaigns.

Tony M. Lentz, author of *Orality and Literacy in Hellenic Greece,* teaches oral performance at the Pennsylvania State University and consults on media performance. He helped establish India's first public speaking course.

John T. Llewellyn is an assistant professor of speech communication at Wake Forest University. Before graduate school, Llewellyn served as media advisor and speech writer for politicians and government agencies in North Carolina.

Greta R. Marlow is an assistant professor of communication at the University of the Ozarks, Clarksville, Arkansas. She is completing work on a Ph.D. at the University of Kansas.

Janette Kenner Muir is an assistant professor of communication at George Mason University in Fairfax, Virginia. She has published several articles on presidential campaigns. She also serves as an educational consultant for the C-SPAN cable networks.

Irving J. Rein is a professor of communication studies at Northwestern University. He has served as communications advisor for many political candidates, including Richard M. Daley, Paul Simon, Adlai Stevenson III, and Harold Washington. His most recent books are *High Visibility* (1987) and *Marketing Places* (1993).

Thomas Rosteck is an associate professor of communication at the University of Arkansas, Fayetteville. Interested in connections between rhetoric, media, and culture, he is the author of *See It Now Confronts McCarthyism: Television Documentary and the Politics of Representation.*

Philip Seib is an associate professor of journalism at Southern Methodist University and is a veteran print and television journalist. His most recent book is *Campaigns and Conscience: The Ethics of Political Journalism.*

Craig Allen Smith is a professor of communication studies at the University of North Carolina at Greensboro, where he teaches courses in contemporary American rhetoric. His books include *The White House Speaks: Presidential Leadership as Persuasion* (1994), *Persuasion and Social Movements* (1994, 1989, 1984), *Political Communication* (1990), and *The President and the Public* (1985).

Larry D. Smith is an associate professor of communication at Purdue University. He teaches political communication and is the author of numerous articles and books.

Rita Kirk Whillock is a professor of communication at Southern Methodist University. Her research combines her interests in applied communication and politics. Her most recent book is an analysis of political strategies in state and regional elections.

INTRODUCTION

The Rhetorical Invention of Bill Clinton

STEPHEN A. SMITH

When Bill Clinton announced his campaign for president, he did so with a splendid speech, and even the first press analyses considered his rhetorical performances as defining his public persona. Morton Kondracke of the *New Republic,* for instance, said, "Clinton is known to the general public, if at all, for his legendary bad speech to the 1988 Democratic National Convention (when the only applause he got was for the words 'in conclusion'). In fact, he is a compelling orator and has now got himself a crackling good speech."[1]

During the 1992 presidential campaign, Bill Clinton often denigrated the opposition camp's speeches as only rhetoric. Clinton's campaign speeches were certainly rhetorical (in the best and true sense of the word), and his extemporaneous comments were models of eloquence contrasted with Bush's frequent problems with syntax. One reporter recalled that candidate Clinton was a "man who spoke not only in complete sentences, every word chosen with intelligence and vision, but in fully articulated paragraphs, seamlessly arranged."[2] Another observed Clinton's impressive combination of substance and style and said, "He's Elvis Presley with a calculator on his belt, an outsized candidate with a drawl as big as his brain, a would-be president of both pie charts and Moon pies."[3]

Early in his first year as president, both news reporters and rhetorical scholars were divided in their judgment of Clinton's communication skills.[4] Still treating the term "rhetoric" with disdain, President Clinton expressed dismay that it was not "easy to reach out directly to the people and cut through the cacophony of noise and rhetoric. Sure, the President can give an address to the nation, but you can only do that every so often. . . . So there have been times when I've been surprised by my inability to shape the agenda on a daily basis or to shape the message that's going out to the folks."[5] Nonetheless, in an interview with Helen Thomas at the end of his first year as president, Clinton said he was surprised at how much "the words of a president count."[6] Political columnist David Broder noted that Clinton was now well aware of the rhetorical impact of certain speeches delivered during the first year of his term and said, "The most encouraging thing about President Clinton . . . is the serious reflection he is doing about the use of the rhetorical powers of his office."[7]

This collection of essays on President Bill Clinton's quest for the White House examines his rhetorical efforts before he took office and presents a unique perspective on the words and texts that brought him to the presidency, one that privileges the speakers, the messages, and the audiences in that most public of communication campaigns. Other books by other authors have and will attempt to tell the story in either more traditional or more explicitly ideological ways, and they will not be without value. In fact, I first imagined that this volume might be an argument by a single author in a single voice offering a confident explanation of Clinton's success as a public persuader. Circumstances of time and distance prevented that project, and it would have been a bad idea anyway.

Objectivity in studies of political communication is always elusive, perhaps impossible, and probably undesirable. One does not have to join the disconnected deconstructionists in ignoring context and intent to understand that individuals often derive different meanings from the same texts. My reading of his rhetoric is only one such interpretation, and it is colored by my particular experiences and observations of his early career. I have known Bill Clinton since 1971, and I will confess up front that I like, respect, appreciate, and admire the president. I worked with and for him in campaigns and in office for almost a decade, I consistently gave him my money and my vote, he was my closest friend for much of that time, and he and Hillary are the godparents of my son.[8] I do not now claim any special connection or relationship not shared and enjoyed by any other citizen of the republic; however, I believe that my brief career in public affairs and my academic training in communication studies provided an unusual view of Clinton as communicator during the early years of his political odyssey. At least, it was an educational experience for me, and this seems an appropriate place to share those lessons as backgrounding for the more detailed essays in this book.

I was a member of the Arkansas House of Representatives and was introduced to Bill Clinton in March 1971 by the Speaker, Ray Smith Jr. of Hot Springs. Clinton was visiting home during his spring break at Yale Law School and had already considered the state capitol an important part of that visit home. We became better acquainted and became friends during the Democratic State Convention and the Democratic National Convention of 1972. I was a delegate to those conventions, and Clinton was a member of George McGovern's national campaign staff. We spent considerable time together during the national convention in Miami, and I was thoroughly impressed at how well this twenty-five-year-old Yalie moved among the famous and powerful in the party. I also enjoyed getting to know him and the chance to talk politics with a kindred soul from Arkansas. We seemed to share a number of views on national issues, such as the futility and injustice of American involvement in Vietnam, and about state politics, hoping that a progressive New South was rising from the shame of the ashes of its racist leadership in the past. I was glad to know that he wanted to come back to Arkansas and to be a political player.

Clinton graduated from Yale Law School in 1973 and in August accepted a position as assistant professor of law at the University of Arkansas, but politics was foremost in his mind. On 25 February 1974 he announced as a candidate for Congress. In his opening speech he declared, "The overriding issue of this campaign is clear; we need a stronger Congress," and his campaign literature echoed the theme, "We must elect men to Congress who are not afraid to take responsibility for the future of our country." While the first argument was a reflection of the contemporary political crisis, the second might be read as the germ of his recent call for responsibility in the presidential campaign or in his inaugural address. He led a field of four candidates with 44 percent in the primary, then handily defeated state senator Gene Rainwater in the run-off two weeks later.

The issues articulated during the primary campaign reveal both similarities and differences between that campaign and his most recent run for the White House. Clinton led with a pledge to "give the highest priority to improving the quality of education," because it would bring "more rapid economic growth, a higher standard of living, and the general enrichment of people's lives." Next he called for tax reform, claiming that "the average working family carries too much of the tax load" and that the tax laws encouraged and rewarded corporate investment in low-wage countries. He also addressed the need for public-works funding and warned against the dangers of concentrations of power in uncaring government bureaucracies and irresponsible private corporations.[9] Those issues and arguments are still prominent in Clinton's vision for America, but other issues stressed during the primary campaign—inflation and the energy crisis resulting from the oil embargo—were tied to the particular times.

I was excited by his campaign and the primary victory, and I joined the campaign staff in July as an unpaid volunteer in charge of issues research, speech writing, media coordination, travel aid, and all-purpose gopher. The campaign materials in the primary carried Clinton's message with a lack of sophistication that reflected the shoestring budget, and they are now amusing items in my personal collection of campaign memorabilia. During the general election, with help from the Democratic Congressional Campaign Committee, the campaign had the benefit of advice from Jody Powell (the future White House Press Secretary), numbers from Pat Cadell, and television spots produced by Sandy Kaplan.

Events, especially the resignation and pardon of Richard Nixon, also shaped the issues of the general-election campaign in 1974. The first speech to which I contributed was Clinton's keynote to the Democratic State Convention in September in which he framed the issues of the fall campaign. He opened with a blast to Gerald Ford's pardon of Richard Nixon, then attacked the Republican administrations' record on economic issues during "six long years" and their impact on "small businessmen, family farmers, working men and women, the poor, and the elderly," closing that theme by suggesting, "In the face of this sorry record, if President Ford wants to pardon anybody, he ought to pardon the Administration's economic advisors." He grounded his proposals for needed changes by placing the solutions in the voices of citizens he had met during the campaign. "In short," he said, "in the words of a friend of mine who works on the

Scott County road crew, 'The people want a hand up, not a hand out.'" The only problem, he said, in words resonant with his most recent bid for national office, was that "the good Government we love has too often been made use of for private and selfish purposes. Those who have abused it have forgotten the people."[10]

The incumbent Republican, John Paul Hammerschmidt, had coasted to easy victories in the last two elections, and his political popularity in the district was based upon his perceived successes at the pork barrel and his skillful use of publicity through newsletters and questionnaires. Clinton confronted the questionnaires in the convention speech and throughout the campaign by suggesting that the people never responded with requests for votes against their interest, citing for example votes to uphold vetoes of water and sewer construction funds or education funding. In a series of weekly news conferences, he also contrasted his positions with Hammerschmidt's voting record in such areas as agricultural policy, education, public-works projects, and programs for senior citizens.

Hammerschmidt responded that Clinton was a liberal McGovernite, was a tool of big labor and special interests, and was distorting his voting record. Clinton's position on Vietnam also became an issue in the campaign, with opposition supporters manufacturing the rumor that Clinton had perched in a tree at the University of Arkansas to protest the war in 1969. It was the type of campaign that Clinton would face again, but in the future he would fare better. In the 1974 congressional campaign he carried fifteen of the twenty-one counties but lost by 6,000 votes out of 170,000 cast.

It was a wonderful, if unsuccessful, campaign. Two days after the loss I received a note from Clinton in which he said, "You and I started this together, ended the poorest losers, waiting for a newer day. I am filled with gratitude and affection and no regrets." My feeling exactly. In that campaign, an experience of more than four months of eighteen-hour days, I had learned much about politics and much about Bill Clinton. I had first been impressed by his knowledge of such a broad range of issues and the energy he devoted to the task, but I soon came to regard him as one of the most intelligent and thoughtful people I had ever met in public life (and I still think he is). Energy and reflective judgment in combination to that degree are rare qualities, indeed. I would spend a week—probably over one hundred hours—reading and analyzing documents and data related to a particular campaign issue; in briefing him on my conclusions, I found that he absorbed it all in the first pass, remembered every statistic, and drew conclusions that I had missed. I also found myself able to anticipate his responses to what was important and why it mattered, making the job of speech writing a breeze, even if the set texts seemed weak by comparison to the speeches he was able to deliver without notes at any civic club or coffee shop in the realm.[11]

In 1976 Clinton announced his campaign for state attorney general. I again became a campaign volunteer, this time with the title of campaign manager, although in fact Clinton was always his own campaign manager. That campaign was the shortest in Clinton's career, announced in March and over in May, as he won a clear majority in the primary and faced no Republican opposition. The victory was clearly a result of Clinton's superiority as a campaigner, combining broad knowledge and clear articulation of issues, unbounded personal energy, an adequate media campaign, and a strong traditional organization advantage.

The obvious plan was to build on the organizational strength in the Third District, and Clinton won clear majorities in thirty-eight counties, led the field in twenty, and finished second in the remaining seventeen. Extensive personal contact and impressive public speaking by the candidate were supported by respectable direct mail, campaign literature, outdoor advertising, considerable radio, adequate newspaper ads, and minimal television, primarily talking-head studio spots and a paid thirty-minute interview on campaign issues.

Clinton's persona was that of energy and dedication, captured by the slogan, "Character, Competence, and Concern." Even for such a low-visibility office, he articulated a platform that included minimum sentences, victim compensation programs, improved work release, and rapid assistance to law enforcement agencies in interpreting the new criminal code, issues related to criminal justice and the office. More politically revealing, however, were his points calling for fair utility rates, citizens' rights to consumer protection in small-claims courts, effective antitrust laws, and a right to privacy. These were issues that revealed a political stance aimed to "significantly improve the quality of life in Arkansas" and which were directed toward a constituency group that in 1992 would be labeled "the forgotten middle class."

Clinton called the attorney general "the guardian of our people's interests" with "a broad range of responsibilities," and said, "I want to shoulder these responsibilities." His campaign literature stressed his educational qualifications, even revealing that he had been a Rhodes scholar, and balanced his past work for housing assistance and affirmative action with membership in the Jaycees and the Baptist church. In explaining his commitment, he said, "For years I have worked hard to acquire the knowledge and habits of discipline necessary to do this or any other job well. Every person I will hire to work in the Attorney General's office for you will have to demonstrate the same devotion to excellence and willingness to put in long hours. Every decision will be the product of these forces and not of political pressures."[12]

The campaign reinforced my respect for Clinton's dedication to the task and his abilities as a tireless and effective campaigner. The only policy speech that I can recall was a Law Day Address at Arkansas Tech University on "Free Press and Fair Trial," in which he championed the First Amendment and proposed several solutions for harmonizing and maximizing the strengths of the often-conflicting First and Sixth amendments. It was a talent for political resolution that I would come to see and appreciate more fully in the future.

When Clinton took office as attorney general, I bellied up to the public trough and went to work on his staff, and there I had the opportunity to watch him work. He applied the same energy to public service that he did to political campaigns, and the results were impressive. Consumer protection activities and recoveries increased; the office issued a record number of official opinions; new divisions were funded to control energy rates and investigate antitrust violations; Clinton chaired a new board to protect individual privacy on information in government records and produced several publications explaining the Freedom of Information Act for public officials; he supported victim compensation legislation, called for regulation of lobbyists, and issued opinions against state regulations restricting price and professional advertising. He headed a national panel on rights of the elderly and testified against age discrimination.[13] It was a record of which he could be proud—and one on which he could and would be elected governor. In September, only nine months after Clinton took office, that wise and skeptical columnist, Bob Lancaster, was already opining that the governor's office was his for the taking, the U.S. Senate seat was a real possibility, and the national ticket was not out of the question for 1988 or 1992.[14]

Clinton announced for governor in March 1978, with a speech grounded on the state's heritage and filled with optimism about the future. "As a people, we have come a long way in a little time. We have put aside so many of the fears and prejudices which crippled us in the past. But we have held fast to our heritage of proud individualism, love for nature's bounty, and firm faith in hard work, discipline, and respect for each other. . . . Our best days are before us if we will forge our own destiny." He emphasized economic development, a road program, education, supporting family farms, assisting senior citizens "and others who are being swamped by inflation and do not have enough to live on." He also stressed a theme in that speech that I believe has been consistent in all of his campaigns, including the latest one. "Most important of all," he said, "I will try to bring out the best in all of us. From this day forward, I will campaign with that goal in mind. I will continue to do my job with that goal in mind. I will try to be honest about what cannot be done, but I will direct our visions toward what must be done."[15]

The campaign was virtually flawless, although some would contend that the opposition was not particularly formidable. Clinton swept to a clear victory over four opponents in the primary and embarrassed the Republican scrub in the general election. Despite the ease with which he won, he campaigned as vigorously as always. His campaign literature offered a fairly detailed vision for economic development, senior citizens, improving health care, moderating utility rates, promoting family farms, preventing chemical spills, building and improving roads, strengthening public education, and revising the state's constitution. Perhaps these were safe issues, but they were neither easy ones nor inconsistent with his political goals.

In a personally revealing campaign message, Clinton expressed a feeling and a commitment that I believe to be very honest on his part. "All my life," he said, "I've wanted to be involved with people and help them with their problems. I've been very interested in all kinds of people. Politics has just given me a way to pursue my interest and my concern on a large scale. I've given it all the energy and spirit I can muster; I've tried to bring out the best in people through politics; and I've really been very happy doing it."[16] I believe that was true then, and I think it is true today.

Clinton delivered a wonderful inaugural address, again calling on the best in the people of Arkansas, then he plunged into trying to fulfill the promises of the campaign. That effort did not lack energy, but it sometimes lacked the appropriate political craft. He secured passage of an overwhelming portion of an ambitious legislative package; he appointed a record number of women and minorities to his staff and to public boards and commissions; he assumed leadership in several national organizations. It was an amazing display of rhetoric shaping and changing realities.[17]

During the 1980 reelection campaign, Clinton proposed to run on the record of his accomplishments in the areas of economic development, energy and utility rate reform, government efficiency, education, transportation, health care and human needs, and environmental protection. In a statement Clinton personally drafted for the campaign tabloid, he said, "My first year and five months in office have not been free of error by any means. I have made mistakes. But the only way to avoid errors is to do nothing. I am trying to be a doer and I am working every day to move Arkansas forward, to do things of real benefit for our people. More important, I think that the record will show that in this short time we have made remarkable—and in some cases unprecedented—gains in education, energy, economic development, and efficiency in government."[18]

The Republican candidate, Frank White, ran a simplistic and often negative campaign against Clinton that fall, and the campaign staff underestimated its impact until too late to respond adequately. Clinton lost that election and, as a consequence, he learned several valuable political lessons, not the least of which was that negative advertising, regardless of how irrational it might appear, must be countered, and that understanding has served him well in all subsequent campaigns.

The roots of Clinton's approach to national politics were evident in the speech he gave at the Democratic National Convention in 1980, and it is much like the argument he advanced in his own campaign for president in 1992. "We must speak," he told his party, "to the millions who are not here—who do not even watch us on television or listen to us. Who do not care. Who will not bother to vote, or if they do, will probably not vote for us. For it is these people who will decide the election of 1980. And they cannot be moved by the symbols and accomplishments of the past." The party has proven its commitment to equality and justice, he told the delegates, "But now we must prove that we offer more in the way of creative and realistic solutions . . . and that we have a vision that can withstand the erosion of special interest politics that is sweeping the land."[19]

Clinton warned that the party "cannot win this election simply by putting together the old elements of the Democratic coalition and repudiating Ronald Reagan. It is not enough." He then argued that there were "answers which will ring true to millions and millions of Democrats and Independents and thoughtful Republicans. They can be found in the words and works of a new generation of Democratic leaders . . ." Admitting that the country was facing serious problems that other politicians might ignore or deny, he cautioned that "we did not get into these difficulties overnight, and we will not emerge from them immediately." As the example of the approach needed, he drew then on the 1936 election of Franklin Roosevelt and shared the lesson he saw, contending that Roosevelt was successful because "people knew what sort of vision he had for America. They knew what action he was taking to transform the country. And they were willing, most importantly, to accept hardship for the present, because they believed they were part of a process that would lead them to a better tomorrow."[20]

Clinton then asked key questions. "What is our vision—what is our hope? We must speak to the American people who do not listen tonight. First we must say forthrightly that we are in a time of transition, a difficult and painful time from which no one can escape the burden, and in which no one can avoid a responsibility to play a part. Secondly, we must say we are committed to the economic revitalization of America, but it will require . . . a redefinition of the relationship between the federal government and big business and labor. It will require a revitalization of our basic industrial structure."[21]

I am inclined to see a certain continuity in Bill Clinton's rhetorical and political career. Perhaps I was too close to get an accurate reading on the public interpretation of the text, and, even more likely, this narrative suffers from trying to force order upon the chaos of politics. I am inclined to think that James Carville's comment on the execution of political campaigns—big theories are "mostly shit"—is equally applicable to their interpretation.[22] But, that's my story, and I'm stickin' with it.

The contributing authors in this volume tell other versions, and their stories are the real strength of the book and what make this collection worth serious attention from anyone hoping to understand how and why Bill Clinton became president of the United States and the process of political communication in America at the end of the twentieth century. It is not a single narrative but a collection of original, valuable, and deeply insightful analyses and interpretations. I solicited this group of outstanding scholars, asked them to apply their craft to particular aspects of Clinton's communication career in Arkansas and the 1992 campaign for president, and placed no further restrictions upon method, content, or stance. The result is a symphony, not merely a rhetorical arcade of independent carnival barkers. The diversity of voices and views mirrors in many ways the first campaign for the postmodern presidency where form followed function. Furthermore, it is a wonderful collection of careful scholarship and fine writing, one sure to provide both personal enjoyment and public enlightenment.

NOTES

1. Morton Kondracke, "Slick Willy: Bill Clinton, Postliberal Man," *New Republic* 205.17 (21 October 1991): 18.

2. Lloyd Grove, "Clinton's Sudden Visit to Babble-On: What Happened to the Great Articulator?" *Washington Post*, 12 May 1993, B1.

3. David Von Drehle, "Letter from the Campaign Trail: Clinton's Political Persona Blends Redneck, Policy Nerd," *Washington Post*, 7 March 1992, A1.

4. Burt Solomon, "Clinton's Rhetoric May Not Be Pretty, but So Far, Anyway, It's Working," *National Journal* 25.13 (27 March 1993): 774; Grove, "Clinton's Sudden Visit to Babble-On."

5. Jack Nelson and Robert J. Donovan, "The Education of a President: After Six Months of Quiet Success and Loud Failure, Bill Clinton Talks about the Frustrating Process of Figuring Out His Job," *Los Angeles Times Magazine*, 1 August 1993, 12.

6. Helen Thomas, United Press International wire story, BC cycle, 23 December 1993.

7. David S. Broder, "Clinton Finds His Voice," *Washington Post*, 12 December 1993, C7. For discussion of one of those speeches, called "the most important of his 10-month-old presidency," see E. J. Dionne Jr., "Clinton's Bully Pulpit," *Washington Post*, 16 November 1993, A21; for a more general analysis of Clinton's evolving rhetorical choices, see David Lauter, "Clinton Defines Presidency with Preacher's Voice," *Los Angeles Times*, 31 December 1993, A1, A10–A11.

8. A more detailed disclosure of my biases toward Clinton can be found in Stephen

A. Smith, "Compromise, Consensus, and Consistency," in Ernest Dumas, comp., *The Clintons of Arkansas: An Introduction by Those Who Know Them Best* (Fayetteville: University of Arkansas Press, 1993), 1–16.

9. Clinton for Congress campaign pamphlet, 1974. The campaign materials and manuscript or typescript cited here are in the personal collection of the author.

10. Bill Clinton, Keynote Address to the Arkansas Democratic Party State Convention, Hot Springs, September 1974. Typed transcript from audio recording.

11. For a similar analysis by Clinton's speech-writing team in the 1992 campaign, see David Maraniss, "For Man of Many Words, The Power of 'I Accept'; According to Top Aides, Clinton Is His Own Best Speechwriter," *Washington Post*, 16 July 1992, A11.

12. Clinton for Attorney General campaign pamphlet, 1976.

13. Office of the Attorney General, *The Attorney General's Report* (Little Rock, 1977).

14. Bob Lancaster, "Clinton's Quandary: Choosing Best Route to Bright Future," *Arkansas Democrat*, 25 September 1977.

15. Bill Clinton, "Announcement of Candidacy for Governor," 6 March 1978. Manuscript copy.

16. Clinton for Arkansas campaign brochure, 1978. This quote was from an extensive preproduction audiotaped interview conducted in Clinton's Little Rock home by his media consultants, Marvin Chernoff and Rick Silver, Columbia, South Carolina.

17. The best scholarly analysis of Clinton's first term is Phyllis Finton Johnston, *Bill Clinton's Public Policies for Arkansas: 1979–1980* (Little Rock, Ark.: August House, 1982).

18. "Bill Clinton Is Fighting for Arkansas, and It's Paying Off for You," campaign tabloid, May 1980.

19. Gov. Bill Clinton, "Address to the Democratic National Convention," New York, August 1980. Typescript.

20. Ibid.

21. Ibid.

22. Charles Laurence, "The Man Who Put Clinton in the White House," *Telegraph Magazine* (London), 16 January 1993, 17.

BILL CLINTON'S CAMPAIGNS FOR GOVERNOR OF ARKANSAS

Prelude to a Presidency

DIANA B. CARLIN AND CHARLES C. HOWARD

On 5 November 1980 Gov. Bill Clinton stood on the patio of the governor's mansion in Little Rock and responded to the reelection loss he had suffered the evening before. He acknowledged the tears he and Hillary had shed, congratulated his opponent, Frank White, pledged a successful transition, and defined the legacy of his administration:

> As time goes on, many more will know that the real legacy of my administration is that in these hard times I made the hard decisions and pursued a vision of the future of our State that is worthy of our best hopes and values, worthy of the future of my daughter and all of the other children of Arkansas.[1]

It was the low point in Bill Clinton's political career. He went from being the nation's youngest governor to the nation's youngest former governor. But it was also a defining moment in a political career that was far from over. While he was the first Arkansas governor since 1954 to be denied a second two-year term, two years later he made political history again by becoming the first Arkansas governor to serve non-consecutive terms. The general-election rematch between Clinton and Frank White was one of the most dramatic in Arkansas politics. Clinton's inauguration in January 1983 served as the beginning of the "Clinton decade" in Arkansas, which ended in January 1993 when Clinton resigned to let his 1982 primary opponent and the then lieutenant governor (Jim Guy Tucker) take over in Arkansas as Clinton prepared to lead the nation as its forty-second president.

In this essay, we explore the Clinton decade in Arkansas through an analysis of his successful return to politics in 1982, the three subsequent reelections between 1984 and 1990 that brought about his domination of Arkansas politics and made possible his rise to national prominence.

1982: THE APOLOGIA CAMPAIGN

In 1982 Bill Clinton faced three Democrat challengers for the party's nomination and the opportunity to face incumbent Frank White: conservative state senator Kim Hendren of Gravette; Jim Guy Tucker, a former state attorney general and congressman who lost the 1978 primary for a U.S. Senate seat; and Joe Purcell, a former attorney general and lieutenant governor. Many assumed that the real contest would be between Clinton and Tucker, both of whom shared a youthful, reformist image. Purcell was considerably older than the two front-runners, had been in Arkansas politics longer, but had a clean slate with the state's large rural population and was untainted by either the racism or corruption charges which had doomed the Orval Faubus machine. Hendren was not well known and throughout the campaign would repeatedly alienate strong constituency groups within the party.

Clinton's approach to the race was unorthodox and stood in marked contrast to the way he acknowledged his defeat two years earlier. Clinton's speech the day after his defeat extolled the accomplishments of his term: better schools, better roads, better health care, better programs for the elderly, and the beginnings of improvements in energy and environmental policy. Clinton told Arkansans that their state survived tough times "because of the leadership of this administration and that is something that will endure. I am proud of it and I want you to be proud of it."[2] However, he began his political comeback with an apology.

In television spots that aired before he officially announced his candidacy for the Democratic nomination, Clinton looked straight into the camera and apologized for the mistakes made in his first administration. According to John Brummett of the *Arkansas Gazette*, "Never before had this been seen. A politician skipping the traditional formalities and going directly to the voters' living rooms and saying—in a way that was designed to be intimate—that he sure was sorry he had let them down, but now he wants to be their Governor again."[3]

This preemptive strike was a savvy move, as Jim Guy Tucker was determined to prove that Clinton didn't deserve a second chance. Tucker argued that he was the only one who could defeat Frank White. Tucker's advertising featured him in rural settings, hunting and playing the guitar on his front porch. This contrasted sharply with his image as a liberal reformer in Congress and a high-priced Little Rock attorney at home. At a major political rally in April, sparks flew between Clinton and Tucker. After Tucker attacked Clinton's record, Clinton told the crowd, "It seems every time Jim Guy Tucker talks he reminds you that I'm seeking a second chance. I've had to ask my wife for a second chance. My daughter for a second chance. Give me a second chance so Arkansas can have a better chance."[4]

The 26 May primary election made it clear that many voters were eager for a Clinton-White rematch. In the voting, Clinton led with 42 percent, followed by Purcell with 29 percent, Tucker with 23 percent, Hendren with 4 percent, and minor candidate Monroe Schwarzloss with 2 percent. Arkansas law required a run-off between Clinton and Purcell. The run-off was calm compared to the primary, and Clinton finally won the right to face White again.

With the apologies out of the way, and vindication through a primary victory, Clinton followed a more traditional approach to campaigning. His print ads emphasized the strong points of his previous administration and singled out the issues he felt were important. In one widely circulated brochure, Clinton focused on "more jobs" (this was the height of the 1982 recession, and Arkansas was hit hard), utility rates (a perceived weakness for White since the public service commissioners he appointed had awarded utility companies large rate increases), and education (a traditional Clinton concern).

The issues resonated, and Clinton's comeback was complete on election night 1982 when he was again elected governor, this time by a 55 percent to 45 percent margin. Analysts cited four reasons for his success: (1) favorable voter response to his television apologia; (2) a hard-working statewide campaign organization; (3) courtship of party rank-and-file who were alienated two years previously; and (4) fund raising that allowed him to match White's negative television spots.[5]

According to Mike Trimble of the *Arkansas Times*, "It's entirely possible that two years of Uncle Frank would have been enough for Arkansas voters no matter what approach Bill Clinton had taken in the 1982 general campaign, but the approach that he did take was as effective as it was surprising."[6]

By going directly to the voters and assuring them that he had learned from the mistakes that sent him out of office in 1980, Clinton was able to do as Linkugel and Ware suggest is consistent with an apologetic stance of transcendence: to "move the audience away from the particulars of the charge at hand in a direction toward some more abstract, general view of his character."[7]

1984: THE STEAMROLLER ROLLS ON

The election year of 1984 was particularly dull for Arkansas voters. After the power politics associated with Clinton's program to overhaul the state education system, the elections were anticlimactic. Indeed, Clinton would turn the election of 1984 into a referendum on his controversial education plan which included a tax increase and testing of public schoolteachers. The plan was bitterly fought by the Arkansas Education Association as an assault on the professionalism of teachers. The plan was put together after months of town hall-type meetings, and the recommendations were made by a special commission appointed by Clinton and chaired by the state's First Lady, Hillary Rodham Clinton.

Clinton's only significant rival in the Democratic primary was Lonnie Turner of Ozark. Turner, an attorney, had been appointed to a state board by Clinton in his first term. Another candidate was Kermit Moss, sixty-four, of Monticello. Moss, a former professor of economics at the University of Arkansas at Monticello, was perceived as the candidate of Arkansas teachers.

Turner announced on 30 March 1984, saying that the people had lost confidence in Clinton.[8] Turner attacked the educational standards as "hastily enacted," teacher testing as "a cover-up and a decoy for the real purpose of increased taxation," and listed a number of other issues from excessive state spending to banning the use of dogs during deer season.[9]

Clinton announced on 31 March 1984, saying, "I'm gonna run as if I were starting out unknown and as if I were behind. I enjoy this, and

I'm ready."[10] Clinton spent much of the primary campaign defending his educational reform package and responding to old allegations about antiwar activity. The allegation that Clinton had led antiwar demonstrations at the University of Arkansas at Fayetteville was first raised in Clinton's unsuccessful congressional race in 1974. Clinton responded to the resurrected claim by consistently denying any such activity since he was studying at Oxford in England during the period of time in question. The rest of the campaign was routine, and Clinton won with 64 percent of the vote. In the general election, Clinton faced Elwood (Woody) Freeman, the Republican candidate from Jonesboro. Freeman was a member of the State Board of Education and focused his campaign on traditional Republican versus Democrat rhetoric. In one ad he listed a twenty-one-plank platform which gave his views on a variety of subjects, from casino gambling to abortion. He told the Benton County Farm Bureau:

> I'm a businessman; I've been in business since I returned from Vietnam in 1971. And I believe it is time to put some business, some common sense back into state government; it's time to put some conservative government back in Little Rock; and, my friends, I offer to you this day the candidacy of Woody Freeman to do that—because I tell you, as I said before, it's time for that change for good, conservative government to bring those jobs, put common sense back in, and I'm gonna do it![11]

The 1984 race was cast by Clinton as a referendum on his education proposals, but by the general election little attention was given to the ins and outs of policy matters. Clinton defended his education proposals, argued that tax increases were necessary, defended teacher testing, and promised that the resulting improvements in the education system would benefit Arkansans in the long run through improved economic development and job opportunities. Clinton captured 63 percent of the vote in the general election despite a low voter turnout.

1986: OLD FRIENDS AND OLD ENEMIES

The 1986 election was the first in Arkansas with a four-year term at stake. The election was enlivened somewhat by the presence of two old war horses from Arkansas's political past. On 21 March 1986

Orval E. Faubus, seventy-six, governor of Arkansas from 1955 to 1967, announced he would be a candidate for the Democratic nomination. Faubus had attempted comebacks before, one in 1970 and another in 1974, and was rebuffed by voters. Frank White had appointed Faubus to be the state's director of Veteran's Affairs during his administration, but for most of the previous twenty years, Faubus had spent his time writing memoirs and giving speeches about the integration crisis of 1957. By 1977 when Ernest Green, one of the students in the Little Rock Central High integration crisis, had been appointed Assistant Secretary of Labor by Jimmy Carter, Faubus had been reduced to working as a teller in a bank in Huntsville, Arkansas.

In his announcement Faubus said he would concentrate on issues of importance to families, such as insurance rates, job creation, utility rates, and hazardous waste.[12] The other candidate in the primary was W. Dean Goldsby, fifty, of Little Rock. Goldsby was the first African-American candidate for governor in Arkansas history. He had served as director of the Pulaski County Economic Opportunity Agency since 1970 and had left under charges of mismanagement of public funds.

For one of the first times in Arkansas history, the Republican party had a serious primary. The pack was led by former-governor Frank White, who was attempting a comeback. The other Republicans were Maurice (Footsie) Britt, a former star football player who had served as lieutenant governor from 1967 to 1971; Wayne Lanier, a dentist from Fort Smith; and Bobby Hays, an oak-flooring manufacturer.

The primaries involved little serious discussion of issues and concentrated on the novelty of individuals from Arkansas's political past, namely Faubus and Britt, challenging two front-runners, Clinton and White. On primary election day there were no surprises. Clinton won with 60.5 percent of the Democratic vote, while White claimed the Republican nomination with 62 percent of the vote, but only one-third the number of votes cast for third-place finisher, Dean Goldsby, in the Democratic primary. Thus, a third Clinton-White confrontation was set.

One of the most important issues in 1986 was utility rates. The federal courts had ordered that Arkansas Power and Light be allowed to increase rates so that its parent company, Middle South Utilities, could pay for the Grand Gulf Nuclear Power Plant located in Mississippi. The issue was a political hot potato with every side blaming someone else for the rate increase. Clinton took the track of blaming the federal courts for stomping on a state's right to regulate local utilities. In the eyes of many, Frank White's candidacy suffered serious damage from his missteps on the issue.

On 2 July 1986 White, who was a member of Middle South's board of directors, appeared as a witness before the state Public Service Commission at a public hearing on Grand Gulf. Before White was finished with testimony attacking the agreement endorsed by Clinton, Patricia Qualls, a music teacher and Clinton appointee, verbally attacked him. She called the former governor a "coffee shop quarter-back," and "riverboat gambler," who was manipulating the issue for political gain. The attack was so fierce and unexpected from the nor-mally demure Qualls that White seemed stunned, and the witnesses who followed him were visibly shaken.[13]

What the 1986 general election lacked in substance, it made up for in mud. Charges were hurled back and forth over a number of issues. The most serious charges launched by the White campaign were attacks on Clinton for his relationship with Daniel Lasiter, an invest-ment banker to whom he had given state bond business. Lasiter had made campaign contributions to both White and Clinton in the past. He was indicted and convicted for cocaine possession. Both White and Bill and Hillary Clinton took drug tests during the campaign. But the "battle of the urine bottles" did not stop the issue. Other tactics included bringing up the fact that Clinton's brother, Roger, was in reha-bilitation for cocaine use. Phone banks were set up to charge that Clinton would be indicted for money laundering. Clinton developed a style of quickly answering charges and hurling back charges of his own. His charges focused on White's business ties to utilities and to the wealthy Stephens brothers' investment banking firm.

On election day, Clinton scored a strong mandate by carrying 64 percent of the vote. Political columnist John Brummett analyzed the vote the following day:

> White's entire campaign has been perceived as such [mudsling-ing]—mainly because of the drug innuendoes, which seem to have stuck only with voters who disliked Clinton in the first place and wanted to believe them. Clinton, as slick as ever this year, has managed to enhance the perception of himself as the nice guy in the race, the one victimized by pure meanness and vicious attacks on his person and family.[14]

1990: THE BATTLE OF THE ELEPHANTS

In 1990 the Democratic primary was duller than usual, while the Republican party provided the excitement for Arkansas voters. The first sign of what kind of election year it was going to be came when Steve Clark, Arkansas attorney general since 1979, announced that he would run for governor in the Democratic primary. Clark was soon plagued by newspaper accounts that he had illegally padded his expense account and claimed personal expenses as business related. One day after Clark made his official announcement, columnist John Brummett said, "He is dead, sordid history—a bad joke. He will be remembered as the dimpled jogger and rip-off artist who had so many $500 dinner dates on your tab and mine that he couldn't remember them all."[15] Clark withdrew shortly thereafter. Jim Guy Tucker also made noises about running again, but soon filed for lieutenant governor. Clinton's only real challenger was Tom McRae, a young reformer who had been at odds with Clinton over the pace of the governor's program.

The Clinton-McRae race had little excitement. Both were reformers arguing about the pace of change, the importance of protecting the environment, and other policy issues. On election day, however, McRae captured 39 percent of the vote compared to Clinton's 55 percent. This showing made some people feel that Clinton was more vulnerable in November than some had expected.

In contrast, the Republican primary was the most spirited and hard fought in the state's history. The combatants were two former Democrats who had switched parties. Sheffield Nelson was well known as the former president of Arkansas Power and Light, the state's most powerful utility. As a successful businessman he was active in community affairs and had been appointed by Clinton to the Arkansas Industrial Development Corporation, a state agency designed to attract industry to Arkansas. Nelson's opponent was Congressman Tommy Robinson. Robinson was one of the most colorful characters in Arkansas politics. Starting off as Sheriff of Pulaski County, he was constantly involved in one controversy after another, including threats to arrest the district attorney and to chain prisoners to a tree. In 1984 he was elected to Congress as a Democrat, and in 1989 he switched parties.

The Nelson-Robinson feud was a novelty for the state's small Republican party, and the two former Democrats attacked each other with gusto. Robinson's controversial career and colorful language made him a hero to populist rural voters, but the state's base of "country club" Republicans had difficulty tolerating the crude rustic. Nelson, who was a major player at the highest level of business and politics in the state, was settled with the image of a tycoon and utilities executive. To enliven the already lively contest, the state's most powerful political brokers and financial bigwigs were at war with each other over the election.

Jerry Jones, multimillionaire owner of the Dallas Cowboys football team, was a childhood friend of Robinson's but was supporting Nelson. Nelson, on the other hand, had made enemies of his old mentor, Jack Stephens, of the powerful Stephens, Inc. On primary day, Nelson won the election with 55 percent of the vote. The Clinton-Nelson campaign lacked the excitement of the Republican primary. Nelson hammered away on a "liberal" charge and contrasted Clinton's liberal leanings with his own business experience. In a televised debate, Nelson said that Clinton was for abortion, gun control, and higher taxes and tied him to the 1988 presidential campaign of Michael Dukakis.[16]

Clinton focused on job creation and rural health care in his campaign. Again he was quick to respond to charges but did not attack Nelson with the same intensity with which he had attacked White four years earlier. In the end, however, Clinton won once again, but with 57.6 percent, his lowest percentage since his comeback in 1982.

CONCLUSION

Several strategies from Clinton's years of running for governor between 1982 and 1990 were evident in the 1992 presidential campaign. His ability to admit to mistakes and to redefine the nature of his character was crucial to turning around attacks on his personal life at the beginning of the primary and on his avoidance of military service during Vietnam throughout both the primary and general elections. His quick response to attacks, with explanations and/or counter charges was honed to a fine edge during the general election, but had its roots in several of his tough political wars in Arkansas. Clinton's ability to focus and translate issues of national importance into clear and highly personalized anecdotes was seen throughout the presidential race, and many of the issues he addressed were the same ones he had talked about in Arkansas for a decade.

The Comeback Kid of the 1992 presidential campaign had his beginnings in the time between the 5 November 1980 speech on the patio of the governor's mansion and the day he faced a camera in 1982 to admit his mistakes and ask for another chance to prove his mettle.

NOTES

1. Bill Clinton, "Speech on the Patio of the Governor's Mansion," Files Office of the Governor, State of Arkansas, Little Rock, Arkansas, 5 November 1980, 2.

2. Ibid., 1.

3. John Brummett, "Clinton's Television Ad Sparks Interest; Apology Appropriate, Tucker Asserts," *Arkansas Gazette*, 10 February 1982, 1B.

4. John Brummett, "Two Clark Foes Highlight Rally at Russellville," *Arkansas Gazette*, 4 April 1982, 1B.

5. John Brummett, "He Is Silent on Transition, Specific Plans," *Arkansas Gazette*, 4 November 1982, 1A.

6. Mike Trimble, "Bill Clinton's Campaign to Become One of Us," *Arkansas Times*, November 1985, 70.

7. B. L. Ware and Wil A. Linkugel, "They Spoke in Defense of Themselves: On the Generic Criticism of Apologia," *Quarterly Journal of Speech 59* (October 1973): 280.

8. "Ozark Lawyer Announces Bid for Governor," *Arkansas Gazette*, 31 March 1984, 1A.

9. "Lonnie Turner for Governor," campaign pamphlet reproduced from the Holdings of the Special Collections Division, University of Arkansas Libraries, Fayetteville, Arkansas.

10. John Brummett, "Clinton Announces, Says Truck Tax Is Issue," *Arkansas Gazette*, 1 April 1984, 3A.

11. "Mr. Woody Freeman, Republican Candidate for Governor," reproduced from the Holdings of Special Collections Division, University of Arkansas Libraries, Fayetteville, Arkansas.

12. Maria Henson, "Faubus 'Goes for It,' Ready for Uphill Battle," *Arkansas Gazette*, 21 March 1986, 1A.

13. Scott Van Laningham, "PSC Member Lets Loose at White on Grand Gulf," *Arkansas Gazette*, 3 July 1986, 1A.

14. John Brummett, "Safest of All Predictions Foresee Clinton, Bumpers Being Re-elected," *Arkansas Gazette*, 4 November 1986, 3A.

15. John Brummett, "Clark's Tale Leaves Us Unsatisfied," *Arkansas Gazette*, 1 February 1990, 1B.

16. Mark Oswald, "Nelson Scores Final Debate Point," *Arkansas Gazette*, 15 October 1990, 1A.

Rhetoric and Ritual in the Arkansas Inaugural Addresses

GLENN C. GETZ

During the 1970s many southern states elected such moderate to progressive politicians as Mississippi's William Waller (1971), Louisiana's Edwin Edwards (1975), Alabama's Fob James (1978), and Arkansas's Bill Clinton (1978) to sit in the governor's chair. These governors became "potent symbols in a new mythology" which rejected "the politics of race baiting, white supremacy, and massive resistance to change."[1] Indeed, argues Stephen A. Smith, Governor Clinton and his colleagues "became symbols of confirmation in the mythic vision of equality."[2] Significantly, the new rhetoric of these governors influenced the entire nation as well as the South. Arkansas's Bill Clinton, in particular, "had an impact on the image of his home state and the image of the South that seemed representative of the emerging new leadership."[3] In light of this phenomenon, then, Clinton's rhetoric as a southern governor warrants the attention of rhetorical critics. The most central addresses by Governor Clinton, those delivered regularly for the most public of audiences, can provide access to the myths developed through his rhetoric.

A volume on the rhetoric of Bill Clinton would not be complete without consideration of the five inaugural addresses he delivered while occupying this highly rhetorical position as a progressive southern governor. The speeches are significant in at least four ways. First, they can help us better understand southern political change during this time period. Clinton and the other governors, most notably through their public discourse, replaced old myths of intolerance with new myths of equality, fairness, and compassion. Second, the speeches can give us specific insights into the particular mythic vision offered by Governor Clinton to his home state. Inaugural addresses function ritualistically— in part—as epideictic directives that create an image of an administration's leadership and project that image into the future.[4] Understanding the myths present in these speeches may also help us predict the future of Clinton's rhetoric as president. Third, the speeches can provide valuable insights into a neglected genre of public address: the gubernatorial inaugural. Although many have examined the presidential version of this important epideictic,[5] few have contemplated its significance in other levels of government.[6] Fourth, an examination of the epideictic and deliberative components of the speeches will improve our knowledge of how public address functions ritually and rhetorically.

To those ends, in this essay I will discuss a ritual view of politics, review research in presidential and gubernatorial inaugural addresses, explore the rhetorical and ritual functions of the gubernatorial inaugural, analyze the five Clinton speeches with particular attention to patterns of argument, style, and audience adaptation, and conclude with some general implications for future research.

RITUAL IN POLITICAL RHETORIC

One of the most troubling catch-phrases for public address scholars may have its origins in the ritual dynamics of political rhetoric. The words "mere rhetoric" are sometimes used to dismiss as self-serving, predictable, and (therefore) irrelevant the public discourse of political officials such as presidents and governors. The first part of this argument may be true, at least to some extent. Political rituals are used for particular social and individual purposes that can sometimes seem fairly transparent. When a group of speeches develop some degree of regularity in response to a rhetorical situation they may become a genre: "a complex, an amalgam, a constellation of substantive, situational, and stylistic elements."[7] Lloyd Bitzer argues that as a genre develops over time the resulting rhetorical tradition not only contains symbolic resources useful for speeches to come, but simultaneously constrains future speakers as they attempt to remain faithful to the tradition.[8] For example, Clinton's presidential inaugural is influenced by a rich generic history of previous such addresses. Arguably, Clinton as president also hopes to pursue a rhetorical and social agenda consistent with his previous discourse. In trying to be true to his own words, Clinton must consider the five gubernatorial inaugurals as he develops future rhetorical messages. A speaker's own past discourses, then, possess the power of constraint similar to a rhetorical genre. Regularity has rhetorical power over future communications.

The second part of the "mere rhetoric" argument, that self-serving, generic discourses are irrelevant by nature, fails to perceive the real impact of speech as a form of action. Scholars who study symbolic forms have struggled with this view by examining the links between culture and politics. Ritual studies provide a perspective on this relationship that is invaluable when considering genres of public address.[9] In *The Symbolic Uses of Politics,* Murray Edelman argues for a definition of ritual which is useful here:

> Ritual is motor activity that involves its participants symbolically
> in a common enterprise, calling their attention to their related-
> ness and joint interests in a compelling way.[10]

Public involvement in compelling political rituals, for Edelman, is "the most potent form of political persuasion" that, empowered with the force of myth, maintains a particular social order.[11] Far from being "mere rhetoric," political rituals such as inaugural addresses have a profound impact on society and culture.

Another theorist, James Combs, cites Orrin Klapp when he defines ritual as a "nondiscursive gestural language, institutionalized for regular occasions, to state sentiments and mystiques that a group values and needs."[12] Combs sees the often magical and transformative process of ritual as a central component in the public experience of political figures and institutions. Like Edelman, he argues that ritual plays a vital role in the legitimation, reproduction, and repair of cultures and ideologies. In fact, Combs reports, some government officials are paid to ensure that political ceremonies are carried out smoothly, operating with the "idea that the correct observation of ritual precautions is crucial to the group's success."[13] Failed rituals can become stimuli for public debates in which the effectiveness and very nature of a political system is questioned. Powerful political interests, including an incoming administration, may fear that such discussions will damage the institution's stability and their own future credibility with the electorate. When stated in its strongest terms, Combs' dramaturgical perspective implies that it matters less which specific persons and groups are involved in the political system and more that these people participate in complex ritual practices. Essentially, these practices are performative communications that celebrate cultural values and some-times transform individual citizens into leaders through state dinners, ticker-tape parades, and inaugural speeches. Still, individual charac-ters with access to powerful rhetorical resources within ritual dramas (i.e., governors who have access to inaugurals) can, within certain con-straints, shape both their own roles and the roles of social institutions such as the government.

Of the three types of rhetorical messages identified by Aristotle (deliberative, forensic, and epideictic), the epideictic may be most closely related to a ritual view of politics. The epideictic address is observed at public ceremonies such as dedications, funerals, gradua-tions, and holidays, which are all ritual events of some importance. The purpose of the epideictic address is to establish praise or blame. While deliberative and forensic speeches are delivered respectively to legislative or judicial audiences and focus on the future or the past, epideictic speeches are presented to a more general group of observers who evaluate the rhetor's skill. Aristotle maintains that the epideictic evaluates the present, but also recalls the past and contemplates the future to accomplish that task.[14] An effective funeral oration, for example, pays tribute to the deceased's past achievements and com-forts those left behind in the present by asserting that the deceased, their accomplishments, and our memories of them live into the future in meaningful ways. As we consider forms of public address that par-tially constitute important political rituals, Aristotle's epideictic genre must enter these discussions.

PRESIDENTIAL INAUGURAL AS TRANSITION RITE

The expressive, celebratory aspects of epideictic rhetoric are pro-foundly present in political rituals such as the presidential inaugural. Karlyn Kohrs Campbell and Kathleen Hall Jamieson, scholars who have written extensively on rhetorical genres, assert that the presi-dential inaugural, a potent political ritual itself, is a form of epideictic.

They explain:

> Presidential inaugurals are epideictic speeches because they are
> delivered on ceremonial occasions, fuse past and future in pre-
> sent contemplation, affirm or praise the shared principles that
> will guide the incoming administration, ask the audience to "gaze
> upon" traditional values, employ an elegant, literary language,
> and rely on "heightening of effect," that is, on amplification and
> reaffirmation of what is already known and believed.[15]

Like many epideictic ceremonies, the inaugural ritual is a highly
enthymematic form of communication, one which celebrates a tradition and body of knowledge already valued by listeners.

Five related elements characterize the presidential inaugural,
according to Campbell and Jamieson, and distinguish it from other
kinds of epideictic messages. The inaugural address unifies an audience, celebrates traditional values, communicates political principles
of a new administration, demonstrates that a president understands
the responsibilities and limitations of the office, and achieves this
through epideictic forms by "urging contemplation not action, focusing on the present while incorporating past and future, and praising
the institution of the Presidency and the values and form of the government of which it is a part."[16] They further identify the presidential
inaugural as a particular type of political ceremony: a rite of transition that "invests" the president in the office of the presidency.[17] Mircea
Eliade claims that such ceremonies, which he calls "rites of passage,"
involve "a radical change in ontological and social status" for persons
engaging in them.[18] Rituals of birth, initiation, marriage, and death
move people from one state of living to another. Similarly, the presidential inaugural ceremony changes the ontological status of a winning candidate from citizen to president through symbolic means.

In an argument more rhetorical in character than Eliade's, Bruce
Gronbeck explains that "ceremonies of cultural transition" are
required to repair systems in either unexpected or cyclical crisis.[19] The
shocking assassination of President Kennedy called for a complicated
set of symbolic events to heal the cultural fissure that developed as a
result of the sudden change. Normal changes in national leadership
brought about through the election process also create ruptures that,
though regular and predictable, nevertheless require ritual attention.

In this situation the expressive or ritual functions of public address and the instrumental or rhetorical functions merge; ritual communication gets important rhetorical work done.

Gronbeck's examination of the 1981 Reagan inaugural reveals three important components of the transition ceremony which link past, present, and future through "symbolic acts of remembrance, legitimation, and celebration."[20] Acts of remembrance in these ceremonies recognize cultural values in particular ways while acts of legitimation attempt to restore public commitment to the system and acts of celebration offer up the political process and the transition itself to be revered. Significantly, the presidential farewell address may further reinforce such ritual transitions by transforming the outgoing president from national leader to individual citizen, thus paving the way for the inaugural ceremony.[21]

THE GUBERNATORIAL INAUGURAL

Presidential and gubernatorial inaugurals are similar as rhetorical genres and serve comparable ritual functions, but interesting differences remain that deserve attention. Gubernatorial inaugurals, like their presidential counterparts, are founded in tradition rather than in law. None of the fifty state constitutions provide for an inaugural address by the governor.[22] Like the presidential formula, the inaugural address at the state level is used to unify an audience, create an image of an administration, and convey a set of political principles. Structural similarities also exist. Richard Cheatham examined the significance, style, and structure of forty-seven gubernatorial inaugurals delivered between 1963 and 1967. He observes:

> The structure of the contemporary gubernatorial introduction is usually comprised of a formal salutation, reference to the occasion, expression of gratitude to the electorate, and an appeal for unity. The body of the speech is reserved for a discussion of the problems and plans of the new administration, and the concluding remarks are used to strike a note of confidence in a promising future and to appeal for Divine Guidance.[23]

Many of these elements can be seen at work in presidential inaugurals, but some notable differences exist. In some states, such as Arkansas, the gubernatorial address prepares the audience for a more detailed policy address to be delivered later. It serves "as an 'index' to the forthcoming State-of-the-State Message."[24] Even in those speeches which serve an indexing role, policies and plans discussed in gubernatorial inaugurals tend to be considered in more concrete terms than in presidential inaugurals, perhaps due to the nature of the audience. Presidential inaugural speakers address the most general of audiences and communicate at high levels of abstraction. The influence of television in attracting and shaping a broad, national audience has been considerable. Governors, however, address more specific audiences of a regional character and tend to use the inaugural as an opportunity to discuss what they will try to accomplish while in office. Cheatham writes:

> The major portion of these gubernatorial inaugurals was devoted
> to a discussion of the problems which faced the new administra-
> tions and the solutions which the new governors were proposing.[25]

This is certainly true of Bill Clinton's five inaugural addresses, in which a great deal of time is spent discussing ways to improve education, health care, jobs, and public safety in Arkansas.

CLINTON'S ARKANSAS INAUGURALS

Arkansas's first governor, James Sevier Conway, delivered his inaugural address to a gathering of legislators and other spectators during the first session of the General Assembly on 13 September 1836. During the state's 155-year history the traditional ceremony has endured and "each elected governor, in his turn, has repeated the oath of office and turned to his audience to express gratitude to God and to the people and to share his dreams and programs for the state."[26] In a collection of the Arkansas inaugural addresses, Marvin E. De Boer contends that these speeches tell an important philosophical and political history of Arkansas. Governor Clinton writes in the foreword that the volume contains "some of the ideas and principles which have built the foundation on which Arkansas now stands."[27] The inaugurals not only tell the tale of Arkansas's "proud past" but, in true epideictic form, also envision the future "in (their) ability to reflect the dreams and hopes of all Arkansans for a better tomorrow."[28] The contributions of Bill Clinton to this mythic history merit special attention, especially when considering the significant events of November 1993. I will provide some basic background information, summarize major elements in each of the five addresses, and discuss some overarching themes in Clinton's rhetoric.

Bill Clinton was born 19 August 1946, in Hope, Arkansas, and grew up in the nearby town of Hot Springs. Degrees from Georgetown and Yale, as well as a Rhodes scholarship at Oxford University, prepared him well for a career in law. Later, in 1973, he joined the University of Arkansas School of Law in Fayetteville. Clinton won the 1974 Third District Democratic primary for state congress but lost in the general election. He successfully ran for attorney general in 1976 and held that position until becoming Arkansas's fortieth governor (and the nation's youngest governor at thirty-two) in 1978.[29] Clinton delivered his first inaugural address 7 January 1979.[30] Note the chart below for important rhetorical dates during his political career.

TIME-LINE OF THE ADDRESSES

9 January 1979:	First Clinton inaugural address
13 January 1981:	Frank White inaugural address
11 January 1983:	Second Clinton inaugural address
15 January 1985:	Third Clinton inaugural address
13 January 1987:	Fourth Clinton inaugural address
15 January 1991:	Fifth Clinton inaugural address
20 January 1993:	First Clinton presidential inaugural

The first inaugural address begins, true to the gubernatorial inaugural form, with a formal salutation to the audience. Next, through a reference to his campaign, Clinton both thanks his supporters and constructs a unified audience:

> At the outset, I wish to acknowledge what we all know well: I did not come here alone. I was carried by the people of our State, through the efforts of those who have known and nourished me, in the hope that together we might make a difference to the future of Arkansas.[31]

After establishing good will and thanking his family, friends, and staff, Clinton clarifies his purpose in the address which is to define his role as governor: "I want to explain as clearly as my command of the language will allow what kind of Governor I will try to be."[32] The speaker assures those gathered that he is aware of the responsibility that comes with this authority. Clinton states that decisions will be difficult and, though he "will seek and often will follow advice and counsel," sometimes he will have to say "No" even to his compatriots.[33] This warning helps demonstrate to the audience that Clinton will not play "good old boy" politics, but will instead exercise fair and impartial judgment: "I will do all that I can, in good faith and humility, to exercise your power well."

In the first substantial section of the speech's body, Clinton offers a list of values that later in his career will become common themes: a belief in equal opportunity, a disgust for abuses of power and government waste, a love for the environment, a concern for the burdens of the needy, and an interest in "industrious people working too hard for too little." After considering these values, Clinton examines social problems that make life "confusing, uncertain, and sometimes difficult to understand."[34] In a reference to the past, he admits that governments and individuals have limited control over change. Finite resources, complex social problems, and powerful forces beyond our control aggravate attempts to influence the world. Still, Clinton retorts, many strengths exist in the community that make it worthwhile "to believe in and work together for the elusive common good."[35] He lists some of these strengths which include pride, hope, prospects for economic growth, and the state's small and diverse population, then expresses excitement at the chance to make a difference:

> We have an opportunity together to forge a future that is more remarkable, more rich, and more fulfilling to all Arkansans than our proud past, and we must not squander it.[36]

Clinton exclaims that "there is much to be done" and suggests five areas for improvement: education, energy, heath care, economic development, and government management. In each of these areas the governor discusses both general goals and the specific proposals he plans to pursue. For example, in health care Clinton asserts that his administration will seek a variety of benefits for senior citizens, including tax relief, improved home health care, and better nursing home care. Clinton is less specific in the area of government management. Though he admits "there is a crying need for more effective management, more efficient delivery of basic services, and a renewed spirit of dedication" from state workers, he offers no proposals other than an expectation that the government will "move us forward in these areas."[37] In the conclusion of his inaugural, Governor Clinton calls upon two strengths observed earlier: pride and hope. He does not explain what they mean in the context of the speech or the state, but uses this final section as a unity-building "pep talk" in which he calls upon the Divine to support his project: "With pride and hope, and the grace of God to take our hands and lead us on, we shall not fail! Thank you, and God bless you all."[38]

Clinton lost the 1980 election to Frank White, a Little Rock banker and former Democrat. White, born 4 June 1933, won the governorship with 52 percent of the vote and delivered his inaugural address 13 January 1981. Although the address and the policies that followed it are not a focal part of this essay, they are relevant through their influence on Clinton's later inaugurals. White's address contains some familiar generic components. He expresses gratitude to the people of Arkansas, enlists the support of a unified audience, discusses some general goals of his administration, and promises to do well at the job. What is most striking about this address is that it defines itself negatively over and against the policies and goals of the previous administration. Early in the speech, White pronounces his recent election "a victory for a conservative philosophy." Like Clinton he admits that there are no simple solutions to Arkansas's problems, but White identifies the previous administration as contributing to Arkansas's unfortunate circumstances. "The people don't want to hear more rhetoric," he contends, but want responsible spending and more focus on "the quality of state government and not the quantity of state government." White describes the time as an "era of realism" in which government spending "will be responsible, austere and, most importantly, accountable."[39] He criticizes Clinton's goals somewhat implicitly here:

> The next two years will be an era of realism, knowing that our
> state government cannot fulfill the bureaucratic dream at the
> expense of the hard-working people of this state.[40]

This inaugural lacks the vision of Clinton's earlier speech and shifts attention from idealistic goals to criticisms of the "serious fiscal problems" of the previous administration. Aside from his dedication to responsible management and his opposition to new taxes and special interests, White discusses few positive goals or policies in the address. He concludes his speech by reinforcing the theme of realism, asking Arkansans to "work together," and promising to approach the task with enthusiasm and commitment.[41]

Following his earlier loss to White, Clinton joined a Little Rock law firm. Later, upon his election in 1982, Clinton became the first person to serve a second nonconsecutive term as Arkansas's governor. In his second inaugural address, delivered on 11 January 1983, Clinton reinforces some values and goals discussed in the first inaugural.[42] He forgoes the customary greetings, thanks, and unity-building rhetoric, and instead begins the speech with an analysis of the social situation, which he calls "hard times," through a personal narrative:

> The most moving story of my childhood was that of my grandfather coming home on Good Friday afternoon during the Depression and crying on his knees to my mother because he could not afford a $2 Easter dress.[43]

This story helps to establish Clinton's ethos by identifying with the struggles of the audience and by demonstrating his personal values for God and family. The governor cites a variety of factors contributing to "hard times," including three bad farming years, dependence of the work force on automobiles and housing, foreign competition, and "a national recession made worse by the national Republican economic policies." He responds to criticisms in White's inaugural both defensively, by demonstrating he is willing to cut government programs, and offensively, by arguing that "austerity is not enough."[44] Interestingly, one can observe a kind of debate in these inaugurals, a series of interactive exchanges in which the arguments of one administration are answered and refuted by the following administration in the same political ritual.

Before Clinton examines specific policy areas in the second inaugural, he defines good government:

> We must give the people a government that solves problems and seizes opportunities; a government that will fight for the people's interest, not just respond to the special interest; most importantly, a government that will give our people a better chance to fight for themselves.[45]

Clinton carves out a role for himself and his position and then identifies four priority areas: jobs, education, utility reform, and prisons. In the area of education he promotes some of the same general goals as in the first inaugural, such as higher teacher pay, increased opportunity in poor and small school districts, and improvement of vocational and high-technology programs. Apparently sensitive to economic issues, Clinton points out that while some of his programs require more money, the state "can move on the basic problems" with current resources. He anticipates and dispels the concerns of those who argue that Arkansas "can do nothing significant without large tax increases" and maintains that although it will be difficult to balance competing forces and "forge a forward march," the state can do it.[46]

Clinton refers to the past in this address not to criticize previous administrations but to dispel a self-defeating "southern hillbilly" myth:

> Too often in the past, we have helped our old foe hard times to defeat us by working against ourselves—by fighting among our-selves, by thinking too little of ourselves and what we can achieve.[47]

The governor admits he has "set an ambitious agenda for Arkansas in hard times" and responds to critics who say his program is "too full of promises" by arguing "it is far better to fall short of a lofty goal than to stand by in self-satisfaction while good people are pained by present conditions." He concludes the address with traditional words of thanks to his constituency, who "labored so that together we might lift our vision and move forward again."[48] After a final appeal to unity Clinton asks for the prayers of the people, promises to work hard, and offers a Divine blessing.

Clinton begins his third inaugural address, delivered 15 January 1985, with a recognition of the occasion and an expression of honor at being elected to another term.[49] After briefly acknowledging the "limitations of speech" he smoothly moves into considering the problems of the day, as in the previous address:

> [W]e live in a complex and challenging time, the essence of which cannot be quickly grasped, a time in which swift currents of change are sweeping through our state and nation, drawing us inexorably into a future very different from even the immediate past.[50]

The governor paints a picture of society changing quickly due to a num-ber of different social forces and implicitly asserts that government must also change and "move forward on some of the most difficult problems facing America today" or be swept away by those same problems.[51]

Clinton reviews several values which should steer the state into the future. Arkansans must believe in themselves, work toward economic growth, realize that neither political party has the entire answer, and understand that solutions take time. He criticizes the Democrats, for being too receptive to special interests, and the Republicans, for being too willing to "leave people and places behind that are unprepared to compete in the world marketplace."[52] Through an ingenious turn of a phrase, he rejects a popular Reaganesque slogan by claiming: "We may want the government off our backs but we need it by our sides." Clinton's concept of government has a conscience and is devoted to change, which he claims is the strength of democracy:

> Our democracy has lasted longer than any other because in times of crisis our system permitted change when the alternative was defeat, and our people worked for change.[53]

Three basic principles should guide the government in order for positive change to succeed in Arkansas. Government must act in partnership with the private sector, be committed to excellence and accountability, and increase public participation in government by communicating with the people when considering new taxes. Clinton promises not to support a tax unless the people of the state are convinced of its necessity and informed of its nature.

Clinton reviews several familiar components of his political agenda in the next section of the inaugural, which include increasing economic growth, improving education, and maintaining public safety. After a brief preview, he discusses each area as a "program," developed by the administration as a group (i.e., "our educational program"), that has certain goals and outcomes. For example, Clinton's economic program aims to make Arkansas competitive with other states for jobs, increase funds available for investment, and provide better job training. He celebrates the occasion of the address, given on Martin Luther King Jr.'s birthday, and promises public access to the proposed economic and educational programs.

Governor Clinton concludes this speech by appealing to the "strong support of all our people, regardless of party, region, race, age or economic situation."[54] Arkansas, which will soon realize its 150th anniversary, must "move forward." Clinton urges the audience to celebrate Arkansas's history and here compliments the state's past. Although he does not give the characteristic Divine blessing at the end of this inaugural address, the metaphor he uses seems almost spiritual in character:

> [I]f our vision is as clear as our purest stream, our will as strong as our hardest rock, our dreams as lofty as our highest peak, I believe we will succeed. We owe it to ourselves and to our children to try.[55]

This closing statement makes accepting Clinton's proposals and leadership seem a compelling and necessary step toward increasing the quality of life in Arkansas.

Clinton continued to break records as an Arkansas politician, and when reelected in 1986 he became one of only three governors (including Jeff Davis and Orval Faubus) to serve more than two consecutive terms. Additionally, an amendment which passed in 1984 took effect at this election and extended the governor's term of office from two years to four. Clinton's fourth inaugural address was delivered 13 January 1987, on the steps of the state capitol.[56] It follows a similar pattern as the other three inaugurals, in which Clinton examines the complexities and problems of the social landscape, appeals to strengths in the audience, argues for a set of guiding principles, presents a political agenda, and asks for the state's commitment to "moving forward" in a spirit of positive change.

This speech begins with a brief reference to the occasion as "a day for decision" and offers up two accomplishments of the past, in the areas of education and job growth. However, notwithstanding these achievements, Clinton contends that problems still require continued vigilance: the collapse of agriculture, rural unemployment, poor children with uncertain futures, and unskilled labor. The state has an obligation to prepare Arkansas for the twenty-first century, he argues, and it must avoid the mistakes of the past, when "in hard times, we have tightened our belts and waited for things to improve." He continues with the metaphor of change as a swiftly flowing current that presents only two alternatives: either press ahead or be pushed back. The challenges of today demand "common investments in education and human development" that allow success in a "highly integrated, highly competitive world economy."[57]

Before discussing his political agenda for the next four years, Clinton links the children of the present with the struggle for tomorrow:

> Every time a child is born with an avoidable problem; fails to learn to read; drops out of school; falls prey to drug abuse; enters the work force illiterate, your future and mine are diminished. We are in the struggle for tomorrow together.[58]

Clinton claims that Arkansas, like its children, needs three basic things to flourish: good beginnings, good schools, and good jobs. In each area, the governor presents a problem that can be improved through a particular set of policies and programs. In response to the problem of children born to poor mothers without access to education or health care, Clinton suggests six policies that are "affordable within the present tight budget, and are far less expensive than neglect."[59] De Boer notes Clinton's reference to the past in the section on good schools:

> Obviously aware of his role as the state's first sesquicentennial governor, Clinton looked back to Governor James Conway's 1836 inaugural address to reaffirm the state's obligation and commitment to education.[60]

Apparently interested in celebrating Arkansas's past, Clinton cites some of Governor Conway's statements about knowledge as a form of power. He then mentions the accomplishments of the past and proposes a number of general changes, including efforts to combat both drug abuse and adult illiteracy. Clinton asserts the third problem, that too many educated young people leave Arkansas to seek better jobs elsewhere, has already improved somewhat. He reviews a number of successes in this area and then presents nine additional programs to create more employment opportunities in the state.

Like in previous addresses, Clinton considers costs to the state immediately after submitting his plan for the future. He suggests three methods for paying for these programs: cut unnecessary state spending, more effectively enforce existing taxes, and "raise new revenues in ways that promote tax fairness and broaden the tax base." He concludes the speech by reminding the audience of their obligation to their children and their own future, asking for their support, and encouraging change:

Let us now gladly take responsibility for our own future. When the history of this year is written, let it be recorded that we did our duty, and moved our state forward into a brighter day.[61]

The fifth address, a twenty-eight-minute speech at least four times as long as any previous inaugural, was delivered 15 January 1991.[62] The inaugural ceremony was originally scheduled for the steps of the Capitol, but took place in the second-floor rotunda due to rain. Press and legislative response to the inaugural was generally favorable. Scott Morris, a reporter for the *Arkansas Gazette,* called the address "vigorous."[63] Michael Arbanas wrote that legislators were "impressed with the energy" of the speech, and they confessed "it was more specific than they had expected."[64] Ernest Dumas wrote that the fifth inaugural "was like each of the others—sweeping vision, perfect tone, masterly delivery, and more impressive for its seeming to be so effortless." Although Dumas criticized fallen promises made in previous terms, he admitted that "the prospects for Clinton's passing a major program seem brighter this time than any except the 1983 session that followed his return to grace."[65] Certainly, something distinguishes this inaugural from the other four. Perhaps Clinton had achieved a new degree of confidence and purpose in his reelection. Perhaps he hoped to use his increasing rhetorical skills to build public support for his state agenda. What seems more likely is that the governor was motivated by his increasing visibility in national politics and the possibility of a 1992 campaign for the presidency.

Clinton begins the final inaugural address rather uncharacteristically with a sense of humor:

> Every inaugural is a little different. It will be noted that this year I did know my right hand from my left, but the chief justice almost took my speaking notes away. Mr. Foster reminded me that I should always speak from the heart and never from notes. The last time I spoke from a written text, it didn't work out so well.[66]

Governor Clinton's reference to his lengthy and much-discussed introduction of candidate Michael Dukakis at the 1988 Democratic National Convention, which earned him valuable publicity in a "Tonight Show" appearance, calls attention to his national character. Following a reference to the familiarity of the occasion, Clinton tells the audience about a special service he attended at Immanuel Baptist Church "where the music raised the roof and the preaching and prayers made us all think a little more about our responsibilities."[67] It seems appropriate that he begins with the theme of social responsibility, a frequent value expressed in various forms throughout the addresses. The comment also foregrounds Clinton's Christian convictions, a definite credibility-booster for the people of Arkansas and for mainstream voters across the United States.

Clinton creates identification with the state's sometimes-disagreeable legislature through his pledge to a "new partnership" with them "for a better Arkansas." He expresses excitement at the opportunities available during the coming session, mentions Martin Luther King Jr.'s birthday, recognizes and compliments the racial diversity of the legislature, and asks those gathered to "work together in a spirit of harmony and brotherhood and sisterhood" for the good of the people.[68] In a familiar way, the speaker then reflects on difficulties in the preceding decade, a time in which farmers, factory workers, and small towns suffered and the income of 40 percent of Americans decreased after inflation. He offers hope for the future by reviewing past accomplishments, then reminds the audience that they will be repeatedly tested during the 1990s. His references to the future seem particularly appropriate for a ritual that provides guidance through time:

> Much of our future, I believe, is in our own hands. Therefore, our best, which is what we owe the people, cannot be timid or cautious even though these are troubled and uncertain times. Our best does not permit us to deny our problems or ignore our possibilities, and if all of us would be perfectly honest, we've done too much of both as a state for far too long.[69]

Change seems to be the only answer in this situation, at least as Clinton expresses it here. Next, he presents "a few simple but powerful truths" that should counsel the community through this change. Using the repeated phrase "our destiny is in our own hands," Clinton argues that improving the quality of health and education in Arkansas will raise individual incomes. "What you can earn depends on what you can learn" in a global, mobile economy. The second "powerful truth" appeals to a traditional value in the Democratic party that is expressed most profoundly in national convention rhetoric, namely that all in a community must "go forward together or not at all."[70] In his 1984 keynote address, Mario Cuomo used the metaphor of the wagon train to give considerable rhetorical force to this value.

The use of the term "investment" to describe government spending enters both the fourth and fifth addresses. Here, Clinton uses it in the policy section of his address as a justification for increased public spending on education, health care, and economic development. Clinton states:

> [T]here must be more investment. . . . whenever someone tells you it's not a money problem, they're almost always talking about someone else's problem. It is a money problem. We do need to increase our investment if we want to increase opportunity.[71]

Clinton examines each of the three areas and recommends that a variety of programs be pursued. In education, he promises to create a "trust fund" to promote opportunities in adult literacy programs, create apprenticeships for those who do not make it to college, retrain math and science teachers, provide academic scholarships for middle-class high school graduates, and increase teacher pay. In health care, he focuses on pregnant mothers, children, rural communities, and alternatives for insurance coverage. Clinton contends that America, unlike any other advanced economy, does not provide health-care access to all its people, and that we "spend a higher percentage of our income on health care than any other country in the world."[72] He criticizes the national government for not taking leadership in response to this problem, but insists that Arkansans cannot wait for change from above. Clinton spends less time discussing the third area of investment, economic development, which includes programs to improve highways and bridges, small businesses, and the environment.

Instead of dealing with programs then addressing sources of funding, as he does in other speeches, here Clinton concludes the investment proposals with a community-building section in which he asserts that money is not enough:

> If we're going to have a real new sense of community, the people who are paying the bill have got to be convinced that government is taking the money only to do those things which government has to do . . . and that we are holding ourselves accountable for the way we're doing business.[73]

He then reviews a number of "spontaneous applause lines" that he has received during eight months of community meetings around the state. According to Clinton, Arkansans applauded when he suggested that child-support laws be stiffened, that nonviolent offenders be put in boot camps to pay back the community instead of "being rewarded" with prison money, that the children of working families have access to college scholarships, and that procedures for getting a driver's license be simplified.[74] Clinton urges legislators to do something for the community—for the people—in order to renew trust in government. He suggests a number of other programs in the final section of the speech, then refutes those who claim the state should wait until the Persian Gulf conflict has ended before acting. The governor insists that events in the Gulf will not change Arkansas's situation. He maintains:

> The best thing we could do in this legislative session for America is to do Arkansas's part to guarantee that we can compete with anybody anywhere for anything that's worth having. And the best thing we can do for all those wonderful men and women from this state who are in the Persian Gulf today, the very best thing we can do, is to give them a better Arkansas to come home to.[75]

Unlike previous inaugural addresses, Clinton ends this speech without a Divine blessing, instead opting for a simple "Thank you."

RHETORICAL AND RITUAL ANALYSIS

Early during Bill Clinton's years as governor of Arkansas, his inaugural addresses followed Cheatham's model closely. In the first speech he recites the greetings, thanks, and unity-building statements one might expect from a freshly elected state official in a democratic culture. He ponders the challenges facing the state and offers a number of programs to meet those challenges. Finally, he expresses confidence that the people and the legislature are up to the task and seeks Divine support and guidance in that process. Still, as is true of any generic representative, a distinct style emerges from Clinton's rhetoric as he responds to Arkansas's unique political context and gains experience in epideictic communication.

Interestingly, each of the Clinton inaugurals have some unique traits. The first address is highly formulaic, filled with blunt parallel phrasing, is less specific in the policy section than other speeches, and lacks components that eventually become part of Clinton's commanding style. Though it meets the requirements of the situation, it seems immature and does not inspire the same interest in change that works so well in other speeches. The conclusion's appeals to the virtues of pride and hope are oddly vague and not very compelling. The second address is filled with responses to Clinton's critics in Frank White's administration and in the legislature. The argumentative tone of this address interferes with more visionary functions of the inaugural; although it, too, is a competent speech. The third and fourth addresses are, perhaps, most uniquely Clinton in tone and expression. In these two speeches one can see the governor at a distinct moment in forming his rhetorical appeals. Unfortunately, the fourth address is dominated by discussion of specific programs to the detriment of other parts of the speech. In the fifth inaugural address Clinton seems distracted from his primary epideictic and deliberative purposes by thoughts of a run for the presidency. This speech is much longer than any of the others, includes talk of the Gettysburg Address (which could suggest an attempt to sound presidential), and addresses both a state and national audience. For example, Clinton broadens the "Arkansas problem" section of the speech to include the difficulties of all Americans.[76] After reviewing social problems, citing recent accomplishments, offering up a set of values, and promoting a particular agenda, the governor launches into unfamiliar territory here. Clinton reports that he has traveled throughout the state and listened to the concerns of "the people," then reviews a long list of additional programs that appeal to various segments of his audience, apparently trying to appear on top of every problem in the state. The final inaugural ends on an odd note of refutation in which Clinton argues that Arkansas should move forward on his agenda despite developments in the Persian Gulf.

Although each of these speeches are different in some ways, key elements exist that characterize Clinton's rhetorical style. Clinton speaks in a relatively plain style in these addresses, only occasionally using metaphors or lofty language. He uses parallel phrasing extensively in the first inaugural, then more subtly and less often in the other speeches. Occasionally, he tells a personal narrative, usually to inspire emotion in his audience. Governor Clinton almost always examines the causes and complexities of Arkansas's problems in these speeches and sometimes discusses such things at the beginnings of his addresses, as in the second and third inaugurals. With the exception of the first speech, which is an anomaly in many ways, the inaugurals also include criticisms of the past. The Arkansan past, for Clinton, represents in-fighting, low state self-esteem, economic backwardness, failure, inaction, and denial. However, the governor often finds achievement in the more immediate past and in several speeches reviews the success of state programs, presumably to justify continued public trust in his policies. Clinton celebrates the strengths of the people in several of the addresses, which include pride, hope, diversity, community, stability, and potential. He usually advances a set of values or truths to guide the state's future decisions, and arranges political proposals in three to five discrete categories directly following that discussion. For example, in the third address Clinton provides a list of basic principles, which includes belief in self, growth as a goal, unity beyond party differences, and patience. After defining principles that should guide the state, Clinton presents his political agenda for the coming term. In the final section of several inaugurals, Clinton implies that though times have been difficult the people have survived. He repeatedly concludes his addresses by challenging the community to "move forward" in a unified spirit of change.

Clinton celebrates the concept of change throughout the inaugural addresses in a powerful way by criticizing the past, using two influential metaphors, and directing the state's vision toward a positively valorized future. In all but the first address, he portrays the past as a failure of some sort. In the second inaugural he states that in the past "we have helped our old foe hard times to defeat us by working against ourselves . . . by thinking too little of ourselves and what we can achieve."[77] In the third inaugural he claims the state has not taken politics seriously. Clinton also asks the people to "move Arkansas from the economic backwaters to the crest of prosperity and opportunity in America."[78] The state has cut investments during hard times and "put off progress in favor of survival."[79] Each of these criticisms of the past, if accepted by the audience, make it difficult to look for the common good in Arkansas's history. Equally difficult is the struggle to find answers in the present, which as Clinton describes it in the speeches contains much struggle and hardship. Clinton's metaphors for change fit into a positive portrayal of the final possibility—the future—quite well. Arkansas must "go beyond the prison of past thinking"[80] or be swept away by a stream called change:

> Survival *requires* progress. We are swept along on currents of change which are too swift and too strong. No one can stand still in the middle of the stream. Either we press ahead or we are pushed back. There is no status quo.[81]

Clinton offers only two choices with the metaphor of change as a forceful current; Arkansas can move and adapt to changing times or be pushed deeper into the mud of poverty and ignorance. The second metaphor uses the image of change as a "forward march." Clinton constantly urges his audience to "move forward."[82] He combines the movement metaphor with a weather metaphor in the closing statement of the fourth inaugural:

> Let us now gladly take responsibility for our own future. When the history of this year is written, let it be recorded that we did our duty, and moved our state forward into a brighter day.[83]

Throughout this rhetoric Clinton locates opportunity and promise in the future as an avenue for progressive change.

As Edelman suggests in his definition of ritual, ceremonies such as the inaugural unify an audience by calling attention to their common interests and connectedness. Clinton uses a variety of rhetorical techniques to build a community which will accept his leadership in the future. He uses words like "we," "us," and "our" to symbolically create a group and include himself among the people. In the second inaugural, Clinton's statement "Now the election is over, and we are one people again" calls attention to audience unity and identifies all people in the state as Arkansans.[84] In the first inaugural, Clinton effectively positions the power of government with the people of Arkansas:

> I will do all that I can, in good faith and humility, to exercise your power well. I must ask you to abide with me, through differences and disappointments, for only then can we move our State forward in these promising but difficult times.[85]

Later in the same speech he celebrates strengths of the people using the word "we" at the beginning of each phrase.

Governor Clinton constructs an ideal audience through his rhetoric in the inaugural speeches and identifies their characteristics, their strengths, even their weaknesses. His use of the word "Arkansan" to depict their connectedness in the third inaugural is especially effective as he describes plans for the state's 150th birthday celebration, to which "we will welcome every Arkansan around the world to come home and take part." Clinton foregrounds the state identity of those who consider themselves Arkansans in order to further unify the audience. Unlike most of his references to the past, he declares in one speech that "there is so much in our rich past to be proud of, to learn from, to honor."[86] The people of this state share a history, a set of qualities, and a geographic area which is portrayed as a kind of home. In a more complex argumentative form Clinton points to common interests to create unity. He asserts that the success of the state's children is connected to everyone's future and declares that "we are in the struggle for tomorrow together."[87] Finally, Clinton makes some overt pleas for unity. After mentioning Martin Luther King Jr.'s birthday in the fifth inaugural, he asks those gathered to commit themselves "to working together in a spirit of harmony and brotherhood and sisterhood for what is best for all of our people."[88]

Unity among the observers of such performances is critical for acceptance of a given ritual as genuine. This is very important because, as Combs argues, when rituals are genuine they provide structure and stability to a system through legitimation. One important way that rituals legitimize political systems is by defining the social roles which organize relations in that system. In the first inaugural Clinton rather overtly begins to define his role as governor and the role of government in general. Throughout the addresses he elaborates on his view of the link between state and citizen, a relationship dominated by themes of responsibility and obligation. As a state, Clinton insists, Arkansas should not "forget what we can and should do" in response to the struggles of its people.[89] The government has an imperative to accomplish more than simple austerity:

> We must give the people a government that solves problems and seizes opportunities; a government that will fight for the people's interest, not just respond to the special interest; most importantly, a government that will give our people a better chance to fight for themselves.[90]

The "government with a conscience" cannot ignore the difficulties of Arkansans but must advocate positive change.[91] It must be "responsible and caring," meet "basic responsibilities," and move Arkansas to the twenty-first century.[92] After developing this role for government early in his inaugural rhetoric, Clinton uses it as a criterion for evaluating proposals. In the fourth speech he defends programs which "will allow us to meet our obligation to our children and to our future."[93] In the fifth inaugural Clinton contemplates a recent church service which "made us all think a little bit more about our responsibilities."[94] There are other references to duty in the five inaugural addresses that contribute to a particular image of government as a caring parent with moral, social, and legal obligations to all of its family members.

CONCLUSIONS

The moderate southern governors offered a new mythic vision of society to the electorate, one more progressive and compassionate than previous philosophies which were driven, in part, by racial hatred. Bill Clinton's particular vision manifests itself in his five gubernatorial inaugural addresses; it looks to the future for hope, understands change as a positive force, and values a government with social responsibility. The gubernatorial inaugural address, though similar in many ways to the presidential inaugural, functions somewhat differently. Unlike the presidential inaugural, which seems almost completely epideictic in character, in this address epideictic merges with deliberative in a compelling way. Clinton refutes specific and general criticisms in these speeches and even engages in critique himself. The presidential form of this address discourages such conflicts, instead foregrounding decorum and modesty in the speaker's ethos and unity as an organizing principle. Not surprisingly, one can also find specific proposals for future change in gubernatorial addresses, as legislators noted after hearing Clinton's fifth and final speech. Although Clinton certainly hopes—in an epideictic fashion—to respond to the ritual requirements of a given rhetorical situation through the gubernatorial addresses, he also aims to convince people to accept his agenda and he anticipates and refutes criticisms. This demonstrates that political rituals can have instrumental as well as expressive functions. The gubernatorial inaugural accomplishes material tasks through deliberative rhetoric, such as persuading legislators to approve funding for an adult literacy program, while simultaneously fulfilling its epideictic function by weaving a mythic story that guides a community.

Several questions arise from this examination of Clinton's rhetoric. First, this analysis is far from complete. To truly understand the influence of Clinton's inaugurals on a particular group in a particular political context, one would have to engage various audiences. This might involve analytical investigations of press responses to the speeches, study of voter polls, even ethnographic research on how audience members actually understood and reacted to Clinton's rhetoric. Additionally, to truly understand the nature of political rituals in a dramaturgical paradigm all forms of communication would need to be considered. What kind of movements and nonverbal exchanges took place during the ceremonies? Who was present? What costumes and props were involved? Besides the speeches, what other words were spoken? Most important, what do all of these things mean in the context of the rituals themselves?

Second, the influence of Clinton's inaugural rhetoric on the southern myth requires more analysis. How does Clinton compare to the other southern governors identified in Smith's work? What unique contributions has Clinton made? In what ways are these governors similar in their discourse and in what ways are they different?

Third, one can not help but wonder how the former governor's communication in these speeches has influenced—and will continue to influence—his rhetoric as president. As I stated previously, not only do rhetorical genres constrain future examples of the same genre, but one's public discourse constrains one's own future public discourse. Themes exist in the presidential inaugural that are also common to the gubernatorial inaugurals, such as the recurring motif of change as a necessary part of a healthy democratic society.[95] One could certainly examine Clinton's presidential inaugural to search for other examples of stylistic devices, rhetorical forms, mythic themes, and political agendas similar to those expressed in his gubernatorial inaugural addresses.

NOTES

1. Stephen A. Smith, *Myth, Media, and the Southern Mind* (Fayetteville: University of Arkansas Press, 1985), 73–74.

2. Ibid., 74.

3. Ibid., 73.

4. Ibid., 73, 124; See also Richard Cheatham, "An Overview of Contemporary Gubernatorial Inaugurals," *Southern Speech Communication Journal* 40 (Winter 1975): 191–203.

5. For analyses of the presidential inaugural, consult Karlyn Kohrs Campbell and Kathleen Hall Jamieson, "Form and Genre in Rhetorical Criticism: An Introduction," in *Form and Genre: Shaping Rhetorical Action*, ed. Karlyn Kohrs Campbell and Kathleen Hall Jamieson (Falls Church, Va.: Speech Communication Association, 1978), 9–32; Karlyn Kohrs Campbell and Kathleen Hall Jamieson, "Inaugurating the President," in *Essays in Presidential Rhetoric*, ed. Theodore Windt and Beth Ingold (Dubuque, Iowa: Kendall/Hunt, 1987), 23–42; Bruce E. Gronbeck, "Ronald Reagan's Enactment of the Presidency in His 1981 Inaugural Address," in *Form, Genre, and the Study of Political Discourse*, ed. Herbert W. Simons and Aram A. Aghazarian (Columbia: University of South Carolina Press, 1986), 226–45; Robert N. Bellah, "Civil Religion in America," *Beyond Belief: Essays on Religion in a Post-Traditional World* (New York: Harper and Row, 1970), 168–89. For a more general rhetorical discussion, consult James W. Ceaser, Glen E. Thurow, Jeffrey Tulis, and Joseph M. Bessette, "The Rise of the Rhetorical Presidency," in *Essays in Presidential Rhetoric*, ed. Theodore Windt and Beth Ingold (Dubuque, Iowa: Kendall/Hunt, 1983), 3–22.

6. For analyses of the gubernatorial inaugural, consult collections of addresses such as Marvin E. De Boer, ed., *Dreams of Power and the Power of Dreams: Inaugural Addresses of the Governors of Arkansas, 1836–1986* (Fayetteville: University of Arkansas Press, 1988). See also Cheatham, 191–203; R. Thomas Quinn, "Out of the Depression's Depths: Henry H. Blood's First Year as Governor," *Utah Historical Quarterly* 54:3 (1986): 216–39.

7. Campbell and Jamieson, "Form and Genre in Rhetorical Criticism," 18.

8. Lloyd Bitzer, "The Rhetorical Situation," *Philosophy and Rhetoric* 1 (1968): 1–14; See also Leo Finkelstein Jr., "The Calendrical Rite of the Ascension to Power," *Western Journal of Speech Communication* 45 (Winter 1981): 51–59; Martin J. Medhurst, "American Cosmology and the Rhetoric of Inaugural Prayer," *Central States Speech Journal* 28 (Winter 1977): 272–82.

9. For a more comprehensive review of such theories, consult Benita Dilley, "A Dramaturgical Analysis of the 1989 Inauguration of George Herbert Walker Bush: 'Engaging' a Smooth and Successful Role Transition." Unpublished paper presented at the Central States Speech Communication Association Convention, 1991.

10. Murray Edelman, *The Symbolic Uses of Politics* (Urbana: University of Illinois Press, 1985), 16.

11. Ibid., 18.

12. Orrin E. Klapp, *Collective Search for Identity* (New York: Holt, Rinehart, and Winston, 1969), 121; cited in James E. Combs, *Dimensions of Political Drama* (Santa Monica, Calif.: Goodyear, 1980) 19.

13. Combs, *Dimensions of Political Drama*, 25. For a model of ritual as practiced, consult Ronald L. Grimes, *Ritual Criticism: Case Studies in Its Practice, Essays on Its Theory* (Columbia: University of South Carolina Press, 1990).

14. Aristotle *Rhetoric,* trans. W. Rhys Roberts (New York: The Modern Library, 1984), 1358b.12–20.

15. Campbell and Jamieson, "Inaugurating the President," 24.

16. Ibid., 24–25.

17. Ibid., 24. See also James L. Hoban Jr., "Rhetorical Rituals of Rebirth," *Quarterly Journal of Speech* 66 (October 1980): 282–83.

18. Mircea Eliade, *The Sacred and the Profane: The Nature of Religion,* trans. Willard R. Trask (San Diego, Calif.: Harcourt Brace Jovanovich, 1959).

19. Gronbeck, "Ronald Reagan's Enactment of the Presidency in His 1981 Inaugural Address," 226.

20. Ibid.

21. Glenn C. Getz, "Presidential Address as Ritual Transition: An Evaluation of Carter's Farewell." Unpublished paper presented at the Speech Communication Association Convention, 1993.

22. Cheatham, "An Overview of Contemporary Gubernatorial Inaugurals," 192.

23. Ibid., 202.

24. Ibid., 193.

25. Ibid., 201.

26. De Boer, *Dreams of Power and the Power of Dreams,* xiii.

27. Ibid., xi.

28. Bill Clinton, "Foreword," in ibid., xi.

29. Biographical data from De Boer, *Dreams of Power and the Power of Dreams,* 1155. For a discussion of specific people and events in Clinton's political career, consult Charles F. Allen and Jonathan Partis, *The Comeback Kid: The Life and Career of Bill Clinton* (New York: Birch Lane, 1992).

30. De Boer, *Dreams of Power and the Power of Dreams,* 1157–60.

31. Ibid., 1157.

32. Ibid.

33. Ibid., 1158, 1157.

34. Ibid., 1158.

35. Ibid., 1159.

36. Ibid.

37. Ibid., 1160.

38. Ibid.

39. Ibid., 1165–67.

40. Ibid., 1166.

41. Ibid., 1167.

42. Ibid., 1173–75.

43. Ibid., 1173.

44. Ibid., 1173.

45. Ibid., 1173–74.

46. Ibid., 1175.

47. Ibid.

48. Ibid.

49. Ibid., 1176–80.

50. Ibid., 1176.

51. Ibid., 1176.

52. Ibid., 1177. This criticism seems to echo Mario Cuomo's "wagon train" metaphor in the 1984 keynote address to the Democratic National Convention.

53. Ibid., 1177.

54. Ibid., 1180.

55. Ibid.

56. Ibid., 1182–87.

57. Ibid., 1182, 1183.

58. Ibid., 1183.

59. Ibid., 1184.

60. Ibid., 1181.

61. Ibid., 1186.

62. "State's Future Is in Our Hands," transcript of Clinton's fifth gubernatorial inaugural address, *Arkansas Gazette*, 16 January 1991, 4H.

63. Scott Morris, "Clinton Sworn In for Fifth Term," *Arkansas Gazette*, 16 January 1991, 1A.

64. Michael Arbanas, "Legislators Impressed with Education, Highway Plans," *Arkansas Gazette*, 16 January 1991, 4H.

65. Ernest Dumas, "Inaugural Address Sounds Familiar," *Arkansas Gazette*, 16 January 1991, 5H.

66. "State's Future," 4H.

67. Ibid.

68. Ibid.

69. Ibid.

70. Ibid.

71. Ibid.

72. Ibid., 5H.

73. Ibid.

74. Ibid.

75. Ibid.

76. Ibid., 4H.

77. De Boer, *Dreams of Power and the Power of Dreams*, 1175.

78. Ibid., 1177, 1180.

79. Ibid., 1182.

80. Ibid., 1177.

81. Ibid., 1182.

82. Ibid., 1175.

83. Ibid., 1187.

84. Ibid., 1175.

85. Ibid., 1158.

86. Ibid., 1180.

87. Ibid., 1183.

88. "State's Future," 4H.

89. De Boer, *Dreams of Power and the Power of Dreams*, 1158.

90. Ibid., 1173–74.

91. Ibid., 1177.

92. Ibid., 1180, 1182.

93. Ibid., 1186.

94. "State's Future," 4H.

95. "Text of President Clinton's Inaugural Address," transcript of Clinton's presidential inaugural address, *Cedar Rapids Gazette*, 21 January 1993, 8A.

BILL CLINTON'S
STUMP SPEAKING

Persuasion through Identification

JOHN T. LLEWELLYN

Old speechwriters wait for the speech—one that a politician knows by heart and believes moves his audiences—to see if candidates grasp the dynamics of their own campaigns.
—William Safire

For its detractors, the political stump speech is cotton candy for the mind. It is the noise a candidate makes while the media listen for a sound bite and while handlers pray that reporters will "discover" the theme for the day. Those charges against the stump speech have some merit; Safire is alluding to the transitory and inconsequential nature of such events in describing the setting for a Clinton stump speech at a community college in Maryland as "a useful suburban backdrop" and the attendees as "a couple of thousand nice people on a pleasant day . . . festooned in ribbons of momentary authority."[1]

However, these criticisms are ultimately superficial and ill-advised. They miss the point that in the enactment of the humble stump speech by presidential contenders is to be found the linchpin of the modern campaign. This form of campaign speaking that has evolved over two centuries brings candidates and the populace together as no other method can. The campaign stump speech is the single clearest presentation of the candidate's world view. While discounting the scene itself, Safire's observations underscore the fact that campaign analysts understand well the significance of these little performances, perhaps even better than the campaigns which craft the words and the candidates who speak them.

With a fuller appreciation for the stump speech, this essay will examine Bill Clinton's standardized message and consider how it employed the rhetorical technique of identification to persuade listeners. To create a context for the examination, I will discuss modern campaign speaking, the set speech, historical and current applications of stump speaking, and the utility of identification as a persuasive technique.

THE EVOLUTION OF CAMPAIGN SPEAKING

Modern presidential campaigns consist of traveling from city to city and state to state delivering essentially the same message to rallies at shopping malls, airports, and civic centers. Media representatives who soon come to know the candidate's stump speech as well as the candidate does tag along to monitor public response to the campaign's message and to be handy if someone takes a shot at the candidate.

As the name may suggest, the origins of the term "stump speech" are to be found in campaigns on the American frontier. Despite the hardships of frontier life, oratorical skill was highly prized and diligently sought. Competing candidates would travel to the hamlets where they might share a platform or literally mount a stump; each speaker would hold forth for an hour or more, only to be replaced by his opposite number who would speak with similar zeal and endurance.[2]

In the modern era of glitzy consultants and million-dollar media buys, ponderous railroad tours to small-town sidings and bus caravans to an endless chain of shopping centers and school gymnasiums seem dull indeed. Yet few candidates are willing to bypass this important electoral work. While they may not have read about Gladstone and the Scottish campaign of 1879, they feel its power in their bones: "Stump oratory, heretofore unknown in British politics, had toppled the entire Conservative majority and carried the Liberals into power."[3]

Gladstone broke ground in media relations; his ostensibly local campaign was covered nationally; the nineteenth-century press pool even included a New York reporter. The fact that Gladstone made many speeches while en route to his Midlothian constituents introduced the concept of national whistle-stopping to raise issues even outside the voting area of greatest concern.[4] Some scholars dispute the depth of innovation reflected in Gladstone's tactics.[5] However, there is no disagreement that he proved the persuasive power of one eloquent speaker with a mission.

One of the charges leveled at Gladstone was the derisive assertion that he was behaving like an American. His critic was none other than Queen Victoria.[6] But this assessment of American political practices was misguided, at least as it characterized presidential campaigns. There was in the nineteenth century a convention that presidential candidates should be called, nominated, and then seated on a porch for the balance of the campaign. The *Atlantic Monthly* explained this practice with an analogy: "It is thought a dignified part in a lady or a candidate in so serious an affair as marriage or the Presidency, to wait till they are asked, and it is believed that they would only hurt their cause by making advances."[7]

It fell to Horace Greeley to break this convention of silence in his 1872 campaign to defeat incumbent Ulysses S. Grant. He tried something new—a speaking tour of eight states. In the long term this innovation proved revolutionary to American political life; in the short term Greeley paid the price. His actions "shocked the nation," as evidenced by the fact that his popularity was highest *before* the speaking tours and his defeat most pronounced in states where he spoke. In all, he carried only six of thirty-seven states. Perhaps it was a relief that Greeley died 29 November 1872, before the electoral college met. It would be a quarter century before anyone again tried stumping in support of his presidential aspirations. In 1896 William Jennings Bryan spoke out in the first of his three unsuccessful bids for the presidency. Although he never won that office, his candidacy was taken seriously when he addressed the public in his campaigns.[8]

Despite its impact on American political campaigns, the stump speech is often suspect due to questions about its authorship. Although "ghost writing" has become so widespread as to be the norm in campaigns, pundits publicly decry the practice. Modern campaigns are haunted by the folklore that Adlai Stevenson authored his own rhetoric in the frenzy of the campaign. The facts reveal the truth: "one of Stevenson's speechwriters in the 1952 presidential campaign describes a crew that numbered as many as 12 writers at times."[9] However, these revelations neither dispel the myth of the ideal candidate as rhetorical dynamo nor weaken the implication of lesser status for candidates who consult others in their speech preparation.

Potential benefits from stump speaking include generating publicity, emphasizing issues, and energizing the troops. However, the precise impact of stump speaking is impossible to quantify: "No one really knows how much value in changed votes or turnout is gained by personal visits to a particular state. . . . Yet no one is absolutely certain that whistle-stop methods produce no useful result."[10]

Consider John Kennedy's 1960 campaign in Ohio. He visited that pivotal state several times but lost it, although with a better Democratic showing than in 1956. Subsequent analyses showed that the population of Roman Catholics, not campaign appearances, was the best predictor of electoral outcome.[11] However, it may be that stumping in Illinois turned the tide for Kennedy in that state.

Some candidates are well advised, as was Warren Harding, to stay home and keep their feet out of their mouth. Generally, however, front-runners and challengers alike are inexorably drawn to the stump: "The spectacle of seeing one's opponent running around the country at a furious pace without following suit is too nerve-wracking to contemplate."[12]

THE SET SPEECH—POLITICAL MANTRA

The stump speech is the mantra of modern political campaigns. Candidates repeat these remarks at whistle stops, in nursing homes, and to crowds at rallies. Although reporters soon know the speech by heart, it is not overhauled because its purpose is not information transfer. The stump speech is the foundation of a ritual interaction; the performance continues as candidates refine their messages and craft a rapport with the audience. The rhetorical device of identification is one of the primary tools through which this rapport is created.

There are many terms for the standard campaign speech: "set speech";[13] "module" or "stock" speech;[14] or "stump speech." The multiplicity of names should not disguise the fact that all of these are terms for a speech composed of clusters of ideas to mix and match for ease of delivery. These speeches catalyze the crucial audience-candidate interaction, according to Kessel, who argues: "The speech given most during the campaign is not written at all. It evolves—a pastiche of applause lines the candidate has discovered in previous months of campaigning, a 'theme song' made up of phrases that the candidate likes and that have demonstrated their ability to spark crowd reaction."[15]

As the campaign progresses, audience reactions to stump speeches take shape, and candidates winnow these ideas and phrases. These refined remarks then become useful in a number of formats: talk shows, candidate forums, debates, and even campaign commercials.[16] So it happens that the core ideas for these more high-profile performances are derived from the lowly stump speech where the campaign's ideas were first expressed.

Candidates handle stump speeches in a variety of ways. Jimmy Carter chose to give one canned speech and then take audience questions rather than adapt a core or module speech. As a result, reporters learned to listen closely to his question-and-answer sessions. Carter was spontaneously answering questions on difficult issues that might have been carefully managed in a module speech. Thinking on his feet led Carter to such unconsidered statements as his allusion to "ethnic purity" and jeopardized his campaign and its focus.[17]

In his 1966 U.S. Senate race against incumbent Paul Douglas, Charles Percy ran no such risk of substantive error. He delivered ten to fifteen minutes of remarks from the back of the train during his whistle-stop tour. Half of this time was taken up with the introduction of his family; then came comments on one or two campaign issues, followed by one of three humorous, writer-prepared anecdotes about himself or his family. Finally, Percy waved to the crowd as the train departed fifteen to twenty minutes after its arrival.[18]

Nelson Rockefeller's stump speaking procedures during his 1970 New York gubernatorial campaign allowed him to blend local influence and statewide policy. His speech writers relied on County Data Books, compilations of politically useful information on each county, in preparing his informal remarks on data-rich note cards: "These cards enabled the Governor to mount the stump at a county fair, for example, and move immediately to local issues on an informal, conversational basis."[19]

The most politically significant speech in America in the last thirty years was given on 27 October 1964. On that night the nation watched as a stump speech was born. Ronald Reagan delivered a half-hour television address in support of candidate Barry Goldwater and Republican values. While Goldwater's candidacy was not saved, Reagan fared better: "With this speech, Reagan rose out of a disastrous Republican defeat to establish himself as a potential candidate for Governor of California, and the 'hottest new product on the Republican horizon.'" In 1965 Reagan fleshed out his potential by expanding the speech to forty-five minutes and stumping with it across ten thousand miles to keep 150 engagements with conservative audiences reeling from the Johnson landslide.[20]

It remains for Horace Greeley to remind us that audiences look for something more than a good performance from stump speakers. The *Atlantic Monthly* observed that during his campaign Greeley deservedly drew large and responsive crowds due to his status as a great actor and stage manager, but concluded: "These qualities ought not be passed over without some recognition; but after all, we do not covet them in a President." In the end, Greeley suffered the ultimate embarrassment of the candidate on the stump: Audiences laughed at his jokes, shook his hand, and then "watched the queer old whirligig disappear round a bend of railroad track, and voted against him."[21]

STUMP SPEAKING—HISTORICAL ROOTS, MODERN INCARNATIONS

According to Gold, election speeches emerged in Great Britain as early as 1806. Apparently, the new tactic caught on. During the 1812 elections a candidate for the House of Commons from Liverpool delivered 160 speeches in less than two weeks. In 1830 candidate Henry Brougham addressed crowds of ten, fifteen, and twenty thousand in Yorkshire in the course of three days. He traveled one hundred miles and made eight speeches in a single day.[22]

Over time, discussing public policy "out of doors," that is, outside the House of Commons, became more acceptable. "Agitation," as social movements were then known, also promoted stump speaking as groups sought first to influence public policy and later to elect sympathetic members to the House of Commons.[23] Gladstone's 1879 Midlothian campaign gave "out of doors" new meaning; in a two-week span he spoke to eighty-seven thousand persons in Scotland and the *Times* printed eighty-five thousand of his words.[24] Gold summarizes Gladstone's impact: "Given the frequency and the location of Gladstone's little whistle stops, I think we must conclude that these comprised the innovative aspect of the Midlothian campaign." The transformation of norms concerning political speaking in public was so complete that one observer could comment, "Mr. Disraeli himself had taken to going around the country, doing what would be called in America stump oratory and doing it remarkably well."[25]

In the modern era, perhaps the most famous American encounter with stump speaking or whistle-stop touring is Truman's 1948 presidential campaign. Truman's underdog status and comeback victory are well remembered. The tour covered twenty-two thousand miles in thirty-five days and included 275 speeches with as many as 16 given in a single day. In these efforts, Truman spoke from notes, which allowed him to adapt to individual audiences. The influence of Truman's stump speaking on his comeback is reinforced by Press Secretary Charles G. Ross: "In the aggregate, these little speeches were perhaps more important than the major addresses. They got him close to the people."[26]

While Truman took to the rails to reinforce his identity, Percy was seeking a new image. Following his defeat by Otto Kerner in the 1964 Illinois gubernatorial race, Percy sought to rehabilitate his image; he wanted to be warmer, more articulate, and more persuasive. In the 1966 campaign Percy also wanted to convey an "action" image and to differentiate himself from an aging incumbent. A sixteen-hundred-mile, twenty-three-city, four-day tour was selected as an image and differentiation device. In explaining the four-hundred-thousand-vote margin for a candidate who had never held elective office, the campaign manager concluded: "Percy's ability to project his action image and his speaking on the 'whistle-stop' tour were key factors in his victory."[27]

Stump speaking has a distinguished political heritage, but how is it relevant to the modern mass-mediated politician? Public expectations sustain the practice even though political spot advertisements and talk show appearances may reach many more voters. As a consequence of media coverage, campaign speeches are no longer subject to massive alteration because local audiences are primarily part of the broad national audience.[28] Modern stump speaking techniques have become part of what Kathleen Jamieson labels a new eloquence for an electronic age. In this new era the fire of the orator has been replaced by the warmth of intimate disclosure which targets not conquest but conciliation (read: identification). Five features of this modern eloquence are specified: brevity (the media will not cover long-winded orations, so speeches are short—twenty minutes or so); reductionism (issues are no longer multifaceted, the universe has been reduced to two sides—

good and evil); conversational tone (speeches have become talks between friends, more suited to the living room that to the lecture hall); an autobiographical cast (public issues are understood and discussed by speakers through the lens of their personal experience—what Jamieson labels "the interiorization of public discourse"); and, directness (that is, not delivered from a scripted text).[29]

IDENTIFICATION AND PERSUASION

Rhetorical scholar Kenneth Burke first underscored the power of identification as a modern persuasive tool.[30] His notion holds that all effective argument, including political argument, aims to convince listeners that the speaker is like them in some essential way. The classic (and somewhat hackneyed) example is the politician's claim offered when addressing a group of farmers: "I was a farm boy myself." That identification between speaker and audience, if accepted by the audience, serves as the cornerstone of trust which may make later policy proposals more attractive.

As Burke has noted, "Identification is affirmed with earnestness precisely because there is division."[31] Presidential campaigns are attempts to carve a majority out of the electoral college. That majority is sought through appeals to geographical, racial, economic, and ideological interests. Those appeals bring into relief significant differences within the body politic; those differences are the division of which Burke speaks. He explains how property distribution generates classes, the members of which in turn become mysteries to one another and feel guilt about the estrangement. It falls to experts in advertising, journalism, and politics to orchestrate a courtship among the classes; courtship does not transcend these mysteries, it only manages them.[32] So while politicians craft messages to appeal to the masses, they are also conscious of the tensions inherent in our political structure.

Candidates, and very often voters, do not wish to be confronted with the untidy realities of divergent interests. Public reluctance even to recognize class differences leads to some interesting contortions: For instance, media representatives highlight candidate preferences in food and drink as subtle markers for class affiliations.[33] Identification is one mechanism, used here in a courtship process, for creating political unity while blunting unpleasant realities. Identification draws its power from the fact that we are more likely to find attractive the positions presented by people we also find attractive or with whom we otherwise feel connection. When candidates seek political support from the broader society, they must grasp Burke's central tenet of identification: "You persuade a man only insofar as you can talk his language by speech, gesture, tonality, order, image, attitude, idea, *identifying* your ways with his."[34]

In reality, identification processes can be very subtle. In the hands (and mouth) of a skillful politician the sophisticated identification process has an elasticity and malleability which makes it particularly ephemeral, as Burke illustrates:

> He was a sincere but friendly Presbyterian—and so
> If he was talking to a Presbyterian,
> He was for Presbyterianism.
> If he was talking to a Lutheran,
> He was for Protestantism.
> If he was talking to a Catholic,
> He was for Christianity.
> If he was talking to a Jew,
> He was for God.
> If he was talking to a theosophist,
> He was for religion.
> If he was talking to an agnostic,
> He was for scientific caution.
> If he was talking to an atheist,
> He was for mankind.
> And if he was talking to a socialist, communist, labor leader,
>   missiles expert or businessman,
> He was for PROGRESS.[35]

Politicians must be seen as exceptional men and women in some dimension to be worthy of high office. Yet, in a democracy, signs of elitist tendencies are anathema to a successful campaign. Political campaigning, "pressing the flesh," is an interminable series of attempts at identification through speaking strategies, handshaking, consuming ethnic delicacies, and taking a turn at the plate in a local softball game.

One dimension of the identification process which has received scant examination is the effect of meeting a candidate on electoral outcomes.[36] By extension, seeing a candidate in person may also be influential. Thus, increased attraction may result from the nonverbal impact, as well as the verbal content, of the stump speech.

To measure the effect of interpersonal communication on electoral politics, Kaid studied a personal contact campaign conducted by Ken Buzbee in a race for Illinois House of Representatives. Having met the candidate proved to be the single strongest factor in explaining pre-election voter decisions, especially for voters who were not members of the candidate's party. While presidential campaigns are far more complex than state legislative races, interpersonal contact or even sharing space at a campaign rally may represent particular invitations to identification. Kaid seems to sense as much when she suggests extending her study to analyze the effect of media forums (e.g., stump speeches) on political campaign communication because these settings combine mass media with interpersonal communication.[37]

Identification is used in many communicative settings—political campaigns, organizational persuasion, and public service announcements, for example. The easiest cases in which to illustrate the workings of identification are sometimes extreme. Identification, like rhetoric itself, is an inherently neutral device which can advance the arguments of the saint or the scalawag, if the audience chooses to be receptive to the strategy. These illustrations sharpen the understanding of identification; however, such tactics are used in many settings less flamboyant than the instances that follow.

Despite being a seven-term incumbent, Rep. George Hansen of Idaho's Second Congressional District faced severe problems as he ran for reelection in 1984. The problems centered around his four felony convictions for filing false financial reports and a five- to fiteen-year prison sentence, which was under appeal at the time of the election. Morcover, this was not Hansen's first brush with the law. In 1974 Hansen pled guilty to violating federal campaign disclosure laws, and in 1976 the Internal Revenue Service charged him with violations of information and disclosure laws. One would assume that any candidate running under these disadvantageous conditions would be crushed. However, Republican Hansen lost to Democrat Richard Stallings by 133 votes out of 200,000 votes cast, a margin of less than one-tenth of 1 percent.[38]

How does a candidate successfully campaign under such conditions? Hansen mounted a masterful campaign in which he identified himself with the interests of his constituents; he explained his troubles as evidence that the government wanted such an effective critic out of the way; he reminded his constituents that he shared their values and their Mormon faith while his critics respected neither of these; and, he cast himself in the role of Saint George seeking to protect his district from the dragon of a distant and malicious federal government. To observers outside this rural Idaho district, Hansen's claims may sound fanciful; regardless, Hansen knew his audience and created messages that led them to identify with and support him even in the face of felony convictions. Kelley concludes: "If identification is the aim of rhetoric, then Hansen's choices were fundamentally sound and may even have been judicious."[39]

The second example of the power of rampant identification is presented by a famous class of political rascal, the southern demagogue. Braden observes that men like Ben Tillman, Theodore Bilbo, and Eugene Talmadge adopted rustic dress and countrified manners to win political support. He concludes: "They became masters at establishing the impression that they were 'just one of the boys,' or at making 'plain folks' appeals. In other words, they knew that identification constitutes powerful persuasion."[40] Gibson examined Talmadge's 1934 gubernatorial campaign in Georgia and found red suspenders and a red bandanna used as identification devices.[41] Talmadge used his very body as evidence in appeals to agrarian voters (rural counties had disproportionate political power in Georgia):

> I resent anyone on earth saying they are closer to labor, or a better friend to labor, than I. I am a laborer myself. You can look at my hands, and the color of my skin and tell it. The first little poem I remember, when I was a small boy, went something like this: Mother told me, father showed me; Hard labor makes a man.[42]

Candidates more staid than the Talmadges of the world also employ identification strategies. Sillars notes that Dwight Eisenhower was a powerful unifier for the Republicans in their 1952 campaign. However, even the strength of the electorate's identification with Eisenhower could not be transferred to the broader Republican ticket; the principle is that identification is interpersonal and non-transferable.[43] Freeley confirms Ike's popularity and makes clear that it was the product of much more than shared policy preferences. He quotes an observer of an Eisenhower rally who notes that middle-aged women "assume the same look of ecstatic transport that their daughters wear when they are being 'sent' by Elvis Presley." Charisma notwithstanding, communication scholars have identified four Eisenhower strategies which promote identification: (1) he opened and closed speeches with references to the audience and the place; (2) he referred to his office often and cited soon-to-be-released statistics; (3) he evidenced concern for the individual; and (4) he enacted the answer to the health issue by the number of speeches he gave and the vigor he displayed.[44]

Despite his problems with fielding questions after stump speeches, Jimmy Carter was ultimately successful because he adapted the persuasive strategy in his stump speeches to the national mood. He identified himself with national renewal and gave the voter the opportunity to identify with him. This strategy succeeded by giving Americans the opportunity to vote for themselves and their faith in the country by voting for candidate Carter.[45]

It might seem that identification is an electoral panacea. Candidates should line up to be just like the common man and their problems will be solved. While voters want a candidate who embraces common practices and values, they are also wise enough to know that there is more to elective office than being "average." In fact, Trent has documented a successful electoral strategy rooted in a retreat from identification. She studied identification strategies employed in Richard Nixon's 1960 and 1968 campaigns and found that in his second, and successful, campaign Nixon markedly reduced his linkages to the audience.

For all of his earnestness as a campaigner, Nixon may not have been well served by some of his efforts at identification in the 1960 campaign. He is the only national candidate I have discovered who has frontally demonstrated the shallowest form of Burkean identification, the "I was a farm boy myself" gambit. While speaking at the National Plowing Contest site in Sioux Falls, South Dakota, on 23 September 1960, Richard Nixon said to the assembled agriculturalists: "I grew up on what we call a ranch in California. It was a citrus ranch. I know what it means to dig a burrow, and hoe weeds out from under the trees . . ."[46]

Identification was used in 45 percent of Nixon's sample sentences in 1960 but in only 26 percent of the 1968 sentences. While it is impossible to say precisely why this change occurred, Trent speculates convincingly that in 1968 the goal of the campaign was no longer to present Nixon as a next-door neighbor. He had not won elective office on his own since 1950, and one more defeat might demote him to the status of neighbor in fact. To counter his 1960 defeat, in 1968 Nixon ran not *for* president but *as* president, stressing experience and exuding a presidential aura.[47]

Trent did not find that all identification strategies vanished from the 1968 Nixon campaign. She describes three standard identification strategies: (1) obvious relations (allusions to local persons, places, etc); (2) common ground, including common man appeals (references to shared beliefs, etc.); and (3) American values (alignment with national values and goals). While the first two categories declined significantly between 1960 and 1968, Nixon conducted what identification he used through appeals to American values, even though this category also declined. So rather than stand among the voters via an identification strategy in 1968, rhetorically Nixon stood authoritatively above them, while praising the view of the American panorama that was available from both levels.[48]

In studying the organizational persuasion offered employees through company newsletters, Cheney has advanced Burke's notion by specifying three common modes of identification: explicit identification (common ground); antithesis (common enemy); and transcendence (the assumed "we").[49] These modes are also evident in political discourse. In summary, Burke reinforces the unavoidable connections among identification, communication, and persuasion: "So, there is no chance of keeping apart the meanings of persuasion, identification ('consubstantiality') and communication (the nature of rhetoric as 'addressed')."[50]

IDENTIFICATION AS PERSUASION IN CLINTON'S STUMP SPEECHES

On 22 April 1992 candidate Bill Clinton addressed a rally in Johnstown, Pennsylvania, at a branch campus of the University of Pittsburgh. He spoke for twenty minutes and ranged with the audience through a discussion of health-care costs, German tax laws, and his upbringing in his grandparents' simple grocery store. Ten of the sixty-seven paragraphs make explicit reference to the presidential campaign, and in only one, the penultimate, does he overtly solicit votes. But of course candidate Clinton had been soliciting audience votes for the entire twenty-minute oration. In fact, every time he gave this speech in its various incarnations he was similarly motivated; he was discussing the issues, but the real issue behind all of these policy questions was "Who should run the country?"

This discussion of identification strategies offers a way to understand the methods used by Bill Clinton (and any other candidate with a scintilla of rhetorical subtlety) to persuade voters to support his candidacy. The campaigner as rhetorician will seek every means to make policies and the politician presenting them attractive to voters.

The first point to be made is that Clinton's Johnstown remarks are entirely consistent with Jamieson's five-element template for the new eloquence. The presentation was brief by stump standards, roughly twenty minutes. It presented a clear dichotomy between the sitting administration and the vision Clinton articulated for America: "We elected people to high office who had the wrong response to the problem. And that's what this election is all about. Three or four big, simple ideas, even though the problems are complex." There can be no doubt that Clinton is using a conversational, as opposed to an erudite, tone: "Then you start your plant overseas and you lose money the first couple of years when you start the plant. You get to deduct those losses from your American income tax. Then when you start to make money, if you leave your money in a foreign bank, you never have to pay a penny of tax on it."

That Clinton's remarks have an autobiographical cast is clear. As he subtly offers himself as evidence for his theories of education, social mobility, and playing by the rules, Clinton recounts tales of his widowed mother and his nurturing, although poorly educated grandparents and their "tiny grocery store in an integrated neighborhood in a little southern town." Gwen Ifill, who covered the Clinton speech in Johnstown, noted that Clinton usually delivered the stump speech without notes.[51] For all of these reasons, candidate Clinton is a fitting exemplar of the electronic age's new eloquence; that is, a brief, dichotomized discussion of issues as presented extemporaneously and explained autobiographically.

Beyond its conformance to Jamieson's predictions, there are other salient features of Clinton's foray into persuasion through identification. The central and most surprising feature of these remarks is that they rely upon throwing up to Americans the successes of other nations. Few speeches by effective national politicians are so full of adulation for the efforts of others. This is an outsider strategy to be sure and a somewhat risky one in that ethnocentric appeals are readily available to one's opponent. These comparative moves could be made only when the audience believes something is seriously wrong with the status quo. The strategy is made more palatable by its connections to a rebirth of the American dream.

The Clinton identification devices, in the order of their impact, include personal language and pronouns, enactment, contrasts, low-tech talk, and the cast, location, and timing depicted in these remarks. These issues will be dealt with in turn.

The most striking feature in the Clinton stump speech is its intensely personal language. This feature is also the central element of the speech in terms of its identification strategy. To be sure, any public-speaking situation is uni-directional; one person, usually of higher status, speaks while a group of others listen. Bill Clinton's standard campaign remarks as exemplified in his speech in Johnstown have all the trappings of a conversation. Surely this is a very powerful identification strategy; the candidate is speaking to the audience and about the audience as though he were everyone's uncle or wise older brother. Consider this paragraph: "The last thing I'm going to tell you is this. You've got to decide whether you believe in citizenship or not. It's always so fashionable to hate politicians today. Especially me, look at all the stuff you've heard about me."

Pronouns count for a great deal in this Clinton speech. Of the 3,609 words in the body of the Johnstown remarks, 382 (roughly 11 percent) were pronouns or pronoun forms. In descending order of frequency, there were 114 instances of second-person pronouns (you, your); this represents 30 percent of the total. There were 95 first-person-singular pronouns (I, me, my), 25 percent of the total. There were 65 instances of first-person-plural pronoun forms (we, us, our), 17 percent of the total. Third-person-plural pronouns (they, them, their) were used 59 times, 15 percent of the total. "It" and "its" occurred 37 times in the remarks, 10 percent of the total. Third-person-singular pronouns (he, she) were found 12 times, 4 percent of the total.

This approach to examining Clinton's remarks is not a remote exercise in accounting. In a much more detailed analysis Hart has established the probative value of paying close attention to the "little" words in a message.[52] For the critic, the most striking feature of this stump speech is its personal tone; the speech "feels" interpersonal and conversational. The extensive use of pronouns is the marker of this tone. An address in which one-tenth of the words are pronouns is going to be personal. Clinton is speaking often about the listener ("you") and clearly staking out his own positions ("I," "me"). The speech is intensely about "you" and "I" becoming "we." This is a classic presentation of Burke's notion of courtship.

Cheney's designation of the transcendent "we" as a persuasive move finds fertile ground in these remarks. Clinton is inviting the audience to stand with him in conducting the campaign and in taking this perspective on the nation and its ills. This speech is literally and figuratively about you, it is about me, and it is about us. This is Clinton's message independent of the more substantive content of the speech. This direct plain-spoken relationship with his listeners is revealed in this pattern in the use of pronouns, which is Clinton's dominant mode of identification. Late in his remarks Clinton spotlights the audience when he asserts that "this system begins with you, and this election is about you. It isn't about me. It's about you and your problems and your promise and your future . . ." While the election is about the audience rather than Clinton, this claim comes only after twenty minutes of remarks from the stump in which he has forged a strong bond with listeners.

Enactment is the second instance of identification employed by Clinton. It is already clear that Clinton is invested in his message. Enactment suggests that Clinton is also wrapped up in his argument. The speech explains what has gone wrong in the country over the past eleven years and outlines policy steps to correct these errors and reanimate the American dream. But in telling the audience the story of his early years, he is transcending his personal rags-to-riches or at least rags-to-prestigious-service story; Clinton is showing the future efficacy of his policy proposals through the story he tells of his own life. He is subtly telling the audience that the path represented by these proposals, though challenging, is not to be feared because he has already been there:

> But when I was a kid, my mother was widowed . . . left me to be raised by my grandparents until I was 4. . . . Franklin Roosevelt was President and gave people hope again by giving them jobs again and giving them work to do.

> And they told me if I worked hard and studied hard and
> played by the rules I could do anything. . . .
> Then I came up through the public schools because of the
> Government. . . . I had to have a loan, and I paid back every
> penny of it. Because that gave me a chance to make a decent
> living and have a future.

Without being overt in its approach, this speech is intense in its dichotomizing. The speech has an embedded point-counterpoint structure. Audience members are given numerous opportunities to identify with the positive polarities and to decry the negative halves recounted in Clinton's descriptions of the recent American scene: one percent of the population with more wealth than the bottom 90 percent; the American tax code, which is fraught with disincentives, versus the German tax code, which promotes retraining of workers; and people who sold their companies "down the drain" during the eighties in contrast to factory workers whose futures were devastated. If identification is compensatory to division as Burke asserts, then Clinton is showing his audience volumes of division for which identification with his plans is the only logical answer.

Burke identifies style and word choice as avenues for identification. Clinton's stump speech is not fancy oratory; it is written at a simpler level than a daily newspaper. This is low-tech talk designed to allow listeners to understand and identify with Clinton's message. This style of writing is premised on the idea that common sense ideas should be conveyed through common sense language. Here are examples of Clinton's conversational, low-tech talk:

> I want to make just a few sort of basic points about this
> election. . . .
> Well, everything is not fine. We have had it their way for 11
> years. And we're going downhill as a nation. . . .
> High school dropouts in the work force—out there working
> for a living—what's happened to them?

Finally, it is instructive to look at how the speaker constructed the cast, location, and time line of his remarks. One of the resources of rhetoric is that speakers can reach forward or back in time for ideas and allusions. They can mention many people or no one as they construct their message. Speakers also are free to choose where the key places are to be. So, who does Clinton mention in his remarks? Even without reference to the adjectives and verbs which surround these proper nouns, the astute observer can grasp the flow of the action. Clinton's named cast includes the Federal Reserve Board, the Federal Government, President Bush (three mentions in all), Texas senator Lloyd Bentsen, newly elected Pennsylvania senator Harris Wofford, Europeans, Japanese, Republicans, and Franklin Roosevelt. Clinton reaches back to talk about the Great Depression (two mentions), the 1920s, a decade ago, eleven years ago (twice), and two years ago; he reaches forward to discuss "next year" and Tuesday. The locations he names include Pennsylvania, New York State, the Bronx, Brooklyn, Washington, Texas, Johnstown, overseas, Europe, and Little Rock. This exercise identifies who, where, and when are the significant elements in Clinton's message; to the extent that we willingly adopt the elements of this narrative, we identify with Clinton's storyline and thence with his conclusions. While rhetoric braids all of these elements together seamlessly, the astute critic can make much from these pieces, even absent the verbs and adjectives the speaker would supply in the original.

CONCLUSION

Candidate Clinton joined the long line of stump speakers when he took to the campaign trail. The tradition rooted in Gladstone's success and Greeley's failure has evolved into interpersonal communication events reported through mass media channels. These events and channels play out candidates' efforts to embody Jamieson's new eloquence for the electronic age.

Identification is a persuasive strategy that is used by demagogues and more staid politicians as well. It represents a means of assuaging the divisions inherent in the social order. By building links between themselves and audiences, leaders can tap positive regard as a form of political capital.

Candidate Clinton made effective use of identification as a persuasive tool in his stump speeches during the 1992 campaign. His most remarkable feat was making attractive to American audiences a string of examples of how social and economic problems are handled better elsewhere in the world. Clinton then promised voters that he would adopt the policies behind these examples and reinvigorate the American dream. The Clinton identification devices included an intensely personal connection with the audience through his language and life story. He subtly stresses identification through antithesis by presenting contrasting data pairs; listeners can easily see which side of the pair they want to endorse. Candidates, especially challengers, enjoy few advantages in presidential campaigns. One such advantage exists in the realm of identification where challengers may encourage voters to identify with the dreams embodied by the campaign while incumbents are held accountable for the realities and frustrations of daily life. In part as a consequence of successful campaign identifications, candidate Clinton's next campaign will be undertaken as an incumbent. At that time, his identifications will have to blend his dreams of "four more years" with the realities created by his first term.

NOTES

1. William Safire, "I Am a Pencil," *New York Times*, 3 September 1992.

2. Frances L. McCurdy, *Stump, Bar, and Pulpit: Speechmaking on the Missouri Frontier* (Columbia: University of Missouri Press, 1969), 47, 83.

3. Newell D. Boyd, "Gladstone, Midlothian, and Stump Oratory," *Central States Speech Journal* 30 (1979): 144–55.

4. Ibid., 149.

5. Ellen Reid Gold, "Gladstone's Role in the Development of Stump Oratory," *Communication Studies* 33 (1982): 379–93.

6. Boyd, "Gladstone, Midlothian, and Stump Oratory," 154.

7. William E. Rickert, "Horace Greeley on the Stump: Presidential Campaign of 1872," *Western Journal of Speech Communication* 39 (1975): 175–83.

8. Ibid., 183.

9. Joseph E. Persico, "The Rockefeller Rhetoric: Writing Speeches for the 1970 Campaign," *Communication Quarterly* 20 (1972): 57–62.

10. Nelson W. Polsby and Aaron Wildavsky, *Presidential Elections: Strategies of American Electoral Politics*, 6th ed. (New York: Scribners, 1984), 172.

11. Ibid.,172.

12. Ibid.

13. Michael Pfau and Roxanne Parrott, *Persuasive Communication Campaigns* (Boston: Allyn and Bacon, 1993), 234.

14. Judith S. Trent and Robert V. Freidenberg, *Political Campaign Communication: Principles and Practices* (Westport, Conn.: Praeger, 1983), 171.

15. John H. Kessel, *Presidential Campaign Politics*, 4th ed. (Pacific Grove, Calif.: Brooks/Cole, 1992), 134.

16. Trent and Freidenberg, *Political Campaign Communication*, 171.

17. Polsby and Wildavsky, *Presidential Elections*, 175.

18. Jerry E. Mandel, "The Presentation of Image in Charles H. Percy's Whistle-Stop Tour of 1966," *Communication Studies* 21 (1970): 209–16.

19. Persico, "The Rockefeller Rhetoric," 60.

20. Kurt Ritter, "Ronald Reagan and 'The Speech': The Rhetoric of Public Relations Politics," *Western Journal of Speech Communication* 32 (1968): 50–58.

21. Rickert, "Horace Greeley on the Stump," 179.

22. Gold, "Gladstone's Role in the Development of Stump Oratory," 382.

23. Ibid., 379.

24. Boyd, "Gladstone, Midlothian, and Stump Oratory," 150.

25. Gold, "Gladstone's Role in the Development of Stump Oratory," 386, 390.

26. Malcolm O. Sillars, "Harry Truman at the Whistlestop," *Quarterly Journal of Speech* 38 (1952): 42–50.

27. Mandel, "The Presentation of Image in Charles H. Percy's Whistle-Stop Tour of 1966," 210.

28. Robert G. Meadow, "Televised Campaign Debates as Whistle-Stop Speeches," in William C. Adams, ed., *Television Coverage of the 1980 Presidential Campaign* (Norwood, N.J.: Ablex, 1983), 93.

29. Kathleen Hall Jamieson, *Eloquence in an Electronic Age* (New York: Oxford University Press, 1988), 65.

30. Kenneth Burke, *A Rhetoric of Motives* (Berkeley: University of California Press, [1950] 1969), 20.

31. Ibid., 22.

32. Ibid., 208.

33. Barry Brummett, "Gastronomic Reference, Synecdoche, and Political Images," *Quarterly Journal of Speech* 67 (1981): 138–45.

34. Burke, *A Rhetoric of Motives*, 55.

35. Kenneth Burke, quoted in Roderick P. Hart, *Modern Rhetorical Criticism* (Glenview, Ill.: Scott, Foresman, 1990), 361.

36. Lynda Lee Kaid, "The Neglected Candidate: Interpersonal Communication in Political Campaigns," *Western Journal of Speech Communication* 41 (1977): 245–52.

37. Ibid., 252.

38. Coleen E. Kelley, "The 1984 Campaign Rhetoric of Representative George Hansen: A Pentadic Analysis," *Western Journal of Speech Communication* 51 (1987): 204–17.

39. Ibid., 215.

40. Waldo Braden, *The Oral Tradition in the South* (Baton Rouge: Louisiana State University Press, 1983), 89.

41. Chester Gibson, "Eugene Talmadge's Use of Identification during the 1934 Gubernatorial Campaign in Georgia," *Southern Speech Communication Journal* 35 (1970): 342–49.

42. Ibid., 347.

43. Sillars, "Harry Truman at the Whistlestop," 99.

44. Austin J. Freeley, "Ethos, Eisenhower, and the 1956 Campaign," *Communication Studies* 9 (Spring 1958): 24–26.

45. Christopher L. Johnstone, "Electing Ourselves in 1976: Jimmy Carter and the American Faith," *Western Journal of Speech Communication* 1978 (42): 241–49.

46. Judith S. Trent, "Richard Nixon's Methods of Identification in the Presidential Campaigns of 1960 and 1968: A Content Analsis," *Communication Quarterly* 19 (Fall 1971): 23–30.

47. Ibid., 25.

48. Ibid., 23.

49. George Cheney, "The Rhetoric of Identification and the Study of Organizational Communication," *Quarterly Journal of Speech* 69 (1983): 143–58.

50. Marie Hochmuth (Nichols), "Kenneth Burke and the 'New Rhetoric,'" *Quarterly Journal of Speech* 1952 (38): 133–44.

51. Gwen Ifill, "Clinton's Standard Campaign Speech: A Call for Responsibility," *New York Times*, 26 April 1992. All quotations are taken from the *New York Times* transcription.

52. Roderick Hart, *Verbal Style and the Presidency: A Computer-Based Analysis* (New York: Academic Press, 1984).

THE JEREMIADIC LOGIC OF BILL CLINTON'S POLICY SPEECHES

CRAIG ALLEN SMITH

Bill Clinton's campaign for the presidency was unusual because of its attention to policies. Usually, presidential campaigns introduce their candidates first and their positions later, if at all. However, Frank Greer, who headed the Clinton advertising team, noticed that 1991–92 voters cared more about solutions than biographies. Consequently, the Clinton campaign stressed "The Plan" throughout the campaign, even before introducing the candidate to the public.[1] From Little Rock through New Hampshire, the Super Tuesday states, New York, and California, candidate Clinton spoke in multipoint plans. Moreover, his speeches were distributed through the Internet computer network and saved in the Sunsite archive at the University of North Carolina at Chapel Hill, from which they can be retrieved and studied—free of charge—by anyone with a personal computer and an electronic mail address. Clinton's strategy, the Internet connection, and, of course, C-SPAN coverage converged to offer citizens an unprecedented amount of policy information.

This essay examines twelve of Clinton's most important campaign speeches—ten major policy addresses as well as his announcement and acceptance addresses—to better understand the role of policies in political campaigns and in the Clinton administration in particular. It is based on an intrinsic analysis of Clinton's speech texts independent of extrinsic information about Clinton, his policies, or his strategy. I will argue that Clinton's policy speeches were part of an overarching political jeremiad, and that this jeremiadic logic both framed his critique of the Bush presidency and helped Clinton to consolidate his support. But first we need to clarify the nature of political jeremiads.

POLITICAL JEREMIADS

The jeremiad is a rhetorical form that frames social problems in the logic of God's covenant with a chosen people.[2] In their most inclusive sense, jeremiads depict a people chosen by God who formed a covenant to undertake a sacred mission or errand. The problems afflicting them are characterized as divine tests of their worthiness or as punishment for straying from their mission and covenant. When the Puritan jeremiad could no longer withstand the religious diversity of a changing America, Puritan values and forms diffused into America's cultural tradition. Eventually there reemerged a secular or political jeremiad, in which Puritan doctrine was replaced with the civil religion of the American dream.[3]

Modern jeremiads evaluate progress by our attainment of an American dream that joins the moralistic dimension of life, liberty, and the pursuit of happiness with the materialistic dimension of the work ethic, individual initiative, and the free market.[4] More than two centuries after the Puritans, American jeremiads continue to describe a special people chosen by God who grow from their adversity and attain a better future by conducting themselves in accordance with the covenant. Jeremiads outlived Puritanism because they remained useful. Jeremiadic logic is a culturally acceptable mode of reasoning that organizes the premises of a chosen people, divine sanctions, and ultimate success into a recognizable narrative form. Although many jeremiads use vivid language to describe dangers, apocalyptic language is not a defining characteristic of jeremiads.

The modern jeremiad's rhetorical power has at least three sources.[5] First, they reinforce the chosen people's sense of exceptionalism while enabling them to escape personal blame for their problems. Secondly, jeremiads transcend apparent contradictions such as (1) God's chosen people will suffer; (2) hard times warrant optimism; and (3) future success requires a return to the past. Each of these statements pairs an unpleasant empirical observation with a psychological reassurance, and modern Jeremiahs fuse them together with the fire of jeremiadic certainty. They climb to a different vantage point from which the apparent contradiction becomes a validation of all that the chosen people need to believe in times of trouble. A third source of persuasiveness lies in the jeremiad's ability to stimulate and validate shared fantasies. The shared fantasies and the emotional gratifications that attend shared fantasizing contribute to membership in, and loyalty to, the rhetorical community. Fantasy themes provide discursive gratifications for psychological needs, thereby stimulating emotions and providing people with "meanings and emotions that can be set off by a commonly agreed upon cryptic symbolic cue."[6]

In summary, the secular jeremiad is an important element of America's rhetorical culture. It is a particular narrative logic that recounts the history of chosen people who, as the heirs to a unique covenant between God and the founders, are destined to attain both the moralistic and materialistic dimensions of the American dream. Whenever the chosen people have violated the spirit of their covenant they have been beset by social, economic, and political crises that cannot be alleviated by social, economic, or political changes alone, because those tribulations are divine sanctions. Instead, restoration of an ancient truth is necessary, even sufficient, to resolve the crises. Jeremiads persist because they are persuasive. And they are persuasive because they enable the chosen people to avoid blame for their society's problems; they transcend apparent contradictions; and they provide emotional and psychological gratifications.

Because it presumes divine interest in the chosen people without presuming that each of them receives direct, personal divine guidance, jeremiadic logic requires prophetic leaders. Emergent leaders who cast their messages in jeremiadic logic tap into community logic and don the vestments of secular prophets. Political candidates frequently echo Jeremiah's warnings of false prophets: Crises occurred because the chosen people were led astray by false prophets who must be renounced and replaced by a new prophet who will help them to restore the covenant. Not surprisingly, jeremiads abound in the corpus of presidential nomination acceptance addresses where emergent prophets unify their chosen peoples around their sacred missions to wrest power from the false prophets so that the chosen people can fulfill the promise of the American Dream.

THE CLINTON POLICY JEREMIAD

Bill Clinton's 1992 campaign policy speeches were part of an overarching political jeremiad.[7] The "Slick Willie" moniker obscured the remarkable consistency of Clinton's message, throughout his career and his campaign. The jeremiadic themes pervaded his campaign speeches, and their full flavor can best be appreciated by reconstituting the whole from its parts. This essay will therefore pull together passages from the twelve speeches to illuminate his jeremiadic logic and its rhetorical implications.

Clinton's jeremiad centered around a central truth revealed to him long ago by a scholar at a private religious university in the nation's capital, a revelation thus invested with academic, sacred, and governmental authority. Clinton told this story to four of his ten audiences and implied the themes for the others, but the following passage from his address to the American Association of Retired Persons (AARP) captures it best:

> When I was a freshman at Georgetown University 28 years ago,
> I had a professor of Western Civilization [Carroll Quigley] who
> said that the very special thing about our civilization in general,
> and the United States in particular, is that we had always believed
> that the future could be better than the present, and that each of
> us has a personal, moral responsibility to make it so.[8]

The key themes of Clinton's truth were optimism, confidence, responsibility, and hard work.

The central truth of Clinton's covenant differed from both the Horatio Alger stories (in which hard work and clean living *caused* success), and from the Puritan notion that success was divine recognition of moral worth. In Clinton's view, hard work and clean living *should* lead to success, and prosperity *should* be an indication of moral worth; but it is not always so. This he had learned from his grandfather, who "taught me more about equality in the eyes of the Lord than all my professors at Georgetown, more about the intrinsic worth of every individual than all the philosophers at Oxford," and "more about the need for equal justice than all the jurists at Yale Law School."[9] His grandfather:

> ran a country store in our little town of Hope. There were no food
> stamps back then, so when his customers—whether they were
> white or black, who worked hard and did the best they could,

came in with no money—well, he gave them food anyway—just made a note of it. So did I. Before I was big enough to see over the counter, I learned from him to look up to people other folks looked down on.[10]

A Horatio Alger story would have criticized Clinton's grandfather for undermining the unfortunate shoppers' personal discipline and thrift. But Clinton learned to differentiate among optimism, hard work, and success.

This, then, was the covenant struck between God and the founders of American government: The party of the first part promised that tomorrow would always be better than today, so long as the parties of the second part fulfilled their personal moral responsibility to make it so. This sounds like a bad deal for the parties of the second part, for if they make tomorrow better than today they should have little need for the party of the first part. But it is the party of the first part who makes the covenant work by making the good people prosperous, by punishing the irresponsible, and, like Clinton's grandfather, by providing good things for good people who are short of cash.

The campaign argued that most Americans had been meeting their personal moral responsibilities to make a better tomorrow ever since the Democrats left the White House, but they found themselves bitterly disappointed and frustrated by the 1990s, which were not what had been promised. In short, the chosen people had fulfilled the moral responsibilities of the American dream, but they found themselves unable to reap its material bounty. Clinton told a Georgetown University audience that, "your future—the very future of our country—the American Dream—is in peril. This country is in trouble. . . . I've seen too much pain on people's faces, too much fear in people's eyes."[11] His travels introduced him to many people with stories to tell, and most of their stories told of hard work and disappointment. Candidate Clinton's speeches were peppered with tales of hard-working people whose faith in the covenant had been shaken. He told of a chemical engineer fired a month before his pension was fully vested so that his employer could trim the payroll. He told of a husband working two jobs and a wife working fifty hours a week in a mill who feared that their straight-A son would be unable to attend college. He told of a twelve-year-old child who had undergone open-heart surgery, and how the child's father could not get work because no company could afford his health insurance.[12] And he told of a man in a hotel uniform who told him:

> Where I came from we were poor, but at least we were free. Here in America we are no longer free. When my boy cannot walk across the street to the park in my neighborhood unless I walk with him, he is not free. When my boy cannot walk down the street to the school in our neighborhood unless I walk with him, he is not free. If I do what my boy asks and vote for you, will you make my boy free?[13]

These were not just the stories of people, these were stories of the *chosen* people.

Clinton's chosen people were the Americans who had believed in the covenant, who had accepted personal responsibility, and who had done their best to forge a better tomorrow. "The people I met," said Clinton, "[are] the backbone of the country, the ones who do the work and pay the taxes and send their children off to war."[14] He observed that:

> Middle-class people are spending more hours on the job, spending less time with their children, bringing home a smaller paycheck to pay more for health care and housing and education. Our streets are meaner, our families are broken, our health care is the costliest in the world and we get less for it. The country is headed in the wrong direction fast, slipping behind, losing our way.[15]

Clinton "worried about the families that live by family values and play by the rules and still get the shaft. . . . and that includes about eighty percent of the people who live in this country today."[16]

How could 80 percent of the country work hard, pay their taxes, shoulder their responsibilities, and still not succeed? The answer is that some Americans had forgotten the eternal truth, lost sight of their sacred mission, and broken faith with the covenant. He told the Democratic Leadership Council that:

> the thing that is killing our country today is that millions of Americans, from New Hampshire to Southern California, from southern Florida to Washington, get up every day and do not believe that tomorrow will be better. They do not believe anything will change. They do not believe politics can make a difference. They do not believe they can make a difference.[17]

And he told the AARP that:

> the plain truth is that millions of our fellow citizens of all ages do not believe the future will be better than the present, and millions more do not believe they have a personal, moral responsibility to make it so.[18]

By straying from their covenant the chosen people had contributed to a general worsening of the situation as "in the face of massive challenges, our government stands discredited, our people disillusioned. There's a hole in our politics where a sense of common purpose used to be."[19]

This lost sense of common purpose—the Puritan's sacred mission to build a shining city on a hill—had to be rediscovered to end what Clinton termed *America's "crisis of community":*

> a spiritual crisis that calls upon each of us to remember and to act upon our obligations to one another. The purpose of community, the purpose of our government, the purpose of our leaders should be to call us to pursue common values and common good, not simply in the moment of extreme crisis but every day in our lives.[20]

This common purpose was the "spirit that built America" from "the barn raisings on the old frontier to the immigrant mutual aid societies" to the "churches that have helped generations of African Americans to make their way."[21] That spirit of community and common purpose was an essential clause of the covenant that Clinton sought to restore:

> I want an America with those convictions to have a renewed sense of community, an America that is coming together, not coming apart. I want to bring back the American spirit that says we're all in this together, and we're going to rise or fall together.[22]

In the closed theocracy of Puritan New England, preachers like Jonathan Edwards could rail against their congregations for straying from their sacred trust. But in the secular political jeremiads of a pluralistic electorate the chosen people are led astray by false prophets, and in this case the false prophets lived at 1600 Pennsylvania Avenue and their initials were GOP.

Bill Clinton's policy jeremiad attacked George Bush, Ronald Reagan, the Republican party and their well-heeled cohorts for shirking their personal, moral responsibilities to make tomorrow better than today. "Everything we believe in, everything we've fought for," he said in his announcement speech,

> is threatened by an administration that refuses to take care of our own, has turned its back on the middle class, and is afraid to change in a world that is changing so fast.[23]

"For 12 years of this Reagan-Bush era," he said at Georgetown,

> the Republicans have let [Savings and Loan] crooks and self-serving CEOs try to build an economy out of paper and perks instead of people and products. It's the Republican way: every man for himself and get it while you can. They stacked the odds in favor of their friends at the top, and told everybody else to wait for whatever trickled down.[24]

The problem was not that these people had prospered, but that they had prospered alone. At Notre Dame Clinton invoked Rabbi Hillel to underscore the moral transgression: "If I am not for myself, who will be for me. If I am only for myself, who am I?"[25] In a community of shared purpose—the community of barn raisings and mutual aid—those who prosper find ways to help the hard-working people. But:

> every step of the way, the Republicans forgot about the very people they had promised to help—the very people who elected them in the first place—the forgotten middle-class Americans who still live by American values and whose hopes, hearts, and hands still carry the American Dream.[26]

Clinton characterized the Bush administration as "reactive, rudder-less, and expedient"[27] and said that Bush's "ship of state lacks a compass and a vision, and the scripture says that where there is no vision the people perish."[28] He depicted Vice-President Dan Quayle's Competitiveness Council as "a group which lets major polluters in through the back door at the White House to kill environmental regulations they don't like."[29] He chastised "Executives at the biggest companies [who] raised their pay by four times the percentage workers' pay went up and three times the percentage their profits went up."[30] He criticized "twelve years of dominance by special interests and big government that have given one percent of the American people at the top more wealth than the bottom ninety percent."[31] False Republican leadership had tricked the chosen people into thinking that they could find the materialistic benefits of the American dream by working hard for selfish purposes.

All jeremiads prescribe ways for the chosen people to rid themselves of their tribulations by getting back to first principles: restoring the covenant, returning to their sacred mission, or reaffirming the central truth. Frequently, the chosen people have been urged to forego practical solutions to their problems in favor of acts of faith: If you get right with God, then God will end your tribulations. In this sense political jeremiads have often confounded political decision making by disconnecting practical problems from practical solutions. However, some recent presidents have introduced practical policies in jeremiadic logic,[32] and this Bill Clinton did throughout his campaign.

The Clinton message throughout the 1992 campaign was the need for what he termed "The New Covenant" between Americans and their government. This New Covenant was intended not to replace the original covenant between God and the founders, but to fulfill it:

> Government's responsibility is to create more opportunity, the people's responsibility is to make the most of it. . . . more opportunity for all, more responsibility from all, and a greater sense of common purpose.[33]

In the spirit of Thomas Jefferson and Theodore Roosevelt, Bill Clinton urged Americans to reaffirm their commitment to the original covenant by reinventing government to make it work.

If the central truth of the American experience was that each American had a personal moral responsibility to make tomorrow better than today, then "America is not just a place, it's an idea."[34] And certainly anyone aspiring to be president of the place would have a personal moral responsibility to articulate policies to make tomorrow better than today, policies that embody the idea of America. Bill Clinton set forth his policy agenda in speech after speech, many of which used "New Covenant" in their titles.

A catalog of Clinton's policy goals and specifics is beyond the scope of this essay, and that is the point to be made. Each of the twelve speeches studied set forth an array of goals and policies for public discussion. The sheer quantity of Bill Clinton's policy suggestions lent support to his contention that he had more ideas than President Bush. The intricacy of his policy formulations demonstrated his intellectual grasp of the problems facing the country. His almost obsessive need to discuss potential policies with citizens dramatized his commitment to empower them with information. In order for people to argue against Clinton's policy initiatives, they had to acknowledge that he had ideas about how to improve life in America and the world, and that acknowledgment alone established Clinton as a worthy alternative to President Bush.

However, the New Covenant was not only about government policies, it was also about accepting responsibility. As Clinton told his Notre Dame audience:

> I want, most of all, to restore the link between rights and responsibilities, between opportunities and obligations. The social contract that defines what we owe to one another, to our communities and to our country, as well as what we are entitled to for ourselves.[35]

Clinton detailed the balance of responsibilities most fully in his Georgetown address on rebuilding America:

> We need a New Covenant that will challenge all our citizens to be responsible. The New Covenant will say to our corporate leaders at the top of the ladder: . . . We'll support your efforts to increase profits and jobs through quality products and services, but we're going to hold you responsible to be good corporate citizens, too. The New Covenant will say to people on welfare: We're going to provide the training and education and health care you need, but if you can work, you've got to go to work, because you can no longer stay on welfare forever. The New Covenant will say to the hard-working middle class and those who aspire to it: We're going to guarantee you access to a college education, but if you get that help, you've got to give something back to your country. And the New Covenant will challenge all of us in public service: We have a solemn responsibility to honor the values and promote the interests of the people who elected us, and if we don't, we don't belong in government anymore.[36]

If all of these Americans would fulfill the terms of the New Covenant, they would reaffirm their common purpose and accept fully their personal moral responsibilities to make tomorrow better than today, thereby fulfilling the original American covenant as revealed to Clinton by his grandfather and Professor Quigley.

Jeremiads describe the utopian world that awaits the chosen people who renew their covenant. As John Winthrop told the Puritans on the deck of the *Arabella* to go forth and build a "shining city on the hill," Clinton described the America of the New Covenant. In education the covenant meant:

> pre-school for every child who needs it, and an apprenticeship program for kids who don't want to go to college but do want good jobs[,] . . . teaching everybody with a job to read, and passing a domestic GI Bill that would give every young American the chance to borrow the money necessary to go to college and ask them to pay it back either as a small percentage of their income over time or through national service as teachers or policemen or nurses or child care workers.[37]

The New Covenant would improve health care by "reforming the health care system to control costs, improve quality, expand preventive and long-term care, maintain consumer choice, and cover everybody." It would develop an energy policy "so all our children will inherit a world that is cleaner, safer, and more beautiful." Public safety would be improved by "making our cities and our streets safe from crime and drugs. Across America," he said, "citizens are banding together to take their streets and neighborhoods back. . . . we'll be on their side—with new initiatives like community policing, drug treatment for those who need it and boot camps for first-time offenders."[38]

This utopian society would be paid for with a utopian economy. It would have a civilian research and development agency "to provide basic research for new and critical technologies" and for ways "to move these ideas into the marketplace," an agency paid for because for "every dollar we reduce the defense budget on research and development, we'll increase the civilian R&D budget by the same amount." The transition from a defense to a domestic economy would occur in a way that "creates more high-wage jobs" without risking either "our most successful high-wage industrial base" or "the careers of many thousands of our best scientists, engineers, and workers."[39] Because "you can't have a healthy economy without a healthy environment, and you don't have to sacrifice environmental protection to get economic growth,"[40] the displaced scientists and engineers could work on environmental problems. Throughout these twelve speeches, Clinton helped his audiences to envision life in the America of the New Covenant, a rhetorical task that George Bush had earlier derided as "the vision thing."

In summary, Bill Clinton's 1992 campaign policy addresses were part of an overarching jeremiad of the New Covenant. His jeremiad spoke to America's chosen people: the hard-working people of the forgotten middle class and those who aspired to it. He reminded them of the central truth that tomorrow would be better than today if they fulfilled their personal moral responsibilities to make it so, and he suggested that they had lost their way during the 1980s by following the false prophets of profit who had led them astray from their common purpose. By rejecting Bush's leadership and "by making common cause" with Clinton "we give new life to the American Dream."[41]

THE RHETORICAL IMPLICATIONS OF CLINTON'S POLICY JEREMIAD

Political situations invite rhetorical choices that have political and rhetorical consequences. Clinton's policy jeremiad had at least two important consequences: it enhanced his critique of the Bush presidency, and it helped him to consolidate support that he might otherwise have lost.

Clinton's Jeremiadic Critique of Bush

Clinton's jeremiadic logic enhanced the persuasiveness of his critique of the Bush presidency in several ways. First, Clinton took advantage of the jeremiad's irony (unity in diversity, finding good in evil) to rhetorically surround President Bush. He did this by advancing an activist policy agenda in conservative rhetoric. The policy initiatives spoke to those who were frustrated with the Bush administration's patient inaction. These audiences included familiar Democratic constituencies such as workers and their unions who wanted more jobs, teachers and parents who wanted improvements in education, and women and minorities who wanted more equitable treatment. For these people Clinton went beyond the usual slogans and shibboleths to articulate ideas like his "domestic GI bill" to finance college educations in return for public service, his "community boot camps" for first-time law breakers, and an increase in the earned-income credit so that people who worked would be above the poverty line.

But unlike Democrats Dukakis, Mondale, and Jackson, Clinton

challenged Bush with a traditional, populist, conservative rhetoric. In his announcement address, he expressed pride in what he and Arkansas had done "without giving up the things we cherish and honor most about our way of life—solid middle-class values of work, faith, family, individual responsibility, and community."[42] Later he said, "We have to honor, reward and reflect the work ethic, not the power grab. Responsibility is for everybody,"[43] and that "Work, family, future—that is what we must honor and reward."[44] He told the Los Angeles World Affairs Council that "It is time for leadership that is strategic, vigorous, and grounded in America's democratic values."[45] These statements and dozens like them could have been made by Ronald Reagan, Alexander Haig, or Pat Buchanan, but they came from Bill Clinton.

It was the logic of the jeremiad that sanctioned the marriage of an activist policy agenda to the traditional rhetoric that guided the candidacy of Bill Clinton. As he told the Democratic Leadership Council:

> My life is a testament to the fact that the American dream works. Leadership, rules, rewards, responsibility, and love. . . . I got to live by the rules that work in America and I ended up here today running for President of the United States of America, because I had the right kind of American community. It went beyond politics, it went beyond programs, it went to values.[46]

Clinton was the product of his grandfather's grade-school education and his own grad-school education. As the result of both backgrounds, Clinton was able to say in his nomination acceptance address that

> We offer our people a new choice based on old values. We offer opportunity. We demand responsibility. We will build an American community again. The choice we offer is not conservative or liberal. In many ways it's not even Republican or Democratic. It's different. It's new. And it will work. It will work because it is rooted in the vision and the values of the American people.[47]

Clinton's jeremiad enabled him to outflank President Bush by using many of the value themes that had previously undergirded the Reagan rhetoric, but now those themes were used to advocate innovative policies as alternatives to Bush's patience.

A second way that Clinton's jeremiad enhanced his critique of the Bush presidency centered around the notion of false leadership.

Modern political jeremiads suggest that the chosen people stray when they are misled by false prophets rather than because of their own way-wardness. Thus Clinton's jeremiad invited citizens to attribute their frustrations to Bush's leadership rather than to their own mistakes or to the failings of Congress, as Bush would have had it. Clinton hung economic responsibility around Bush's neck early:

> Just this week, George Bush said we don't need a plan to end this recession—that if we wait long enough, our problems will go away. Well, he's right about that part: If he doesn't have a plan to turn this country around by November of 1992, we're going to lay George Bush off, put America back to work, and our problems will go away. We need a President who will take responsibility for getting this country moving again. A President who will provide the leadership to pull us together and challenge our nation to compete in the world and win again.[48]

The jeremiadic theme of responsibility served to increase Bush's accountability and to underscore Clinton's determination.

On the twenty-second anniversary of Earth Day, Clinton critiqued Bush's record as the "Environmental President." Clinton contrasted Bush's campaign promises with the record of his presidency for an audience at Drexel University:

> George Bush promised to be the Environmental President, but a photo op at the Grand Canyon is about all we have to show for it. He made Boston Harbor a prop in his negative campaign in 1988, but four years later has done precious little to help clean it up. He promised "no net loss" of America's precious wetlands, then tried to hand half of them over to developers. He invoked Teddy Roosevelt's devotion to preserving our natural heritage, then called for opening the Arctic wilderness to oil drilling. He talked about the need for an energy policy, then went to Detroit on the eve of the Michigan primary to promise American automakers that he wouldn't raise fuel efficiency standards for American cars. He called for an international summit on the environment but now is singlehandedly blocking an historic meeting in Rio de Janeiro of a hundred nations to control global warming. And just yesterday, I read in the paper that he wants to make another attack ad, this time about problems along the White River in Arkansas.[49]

Clinton then adroitly used the president's alleged attack ad not to claim liberal environmentalist tendencies but to reinforce his traditional values:

> We're fighting the battle to clean up the White River, and I welcome the President's attention. So, Mr. President, when you return from Rio, I hope you'll visit Northwest Arkansas and the White River. I'll show you what the problems are and what progress we've made. I'll show you rivers you can fish in, and streams kids can swim in. And if you really want to clean up the problem, I'll make an agreement with you. We'll outline federal and state responsibilities—and we'll get results. Our people are tired of the politics of blame. But this is no Boston Harbor. If you want to place blame, you'll have to shoulder some.[50]

In this portion of his Drexel speech, Clinton was able to critique President Bush's inconsistencies—his unwillingness to accept responsibility, his inclination to "go negative" and to contrast them with his own professed traditional values, his willingness to accept responsibility, and his willingness to work to solve environmental problems.

Even foreign policy, the area of President Bush's most notable success, was subjected to the Clinton critique. In a December 1991 address at Georgetown, Clinton stressed the link between foreign and domestic concerns. In jeremiadic logic the best foreign policy is a sound domestic policy and vice versa:

> Given the problems we face at home, we do have to take care of our own people and their needs first. We need to remember the central lesson of the collapse of communism and the Soviet Union. We never defeated them on the field of battle. The Soviet Union collapsed from the inside out—from economic, political, and spiritual failure. Make no mistake: Foreign and domestic policy are inseparable in today's world. If we're not strong at home, we can't lead the world we've done so much to make. And if we withdraw from the world, it will hurt us economically at home. We can't allow this false choice between domestic policy and foreign policy to hurt our country and our economy.[51]

He underscored this point for the members of B'nai B'rith as it related to Israel, saying that "Without a growing economy, without a strong, stable, and secure American middle class, America's commitment to Israel will always be under pressure."[52]

Clinton's critique of Bush's foreign-policy leadership makes sense only in this jeremiadic logic:

> Our President has devoted his time and energy to foreign concerns and ignored dire problems here at home. As a result, we're drifting in the longest economic slump since World War II, and, in reaction to that, elements in both parties now want America to respond to the collapse of communism and a crippling recession at home by retreating from the world.[53]

Put differently, because the best foreign policy is a sound domestic policy, President Bush failed at foreign policy by devoting so much attention to it rather than to domestic policy. Clinton's argument is unusual, if not downright tautological, but it works as part of a jeremiadic critique because of the jeremiad's embodiment of contradictions.

In remarks before the Los Angeles World Affairs Council in August 1992, Clinton set forth three tests of presidential leadership in the post–Cold War world:

> The first is to grasp how the world has changed. The second test is to assert a vision of our role in this dynamic new world. The third test is to summon all our strengths—our values, our economic power, when necessary our military might—in service of that vision.[54]

These new "tests of leadership" juxtaposed "change" and "vision" and set them against "continuity" in ways that disadvantaged the president. Thus Clinton could announce that

> I do not believe President Bush has met these new tests, despite his effectiveness in organizing the response to Iraq's aggression. Too often the administration has held on to old assumptions and policies, trying to prop up yesterday's status quo, failing to confront our new challenges.[55]

These new tests were so important that despite his agreement with President Bush on some foreign policy issues, Clinton did not believe that Bush had "a vision of our role in this new era. In a world of change, security flows from initiative, not inertia."[56] In this critique, Bush's experience with Cold War politics actually limited his ability to meet the new tests of leadership. Moreover, Bush could fully satisfy Clinton's tests only by pursuing a new foreign policy, thereby sacrificing one of the major advantages to be accrued from the reelection of an incumbent president.

The foregoing examples of Clinton's critique of President Bush's handling of the economy, the environment, and foreign policy all illustrate the importance of his jeremiadic logic. In each case the jeremiad enabled Bill Clinton to attribute responsibility to Bush rather than to Congress or the chosen people. Furthermore, each of these critiques posed a dilemma for the president. If President Bush were to claim personal responsibility for improvements in the economy, the environment, or foreign policy he would have to defend himself against Clinton's critique. But if the president were to attribute responsibility for the economy, the environment, or foreign policy to others, he would have to defend himself against Clinton's charge of evading responsibility. Caught in this dilemma Bush did neither, preferring to attack Clinton and his policy proposals. Thus did the Bush people miss the point of Clinton's jeremiad and his supporters' assent: Where Bush derided the "vision thing," Clinton had a vision; where Bush counselled patient forbearance, Clinton provided energy, initiative, and a fusion of the liberal agenda and traditional values; and where Bush "went negative" in the campaign, Clinton was positive in his affirmation of American values and ideals.

Clinton's Jeremiad and the Consolidation of Support

Clinton's jeremiadic logic helped him to consolidate tentative support that he might otherwise have lost. The "New Deal" coalition has not held together for recent Democratic presidential candidates, and many of the constituencies those Democrats needed have frequently been at odds with one another. Blue-collar workers and their unions, for example, have gone one way, while African-Americans, feminists, gays, and latter-day sixties radicals have gone their own. In the seven presidential elections between John Kennedy's victory in 1960 and Clinton's in 1992, no Democrat was able to win the presidency under normal circumstances: Johnson was buoyed by the national solidarity that followed the Kennedy assassination, and Jimmy Carter benefited from public revulsion toward Watergate and Ford's pardon of Richard Nixon.

Because it is built from contradictions, jeremiadic logic enabled Clinton the Baptist to consolidate Jewish and Catholic support with his quasi-Puritan rhetorical form. At Notre Dame he recounted his fears as a Baptist student at a Jesuit university:

> I wondered when I went there whether I would be out of place, a Southern Baptist who had rarely been far from home. Thankfully, both the students and the faculty there held to the scriptural commandment to befriend the stranger in their midst. And together, we found much common ground that Baptists and Catholics could walk together.[57]

From his Catholic education Clinton learned "The Catholic understanding of history and tradition," and he found the two religions similar in their orientation toward the chosen people:

> Both Baptists and Catholics in different ways are rooted in the spiritual richness of America's working people—people who know the bite of discrimination, people for whom life is a daily struggle in which they must sweat and sacrifice for themselves and their families, for whom life is made worthwhile not only through hard work and self-reliance but through opening their hearts to God and their hands to their neighbors.[58]

But Clinton's ecumenicism was not confined to Baptists and Catholics, because his was the "Judeo-Christian understanding of what it means to be a member of the human society."[59] To buttress that point he invoked Rabbi Hillel, Baptist Roger Williams, Catholic John Kennedy, Baptist ministers, and the pastoral letter of the National Conference of Catholic Bishops. He cited the letter's statement that "our children's future is shaped by the *values* of their parents and the *policies* of our nation" and used it to turn the tables on Bush and Quayle, who had been stressing "family values" to imply that Clinton and his policies were out of the mainstream:

> I want an America that does more than talk about family values. I want an America that values families. I want an America that values families by recognizing that parents have the right to take time off from their jobs when a baby's born or someone is sick. An America that values families by freeing fathers and mothers from the fear that they won't be able to take a sick child to the doctor. An America that values families by helping every parent enjoy the dignity of a job that puts bread on the table, buys shoes for the children and holds the household together in mutual

support. An America that honors and rewards work and family not just in words but in deeds.[60]

In this passage Clinton used the bishops' emphasis on values and policies to stress the interdependence of the two, and he used those values to frame his policies. "I'm not just talking about economic policies," he said. "I'm talking about our moral obligation to help every one of our brothers and sisters enjoy the dignity of useful and productive working lives."[61]

Clinton also stressed the Judeo-Christian heritage when he addressed the international convention of B'nai B'rith. "What guides each of you," he observed, "is a belief in a covenant that we all share to enrich the lives of those around you, to fight bigotry, to protect liberty. . . . [L]et us join together to renew our dedication to the values we share in common."[62] Clinton was generally concerned "by the cynicism, the intolerance, the ugliness that threatens our society today" and, more particularly, by the tone of the Republican convention that "seemed . . . more interested in dividing the American people by claiming that some of us have values while others don't" than in "uniting us in a common effort to overcome our problems."[63] That was not in keeping with the Judeo-Christian covenant:

> I was raised in a different faith than most of you here. But we were both raised in a tradition which champions tolerance and which defends freedom. We both have absolute faith in the primacy of each individual's conscience and judgment. We believe everyone ought to have the freedom to worship God in his or her own way. We believe in the strength our country and our churches and synagogues draw from constitutional separation between church and state.[64]

To restore that covenant and "to reaffirm the relationship of neighbor to neighbor, family to family, this generation to the next,"[65] Americans must reaffirm the central truth and regain their sense of common purpose. Thus, with his Catholic audience at Notre Dame and his Jewish audience in B'nai B'rith, Clinton stressed the Judeo-Christian foundation of his New Covenant.

Clinton's need to win support from African-American voters without losing the white middle-class vote to the ticket that had made Willie Horton a household name in 1988 provides a second important example of consolidated support. He did this by transcending the differences between the problems of the disadvantaged and the middle class with his traditional patriotic rhetoric. He began doing this in his announcement address:

> For 12 years, Republicans have tried to divide us—race against race—so we get mad at each other and not at them. They want us to look at each other across a racial divide so we don't turn and look to the White House and ask, Why are all of our incomes going down? Why are all of us losing jobs? Why are we losing our future?[66]

This rhetoric put both groups in the same boat and blamed their past differences on Republican mismanagement and polarization. Thus, when or if the two communities diverged, their divergence would function as validation of Clinton's analysis.

When riots erupted in south central Los Angeles and tensions mounted across the country after a white middle-class suburban jury acquitted the white Los Angeles policemen who had been videotaped beating a black man named Rodney King, Clinton's rhetorical framework was already in place. "The crisis in Los Angeles is now our fire bell in the night," he told the Democratic Leadership Council. "It is clear evidence once again of the profound divisions in our community— divisions that have been ripped to shreds in Los Angeles."[67] His account of race relations and social progress during his lifetime underscored both the problems of the disadvantaged and the efforts of the chosen people to make tomorrow better than today. "In the 1950s and [19]60s there were arguments over equal access, over race, over poverty, over politics," he said. "We have made a great deal of progress for those of us who live in the mainstream of America. But what progress has been made outside that mainstream? Beneath that there are those who are not part of our community, whose values have been shredded by the hard knife of experience, where there is the disintegration of family and neighborhood and jobs, and the rise of drugs and guns and gangs."[68]

He articulated the fears of white and black Americans toward each other:

> White Americans often fear that violence has only a black face. They see it on the news. They see it in the movies. They are gripped by the isolation of their own experience where, especially

in many of our larger areas, too many white Americans still simply have no friends of other races and do not know any differently. Blacks fear that too often violence has a black face and no one cares.[69]

He then transcended these fears with the simple chilling truth that "We have no place to hide," and he quoted Rodney King's statement that "I never meant my verdict to be an excuse for this kind of behavior." "But," Clinton elaborated:

> neither will his verdict make the streets safer for others, especially for black Americans. After all, more than any other racial group in this country, it is their children who are shot on the street, their neighborhoods that are savaged by crack cocaine, their businesses and dreams that are crushed.[70]

Clinton's point was that the middle class and the growing underclass of disadvantaged were all suffering from the consequences of false leadership that had divided, and thus misled, them from their common purpose of making tomorrow better than today.

These divisions and Clinton's response to them became the climax of his nomination acceptance speech:

> It is time to heal America. And so we must say to every American: look beyond the stereotypes that blind us. We need each other. All of us, we need each other. We don't have a person to waste. And yet, for too long, politicians have told the most of us that are doing all right that what's really wrong with America is the rest of us. Them. Them the minorities. Them the liberals. Them the poor. Them the homeless. Them the people with disabilities. Them the gays. We've gotten to where we've nearly them'd ourselves to death. Them, and them, and them. But this is America. There is no them; there is only us. One nation, under God, indivisible, with liberty, and justice, for all. That is our Pledge of Allegiance, and that's what the New Covenant is all about.[71]

This remarkable paragraph begins by evoking Gerald Ford's *A Time to Heal,* then weaves together the "most of us who are doing all right," the minorities, the liberals, the poor, the disabled, and the gay, ties them to God and country by quoting the Pledge of Allegiance (that had tripped Michael Dukakis in 1988), and then it calls the whole package "The New Covenant." The logic of the jeremiad thus explained that people in apparent opposition were actually bound together by their difficulties, and it attributed their antagonisms to the false leaders.

Candidate Clinton also used these divisions to solidify his centrist position. Democrats such as Mondale and Dukakis had tried to address civil rights issues on Jesse Jackson's terms, a strategy that seemed to drive many white middle class voters to Reagan and Bush. Clinton took a different approach when addressing Jackson's Rainbow Coalition in June of 1992. Clinton praised Jackson and the Coalition "for giving birth to this Rebuild America program" and "for not just pointing the finger of blame but taking up the burden of responsibility."[72] He also praised people who had not rioted in Los Angeles despite their frustration and anger:

> The real story of Los Angeles is in these people we stood up and clapped for. That's the real story. Let's not forget folks, most people who live in that city did not burn, or loot, or riot. Most little children were home with their parents. Even the poorest children were sitting in their houses when they could have been looting goods because their parent told them it was wrong to steal from their neighbors. It violated the Ten Commandments. They could have gotten away with it and they didn't and they were poor. They really live by family values. And we ought to honor that.[73]

None of this was particularly innovative, but it did stop short of blaming the riots on the American system or middle-class indifference.

Clinton began to innovate by stressing his own personal contact with the African-American community "when I was in Los Angeles, three years before the riots and three days after the riots." His own direct contact with local community leaders provided a basis for Clinton himself to articulate their needs without depending on Jackson. Indeed, he had noticed, "the unanimous endorsement of community leaders at the grass roots for bold new steps" that would "bring in money from the private sector as well as the public sector, venture capital, small business loans, start up finances."[74] The people he had talked to "didn't want more big government"; they wanted Clinton's policies:

> They wanted more jobs and they wanted small business. Most people said what they really wanted was a Washington that would support their efforts at work and they knew that Washington had failed them but also that their banks had not met their responsibilities to re-invest in their communities.[75]

By this point in his Rainbow Coalition address, Clinton had managed to praise Jackson even as he subtly declared his independence from him.

Then Clinton took the big step. He broke with recent Democratic candidates by refusing to excuse racial violence as understandable, and he did it before a predominantly black audience with reference to their principles. He urged his audience to "stand up for what has always been best about the Rainbow Coalition which is people coming together across racial lines." He specifically drew his audience's attention to rap singer Sister Souljah who had addressed them the night before. He quoted her 1991 comment that "If there are any good white people I haven't met them" and her post-riot comment to the *Washington Post* that "If black people kill black people every day, why not have a week and kill white people?" Clinton told the coalition that "her comments before and after Los Angeles were filled with the kind of hatred that you do not honor today and tonight."[76] "If you took the words white and black and reversed them," said Clinton, "you might think David Duke was giving that speech. Let me tell you, we all make mistakes and sometimes we're not as sensitive as we ought to be. And we have an obligation, all of us, to call attention to prejudice wherever we see it."[77]

Jackson was grim-faced after the speech, and he told reporters that Clinton's remarks were not helpful. But Clinton's remarks did seem to help him with white middle-class voters who had grown accustomed to the permissive rhetoric of Democratic candidates whom they perceived as overly deferential to Jackson and unwilling to draw the line on unacceptable conduct.[78] The speech and news coverage of it enabled Clinton to establish his commitment to improve the quality of life for the disadvantaged, to establish his independence from Jackson, and to establish that his message of taking personal responsibility applied even in a politically volatile context. Thus Clinton's jeremiad helped him to transcend differences of religion, race, and class with his traditional themes.

CONCLUSION

Bill Clinton's 1992 campaign used an unusually heavy amount of policy rhetoric. To the casual observer, Clinton may have seemed to be another political medicine man with a wagonful of patent medicines to cure anything that ailed people. Perhaps that perception had something to do with the Bush and Perot campaigns' inability to defeat him. Clinton's policy speeches were linked together by the logic of the jeremiad, the primal American rhetorical form. He was not selling individual programs, although most of his policy proposals had been part of his political program for many years. It was Paul Tsongas who had an economic policy to sell in 1992, much as Richard Gephardt had banked on his trade bill in 1988. Their problem was that no *single* policy can establish its advocate as an *all-around* national leader.

Bill Clinton began his jeremiad in his announcement speech and continued it into his inaugural address. His message was that America has always been great because the chosen people had always believed that tomorrow would be better than today and that each of them had a personal moral responsibility to make it so. He used his policy analyses to demonstrate his grasp of the issues and his ability to formulate solutions. He used his policy proposals to differentiate his activist leadership from Bush's passivity and Perot's simplicity. He used his multipoint plans to establish both his vision of a better tomorrow and his strategy for getting us there, as well as to show that he himself had fulfilled his personal responsibility to think about making tomorrow better than today.

Clinton's jeremiad accomplished a number of other objectives as well. Because the jeremiad is a sermonic form, it allowed Clinton to cite scriptures and to refer to God in ways that recent Democratic presidential candidates had avoided. Because the jeremiad directs people to the future by referring them to their heritage, it allowed Clinton to combine liberal activist policies with traditional American values. Because a jeremiad often describes social ills and the coming utopia in graphic language, it enabled Clinton to characterize present ills and his utopia in vivid language. And because a jeremiad unites apparently divergent concepts such as finding hope in one's tribulations, it enabled Clinton to be tough about compassion, to criticize Bush's foreign policy for being overly foreign, and to admit his acquisition of greater wisdom from his grandfather than from his professors at Georgetown, Oxford and Yale.

However, when Bill Clinton began to govern, he found frustration all around. He was criticized widely for trying to do too many things at once, for losing his "focus" on the policies he wanted; and David Gergen was brought into the White House to improve the president's communication. The present analysis suggests that the rhetorical problems of Clinton's first hundred days were quite different. The question was not what happened to Clinton's focus, but what happened to his jeremiadic logic. Almost upon his inauguration Clinton ceased addressing the nation, ceased linking his policies together in relation to a central truth, and ceased showing how his policy proposals fit together. Without his constant sermons about our common purpose and our personal responsibilities to create a better tomorrow, his adversaries were able (1) to unravel his policy package, (2) to tackle his policy proposals individually, thus (3) redividing the supporters he had consolidated during the campaign such that (4) the wheels of representative government ground slowly enough to be construed as more gridlock. No one ever accused Jonathan Edwards or John Winthrop of lacking focus in their sermons, and there can be real systemic dangers when jeremiads emanate from the bully pulpit of the presidency.[79] Where many jeremiads have substituted faith in first principles for rational problem solving, Bill Clinton's 1992 campaign jeremiad used those first principles to frame practical problem solving and to encourage citizens to accept responsibility for implementing those solutions. President Clinton, like candidate Clinton, needs a coherent jeremiadic logic to link his various proposals and to consolidate his supporters if he intends to fulfill his personal moral responsibility to make tomorrow better than today.

NOTES

1. Frank Greer, Remarks at the "Communication in the 1992 Presidential Campaign" Pre-Conference, 27 May 1993. Washington, D.C.: International Communication Association.

2. For additional material on jeremiads, see Sacvan Bercovitch, *The American Jeremiad* (Madison: University of Wisconsin Press, 1978); Perry Miller, *The New England Mind: From Colony to Providence* (Cambridge, Mass.: Harvard University Press, 1953); Ernest R. Bormann, ed., *The Force of Fantasy: Restoring the American Dream* (Carbondale: Southern Illinois University Press, 1985); Kurt Ritter, "American Political Rhetoric and the Jeremiad Tradition: Presidential Nomination Acceptance Addresses, 1960–76," *Central States Speech Journal* 31 (1980): 153–71; Kurt Ritter and David Henry, *Ronald Reagan: The Great Communicator* (Westport, Conn.: Greenwood, 1992); John J. Murphy, "'A Time of Shame and Sorrow': Robert F. Kennedy and the American

Jeremiad," *Quarterly Journal of Speech* 76 (1990): 401–14; and Craig Allen Smith and Kathy B. Smith, *The White House Speaks: Presidential Leadership as Persuasion* (Westport, Conn.: Praeger, 1994), 133–64.

3. Richard L. Johannesen, "Ronald Reagan's Economic Jeremiad," *Central States Speech Journal* 37 (1986): 79–89.

4. Walter R. Fisher, "Reaffirmation and Subversion of the American Dream," *Quarterly Journal of Speech* 59 (1973): 160–67.

5. Smith and Smith, *The White House Speaks*, 134–37.

6. See Bormann, *The Force of Fantasy*, 6.

7. The speech texts studied were retrieved through the Sunsite archive on the Internet computer network. They were accessed with a standard personal computer using the "Gopher" command to reach Sunsite and then printed, single-spaced, on a standard printer. Page numbers refer to these single-spaced personal copies, which should approximate other researchers' personal copies. Among the speeches analyzed were "A New Covenant for American Security," Georgetown University, 12 December 1991; "A New Covenant for Economic Change," Georgetown University, 20 November 1991; "A Vision for America: A New Covenant," New York, 16 July 1992; "Announcement Speech," Little Rock, Arkansas, 3 October 1991; "Earth Day Remarks," Drexel University, 22 April 1992; "Remarks at the University of Notre Dame," South Bend, Indiana, 11 September 1992; "Remarks to the B'nai B'rith 36th Biennial International Convention," Washington, D.C., 9 September 1992; "Remarks to the Democratic Leadership Council," New Orleans, 2 May 1992; "Remarks to the Los Angeles World Affair Council," Los Angeles, 13 August 1992; "Remarks to the Rainbow Coalition National Convention," Washington, D.C., 13 June 1992; "The New Covenant: Responsibility and Rebuilding the American Community," Georgetown University, 23 October 1991; and "Work, Family, Future: Address to the American Association of Retired Persons," San Antonio, Texas, 4 June 1992.

8. Bill Clinton, "Work, Family, Future: Address to the American Association of Retired Persons," San Antonio, Texas, 4 June 1992 (Internet: Sunsite, 1992), 2.

9. Bill Clinton, "A Vision for America: A New Covenant," New York, 16 July 1992 (Internet: Sunsite, 1992), 3.

10. Ibid.

11. Bill Clinton, "A New Covenant for Economic Change," Georgetown University, 20 November 1991 (Internet: Sunset, 1991), 1.

12. Ibid.

13. Bill Clinton, "Remarks to the Democratic Leadership Council," New Orleans, 2 May 1992 (Internet: Sunsite, 1992), 3.

14. Clinton, "A New Covenant for Economic Change," 1.

15. Bill Clinton, "Announcement Speech," Little Rock, Arkansas, 3 October 1991 (Internet: Sunsite, 1991), 2.

16. Bill Clinton, "Remarks to the Rainbow Coalition National Convention," Washington, D.C., 13 June 1992 (Internet: Sunsite, 1992), 3.

17. Clinton, "Remarks to the Democratic Leadership Council," 10.

18. Clinton, "Work, Family, Future," 2.

19. Bill Clinton, "The New Covenant: Responsibility and Rebuilding the American Community," Georgetown University, 23 October 1991 (Internet: Sunsite, 1991), 1.

20. Bill Clinton, "Remarks at the University of Notre Dame," South Bend, Indiana, 11 September 1992 (Internet: Sunsite, 1992), 9.

21. Ibid., 5.

22. Ibid., 4–5.

23. Clinton, "Announcement Speech," 1.

24. Clinton, "A New Covenant for Economic Change," 2.

25. Clinton, "Remarks at the University of Notre Dame," 3.

26. Clinton, "A New Covenant for Economic Change," 2.

27. Bill Clinton, "Earth Day Remarks," Drexel University, 22 April 1992 (Internet: Sunsite, 1992), 2.

28. Clinton, "Remarks to the Rainbow Coalition National Convention," 1.

29. Clinton, "Earth Day Remarks," 4.

30. Clinton, "A New Covenant for Economic Change," 7.

31. Clinton, "Remarks to the Rainbow Coalition National Convention," 3.

32. Smith and Smith, *The White House Speaks*, 148–57.

33. Clinton, "Announcement Speech," 3, 6.

34. Clinton, "Remarks to the B'nai B'rith 36th Biennial International Convention," Washington, D.C., 9 September 1992 (Internet: Sunsite, 1992), 7.

35. Clinton, "Remarks at the University of Notre Dame," 5.

36. Clinton, "The New Covenant: Responsibility and Rebuilding the American Community," 4.

37. Clinton, "Announcement Speech," 4.

38. Ibid.

39. Clinton, "A New Covenant for Economic Change," 8.

40. Clinton, "Earth Day Remarks," 3.

41. Clinton, "Announcement Speech," 6.

42. Ibid., 1.

43. Clinton, "The New Covenant: Responsibility and Rebuilding the American Community," 5.

44. Clinton, "Work, Family, and Future," 9.

45. Bill Clinton, "Remarks to the Los Angeles World Affairs Council," Los Angeles, 13 August 1992 (Internet: Sunsite, 1992), 9.

46. Clinton, "Remarks to the Democratic Leadership Council," 9.

47. Clinton, "Acceptance speech," 7.

48. Clinton, "A New Covenant for Economic Change," 1.

49. Clinton, "Earth Day Remarks," 2.

50. Ibid., 2–3.

51. Bill Clinton, "A New Covenant for American Security," Georgetown University, 12 December 1991 (Internet: Sunsite, 1991), 1.

52. Clinton, "Remarks to the B'nai B'rith 36th Biennial International Convention," 4.

53. Clinton, "A New Covenant for American Security," 2.

54. Clinton, "Remarks to the Los Angeles World Affairs Council," 1.

55. Ibid., 1.

56. Ibid.

57. Clinton, "Remarks at the University of Notre Dame," 3.

58. Ibid.

59. Ibid.

60. Ibid., 6–7 (emphasis added).

61. Ibid., 7.

62. Clinton, "Remarks to the B'nai B'rith 36th Biennial International Convention," 2.

63. Ibid., 5–6

64. Ibid., 7.

65. Ibid., 7.

66. Clinton, "Announcement Speech," 2.

67. Clinton, "Remarks to the Democratic Leadership Council," 1.

68. Ibid., 2.

69. Ibid., 3.

70. Ibid., 4.

71. Clinton, "Acceptance Speech," 9.

72. Clinton, "Remarks to the Rainbow Coalition National Convention," 1.

73. Ibid., 2–3.

74. Ibid., 3.

75. Ibid., 4.

76. Ibid., 7.

77. Ibid.

78. This is but one of several pertinent suggestions advanced by political consultant and speechwriter David Kusnet in his rich and insightful book *Speaking American: How the Democrats Can Win in the Nineties* (New York: Thunder's Mouth Press, 1992), esp. 85–86.

79. Smith and Smith, *The White House Speaks*, 158–61.

THE STYLISTIC PERSONA
OF BILL CLINTON

From Arkansas and Aristotelian Attica

RONALD H. CARPENTER

In 1753 George Buffon articulated his celebrated epigram, "Style is the man himself."[1] As the notion has come to be understood and applied in more recent times, a close examination of style in discourse should reveal something about the emotional and intellectual condition of the individual who spoke or wrote those words in that particular order. Of course, the epigram now requires emendation to read that unique facets of syntax and lexicon may reveal something about the man or woman creating that discourse. And for the style in discourse emanating from a president of the United States, whether on the way to attaining the White House or once therein, any dimensions of presumed personality revealed by style may be less those of the particular communicator *per se* and more of some composite persona reflecting the varied stylistic preferences of speechwriters as well as any advisors from whom that speaker sought suggestions for, or reactions to, what might constitute the best words in their best orders for that particular statement.[2] Nevertheless, stylistic preferences evinced in political and presidential discourse can reflect and project *some* persona, and the style in discourse of Bill Clinton deserves scrutiny, first and appropriately in his crucial acceptance address to the Democratic convention in 1992. After all, the future candidate's earlier, overly long address to the 1988 Democratic convention was a subject of some ridicule, and thus his effort as presidential nominee would require much more careful preparation to achieve positive reactions (beyond his introductory, ironic self-deprecation: "I ran for President this year for one reason and one reason only: I wanted to come back to this convention and finish that speech I started four years ago"). Moreover, Clinton's subsequent inaugural address then is an appropriate focal point for a perspective toward his progression as a stylist, for inaugurals invariably elicit considerable diligence on the parts of their writers to achieve eloquence. The stylistic parameters of the Arkansan's efforts are the subject of this analysis.

An operational definition is in order first, however, for style is the confounding canon of rhetoric. Much about style has been written by theorists over the centuries, and students of rhetorical prowess for eloquence are confronted (if not in many cases overwhelmed) by recommendations about nebulous stylistic qualities such as "grandeur," "sublimity," or "impressiveness," with complementary arcane terminology to describe their syntactical sources in discourse, such as *antimetabole, brachylogy, epizeuxis, hyperbaton, irmus, sinasthrismas,* and *zeugma, hypozeugma,* or *mesozeugma.*[3] For the purposes of this essay, style is defined in a contemporary viewpoint that recognizes that our language habits are organized into *"hierarchies of alternatives"*; for "at both lexical and structural choice points, to the extent that there is choice, certain alternatives will be most probable, others less probable, and others very improbable." From that perspective, *"style is defined as an individual's deviations from norms . . . these deviations being in the statistical properties of those structural features for which there exists some degree of choice in his code"*; and as Charles Osgood also indicates, style more typically evolves from *"how* a person talks about something rather than *what* he talks about."[4] Or as another, contemporary view also asserts, "underlying the very notion of style is a postulate of *independence of matter from manner.*"[5] Therefore, when viewed as a function of form more so than content, any persona projected through style in discourse may be discussed most meaningfully as that "paramessage" whereby some factors, "although peripheral to the ideational content of the message, can materially affect the overall impact upon the receiver" by conveying persuasively favorable "information about the source."

> Inferences about the source also derive from the message, even though it contains no direct personal references. Because it is the product of human thought processes, a discourse can provide *some degree of information about the personality that created it.*

The nature and originality of the subject matter, the quality and organization of the supporting materials, and *the language in which the whole is expressed are forms of "real" evidence* from which inferences about the *competence, values, attitudes, etc.* of the source may be drawn. . . . *the character of his vocabulary and diction—his literacy*—are indicators of personality reflected in the discourse he produces, *quite apart from the representational meaning of the message itself.*[6]

In several of its dimensions but not all—Clinton's style in discourse for the acceptance address evinced a positive persona that served the nominee well in the exigencies of that rhetorical situation.[7] Furthermore, after the election, subsequent adaptations of that stylistic persona likely served equally well, if not more so, in his inaugural address.

As a framework for meaningful interpretation of Bill Clinton's stylistically derived persona, an Aristotelian paradigm is appropriate. Although stemming from the fourth-century B.C. Aristotle's *Rhetoric* offers as good advice today for an aspiring stylist from Arkansas as it did then for orators from Attica who would be eloquent in their *lexis*; and as supplemented by the Greek critic, Demetrius *On Style,* as well as by subsequent disciples among other prominent rhetorical theorists, that classical lore about the pragmatic implications of stylistic prowess remains particularly pertinent for Bill Clinton's acceptance address to the Democratic convention. After all, that speech was his first major one that would be seen by an audience substantially larger than any earlier in the campaign; and although still significantly larger audiences later would assess Clinton's communication prowess during the TV debates with President Bush and Ross Perot, the acceptance address was one in which it was imperative that the candidate project a favorable impression at the outset of his formal presidential bid. For in an age when more and more citizens are unable themselves to articulate well their fears and hopes for the future (or say with complete conviction "Unaccustomed as I am to public speaking . . ."), Americans do respect the abilities of their presidents to be able communicators on their behalf as surrogate spokespersons.[8] Presidential political power often *is* derived from communication prowess. In some cases, that rhetorical source of advantage stems in large measure from abilities to deliver lines well (as in 1980 when an oratorically inept President Jimmy Carter stood in stark contrast to challenger Ronald Reagan, whose stature in some estimates as a "Great Communicator" was linked closely to his well-modulated voice, eye contact, and superb sense of timing capable of "milking" a dramatic pause to its fullest).[9] Herein, however, the focus for analysis is style, and a close reading of stylistic preferences in Clinton's acceptance address reveals its applications of several Aristotelian *dicta* for eloquence.

Underlying the concept of *lexis* or style in discourse in practical affairs is Aristotle's fundamental observation in *The Rhetoric* (1404b) that "words are like men; as we feel a difference between people from afar and our fellow townsmen, so it is with our feeling for language. And hence it is well to give the ordinary idiom an air of remoteness; the hearers are struck by what is out of the way, and like what strikes them." Or, as another translator rendered the same passage, "to alter or vary language in this way invests it with a higher dignity; for we feel towards language just as we feel towards men; 'familiarity breeds contempt' for the words we are constantly meeting in everyday intercourse, whilst 'strangers' assume a higher importance and dignity in our eyes. Hence we are to aim at a 'strange' *i.e.*, unusual, not familiar, novel, out of the common way diction" because with "uncommon" style which "strikes one as singular" communicators can attain a statement which "forces itself upon the attention."[10]

In contemporary terminology, such style potentially embodies a factor of attention known as novelty, which, as "an interaction between stimulus and receiver," stems from "a *discrepancy* between the individual's expectancy about the stimulus and his present perception of that stimulus."[11] Axiomatically, novelty is one of those "factors of advantage" that influence attention, and "a variety of well-authenticated observations" of "ordinary speech" behaviors attest to a "filter" in the human nervous system with a "bias" toward novel stimuli which therefore are "more likely to elicit a response."[12] Readers and listeners expect the words chosen for discourse will be those in the customary, familiar idiom and arranged in habitual patterns of the language system which has been taught—very carefully—throughout our educations. So word choice (lexicon) which deviates from the common idiom, such as Lincoln's "four score and seven," has novelty operative as a potential factor of attention, as is true for word arrangement (syntax) which deviates from the common idiom, such as the *anastrophe* of "Great is Diana," instead of the idiomatic "Diana is Great." Psychologists also agree that the more attention people pay to a stimulus the greater the likelihood it is learned and remembered; and in the psychology of communication, specifically, "a general principle is that the stronger or more potent the stimulus, the greater impress it will make upon the responding person. The best omnibus word to describe this principle in operation is *emphasis*, the special stress or weight given to particular stimuli. In the communication situation this means the emphasis given to particular stimulus units (whole arguments, propositional sentences, key words) by presenting them with special potency."[13] Several examples leap to mind of that "out of the common way diction." Suppose Lincoln had said "87 years ago" instead of "Four score and seven years ago"; or consider Kennedy's inaugural line, "Ask not what your country can do for you—ask what you can do for your country," in contradistinction to his idiomatic campaign version in Detroit on Labor Day, "The new frontier is not what I promise I am going to do for you. The new frontier is what I ask you to do for your country." In their eminently quotable sentences, both Lincoln and Kennedy achieved *lexis* which "forces itself upon the attention." For the Democratic presidential candidate in 1992, however, any emphasis derived from style would have still other pragmatic functions as a paramessage.

Clinton the challenging governor clearly had to set himself favorably apart from Bush the incumbent president. The Democratic nominee would have to appear not only as a person capable of solving the economic problems confronting the country but also as a more effective communicator. Bush was mundane in that no eloquent, memorable lines emerged from his presidential rhetoric, except perhaps for "a line in the sand" about the Gulf War; "a thousand points of light," which in the economic realities of the administration lost its pertinence; and "read my lips," which ultimately backfired rhetorically. Perhaps President Bush understood that he could not hope to compete rhetorically with his immediate predecessor as the "great communicator" in the White House, so why bother? But Bush as a communicator was so mundane as to be ridiculed persistently on TV, particularly on "Saturday Night Live," and the rhetorical situation demanded that his challenger be different, more capable, and in command as a communicator. Moreover, Clinton would have to measure up favorably both to John Kennedy, whose eloquent "summons to citizenship" had inspired the Arkansan as teenager, as well as to Mario Cuomo, former, likely contender for the Democratic presidential nomination whose eminent oratorical capabilities had been displayed prominently in the keynote address to the Democratic convention in 1988 and then in a *tour de force* nominating Clinton in 1992 (which the Arkansan's acceptance address introduction acknowledged as "how a real nominating speech should be given").

A prominent source of ensuing style for the acceptance address was derived from those schemes of repetition whereby successive clauses or short sentences have like beginnings (*anaphora* or *epanaphora*) or like endings (*antistrophe* or *epistrophe*) or a combination of both (*conplexio*). These are deviations from the common idiom. Along with "four score and seven years ago," many Americans remember some other words from Abraham Lincoln's Gettysburg Address: "government of the people, by the people, for the people." This statement utilizes ten words or "tokens" but only six "types" or different words: "government" (1), "of" (2), "the" (3), "people" (4), "by" (5), "the" (used already), "people" (used already), "for" (6), "the" (used already), and "people" (used already). A type-token-ratio, or TTR, for a statement, is derived by dividing the number of different words (or types) by the total number of words (tokens).[14] So for Lincoln's other eminently memorable words from the Gettysburg Address, the six types divided by ten tokens equal a TTR of .60 as a numerical value for the symmetrical proximity of its repetition. For utterances in the common idiom, however, the statistical probability is that in every ten to fifteen words one of them is repeated, for a type-token-ratio of .90 to .93 (some studies used ten-word segments; others used fifteen-word segments of the common idiom).[15] Thus, we *do* repeat some words normatively in our statements—but not with the proximity and symmetry that Lincoln did in "government of the people, by the people, for the people."[16] A TTR of .60 is significantly different from one of .90—and thereby "uncommon" or "singular" in the Aristotelian paradigm.

In addition to being deviations from the common idiom conducing to novelty, those schematic parallel repetitions as used in 1992 A.D. may serve another pragmatic function identified by Aristotle in 336 B.C. Consider the following Aristotelian observation in *The Rhetoric* (1414a) about the effect of schematic repetitions as used in a passage quoted from Homer: "Nireus from Syme brought three curved ships; Nireus, son of Aglaia and of Charopus; Nireus, most beautiful of all the Greeks who came to Troy, saving Achilles only." As Aristotle advised, "If a good many things are said about a person, his name will have to be mentioned pretty often; accordingly, if his name is often mentioned, one has the impression that a good deal has been said about him. By the use of this fallacy, Homer, who mentions Nireus only in this single passage, makes him important, and has preserved his memory, though in the rest of the poem he says never a word more about him."[17] Or, as the Greek critic Demetrius observes in *On Style,* "Nireus is not himself important in the *Iliad,* and his contribution is even less so, three ships and a few men, but Homer makes him appear important and his contribution great. . . . although Nireus is mentioned only once in the action, we remember him. . . . If Homer had said: 'Nireus, the son of Aglaia brought three ships from Syme,' he might as well not have mentioned him."[18] Potentially, stylistic repetition can perform similar pragmatic functions of emphasis in contemporary discourse. Time-honored research attests to communicative values of "the added strength given to the stimulus by repeating it and in the consequent increase of our sensitivity to the stimulus"; and axiomatically, "repetition of a stimulus, up to a certain point, may have a greater effect than a single stimulus, even if the latter is fairly strong."[19] And for style in language specifically, "the probability of recalling a repeated word is just about twice the probability of recalling a unique word"; and that advantage accrues not only for spoken discourse but also for the words we write, whereby "thresholds vary inversely with frequency of prior usage," which is immediate within the communication event (and not to the relative frequency with which these verbal stimuli appear in word counts of more probable lexical items generally).[20]

Such stylized repetition predominates in the Clinton acceptance address, with like beginnings preferred quantitatively. Qualitatively, though, that schematic symmetry seems to be employed sometimes only to achieve parallelism for its own sake, almost mechanistically, as in the *anaphora* with sequential references to "*a government* that offers more empowerment . . . *A government* that is leaner . . . that expands opportunity . . . *a government* that understands that jobs must come from growth in a vibrant and vital system of free enterprise."[21] The address also articulates Clinton's view of this country when he is president, in an almost obtrusively extended passage (in part with *conplexio,* too, but with groups of words between two periods that because of their lack of predicates are not grammatical sentences):

An America with millions of new jobs and dozens of new industries moving confidently toward the 21st century. *An America* that says to entrepreneurs and business people: We will give you more incentives and more opportunity . . . *That's what this New Covenant is all about.*

An America in which the doors of college are thrown open once again to the sons and daughters of stenographers and steelworkers . . . *That's what this New Covenant is all about.*

An America in which health care is a right, not a privilege . . . *That's what this New Covenant is all about..*

An America in which middle-class incomes—not middle class taxes—are going up. *An America* . . . *An America* . . . *That's what the New Covenant is all about* . . .

An America . . . *An America* . . . *An America* that will not coddle tyrants from Baghdad to Beijing. *An America* that champions the cause of freedom . . .

Furthermore, in referring to the previous administration mode of government that "is in the way," limited if any rhetorical advantage is attained from repeating a semantically impotent pronoun as a contraction: "*It's* been hijacked by privileged, private interests. *It's* forgotten who really pays the bills around here. *It's* taking more of your money and giving you less in service."[22] For what pragmatic, rhetorical purpose should "it's" be noticed and remembered? The far more functional application of parallel repetition on behalf of worthy words is that illustrated by Winston Churchill, for instance, during the darkest of days for England in World War Two: "*We shall fight* on the beaches, *we shall fight* on the landing grounds, *we shall fight* in the fields, and in the streets, *we shall fight* in the hills . . ." The words "we shall fight" *are* worthy of repetition.

Despite some instances of inconsequential or unworthy words being repeated, the acceptance address nevertheless evinces a predilection overall to emphasize through schematic repetition other words which, for that rhetorical situation, surely are more worthy of being noticed and remembered in that campaign context. At the outset of his address, as if to emphasize his own capabilities for leadership, Clinton relies on *anaphora* to speak of "*my* hope for the future, *my* faith in the American people, and *my* vision of the kind of country we can build, together." Similarly, to emphasize the scope of a commitment to family values, he envisions "an America that includes *every* family. *Every* traditional family and *every* extended family. *Every* two-parent family, *every* single-parent family, and *every* foster family. *Every* family." Discounting the fact that these are not grammatically complete sentences because they lack predicates, the prevailing sense of style is one whereby repetition is reserved for relatively important words, as also is the case with an *anaphora* to emphasize the dissatisfaction of the American electorate: "So *if you are sick and tired* of a Government that doesn't work to create jobs, *if you are sick and tired* of a tax system that's stacked against you, *if you're sick and tired* of exploding debt and reduced investments in our future, or if, like the great civil rights pioneer Fannie Lou Hamer *you're just plain old sick and tired* of being sick and tired, then join *us*, work with *us*, win with *us*" (also using the like endings, or *antistrophe*, of repeating "us"). Similarly, another appropriate use of *anaphora* is on behalf of "*saving* lives, *saving* money, and *saving* families from heartbreak," instead of the more idiomatic and less emphatic "saving lives, money, and families from heartbreak."

The Clinton style does have brief use of like endings (*antistrophe*) but primarily as a direct quote early in the speech from the party platform: "The most important family *policy*, urban *policy*, labor *policy*, minority *policy* and foreign *policy* America can have is an expanding, entrepreneurial economy of high-wage, high-skill jobs." The stylistic fingerprint in the acceptance address clearly is like beginnings (*anaphora*). Early and then midway in the text, those repetitions tend to be on behalf of single words, such as his praise of the "Arkansas miracle" where "*our* schools are better, *our* wages are higher, *our* factories are busier, *our* water is cleaner, and *our* budget is balanced"; or he prefers repeating very short segments, as in how his grandfather taught him "*more about* equality in the eyes of the Lord than all my professors at Georgetown; *more about* the intrinsic worth of every individual than all the philosophers at Oxford; *more about* the need for equal justice under the law than all the jurists at Yale Law School." As the text progresses toward its ending, those like beginnings tend to be of entire, longer phrases introducing successive clauses or sentences, as in these concluding paragraphs:

> Somewhere at this very moment, a child is being born in America. *Let it be our cause* to give that child a happy home, a healthy family, and a hopeful future. *Let it be our cause* to see that that child has a chance to live to the fullest . . . *Let it be our cause*

to see that child grow up strong and secure, braced by her
challenges . . .

Let it be, let it be our cause that when this child is able, she gives
something back to her children, her community and her country. *Let it be our cause* that we give this child a country that is coming together . . .

The *anaphora* of "Let it be our cause" not only has some overtones
of a scriptural commandment but a more distinct echo of John
Kennedy's inaugural address:

Let both sides explore what problems unite us instead of bela-
boring those problems which divide us.

Let both sides . . . formulate serious and precise proposals for the
inspection and control of arms . . .

Let both sides seek to invoke the wonders of science instead of
its terrors . . .

Let both sides unite in all corners of the earth the command of
Isaiah—to "undo the heavy burdens . . . [and] let the oppressed
go free."

To a critic of style, the Kennedy mode, however, is more active and
forceful, but Clinton nevertheless did have the option of saying instead
"let our cause be that of giving . . ."

The acceptance address does have isolated instances of *polysyndeton*
(the repetition of the grammatically unnecessary conjunction), in "We
can seize this moment, make it exciting *and* energetic *and* heroic to be
an American again" or that about "millions of energetic young men
and women, serving their country by policing the streets, *or* teaching the
children, *or* caring for the sick, *or* working with the elderly and people
with disabilities, *or* helping helping young people stay off drugs and out
of gangs." *Polysyndeton* was a characteristic Kennedy conformation, as
in his inaugural reference to a world "where the strong are just *and* the
weak secure *and* the peace preserved," instead of the grammatically
more idiomatic "strong are just, the weak secure, and the peace preserved." In traditional rhetorical theory on style, this particular technique was often recommended to persuaders as functionally eloquent
for reasons other than being a deviation from the common idiom.
For example, George Campbell in 1776 suggested that an impressive
"multiplicity of the circumstances" is conveyed by adding conjunctions
between each item in series; for by creating the polysyndeton, the

persuader may create "a deliberate attention to every circumstance, as being of importance." After all, "much additional weight and distinctness are given to each particular by the repetition of the conjunction."[23] Hugh Blair in 1787 also recommended that conjunctions should be "multiplied" so that the objects in between "should appear as distinct from one another as possible, and that the mind should rest, for a moment, on each object by itself." Thus, if the communicator's intention is "to show in how many places the enemy seemed to be at one time," the conjunction is repeated or "very happily redoubled, in order to paint more strongly the distinction of these several places."[24] Consider the hypothetical example of a United States senator who might have said, "Behind me in the fight for this legislation are the states of Maine, New Hampshire, Vermont, Massachusetts, and Connecticut." Instead of that customary usage for conjunctions as taught in our schools, the senator could have said, "Behind me in this fight are the states of Maine and New Hampshire and Vermont and Massachusetts and Connecticut." The effect *is* different! Listeners almost want to say to themselves, "Wow, *that* many?" In this context, ruminate about the potential advantage in Clinton's use of the scheme had he changed his sequence from repeating "or" to "policing the streets, *and* teaching the children, *and* caring for the sick, *and* working with the elderly and people with disabilities, *and* helping young people stay off drugs and out of gangs."

A more idiosyncratic species of schematic repetition in the Clinton style evolves from the classical scheme known as *epizeuxis*, whereby a word or phrase is repeated in immediate succession with no other words intervening, as in "Just *think of it. Think of it.*" In some instances, however, that deviation from the common idiom seems accidental, for the immediate repetitions in "the rest, the rest of the world" or the above quoted "Let it be, let it be" serve no rhetorical purpose. Other examples of this usage do seem somewhat more appropriate, though, conforming to the classical *desiderata* that only the most pertinent words are worthy of immediate repetition, illustrated by Demetrius with "The serpents in the Caucasus are large, large and numerous," wherein "repetition of 'large' gives weight to the style."[25] The more likely stylistic usage conforming to this criterion is Clinton's comment about his mother, that "*always, always* she taught me to fight." Less rhetorically advantageous applications occur while praising several facets of improved life in Arkansas after he became governor, saying "*I wish, I wish* I could say the same thing about America under the incumbent President"; and he then adds for "those who would criticize Arkansas: Come on down. *Especially, especially* if you're from Washington." None of these applications of the scheme have as much potency as other instances of *epizeuxis* fixed firmly in our minds, such as the line attributed to Paul Revere, "*To arms, to arms*, the British are coming" or the more singular sentence from Gertrude Stein: "A rose is a rose is a rose is a rose."[26] Still, to preface and amplify upon a warning that "where there is no vision, the people perish," *epizeuxis* is combined with *conplexio:* "*I hope, I hope* nobody in this great hall . . . has to go through tomorrow *without a vision. I hope* no one ever tries to raise a child *without a vision. I hope* nobody ever starts a business or plants a crop in the ground *without a vision.*" The most blatant use of *epizeuxis* occurs, however, as Clinton approaches his peroration, for "we can do it, with commitment, creativity, diversity and drive" is emphasized with seven immediate repetitions *a la* "the little engine that could" succeed: "*We can do it. We can do it. We can do it. We can do it. We can do it. We can do it.*"

An appropriate stylistic counterpoint to the heavy-handed approach of repeating an entire short sentence seven times is the more subtle repetition achieved by the Democrat's alliteration in "*c*ommitment, *c*reativity, *d*iversity and *d*rive." Actually, numerous alliterative sequences appear, as a stylistic fingerprint typically restricted to only pairs of words such as "*p*rivileged, *p*rivate interests," "*s*tenographers and *s*teelworkers," or President Bush who "*d*erides and *d*egrades the American tradition of *s*eeing and *s*eeking a better future" (with that earlier quoted sequence as well founded upon three repetitions of an initial sound in an "*e*xpanding, *e*ntrepreneurial *e*conomy." Indeed, alliteration becomes almost a variant whorl of Clinton's stylistic fingerprint with preferences for sequences such as those in "a *h*appy home, a *h*ealthy family, and a *h*opeful future"; or that coupled with *polysyndeton* in "*f*amily and *f*riends and a *f*aith that in America no one is left out"; or that which characterizes his peroration appeal: "Let that be our *c*ause, our *c*ommitment, and our New *C*ovenant" (with the *anaphora* of repeating "our" as if to emphasize unity between the candidate and his constituents).

Still another potential source of rhetorical effect evolves from parallel repetition of important words in the following passage in which the governor incorporates *conplexio* to contrast himself with the president:

He won't take on the big insurance companies and the bureaucracies to control health costs and give us affordable health care for all Americans, *but I will.*

He won't even implement the recommendations of his own Commission on AIDS, *but I will.*

He won't streamline the Federal Government and change the way it works . . . *but I will . . .*

He won't break the stranglehold the special interests have on our elections and the lobbyists have on our government, *but I will.*

He won't give mothers and fathers the simple chance to take some time off from work when a baby is born or a parent is sick, *but I will.*

As if conforming to the Aristotelian rationale about stylistic repetition helping listeners remember pertinent words, the stylistic device appropriately emphasizes "he won't" in contrast to "I will" and serves well a candidate clearly trying to distance himself from Bush's apparent inactivity on behalf of solving domestic problems. But the stylistic parallelism in itself potentially has other implications for rhetorical affect, and these are derived from the way the passage sets up and then fulfills expectations.

Recall from recent theorists an oft-used example of rhetorical style: "He who controls Berlin controls Germany; and he who controls Germany controls Europe; and he who controls Europe controls the . . ." Most people responding to this *klimax, scala, gradatio,* or *incre mentum* would not have to read the word "world" to know how the statement would resolve. As Kenneth Burke argues, "by the time you arrive at the second of its three stages, you feel how it is destined to develop— and on the level of purely formal assent you would collaborate to round out its symmetry by spontaneously willing its completion and perfection as an utterance"; and this function of style conduces to a rhetorically desirable "identification" achieved by discourse through the persuader's demonstration of "common" sensations, concepts, images, and attitudes with the audience. Moreover, this functional effect may be achieved "regardless of content"; for when "you persuade a man only insofar as you can talk his language," the means to do so often are word orders that are *"deviations from norms,"* as in this formal sequence of antitheses conducing to predictability: *"we do this,* but *they* on the other hand *do that; we* stay *here,* but *they* go *there; we* look *up,* but *they* look *down."*

Once you grasp the trend of the form, it invites participation regardless of subject matter. Formally, you will find yourself swinging along with the succession of antitheses, even though you may not agree with the proposition that is being presented in this form. Or it may even be an opponent's proposition which you resent—yet for the duration of the statement itself you might "help him out" to the extent of yielding to the formal development, surrendering to its symmetry as such. Of course, the more violent your original resistance to the proposition, the weaker will be your degree of "surrender" by "collaborating" with the form. But in cases where a decision is still to be reached, a yielding to the form prepares for assent to the matter identified with it. Thus, you are drawn to the form, not in your capacity as a partisan, but because of some "universal" appeal in it. And this attitude of assent may then be transferred to the matter which happens to be associated with the form.[27]

This notion of a functional effect of style as it achieves advantageous predictability was identified early by Longinus, a classical critic of style, who observed that kind of elation wherein the audience feels as though "it were not merely receiving, but were itself creatively participating" in the assertion being advanced (another translation reads that an audience feels a "joy and pride" as if it had *originated* the idea so expressed stylistically).[28] Of this originally Longinian conception of stylistic effectiveness Burke asks the question "Could we not say that, in such cases, the audience is exalted by the assertion because it has the feel of collaborating in the assertion?"

Parallel repetition is even more effective than a sequence of antitheses for ensuring predictability and resultant identification.[29] After hearing or reading for the very first time "of the people, by the people, for the . . . ," someone most likely "knows" how the statement ends. The repetition of "people" establishes a syntactical pattern by which that closure is virtually assured by end of the third element, as was the case for Hubert Humphrey in 1964. As Democratic candidate for vice-president, his convention acceptance address incorporated successive sentences enumerating values in which he and fellow Democrats believed—all ending alike with "But not Senator Goldwater" (the Republican candidate for president). By the third and fourth of his schematic like endings, Humphrey's audience was shouting in unison with him, "But not Senator Goldwater." The persuad*ees* articulated a conclusion to be reinforced in their minds by the persuade*r*. Walter Mondale emulated his political mentor and tried the same thing in 1980 as the Democratic vice-presidential nominee; but in a convention not as unified, he could not get the same extent of predictive closure from *epistrophe* or *antistrophe* with "But not Ronald Reagan" (Mondale actually had to tell the audience what they were supposed to do vocally). Conforming to the practice of his party predecessors in his own acceptance address for the 1992 vice-presidential nomination, Al Gore attacked the previous Republican administration and utilized the same stylistic technique repeating the successive like endings, "It is time for them to go." So closure as actual vocal participation might function in part as an audience's "leaning" already in a certain direction attitudinally (as in some religious services in which the preacher's stylistic parallelism helps the congregation to utter some words in unison during a sermon). In Clinton's case at the 1992 Democratic convention, the audience legitimately could not shout out with him, "*I will*"; but other, internalized "identification" might occur in the nature of a favorable response to the content introduced within this "pale of assent."[30]

For all its conducing to predictability and then closure, the above quoted *conplexio* utilizing the stylistic symmetry of the "He won't . . . I will" pattern also has this immediately following sequence which offers still another rhetorically advantageous variation:

> We're losing our farms at a rapid rate and he has no commitment to keep family farms in the family, *but I do.*
> *He's* talked a lot about drugs, but he hasn't helped people on the front line to wage that war on drugs and crime, *but I will.*
> *He* won't take the lead in protecting the environment and creating new jobs in environmental technologies for the 21st century, *but I will.*
> And you know what else? *He* doesn't have Al Gore, *and I do.*

By altering the like endings from "but I will" to "but I do," the option is highly reminiscent (to a critic of presidential style in discourse) of that sequence of like endings used by Franklin Roosevelt to stylistic advantage in his *epistrophe* or *antistrophe* about a world founded upon four essential human freedoms: "The first is freedom of speech and expression *everywhere in the world.* The second is freedom of every person to worship God in his own way *everywhere in the world.* The third is freedom from want, which translated into world terms means economic understandings which will secure to every nation a healthy, peace-time life for its inhabitants *everywhere in the world*. The fourth is freedom from fear, which translated into world terms means a worldwide reduction in armaments to such a point and in such a thorough fashion that no nation will be in a position to commit an act of physical aggression against any neighbor, *anywhere* in the world." The subtle variation of "anywhere" from the clearly established pattern of repeating "everywhere"—while still retaining the symmetry of the form—constitutes a discrepancy from what is expected and thereby is even more conducive to novelty for emphasis of the last phrase. After all, with excessive repetitions, any stimulus becomes monotonous, so eloquent stylists may be discrete and inject subtle variation into parallel repetition which at the same time retains its symmetry. Clinton's first "I do" fulfills such a function—and helps "set up" the audience to have another expectation fulfilled with "He doesn't have Al Gore, and I do." The sense of closure is complete and appropriate for lines classical rhetoricians likely would have acclaimed as suitable for persuasive style. As the consummate orator himself, Cicero extolled style "marked by a certain artistry and polish," which in turn would produce "applause and admiration"; and as he went on, "although we hope to win a 'Bravo, capital!' as often as possible . . . the actual ejaculation 'Couldn't be better!' is the one I should like to hear frequently."[31] Although Roman culture believed that "as the glory of a man is the strength of his mental capacity, so the brightest ornament of genius is eloquence," Cicero was pragmatic, arguing that "when a citizen hears an able orator, he readily credits what is said; he imagines everything to be true, he believes and relishes the force of it; and in short, the persuasive language of the speaker wins his absolute, his hearty assent."[32] Moreover, he deemed that impact of style was not only upon other learned people, sophisticated in nuances of eloquence but also upon "the unlearned crowd when it forms the audience. For everybody is able to discriminate between what is right and wrong in matters of art and proportion by a sort of subconscious instinct, without having any theory of art or proportion of their own."[33]

Another feature of the acceptance address style is antithesis, that mode of utterance wherein words with opposing semantic meanings balance one another off neatly (usually within one sentence), as in

Clinton's stylistic contrast of himself with President Bush: "He took the *richest country* in the world and *brought it down*. We took one of the *poorest states* in America and *lifted it up*." Antitheses are not in the common idiom because of psycholinguistic constraints upon people as they choose words and arrange them in sentences. To illustrate this principle, the words "devil," "dark," and "sinister" in a sentence most likely would be followed by use of the word "Satan," "evil," or "Hell" rather than a word opposite in meaning, such as "good" or "angel"; similarly, after using "hot," "sweaty," and "sultry," people likely would not include the word "cold" or "overcoat" in the same sentence but rather "sun," "beach," or "Florida." As an axiom of language behavior, once a context is formed by words with compatible meanings, a successive word which is incompatible or opposite in meaning is unlikely; and this preference for words compatible in meaning to be placed close together is one that operates "automatically and unconsciously."[34] So the common idiom is characterized by sentences wherein words with similar meanings are positioned close together syntactically, and that proximity of semantically compatible words is customary and familiar usage for the English language and thereby what people expect when they hear and read discourse. When a sentence deviates from that normative syntax and places words with opposite meanings in close proximity syntactically, the resultant statement embodies a source of style known as antithesis; and in that discourse which has endured the test of time for memorability and quotability, neatly balanced antitheses are ubiquitous.[35] For example, many Americans remember Neil Armstrong's exact, triple antithesis about "one small step for a man—one giant leap for mankind."

The acceptance address has several antitheses. Too often, however, they do not display that balance which lends itself to epigrammatic statements as quotable and memorable as John Kennedy's, for instance. For example, Clinton (or his writing staff) constructs this sentence: "And yet just as we have won the cold war abroad, we are losing the battles for economic opportunity and social justice here at home." Admittedly, "won" is counterbalanced by "losing"; "abroad" is counterbalanced by "at home"; but "cold war" is offset by "battles" for both "economic opportunity" and "social justice." The line would be better balanced, for instance, as "We have won the cold war for political democracy abroad but are losing the heated battle for economic opportunity at home." In this recast version, elimination of the second "we" helps heighten the effect of the antithesis by bringing the opposites closer together syntactically. Moreover, that omission then destroys the parallel like beginnings which in effect make the two halves of the antithesis sound more alike than different. Of course, the revised version just as well could have substituted "social justice" for "economic opportunity" because either one or the other, alone, contributes to balance; but both terms in the second half make the line unbalanced and less epigrammatic (and the subtle addition of "heated" helps counterbalance "cold"). Similarly, the antithesis is unbalanced in "Soviet Communism has collapsed, and our values—freedom, democracy, individual rights, free enterprise—they have triumphed all around the world." The Clinton style is much more conducive to balanced antitheses and the classical conception of eloquence in his denouncement of a government which is "taking more of your money and giving you less in service."

Another hallmark of an effective antithesis is the sense of style exercised in determining the order in which the two opposing halves are placed. For example, Adlai Stevenson had two options when he eulogized Eleanor Roosevelt: "She lit a candle when other people cursed the darkness" or "When other people cursed the darkness, she lit a candle." The latter *is* better! Antitheses often read better or sound better as they end on the upbeat, emphasizing the positive—although a writer or speaker sometimes just might want to emphasize the negative. For all its being the "best of times," Charles Dickens did want to emphasize that it also was the "worst of times." Similarly, to emphasize the negative impact of a Bush decision on voters Clinton was trying hardest to attract, this line could have been reversed to advantage: "He has raised taxes on the people driving pickup trucks and lowered taxes on the people riding in limousines." Whichever is deemed more pertinent for the situation at hand, however, should be placed syntactically in the second half of the antithesis because of what learning theory calls the laws about recency and primacy. When hearing a series of numbers, alphabet letters, or words read aloud once in random order, two items have an advantage for memorability: the first (primacy) and the last (recency); and of those two, the last is more reliably remembered than the first on the list. So the second, recent half of the balanced antithesis is more advantageous for emphasis. In this context, consider these of Clinton's assertions: that "welfare should be a second chance not a way of life"; that family values should "live in our actions, not just our speeches"; that we must be "exporting products, not jobs"; or his peroration hopes for "a country that is coming together, not coming apart." To stress how people are to view welfare, truly live family values, export products only, and come together as a country, those antitheses should emulate Kennedy's eminently quotable moral which emphasizes by syntactical placement what people *are* to do in "Ask not what your country can do for you—ask what you can do for your country." Part of Ronald Reagan's stylistic ineptness was that his antitheses inappropriately accentuated the negative. For example, to make a moral about the best "government," Reagan said "It is rather to make it work—work with us, not over us; to stand by our side, not ride our back." Those antitheses might end with, and thereby accentuate, positives, as in "not work over us but with us; not ride our back but stand by our side." Similarly, "The future is best decided by ballots, not bullets" might sound better as "The future is decided best not by bullets but ballots."[36] Clinton does conform to that criterion, however, in "These are not just commitments from my lips" but "the work of my life," or his antithetical assertion (albeit with an accidental *epizeuxis*), "When I am your President, the rest, the rest of the world won't look *down* on us with *pity* but *up* to us with *respect* again." Nevertheless, the Arkansan's antitheses overall do not display the epigrammatic quality that characterized those most quotable lines that do stick in our memories.

If the acceptance address to the 1992 Democratic convention is not distinguished in its achievement of epigrammatic antitheses, perhaps a causal factor is a prevailing sense (at some level of awareness) that Clinton had to be cautious about using this particular stylistic device. In the realm of recent presidential style in discourse, the exemplars of antitheses are those in the Kennedy inaugural: the *urbanitas* of the AB-BA reversal format in "Ask not what your country [A] can do for you [B]—ask what you [B] can do for your country [A]" or "Let us never negotiate [A] out of fear [B] but let us never fear [B] to negotiate [A]" as well as in those other, neatly balanced lines such as "if a free society cannot help the many who are poor how can it save the few who are rich?" But a persona projected by the Arkansan's *lexis* could not be that of an immediately apparent, stylistic clone. If one image was particularly vivid from the campaign "documentary" shown at the beginning of the telecast the evening of his acceptance address, it is that showing young Bill as a high-school student visiting Washington, D.C., being invited to the White House, standing in the front row of other boys being greeted by the president, and being in obvious awe of President John F. Kennedy (recall his oratorical counterpoint to the visual imagery of the documentary acknowledging that "as a teenager, I heard John Kennedy's summons to citizenship"). While campaign strategy called for Clinton's being young and assertive in contrast with an old and passive Bush, the Democratic nominee could not be too much like Kennedy. Any stylistic persona projected by the acceptance address had to be one of the Arkansan as his own man. After all, the Kennedy image was tarnished somewhat in recent years by constant stories of his marital infidelities while in the White House, and attempts had been made during the 1992 presidential campaign to suggest that the current Democratic candidate might have similar propensities. So some antitheses could be there, but not to the extent that other discourse emulated the style of John Kennedy and his stylistic alter ego Ted Sorensen.[37] Richard Nixon's 1968 acceptance address, for instance, had "Let us accept this challenge, not as a grim duty, but as an exciting adventure" and a Kennedyesque "If we are to have respect for law in America we must have laws that deserve respect"; and he was fond, too, of quoting the well-turned antitheses of others, such as his favorite "when the going gets tough the tough get going" (Nixon was not above using what worked for others, even admitting that the "Checkers" example imitated Franklin Roosevelt who got so much political mileage in the 1944 campaign from "my little dog Fala").[38]

Clinton's restraint in using antitheses is apparent in the absence of any *urbanitas* derived from those neatly turned AB-BA conformations wherein two key words from the first half are reversed in the second half to create the apposing meaning. Those antitheses often evolve when one of the words can have two grammatical functions. For example, in Kennedy's "let us never negotiate out of fear," fear is a noun; but in the second half, "let us never fear to negotiate," fear is a verb. Clinton had argued that "I want an America where 'family values' live in our actions, not just in our speeches." Because "value" can be both a noun and a verb, an AB-BA antithesis (which also accentuates the positive) well might have been something to the effect that

"Whereas their words praise family [A] values [B] our actions value [B] families [A]"; or to amplify upon the way that the Republicans created a government that "doesn't work" (and "work" can be both a noun and a verb), style could have yielded something like "The work [A] for our government [B] is to become a government [B] that works [A] for us" (and recalling that "place" and "hope" both can be nouns and verbs, the stylistically adventuresome reader here might speculate about epigrammatic possibilities for Clinton's "I still believe in a place called Hope"). After all, if quotability of presidential style is a valid criterion, this is the Ciceronian style for political oratory "marked by a certain artistry and polish" producing that "applause and admiration" whereby the citizen "readily credits what is said; he imagines everything to be true, he believes and relishes the force of it; and in short, the persuasive language of the speaker wins his absolute, his hearty assent." Yet Clinton's stylistic restraint against emulating Kennedyesque antitheses similarly is evinced in the failure to "cash in" on opportunities to make those conformations when an obvious, obverse half appears without stating its apposing counterpart. Where trickle down economics has "failed," identify what would "succeed"; in contrast to "stereotypes that blind us," specify what restores our vision; and offer the "divided" opposite to "when we are united, we are unstoppable."

Although Clinton's use of antithesis is restrained, this is not the case for a unique metaphor which the candidate repeated over and over: His intended campaign theme for the acceptance address was that of offering Americans a "New Covenant." All recent presidential candidates seemingly try hard stylistically for some "cheer line," particular phrase, or metaphor to catch on as a hallmark of the campaign and forthcoming presidency. FDR had his "New Deal"; Kennedy promised us a "New Frontier"; and Bill Clinton obviously had such hopes for "New Covenant." For a carefully crafted address in a speech intended for the most favorable of immediate reactions and ultimate effects, the recurrence of "New Covenant" obviously was intended to achieve status as the slogan for his forthcoming campaign and perhaps presidency. Approximately two-thirds of the way through the address, the Democratic nominee said, "I call this approach a New Covenant"— and then repeated that metaphor ten additional times! Moreover, in its adherence to an Aristotelian-like parallelism, the speech included a substantial segment wherein successive paragraphs (instead of clauses or sentences) had the like endings of "That's what the New Covenant is all about."

In the Aristotelian view, metaphor is a significant source of eloquent *lexis* or style. *The Rhetoric* proclaims its potential virtues many times: "It is metaphor above all else that gives clearness, charm, and distinction to the style" (1405a); metaphor is a source of "dignity" and "impressiveness of style" (1407b); and "it is metaphor that is in the highest degree instructive and pleasing" (1410b). Moreover, Clinton's extensive repetition of his specific, favored metaphor should have contributed to its being noticed; and it was to some degree. When the *New York Times* published the Acceptance Address, its text was followed immediately by a short article comparing Clinton's "Policy Trademark" with FDR's New Deal, Kennedy's New Frontier, and Lyndon Johnson's Great Society.[39] Nevertheless, "New Covenant" did not catch on among the public, either as the slogan for the campaign or for the forthcoming administration. Why? Contrast the phrase with "New Frontier," for example. All Americans are a product of a persistent, popular culture—from dime novels through subsequent motion pictures and years of TV westerns—in which the frontier was depicted as the place of excitement, adventure, and opportunity. Never mind that the reality was one of incredible hardship and disease, if not death. We as a people continue to succumb to the appeal of the frontier in clothing, movies, television advertising for a variety of products, trucks with off-the-road capability in difficult terrain, country-western dancing, and even as a metaphor for our military combat in the twentieth century.[40] The connotations evoked by our frontier experience are virtually always positive in our national experience.

Potential connotations evoked by a "covenant" are not necessarily so universally positive, however. In the more general sense, the word may signify a mutual agreement, vow, or compact between two or more persons about what they will or will not do, and the word also has legal implications in that it can refer to a point or term in a legal document if not the entire document itself. But for Americans, "covenant" is more familiar for its scriptural or religious connotations. Often signifying that relationship entered into by a divine being with another being or persons, the word was in especially wide usage among seventeenth-century American Puritans and subsequent New

Englanders, particularly Calvinists who ascribed to a "covenant theology" as well as those members of the Congregational Church who endeavored to constitute themselves as a distinct religious society. Thus, on the one hand, depicting his political goals metaphorically as a "covenant" might help project a persona of morality if not religiosity for Clinton. After all, the very nature of the term as referring to a religious compact might bestow some aura of moral virtue on Clinton; anyone who makes a covenant must be "good"; and those people who would endorse that covenant by voting Democratic also might be "good." Still the metaphor as used alone has problems. In the American *ethos*, the Puritans bestowed upon themselves an aura of intolerance which persists to this day, as a result not only of American literature but also of history. Although likely more conservative than the way he was characterized by Republicans, Clinton was appealing to Democrats who by their traditional impulses might be wooed to return to the fold of liberalism. America had too many peoples in need of help, and all of these groups had been carefully enumerated in his address: unemployed, underemployed, overtaxed, poorly educated, addicted to drugs, just plain poor, minorities, disabled, gay, elderly, children missing a parent, women seeking their right to choice. But among these are groups whom earlier intolerant Puritans and subsequent heirs among the contemporary Religious Right might shun. In its connotations evolving from American history, "covenant" was linked too close semantically with the type of voters from whom Clinton could not receive support in 1992.

With slight stylistic emendation, the metaphor might have worked better, however. First, the hoped for "catch phrase" could have eliminated "new." After a New Deal, a New Frontier, and Ronald Reagan's tautological New Beginning, any subsequent "new" something or other was banal or trite—if not by now politically meaningless—in the context of having a different president. But if "new" were deleted from the metaphor, the addition of another contextual qualifier was imperative to help ensure that an intended meaning—and not any associated with intolerant Puritans—would be evoked among listeners and readers. Suppose Clinton had proposed simply a "covenant with compassion." In addition to any salience derived from its alliteration, the metaphor then likely would not evoke any connotations linking the term with the intolerance of the past but far more a virtuous commitment to aid those peoples needing help for the future. And the addition of "compassion" to the metaphor also would have complemented his second last sentence, "My fellow Americans, I end tonight where it all began for me: I still believe in a place called Hope." Semantically, hope and compassion are aptly conjoined.'

Admittedly, the acceptance address has a few other modes of metaphor. The maritime figuration Cuomo used the previous night, "we have to steer our ship of state on a new course," was reiterated. Listeners also heard that their government had "been hijacked by privileged, private interests" and that accordingly we must join "in a great new adventure to chart a bold new future." Martial metaphor also occurs when the speaker refers to those millions of Perot's supporters as "an army of patriots for change." In keeping with the religious motif of his "New Covenant," Clinton also called upon his audience to "just remember what the Scripture says: 'Where there is no vision, the people perish,'" a quotation which over the span of the next six sentences was repeated once and then restated substituting the life-cycle metaphor and personification that "America will *perish*." This particular scriptural reference was the same used by Franklin Roosevelt in his first inaugural address, suggesting that FDR might become more the model for a stylistic persona evinced in Clinton's discourse. In the final analysis, though, the 1992 acceptance address is predominantly literal. After all, another rhetorical obligation that evening was to introduce, in the first person, a nominee who still was relatively unknown to the American electorate. Appropriate subject matter for those purposes included an autobiographical account of the candidate's life, including the early death of his father, the influential roles of his mother and grandfather, and the importance of his wife, Hillary. An extended chronology of detail simply does not lend itself easily to being described metaphorically. Thus, from the standpoint of utilizing the rhetorical potency of figurative language, the acceptance address put all its proverbial eggs in one basket, as if not to obscure that one metaphor the audience hopefully would accept as the catch phrase or slogan for the campaign. But for all its overt emphasis from being repeated ten times, the semantic nuances of the "New Covenant" were such that the metaphor did not catch on as hoped. And for that reason, the Arkansan's acceptance address stands as a competent—but not consummate—application of Aristotelian precepts for effective style in discourse.

For the presidential campaign of 1992, the polls were showing more and more that Americans wanted neither more nor less than change. With so many people hurting in various ways from the state of the economy, and the Republican incumbent's ostensible neglect of domestic affairs, one of several important rhetorical objectives for the Democrat's acceptance address was simply that of demonstrating sufficient communication competence to be worthy of having been nominated. Delivered well, the content or substance of Clinton's address was appropriate; and in several of its facets, the form or style of that speech was suitable. The next major hurdle in the communication of the campaign was that of the televised debates with the other two candidates, President Bush and Ross Perot. As seems now to be the case, however, an important criterion to measure any candidate's degree of success in those presidential debates is the extent to which mistakes are avoided in those telecasts with impressively large viewing audiences. Clinton made no mistakes. Memory lapses were absent; he was poised, confident, and articulate; and no mis-statement marred his performance, such as that of Gerald Ford in one of the 1976 TV debates with Jimmy Carter: "There is no Soviet domination of Eastern Europe and there never will be under a Ford administration."[41] For a performance in which verbal behavior is largely extemporaneous (because of a format of responding to questions posed then and there), style in discourse is an inappropriate focus of critical attention; for extemporaneous delivery for the most part relies on the common idiom (speakers cannot phrase well-balanced antitheses at the moment of utterance, for instance). The Democratic nominee obviously was well prepared and had stock lines of argument available for any question he might be asked; some well-worded sentences obviously were phrased ahead of time and memorized to be included as appropriate responses when certain opportunities arose; and in the main his performance was well orchestrated beforehand to refer over and over to the theme that ultimately was responsible for victory at the polls: "change." And observant viewers noticed that before each of his responses, Clinton paused briefly to ensure his having the best words, whether from his prepared repertoire or to avoid any mis-statement from too hasty an extemporaneous response. The candidate remained the competent communicator.

For a Clinton campaign wherein speeches before live audiences were for the most part extemporaneous, a concluding assessment of his stylistic persona therefore must turn to the inaugural address. Unlike a convention acceptance address with its requirements for an autobiographical statement constrained to be idiomatic, inaugurals admit to substantially more possibilities for sweeping generalizations that can be phrased metaphorically; and the Clinton inaugural draws from a rich reservoir of figurations. Reminiscent of John Kennedy, who spoke of a "beachhead of cooperation" or "now the trumpet summons us," this speech also uses some martial metaphors: "we *march* to the music of our time, our *mission* is timeless"; we have "always *mustered* the determination"; and in its conclusion, "We have *heard the trumpets*. We have *changed the guard*." Building metaphors also are present in that we might "*construct* from these crises the *pillars* of our history" and in how America "*rebuilds* at home" or is "*building* democracy" across the world. Even a music metaphor occurs: "You have raised your voices in an unmistakable *chorus*." And the address also capitalizes, but only briefly, on those metaphors with archetypal significations that what is light or high is universally understood as being good. Thus, "our founders saw themselves in the *light* of posterity" and "from this joyful *mountain top* of celebration we hear a call to service in the valley." Not one of these metaphorical types, however, is significant in the inaugural address, either quantitatively or qualitatively.

Just as Clinton had put all his figurative eggs in one basket with "new covenant" for the acceptance address so, too, did he choose a distinct metaphorical motif for the inaugural address. Both quantitatively and qualitatively, his significant metaphor is about spring, its signification of renewal, and the inexorable change of seasons leading to something better. Moreover, to endow that metaphor with enhanced potential for emphasis, the address begins by making the metaphor as an antithesis: "This ceremony is held in the depth of winter. But, by the words we speak and the faces we show the world, we force the spring." Although the line is imbalanced as an antithesis, the prevailing metaphor of the address about "spring reborn" has been established from the outset for a world now "warmed by the sunshine of freedom" after having been "raised in the shadows of the Cold War." Thus, after an alliterative "*e*nd to the *e*ra of *d*eadlock and *d*rift," the audience is reassured that "a new season of American renewal has begun"; and the metaphor can be reassuring because of its archetypal signification that the cold of winter will be replaced inexorably by the warmth of spring, with all the change of season entails for renewal, regrowth, and an eventual harvest as well. Indeed, by their votes for the Democrat, "Americans have forced the *spring*," and "Now, we must do the work the *season* demands." Moreover, "our renewal" thereby entails for young Americans an alliterative "*season* of *s*ervice"; for as "the scripture says, 'And let us not be weary in well-doing, for in *due season*, we shall reap, if we faint not'." In so doing, Clinton now links himself stylistically less with John Kennedy and more once again with Franklin Roosevelt. Admittedly, FDR's first inaugural articulated with martial metaphor both his intent "to *wage a war* against the emergency" as well as "the *lines of attack*" for Americans as a "*trained and loyal army*" But all these endeavors were intended to restore confidence in that wintery "dark hour of our national life" when "values have shrunken to fantastic levels; taxes have risen; our ability to pay has fallen; the means of exchange are *frozen* in the currents of trade; the *withered leaves* of industrial enterprise lie on every side; farmers find no markets for their produce; the savings of many years in thousands of families are gone." Therefore, FDR would lead America out of the dread of winter to the rejuvenated confidence coming with the spring. With their inherent archetypal qualifiers about inexorable seasonal change for the better, these of Clinton's figurations are both safe (from the standpoint of not evoking unintended meanings) as well as compelling lexical choices befitting the rhetorical situation.

Syntactically, however, that inaugural address is restrained in its deviations from the common idiom. Other, occasional antitheses occur, such as "We will act—with *peaceful diplomacy* whenever *possible*, with *force* when *necessary*"; yet those conformations may emphasize the unintended negative in offering "a government for our *tomorrows*, not our *yesterdays*" or retain unnecessary words, as in "There is nothing wrong with America that cannot be cured by what is right with America" (the more epigrammatic version would eliminate the double negative and the parallel repetition that make the halves sound alike: "What is *wrong* with America can be cured by what is *right*"). But "right" also is one of those words capable of dual grammatical functions; and had Clinton been interested in projecting a persona more reminiscent of Kennedy, another potential AB-BA could have evolved from a juxtaposition about "the right [A] of Americans [B] to make America [B] right [A]."

Similarly, the inaugural early had warned against "change for change's sake" so a new president concerned about not appearing too liberal might have alluded to only "guarded changes" once "we have changed the guard." In keeping with previous stylistic inclinations, however, alliteration again occurs characteristically in pairs, as in "*powerful people*," "*communications and commerce are global*," "*profound and powerful forces*," or "*power and privilege*." Nowhere, though, does the inaugural incorporate the heavy-handed, sometimes obtrusive schematic repetition of the acceptance address. The use of *anaphora* is both sparse and in the form of a tri-colon, as in the alliterative "*our hopes, our hearts, our hands*" or the imperatives "*We must* do what no other generation has had to do before. *We must* invest more in our own people . . . And *we must* do so in a world in which we must compete for every opportunity." Only for the peroration, when a more percussive effect actually might be fitting, does style for the inaugural amplify upon "the very idea of America" by going beyond a tri-colon for repetition: "*An idea* born in revolution and renewed through two centuries of challenge; *an idea* tempered by the knowledge that, but for fate, we—the fortunate and the unfortunate—might have been each other; *an idea* ennobled by the faith that our nation can summon from its myriad diversities the deepest measure of unity; *an idea* infused with the conviction that America's long heroic journey must go forever upward."

In its overall tone, the stylistic persona of Bill Clinton in the inaugural is one of restraint in syntax complemented by dignity in lexicon. If television viewers of the address actually did read accurately the lips of President Bush at the conclusion of this inaugural, he leaned over to Barbara and made the critical comment, "good speech." Factors contributing to such an assessment surely reflected the new president's applications of Aristotelian notions of *lexis* or style in discourse. And the final, critical comment here must be that style in the inaugural address in its final effects evinced a stylistic persona of the new president as one who was not only competent but making some substantial strides toward becoming that more consummate orator with style. In its focus on form or style, this critical assessment largely ignores Clinton's content or substance. But others are more appropriate judges of his ideas and issues as articulated in discourse: the polls, the press, and ultimately the populace. Thus, for the merit of judgments rendered in this essay, recall how Aristotle concluded for students in Attica his treatise on rhetoric: "I have done; you have heard; you have the facts; give your judgment." And if your judgment about President Clinton's style in discourse is different from that expressed herein, only one additional observation is warranted: *De gustibus non est disputandum.*

NOTES

1. For a translation of Buffon's *"Discours sur le Style,"* see Lane Cooper, *The Art of the Writer* (Ithaca, N.Y.: Cornell University Press, 1952), 146–55.

2. This is not a categorical disavowal of the likelihood that presidential style in discourse might reveal something about personality. Elsewhere, I have made the case that some statistical descriptors of style well might reveal some aspects of a president's persona, at least in extemporaneous discourse in TV debates as well as in inaugurals in which the speaker is highly involved emotionally. See Ronald H. Carpenter et al., "Style in Discourse as a Predictor of Political Personality for Mr. Carter and Other Twentieth-Century Presidents: Testing the Barber Paradigm," *Presidential Studies Quarterly* 8 (Winter 1978): 67–78.

3. In an attempt to bring some order out of that chaos, I surveyed major treatises in the history of rhetorical theory, from classical times through the nineteenth century, to classify all those usages into but twenty-one discrete conformational modes which deviate from the common idiom of English. See Ronald H. Carpenter, "The Essential Schemes of Syntax: An Analysis of Rhetorical Theory's Recommendations for Uncommon Word Orders," *Quarterly Journal of Speech* 55 (April 1969): 161–68.

4. Charles Osgood, "Some Effects of Motivation on Style of Encoding," in *Style in Language,* ed. Thomas A. Sebeok (New York: John Wiley and Sons and the Massachusetts Institute of Technology, 1960), 293–96.

5. Rulon Wells, "Nominal and Verbal Style," in Sebeok, *Style in Language,* 215.

6. Paul I. Rosenthal, "The Concept of the Paramessage in Persuasive Communication," *Quarterly Journal of Speech* 58 (February 1972): 15–17. Italics mine.

7. Undergirding my discussion here is a frame of reference recognizing that the more effective communicators are those who are constrained to make the most "fitting" rhetorical responses to the exigencies confronting them in discourse. After Lloyd F. Bitzer, "The Rhetorical Situation," *Philosophy and Rhetoric* 1 (January 1968): 1–14.

8. For my more complete discussion of this point, see Ronald H. Carpenter, "The Symbolic Substance of Style in Presidential Discourse," *Style* 16 (Winter 1982): 38–49.

9. For my earlier discussions of this point, see Ronald H. Carpenter, "Ronald Reagan and the Presidential Imperative to Stylize: A - E = Less-than GC," *Speaker and Gavel* 20 (1982–83): 1–6; "Ronald Reagan," in *Fifty American Political Orators,* ed. Bernard K. Duffy and Halford R. Ryan (Westport, Conn.: Greenwood Press, 1986): 331–36; and "The Impotent Style of Ronald Reagan: A - E = Less-than GC *Rediviva,*" *Speaker and Gavel* 24 (Spring 1987): 53–59.

10. See the Lane Cooper translation of Aristotle's *Rhetoric* iii. 2 (New York: Appleton-Century-Crofts, 1932) as well as E. M. Cope's translation of the same

passage in *An Introduction to Aristotle's Rhetoric* (London: MacMillan and Company, 1867): 283–84.

11. William N. Dember, *The Psychology of Perception* (New York: Holt, Rinehart and Winston, 1960), 348.

12. See, for examples, Jon Eisenson, J. Jeffery Auer, and John Irwin, *The Psychology of Communication* (New York: Appleton-Century-Crofts, 1963), 239; D. E. Berlyne, "Novelty and Curiosity as Determinants of Exploratory Behavior," *British Journal of Psychology* 40 (1949): 68–80; Norman L. Munn, *Psychology: The Fundamentals of Human Adjustment*, 3d ed. (Boston: Houghton Mifflin Company, 1956), 319; Judson S. Brown, *The Motivation of Behavior* (New York: McGraw-Hill, 1961), 330–31; and Donald E. Broadbent, *Perception and Communication* (London: Pergamon Press, 1958), 85–86.

13. Eisenson, Auer, and Irwin, *The Psychology of Communication*, 250.

14. As a precise, quantitative index of lexical diversity, the type-token-ratio was formulated originally by Wendell Johnson, "Studies in Language Behavior: I. A Program of Research," *Psychological Monographs* 56 (1944): 1.

15. George A. Miller, *Language and Communication* (rev. ed., New York: McGraw-Hill Book Company, 1963), 89, 122–23.

16. In normative conversation, we tend to get by relatively well with small vocabularies. For example, "statistical studies of telephone speech have suggested that 96 percent of such talk employs no more than 737 words," and "conversation is built out of a relatively small vocabulary." In Colin Cherry, *On Human Communication* (New York: Science Editions, Inc., 1961), 120. With such small vocabularies being used, idiomatic speech therefore must be relatively repetitive.

17. Aristotle *Rhetoric* iii. 12.

18. Demetrius *On Style* 61, in the translation by G. M. A. Grube (Toronto: Toronto University Press, 1961).

19. Eisenson, Auer, and Irwin, *The Psychology of Communication*, 239; and Giles W. Gray and Claude M. Wise, *The Bases of Speech*, 3d ed. (New York: Harper and Row, 1959), 416.

20. See for instance Nancy C. Waugh, "Immediate Memory as a Function of Repetition," *Journal of Verbal Learning and Verbal Behavior* 2 (1963): 109; and Richard L. Solomon and Leo Postman, "Frequency of Usage as a Determinant of Recognition Threshold for Words," *Journal of Experimental Psychology* 43 (1952): 198. Nevertheless, the threshold of recognition also is more efficient according to "the relative frequency with which that word occurs in the Thorndike-Lorge word counts." See also Davis Howes and Richard L. Solomon, "Visual Duration Threshold as a Function of Word-Probability," *Journal of Experimental Psychology* 41 (1951): 410.

21. All quotations from the acceptance address are from the text published in the *New York Times*, 17 July 1992, as transcribed by the newspaper. I italicize those specific segments that create deviations from the common idiom.

22. See my previously cited essays about Reagan, particularly on "The Impotent Style."

23. George Campbell, *The Philosophy of Rhetoric*, ed. Lloyd F. Bitzer (Carbondale: Southern Illinois University Press, 1963), 368.

24. Hugh Blair, *Lectures on Rhetoric and Belles Lettres* (London, 1787), Vol. 1, Lecture 12: 292–93.

25. Demetrius *On Style* 66.

26. In one of the most quoted and remembered lines of poetry in the English language, the eleven tokens and three types yield a TTR of .27. Any writer or speaker would be hard pressed to achieve more unusual proximity of repetition than that. And Stein herself gave a clue as to why such schematic repetition is novel: "Now the poet has to work in the excitingness of pure being; he has to get back that intensity into the language. We all know that it's hard to write poetry in a late age, and we know that you have to put some strangeness, something unexpected, into the structure of the sentence in order to bring back the vitality of the noun. Now it's not enough to be bizarre; the strangeness in the sentence structure has to come from the poetic gift, too. That's why it's doubly hard to be a poet in a late age. Now you have seen hundreds of poems about roses and you know in your bones that the rose is not there. All those songs that sopranos sing as encores about 'I have a garden; oh, what a garden!' Now I don't want to put too much emphasis on that line, because it's just one line in a longer poem. But I notice that you all know it; you can make fun of it, but you know it, now listen! I'm no fool. I know that in daily life we don't go around saying 'is a . . . is a . . . is a . . . is a . . . .' Yes, I'm no fool; but I think that in that line the rose is red for the first time in English poetry for a hundred years." See Gertrude Stein, *Four in America* (New Haven, Conn.: Yale University Press, 1947), v.

27. Kenneth Burke, *A Rhetoric of Motives* (New York, 1958), 49–51, 55–69.

28. Longinus *On the Sublime* 7. See in particular the translation by H. L. Havell (London, 1890). Other rhetoricians attest to the same capability of style. See Campbell, *The Philosophy of Rhetoric*, 121, as well as Blair, *Lectures on Rhetoric and Belles Lettres* Vol. 2, Lecture 19, 35.

29. See Ronald H. Carpenter, "Stylistic Redundancy and Function in Discourse," *Language and Style* 3 (Winter 1970): 62–68 as well as "The Stylistic Basis of Burkeian Identification," *Today's Speech* 20 (Winter 1972): 19–23. See also Ronald H. Carpenter, Idolene Mazza, and William Jordan, "The Comparative Effectiveness of Stylistic Sources of Redundancy," *Central States Speech Journal* 23 (Winter 1972): 241–45.

30. This notion has a literary counterpart in what I. A. Richards refers to as the ability of form in literature to invite an "incipient act" which involves "a leaning or inclination" toward a desired end. See I. A. Richards, *The Principles of Literary Criticism* (New York, 1924), 107. Kenneth Burke also discusses the notion in *A Grammar of Motives* (New York, 1954), 236.

31. Cicero *De Oratore* i. 2.50 and 33.152 as well as iii. 26. 101.

32. Cicero *Brutus* 14 and 50.

33. Cicero *De Oratore* iii. 50.195. As corroboration for this assumption about antitheses such as John Kennedy's "Let us never negotiate out of fear, but let us never fear to negotiate," a college teacher of composition observed that students "*enjoyed* working with a piece of contemporary prose by a man of eminence, and they are *pleased* to discover so much to discuss about Mr. Kennedy's word choice, figurative language, *phrase-making*, and variety of appeals." See Burnham Carter Jr., "President Kennedy's Inaugural Address," *College Composition and Communication* 14 (1963): 36–40, italics mine.

34. See Davis Howes and Charles Osgood, "On the Combination of Associative Probabilities in Linguistic Contexts," in *Psycholinguistics*, ed. Sol Saporta (New York: Holt, Rinehart, and Winston, 1961), 214–15, 219–21, and 226; as well as George A. Miller, *Language and Communication*, rev. ed. (New York: McGraw-Hill, 1963), 187.

35. See my essay "The Ubiquitous Antithesis: A Functional Source of Style in Political Discourse," *Style* 10 (Fall 1976): 426–41.

36. For further discussion of this principle, see my "Ubiquitous Antithesis" as well as the several essays cited earlier about Ronald Reagan.

37. As an undergraduate member of the debate team at the University of Nebraska, Ted Sorensen could speak extemporaneously in intercollegiate contests in the antithetical style he would write for John Kennedy years later. That observation was offered to me by Donald Olson, who was the University of Nebraska debate coach at that time.

38. For other examples of this emulation, see Ronald H. Carpenter and Robert V. Seltzer, "On Nixon's Kennedy Style," *Speaker and Gavel* 7 (1970): 41–43. This essay is reprinted in *Current Criticism*, ed. Robert Weiss and Bernard Brock (1971), 91–93.

39. Karen De Witt, "Clinton's Policy Trademark: 'New Covenant,'" *New York Times*, 17 July 1992.

40. Ronald H. Carpenter, "America's Tragic Metaphor: Our Twentieth-Century Combatants as Frontiersmen," *Quarterly Journal of Speech* 76 (February 1990): 1–22. For still other discussion of the persistent rhetorical appeal of the frontier, see Ronald H. Carpenter, "Frederick Jackson Turner and the Rhetorical Impact of the Frontier Thesis," *Quarterly Journal of Speech* 63 (April 1977): 117–29 and *The Eloquence of Frederick Jackson Turner* (San Marino: Huntington Library, 1983).

41. Implications of that "blooper heard around the world" figure prominently in the way Ford's statistical profile changed with respect to a dimension of verbal behavior as a predictor of presidential character. See Carpenter, "Style in Discourse as a Predictor." That essay as published contained two numerical *errata*: on p. 71, the statement at the bottom of Table 1 should read "The four passives have a mean TTR of .510"; and on p. 76, the sentence should read "Thus, for all three debates, Mr. Carter emerged with an overall mean TTR of .677 whereas a lower .637 characterized the composite TTR of Mr. Ford."

THE VOICE OF CONCERN AND CONCERN FOR THE VOICE

TONY M. LENTZ

The incredible resilience of Gov. Bill Clinton during the 1992 election campaign led reporters to dub him "robo-candidate."[1] The expression raises the image of "Robo-Cop," part man, part machine. This cyborg gets blown away, piece by piece, and then by force of will and mechanical miracle, lifts itself from the pavement to wreak revenge on the bad guys. In like fashion, Clinton faced crisis after crisis in the early months of the 1992 campaign, only to resurrect himself and take out his opponents, one by one.[2] In an odd way the "robo-candidate" image also matches the difficulties with sore vocal cords which shadowed Clinton throughout 1992. What began as a barely noticeable problem with sore throats and allergies simply refused to go away. The candidate found himself able to rebound from one controversy after another, but the strain on his voice remained a continuing and growing problem. The persistence of vocal difficulty eventually led reporters to question whether or not it was symptomatic of more serious health difficulties that the Clinton campaign was hiding.[3]

Viewed in this context, the 1992 presidential campaign of Bill Clinton presents an interesting performance question regarding his admittedly serious vocal problems. That question is, how much of the problem can be attributed to his allergies, and how much to inappropriate use of his vocal mechanism? In other words, to what extent was his sore throat due to allergies, as his physician has argued publicly, and to what extent has this difficulty exposed a chink in the armor of the carefully crafted and mediated public persona of the man critics have called "Slick Willie." Candidate Bill Clinton's efforts to voice his concern for the average citizen in emotionally effective performances led to a serious concern for the well-being of his voice. I argue here that this is more than a simple problem with allergies. Contemporary political campaigns place great demands on the speech performer's ability to manage tension . . . in both voice and body language. Yet in this highly managed campaign, the voice remained one part of "Slick Willie's" performance where real tension and real pain were revealed at particularly tense moments of the campaign. Review of selected campaign performances reveals that Clinton consistently employed his vocal mechanism in ways that exacerbate his difficulties. He employed a high, tense style of projection in emotional high points of speeches aimed at live audiences in large halls. In short, he strained to voice his concern for the public, and that strain led to a serious concern for the welfare of his voice. As a consequence, President William Clinton remains on the horns of a dilemma. He must either change his vocal style and risk sounding less sincere to the public, or remain naturally "sincere" and run the risk of not being able to speak effectively at all.

THE EFFECTS OF MEDIATED PERFORMANCE ON THE VOICE

The national political scene has become reliant upon mediated communication that places tremendous pressure upon speakers as performers. After his retirement in the mid-1970s Sen. William Fulbright noted the importance of the sound bite.[4] There was a time, he told the *Washington Post,* when people read speeches in the newspaper in their entirety. Television, he said, had reduced that to one or two main points. Recent studies have shown that the average sound bite has now been reduced to less than ten seconds in length.[5] This means that a person performing a speech remains constantly aware that any single ten-second gaffe in the presentation of his or her message can replace that message. Any mistake will be singled out for replay on the evening news. As Elizabeth Kolbert pointed out in reporting Clinton's victory speech after the New York primary, candidates have a real problem in attempting to get their message through the news media. NBC's "Today Show," she noted, reduced the fourteen-minute speech to "I love Wisconsin and Minnesota and Kansas, and I really love New York!"[6] The thesis of the speech and the remainder of the content of the speech simply did not exist in the national news media consciousness of the nation.

If the ten seconds chosen happen to present a negative image, the results can be devastating. One obvious example would be the image of Sen. Edmund Muskie crying in the snows of New Hampshire, a moving picture which effectively ended his run for the presidency. Another would be the tasteless language in a reference by former Secretary of the Interior James Watt to the "politically correct" composition of a committee. The replay of that clip ad nauseam on various television outlets sealed Watts fate as a member of Ronald Reagan's administration. Critic Max Atkinson notes that even small details of performance behavior will be recorded and noticed, sometimes to the great discomfort of the politician and with great damage to his or her image.[7] Yet even as the pressures upon performers have increased, the "cool" style that is perceived as most effective on television requires performers to hide all signs of tension.[8] Marshall McLuhan postulated that television was a "cool" medium, and John F. Kennedy's success with an urbane, witty style opened the era of the mediated performer.[9] Richard Nixon consciously crafted his encounters with the media to match the portions of his personal style that were best suited to television.[10] Ronald Reagan became known as the godlike "Great Communicator," as scholars recoined "communication" to be a god term.[11] And Kathleen Hall Jamieson has codified the most effective approach to television performance as the cool "feminine" style.[12] Such national attention led scholars in the speech communication field to recognize performance issues as a significant area in need of research.[13] In all of this it became clear that the performer must literally and figuratively "never let them see you sweat." So campaigners for national office must endure harried schedules, the pressure of potentially terminal land-mine issues like infidelity (or the hiring of illegal household help), lack of sleep, and the numbing repetition of hostile or inane questions from the press. Furthermore, they must never show anger or irritation when the cameras are rolling. This attempt to restrain or manage personal emotional reactions in the middle of the fray can lead to serious vocal difficulty. The neck and throat can become a focus for tension related to everyday life.[14] The problem is exacerbated when the stress of facing an audience is added.[15] Management of this sort of tension has been a continuing concern among those training actors and public speakers.[16] The definition of effective vocal performance generally includes a reference to the production of volume without undue stress related to tension.[17] Much concern for speech training in recent years has been addressed to the use of various techniques to manage tension in general, from talk about speech performance contexts to guided relaxation, desensitization exercises, and skills training.[18] It would seem a simple matter for the Clinton campaign to have their candidate work with a vocal coach. Vocal exercises along with relaxation techniques could lower the candidate's pitch, improve his resonance, and provide a more pleasant voice with a broader range. This in effect creates a larger signal to "project" the candidate to the audience. This could provide ensurance against the obvious and unwanted comparison to the last Democratic president from the South, whose high voice and narrow vocal range surely contributed to the image of an uptight and ineffective leader.[19] High pitch has been perceived as a handicap to women seeking public office . . . their higher voices make them sound less like powerful personalities.[20]

Yet the Clinton campaign already had an image problem because their candidate worked so seamlessly as a performer. Television loved the spontaneous, the natural, the uncontrived.[21] Clinton had created a performance persona that was seen to be so slick that, despite his admitted abilities as a performer, he was perceived as insincere.[22] In that context the voice, and the sense of sincerity in the voice, becomes a key element of relating to other individuals. "*Sound unites groups of living beings as nothing else does,*" Walter Ong argues (his italics).[23] Listeners "feel into" the performer's voice qualities, experiencing sound in their interior, responding almost as if they were imagining, "how would I feel if my voice sounded like this?" Clinton was attempting to create the sense that he was truly concerned about the lives of the individual citizens.[24] A voice perceived as being artificial or overarticulated would become a serious campaign liability. So the attempt to create a "voice of concern" led to "concern for the voice," as Clinton's voice became a noticeable problem at several key junctures in the campaign.

Thus by not opting for drastic change in the candidate's vocal style, not opting for a noticeably "trained" voice quality, the campaign may have exacerbated the candidate's lingering problem with sore throats. The official version of the problem, of course, blamed it on the candidate's serious allergies.[25] Yet clearly the problem was compounded by the candidate's vocal performance style, as we will see below. The audience that would have felt removed from a "slick" vocal presentation was left to feel pain, tension, and tightening of the throat. They responded to the rasping and coughing and squeaking that was a hallmark of many of the most tense portions of the campaign. As pain increases in the throat the tension increases in response, in a fashion similar to the progression from fear to tension to pain described by physicians in other contexts.[26] Thus the candidate became prey to a descending spiral, as pain led inexorably to tension, and forcing performances through the tension led to more pain.

CRISES IN CAMPAIGNING LEAD TO VOCAL CRISES

The references to the voice in the 1992 campaign begin, eerily enough, with questions to Paul Tsongas about his sore throat.[27] This is only an issue for me, Tsongas replied, because I recovered from cancer. Bill Clinton can miss an engagement due to his voice, he said, and no one questions it. In actuality Clinton had already consulted a physician about his voice in December of the preceding year.[28] His voice had not, at that point, become an issue. But it soon did, and it remained so throughout the campaign.

The problems were certainly exacerbated by the personality of the candidate as it was evident during the campaign. First, he loved to talk. As Charles Kuralt put it, "You ask him what he thinks and he tells you everything he thinks."[29] Campaign aides had to fight his temptation to talk at length on airplane trips.[30] At many stops along the campaign trail, one reporter noted, the candidate would rasp "find me people."[31] The voice of concern was something that seemed sincere, and many noted his interactions with ordinary people in New Hampshire. Ironically, it was former Gov. Edmund G. Brown Jr. who spoke directly of the voice of concern, at a time when Clinton was literally unable to speak at all.[32] He quoted a woman from Laconia, New Hampshire, who said, "You have a voice that can be heard. You have to speak for me. Will you promise me that?" It was a theme which appeared again later, when the voiceless candidate Clinton asked crowds to be his voice on 3 November so that he could be their voice for the next four years.[33] The appeal was driven by the candidate's sincere enjoyment of interactions with ordinary people similar to that described by Brown. The sincerity he displayed in such situations impressed even callous journalists. Joe Klein described the phenomenon in *New York*. "The most important element in Clinton's success, though, may be a quality that journalists find hard to communicate without seeming sycophantic or sappy, but—risking all—I'll take the plunge. He actually seems to like people."[34] The kind of moment Brown described became a model for one of the defining moments of the campaign, in the midst of the second presidential debate, when a questioner asked the candidates how the recession had affected them personally.[35] Clinton's direct eye contact and displayed sense of concern contrasted vividly with the behavior of President George Bush, who checked his watch while she asked her question. He gave the impression of being eager to get away from the close contact with questioners which Clinton seemed to relish. But all this led to continuous use of the candidate's voice.

A second difficulty in handling the problem of vocal stress was the candidate's hard-driving personal style and the resulting lack of relaxation for the candidate and his voice. He won the Democratic nomination based on hard work and organization. He had carefully laid the groundwork for the campaign through contacts with people around the country.[36] He went through fifteen drafts of his first important economic address.[37] The famous bus trips following the campaign were reported to be "as choreographed as a Broadway play."[38] The team practiced hard for the debates, despite the candidate's throat difficulties.[39] The debate facilities were checked out early.[40] This was clearly a candidate who liked to avoid surprises.[41]

This passion for detail was driven by the candidate's personal stamina, noted in the opening paragraph.[42] And the events of the campaign handed him serious hurdles to overcome with that energy. As Edwin Diamond wrote in *New York Magazine*, "Even for a postmodern campaign, the velocity of the Clinton story was stunning. Consider that he went, in media world, from unknown to front-runner to de-Flowered goods to 'tested' survivor in a matter of weeks . . . and before a single ballot was cast."[43] Clinton was a person with a passion for organization placed in a whirlwind of stressful events. Yet as a candidate he had to keep that stress out of sight of the cameras, and he wasn't always successful at keeping it completely out of the public eye. Maureen Dowd noted the difference between Clinton's smile and the hard-driving personality beneath: "in person, it is possible to see more: his commanding attitude and his supple political shape-shifting, his fascination with and yearning for the adulation he is getting, and his surliness and finger-wagging upbraidings when something does not go exactly as he likes."[44] Note that the outbursts she cites happened at a time when the Clinton campaign was riding high in the polls.[45] Clinton himself noted the sometimes violent contrast between his inner feelings and the exterior he presented to others.

> When people are criticizing me, they get to the old "Slick Willie" business. Part of it is that I'm always smiling and try to make it look easy and all that. And part of it is the way I was raised. I had such difficulties in my childhood. And I didn't have anybody I could talk to about it. I didn't know I was supposed to talk about it. I was raised in that sort of culture where you put on a happy face, and you didn't reveal your pain and agony. Those were not things you shared with people.[46]

The strain of maintaining that kind of performance exterior for so many hours a day had to show through somewhere, and the most obvious place where it reached public consciousness was in the candidate's vocal difficulties. The press noted Clinton's voice as he rasped his way through a "Nightline" interview following the publication of his famous letter about the draft.[47] The strain on the voice seemed to be accepted as indicative of his strong feelings and sincere emotions about the issue. After driving hard through all of his difficulties to the New York primary, the candidate's voice became so bad that he was ordered to take a full vocal rest for four days.[48] When this rest period was extended a day Clinton's voice was worthy of a *New York Times* byline story, and it continued to be a matter of interest for the rest of the campaign.[49]

Clinton was rested enough before the Democratic National Convention that the voice wasn't noted by the *Washington Post* as a difficulty in his acceptance speech.[50] But as the stress level rose at the beginning of autumn, the voice rose as a noticeable problem again. The Clinton campaign was receiving notes from supporters about how to handle vocal problems in September.[51] The physician he had visited the previous fall was touted in *People* magazine.[52] Articles about preparations for the first presidential debate mentioned his allergy shots.[53] Vocal rest was considered one of his strategies to win the debates.[54] The candidate admitted that his "main problem" in preparing for the debates was his voice.[55]

Then *New York Times*'s Lawrence Altman cited Clinton's voice in an article on 9 October headlined "Clinton, Citing Privacy Issues, Tells

Little about His Health."[56] It had been revealed that Paul Tsongas's physician had hidden a recurrence of the former senator's cancer. Suddenly the raspy voice of candidate Clinton was seen as a possible symptom of something more serious. By the fifteenth, the date of the final presidential debate, the campaign had delivered full medical reports to the press. The question of serious medical problems was resolved in most minds as one of serious allergies.[57] But questions lingered in the minds of some members of the press into 1993. William Safire wouldn't admit to "Clearing Clinton's Throat" until he talked extensively with physician Dr. James Suen that January.[58] Difficulties lingered in the campaign as well, as Clinton gradually lost his voice almost completely in the manic charge toward 3 November.[59]

Thus the record shows noticeable difficulty with vocal performance throughout the campaign. The personality of the candidate and his tendency to drive hard left little room for vocal rest. His tendency to hold back on feelings may have increased the strain on his voice. The most stressful periods of the campaign before winning the nomination and the election were marked by serious vocal difficulty: in one case, complete vocal rest, and in the other, nearly complete loss of the voice. The video record of the campaign depicts the performance style that apparently exacerbated the candidate's difficulties in avoiding undue stress on the voice.

VOCAL SUCCESS IN IMPLICITLY INTIMATE SITUATIONS

A review of nine campaign addresses and the three televised debates reveals a serious performance problem for candidate Clinton in the 1992 campaign. Concern for the voice was evident in speaking to large crowds where the candidate felt the need to increase volume to reach and fire up the energy in a large space. In attempting to inspire large crowds, Clinton employed a high pitch and tense vocal quality which placed strain on his vocal mechanism. He was more successful with the "voice of concern" in televised town-meeting formats. There he lowered his pitch and avoided vocal strain. The suggestion of a more intimate relationship with his questioners made the lower volume and more relaxed vocal quality appropriate. In one major large-crowd situation, the Democratic National Convention acceptance speech,

Clinton adapted the more relaxed, intimate performance style to the large hall successfully. In other cases, however, he was less successful at the adaptation of intimate performance style to large rally situations.

The vocal problems with Clinton's habitually high pitch and his tendency to squeeze his larynx in emotional appeals could be seen early in the campaign, even in short campaign appearances. As the weeks led up to the Democratic National Convention, Clinton had more and more difficulty with his voice. On 30 June he spoke to a National Abortion Rights Action League rally.[60] Even in this short fourteen-minute tape, the source of Clinton's performance problems with his voice became apparent. The candidate spoke in a high vocal pitch level that gives him little vocal range within which to vary his expression. In this short talk his voice cracked a couple of times, indicating that he was in some difficulty with sore vocal cords. Then when he reached his emotional peak, he squeezed his voice through a tense larynx to get greater volume out of the high end of his pitch range. He told the audience that he hoped there would be no more presidential campaigns based on the abortion issue, reaching an emotional high which fueled a big response from the audience. His voice was high and tense.

At a Jonesboro, Georgia, rally in September, he coughed in opening the speech, and his voice was noticeably scratchy at the beginning of his talk.[61] He forced his voice higher and tenser as he spoke to the crowd from notes, with his neck noticeably tense and the voice following suit. This was especially true in moments where he was trying to reach the crowd emotionally. The contrast was dramatically illustrated when he ad-libbed to the crowd over the crying of a baby near the podium, smiling and saying "that's just my musical background." The volume dropped as he relied on the public address system to carry the sound to the audience, the pitch level lowered as well, and thus he reduced the strain on his voice.

In addition to the high pitch and vocal tension exhibited in the campaign rallies, the candidate made the problem worse by shifting his vocal key, or pitch range, upward. In a 23 September address in Albany, Georgia, for example, he stepped up his pitch level as he sought to whip up the crowd.[62] Since he began at a high vocal level, he had little room left to move up comfortably within his vocal range. As a result he squeezed his voice tighter and tighter to increase the volume, and in so doing, he increased the strain on his vocal mechanism.

The effects of the tendency to force higher and tenser sound from his voice can be seen in his continuing vocal difficulties. At a Flint, Michigan, rally on 2 October, Clinton was high and tense at the opening, as if straining to be heard through the pained vocal cords. The voice cracked in the opening two minutes of his talk, and he continually shifted his pitch higher. He was clearly in difficulty, coughing and reaching for the water glass. Yet he continued in a vocal tattoo, a kind of drumbeat of high, tense pounding which clearly exacerbated the pain in his sore vocal cords. By the end of the campaign, he was relying upon surrogate speakers to handle roughly half of the rallies' performance time.[63]

Clinton continued in his high, tense ways, exhorting the faithful to get out the vote in Sterling Heights, Michigan. By the day before the election at Paducah, Kentucky, he was able to speak for less than six minutes, despite having received a cortico-steroid called Vanceril from his throat doctor.[64] He admitted to the crowd that he was losing his voice.[65] "I'm losing my voice," he told the crowd, "but tomorrow if you'll be my voice, I'll be your voice for four years." As he did so, his pitch was high and the quality tense, and the pain was evident to the listener.

In short, Clinton continued to employ a vocal performance style which must have aggravated whatever difficulties he was having with allergies during the campaign. Throughout the long campaign the same style appears at rallies with large crowds, and the problems intensified as the candidate sought to involve his audience emotionally. The candidate was vocally more successful, however, in implicitly smaller performance contexts such as the televised town meetings in which his "voice of concern" could be presented at a lower level of volume and tension. In the performances where he concentrated on the television audience, or on a smaller audience in a televised town meeting, he was more successful in avoiding vocal behavior that was potentially damaging. In all three of the debates, for example, Clinton lowered his pitch and relaxed his vocal quality. He focused on the camera and spoke to it in a more implicitly intimate level, as if speaking one on one with the listener on the other side of the camera. Even within this more relaxed frame, however, he occasionally strained his throat in an effort to reach the audience with an emotional appeal. In the first debate he successfully delivered his counterattack on the patriotism issue, citing President Bush's father, without serious vocal difficulty.[66] But a few moments later the strain became evident as he made an emotional appeal. He continued with near perfect television body language, using direct and focused eye contact with either the questioner or the camera, maintaining a slight smile on his face, gesturing in a clean and uncluttered manner. Further, he was not seen on camera with a water glass in his hand, even though we know he had been advised to drink.[67] Yet by two-thirds of the way through the debate, his voice had begun to break noticeably.

He found a good balance between emotional quality and strain on the voice when Ann Compton asked him what his definition of a family was. The response was moving, but in a conversational way which didn't require the high, tense vocal strain that characterized his performance in large situations. By his closing statement, however, the raspy quality was noticeable, and the performer must have felt additional stress wondering if and when his voice would give way. The Clinton mastery of the town-meeting format was evident in the second debate in many ways.[68] One key to his more relaxed vocal approach was his focus on the questioners. He looked directly at them, spoke at a level appropriate for more intimate conversations, and relied upon the microphones to carry his more relaxed responses to the audience. The scratchiness of his voice, in this softer context, sometimes even seemed to reveal his personal emotional commitment to the issues being discussed.

Even toward the vocally desperate end of the campaign, in a town meeting in Dearborn, Michigan, Clinton was able to maintain a reasonable vocal range throughout an hour-long session.[69] His voice was certainly raspy and painful to hear, and he hesitated often, coughed regularly, and drank water throughout. He remained effective as a performer, however, by keeping the pitch and tension lower than in other performance situations such as the Paducah rally. The performer could not consistently employ his vocal skills as a more intimate communicator, however, in large situations. On one hand there was a remarkable change from his previous performances in the Democratic National Convention acceptance speech.[70] He was able to talk to the cameras effectively, and he showed an ability to rouse the crowd without resorting as often to the high, tense vocal quality he habitually employed at rallies. He was not able to consistently reap the benefits of this more relaxed quality, however. The candidate seemed to lose his more intimate quality in large halls. One interesting example was the National Education Association Convention in early July, where Clinton attempted to adapt the implicitly intimate town-meeting format to a large hall.[71] Clinton had to open the meeting with a cough, and his voice was distinctly raspy in quality. He had already adapted to his problems so well that he generally kept the focus off his vocal difficulty. He slipped sips of water when the cameras were pointed at questioners, and coughed with the microphone held out of range. He managed this so artfully that at one point NEA president Keith Geiger noticed that Clinton was filling his water glass. Geiger apologized that he hadn't poured the glass full after his introduction and before leaving the stage where Clinton was facing the audience. He seemed unaware, in short, that Clinton had been sipping water all through the session.

The candidate led attention even further from his vocal difficulties by responding, to general laughter, that he just wanted Geiger to "carry water for me in November." Thus problems with the voice were well camouflaged by timing coughs and sips of water at times when Clinton was not the focus of attention, but clearly the problem was of concern to the performer. Furthermore, emotional peaks in his responses brought noticeable tension to the veins in the candidate's neck. He persisted in raising pitch and tension in his voice when reaching for emotional responses by the audience. When he spoke of his opposition to "putting public money in private schools," for example, his voice was high and tense once again. Thereafter in the talk his voice broke noticeably. The hall was large, and he was unable to employ the more intimate style of the small-setting town meeting. He felt obliged to raise his pitch and his tension to rouse the large crowd, and in the process put more strain upon an already overworked vocal instrument.

CONCLUSION

The record of 1992 shows a candidate with remarkable stamina, but one whose Achilles' heel may be in his throat. The most striking thing about the campaign is how lucky it was in keeping his voice together in extremely tense circumstances like the debates. How might the campaign have been different, for example, if another controversy had erupted when Clinton was on vocal rest or when his voice was completely dysfunctional? Would a "60 Minutes" interview have had the impact it did if the candidate's voice had been painful to hear? The comparison to George Bush in the debates might have been very different if his voice hadn't held through his reference to Bush's father regarding the draft issue. And his voice might have been completely gone earlier in the end of the campaign if he had been under the stress of being behind in the polls rather than holding a lead into November.

In terms of presidential image for governing and reelection, can Clinton fight off the "wimp factor" problem of a comparison with Jimmy Carter's high-pitched voice? The question of his relationship with the military damages his image as a strong leader, and a tense voice that cracks in awkward places raises the impression of weakness. He lost his voice when he was ahead in the polls. What might happen if he was seriously behind? The public accepted vocal problems as evidence of Clinton's concern for them in 1992. If he is perceived as having disregarded their concerns, if the Republicans are successful in defining him as a weak president unable to deliver, vocal problems in a new campaign will only reinforce that picture.

The dilemma Clinton and his advisors face is as old as the study of speaking itself. *The Rhetoric to Alexander* from ancient Greece offers "one-liners" to the budding orator who is attacked for being too slick as a result of studying with a speech coach. A contemporary voice handbook might offer several strategies open to the new president. He can work to rely even more heavily on microphones and continue the low-intensity speaking he modeled in his convention acceptance address. The volume he wants to rally the crowds, in other words, can be provided by amplifiers. He can drastically reduce appearances, especially live rallies where he tends to strain himself. He can stress even more heavily the intimate "town-meeting" format for televised appearances that limit strain on his vocal mechanism. Or he can begin to work on a regular basis with a vocal coach who can help him learn to relax the larynx and adjacent muscles, lower his pitch, and focus his resonance.

Personally, I believe he will continue to have problems unless he learns to use his voice more effectively, and that means running the risk of sounding "trained" as a speaker. I argue this point based on the hard-driving personality of the man, and on the vocal tension implicit in his tendency to "hold things in." It was clear that he had some vocal work before the Democratic convention, even if it was only advice to play to the television audience instead of the live hall. It was just as clear that he kept forgetting what he was taught in the race to November. Vocal habits are the product of a lifetime, and they are not easy to break. Furthermore, it's clear Clinton has serious allergies, and that they will not go away. Training might, indeed, help here. The lower the tension in the neck, the less the strain on the larynx, and the easier it will be for the president to maintain a strenuous speaking schedule despite the allergies. There is the danger that any new voice quality would be considered phoney. On the other hand, it wouldn't be necessary or desirable to change his southern dialect, and the difference would appear gradually over a period of time.

The critical question in a review of Clinton's 1992 vocal performance is whether the cyborg candidate will eventually handle his vocal problems as deftly as he dodged the myriad "slings and arrows" of the 1992 campaign. If not, strained vocal cords may prove to be a serious weakness in the performance armor of the "manufactured candidate" in future campaigns.[72] The Republicans could keep the pressure on, wait for his vocal problems to materialize, and then arrange an "October Surprise" of sorts when the candidate was crippled by a voice that wasn't functioning. Richard Dyer-Bennet, late performer of traditional song, told the story of a vocalist who kept his voice well into his old age. When asked how he was able to maintain a career when many younger men had to give up singing, he replied that he had never "spent his principal." Other singers had strained their voices to force performances that would impress audiences. He, on the other hand, had been careful never to ruin his voice in seeking public acclaim. The story may bear a message for the new president. If he is to be able to voice his concern for the public, he will have to do so in ways that do not give rise to concern for his voice.

NOTES

1. Ann Reilly Dowd, "Bill Clinton as President," *Fortune*, 4 May 1992, 87.

2. Eleanor Clift, "Testing Ground: The Inside Story of How Clinton Survived the Campaign's Worst Moments," *Newsweek*, 30 March 1992, 34–36.

3. Lawrence K. Altman, "Clinton, Citing Privacy Issues, Tells Little about His Health," *New York Times*, 9 October 1992, 18.

4. Robert G. Kaiser and Walter Pincus, "The Outlook Interview: J. William Fulbright Talks to Robert G. Kaiser and Walter Pincus," *Washington Post*, 18 July 1982, B3.

5. "Sound Bites Become Smaller Mouthfuls," *New York Times*, 23 January 1992, A1. See also Richard Rosen, "For Overloaded Eyes and Ears, Bite Makes Right," *New York Times*, 10 June 1990, II31.

6. Elizabeth Kolbert, "Heard by Few, Clinton Speech Shows Candidates' Quandary," *New York Times*, 9 April 1992, A21.

7. Max Atkinson, *Our Masters' Voices: The Language and Body Language of Politics* (London and New York: Methuen, 1984), 166.

8. Marshall McLuhan, *Understanding Media: The Extensions of Man* (New York, London, Sydney, and Toronto: McGraw-Hill Book Co., 1965), 317.

9. McLuhan, *Understanding Media*, 329–30.

10. Joe McGinniss, *The Selling of the President 1968* (New York: Pocket Books, 1970), 23–26.

11. Tamar Katriel and Gerry Phillipsen, "'What We Need Is Communication'. 'Communication' as a Cultural Category," *Communication Monographs* 48 (1981): 302–17.

12. Kathleen Hall Jamieson, *Eloquence in an Electronic Age: The Transformation of Political Speechmaking* (New York: Oxford University Press, 1988), 81.

13. Gerald M. Phillips, *Communication Incompetencies: A Theory of Training Oral Performance Behavior* (Carbondale and Edwardsville: Southern Illinois University Press, 1991), 61–62.

14. Alexander Lowen, *The Language of the Body* (New York and London: Collier Books and Collier–Macmillan Ltd., 1971), 45, 55–59.

15. Stephen Aaron, *Stage Fright: Its Role in Acting* (Chicago and London: University of Chicago Press, 1986), 59–79.

16. Atkinson, *Our Masters' Voices*, 112.

17. See David Stern, "Teaching and Acting: A Vocal Analogy," *Communication Education* 29 (1980): 259–63; Cicely Berry, *Voice and the Actor* (New York: Macmillan, 1973), 20–21; and Ethel C. Glenn, Phillip J. Glenn, and Sandra H. Forman, *Your Voice and Articulation* (New York and London: Macmillan and Collier Macmillan, 1984), 65.

18. Tim Hopf and Joe Ayres, *Coping with Speech Anxiety* (Norwood, N.J.: Ablex, in press).

19. See James A. Barnes, "The Hard Charger," *National Journal*, 18 January 1992, 126–31; Peter Applebome, "Misleading Echoes of Carter in Clinton," *New York Times*, 19 July 1992, 122; and David Broder, "Clinton Errors Send Global Shock Waves," *Centre Daily Times*, 9 June 1993, 10A.

20. Atkinson, *Our Masters' Voices*, 112–13.

21. Daniel Boorstin, *The Image: A Guide to Pseudo-Events in America* (New York: Harper and Row, 1964), 254.

22. Joe Klein, "Elvis vs. Big Daddy," *New York*, 30 March 1992, 31. See also Joe Klein, "Bill Clinton: Who Is This Guy?," *New York*, 20 January 1992, 32; and Maureen Dowd, "The Faces behind the Face That Clinton's Smile Masks," *New York Times*, 16 March 1992, A1.

23. Walter J. Ong, *The Presence of the Word: Some Prolegemena for Cultural and Religious History* (Minneapolis: University of Minnesota Press, 1981), 122.

24. Klein, "Elvis vs. Big Daddy," 31. See also Chris Smith, "The Player: Rising-Star Media Consultant Mandy Grunwald Comes Out Swinging for Clinton," *New York*, 13 July 1992, 50.

25. Altman, "Clinton, Citing Privacy Issues, Tells Little about His Health," 18.

26. Grantley Dick-Read, *Childbirth without Fear: The Principles and Practice of Natural Childbirth*, 2d ed. (New York: Harper and Row, 1959).

27. Karen De Witt, "Old Queries Greet Tsongas on Climb," *New York Times*, 12 February 1992, A21.

28. Joanne Kaufmann and Jane Sanderson, "Paging Dr. Ossoff: Country Stars Come Calling When the Song Is Over but the Malady Lingers On," *People Magazine*, 28 September 1992, 53–54.

29. Elizabeth Kolbert, "Clinton's Big Moment Is Short on Telegenics," *New York Times*, 18 July 1992, I10.

30. "Doctor Silences the Front-Runner," *New York Times*, 9 April 1992, A21.

31. Clift, "Testing Ground," 36.

32. Kolbert, "Clinton's Big Moment Is Short on Telegenics," A21.

33. Edward Walsh and David Maraniss, "Days Are Merging for Hoarse Clinton as Eight-State Dash Awaits," *Washington Post*, 2 November 1992, A16.

34. Klein, "Elvis vs. Big Daddy," 31.

35. William Clinton, Presidential Debate II, Richmond, Va., 15 October 1992.

36. Andrew Kopkind, "The Manufactured Candidate," *Nation*, 3 February 1992, 116–20.

37. "The Making of a Candidate's Speech," *National Journal*, 18 January 1992, 131.

38. Richard L. Berke, "Democrats Use TV to Ride Momentum," *New York Times*, 23 July 1992, A18.

39. Michael Wines, "Candidates Train for a Key Debate," *New York Times*, 8 October 1992, A1.

40. Lloyd Grave, "Political Spirit of St. Louis," *Washington Post*, 12 October 1992, D1.

41. Mary McGrory, "'No Surprises' School of Debate," *Washington Post*, 20 October 1992, A2.

42. See also Barnes, "The Hard Charger," 26–31.

43. Edwin Diamond, "Crash Course: Campaign Journalism 101," *New York*, 17 February 1992, 28–31.

44. Maureen Dowd, 25 Oct. 1992: I1.

45. Edward Walsh, "Clinton Campaign Is Feeling No Pain," *Washington Post*, 21 October 1992, A1.

46. Eleanor Clift and Jonathan Alter, "You Didn't Reveal Your Pain: Clinton Reflects on the Turmoil in His Childhood," *Newsweek*, 30 March 1992, 37.

47. Ibid., 34–36.

48. "Doctor Silences the Front-Runner," 9 April 1992, A21.

49. Lawrence K. Altman, "Laryngitis Silences Clinton Another Day," *New York Times*, 14 April 1992, A20.

50. Dan Balz, "Clinton Vows to 'Change America' in Accepting Party's Nomination," *Washington Post*, 17 July 1992, A1.

51. David Von Drehle, "For What It's Worth—Free Advice," *Washington Post*, 26 September 1992, A9.

52. Kaufmann and Sanderson, "Paging Dr. Ossoff," 53–54.

53. Michael Wines, "Candidates Train for a Key Debate," *New York Times*, 8 October 1992, A1.

54. Gwen Ifill, "Clinton's Four-Point Plan to Win the First Debate," *New York Times*, 9 October 1992, A21.

55. Ann Devroy, "Rehearsing for Showdown," *Washington Post*, 7 October 1992, A1.

56. Altman, "Clinton, Citing Privacy Issues, Tells Little about His Health," 18.

57. David Brown, "Clinton Given a Clean Bill of Health in Detailed Medical Report," *Washington Post*, 15 October 1992, A18.

58. William Safire, "Clearing Clinton's Throat," *New York Times*, 14 January 1993, A25.

59. Walsh and Maraniss, "Days Are Merging for Hoarse Clinton," A16.

60. William Clinton, "Reaction to [Planned Parenthood vs. Casey]," 30 June 1992, Purdue University Public Affairs Video Archives, Tape 92-06-30-2358-1, 6972-26838.

61. William Clinton, "Clinton Campaign Speech," 9 September 1992, Purdue University Public Affairs Video Archives, Tape 92-09-10- 0157-2, 6972-32219.

62. William Clinton, "Clinton Campaign Speech," 23 September 1992, Purdue University Public Affairs Video Archives, Tape 92-09-23-2158-1, 6972-32698.

63. William Clinton, "Clinton Campaign Rally," 25 October 1992, Purdue University Public Affairs Video Archives, Tape 92-10-26-0102-1, 6972-33587.

64. Safire, "Clearing Clinton's Throat," A25.

65. William Clinton, "Clinton Campaign Rally," 2 November 1992, Purdue University Public Affairs Video Archives, Tape 92-11-02-2158-1, 6972-33985.

66. William Clinton, Presidential Debate I, St. Louis, Mo., 11 October 1992.

67. Kaufmann and Sanderson, "Paging Dr. Ossoff," 53–54.

68. William Clinton, Presidential Debate II, Richmond, Va., 15 October 1992.

69. William Clinton, "Clinton Town Meeting," Dearborn, Mich., 30 October 1992, Purdue University Public Affairs Video Archives, Tape 92-10-30-2158-1, 6972-34280.

70. William Clinton, "Democratic Convention Acceptance Speeches," 16 July 1992, Purdue University Public Affairs Video Archives, Tape 92-07-16-0800-4, 6979-32863.

71. William Clinton, "Clinton Campaign Speech on Education," NEA Convention, 7 July 1992, Purdue University Public Affairs Video Archives, Tape 92-07-07-1558-1, 6972-26935.

72. Kopkind, "The Manufactured Candidate," 116–20.

DODGING CHARGES AND CHARGES OF DODGING

Bill Clinton's Defense on the Character Issue

GRETA R. MARLOW

It seemed to be a staggering blow for presidential candidate Bill Clinton. Only two weeks before the crucial New Hampshire primary, accusations of a twelve-year extramarital affair between Clinton and a state employee, Gennifer Flowers, were splashed across the front of the supermarket tabloid the *Star*. After debating the ethics of using material from a less-than-reliable publication, the mainstream press picked up on the allegations. Flowers even had live coverage on the Cable News Network (CNN) for the press conference in which she revealed her "love tapes." While still scrambling to do damage control over the Flowers incident, Clinton's campaign was dealt a second blow. A former draft board employee told the press Clinton had signed up for Reserve Officers Training Corps (ROTC) at the University of Arkansas to avoid the draft for the Vietnam war, but that he never actually joined the program. A letter written by Clinton in 1970 was released, a letter which explained his decision to give up the ROTC deferment while still expressing protest against the war. To some observers, the letter appeared to be a way to equivocate on the war issue—the attempt of a young man to keep himself out of the war and yet to keep a future in politics alive as well.

Such a combination of problems just before the start of the primary season would seem to spell the end of a candidacy. After all, charges of infidelity led to Gary Hart's withdrawal from the race for the

Democratic nomination in 1988. Despite the questions surrounding his character, Clinton finished a respectable second place to Sen. Paul Tsongas in the New Hampshire primary. Clinton went on to become the Democratic nominee and, eventually, president of the United States. How did the self-proclaimed "Comeback Kid" not only survive but also win?

Although many factors converged to help Clinton become president, this paper will argue that two apologies Clinton made in the period between the first accusation in the *Star* and the New Hampshire primary served as key elements in keeping his young campaign viable. However, it may have been a technique of pre-accusation "inoculation" very early in the campaign that actually allowed Clinton's *apologia* to withstand the pressure of the twin accusations of infidelity and draft dodging.

ACCUSATIONS OF INFIDELITY

Rumors of Clinton's involvement in extramarital affairs had circulated during his tenure as Arkansas's governor. The accusations first surfaced when Larry Nichols, a bureaucrat Clinton had fired, sued Clinton during the 1990 gubernatorial race, alleging the governor had a slush fund of taxpayer money which paid for his affairs.[1] Local media ignored the charges, and the issue was dormant until January 1992, the first opportunity for voters to officially assess Clinton's campaign.

Ironically, the same week Clinton's portrait appeared on the cover of *Time* magazine, the infidelity rumors were featured in a four-page story in the *Star*. The story outlined the information Nichols had presented for his lawsuit in 1990, linking Clinton to at least five women, among them a former Miss America, a reporter, two members of Clinton's staff, and nightclub singer Gennifer Flowers.[2] Also mentioned was Nichols's accusation concerning a slush fund of state money used to "bankroll the governor's bid for the presidency and his illicit romances."[3] Despite its potentially damaging allegations, the initial story in the *Star* received little attention from the legitimate press. A related story in the next edition of the *Star*, however, received more notoriety. The article detailed Flowers's account of her alleged affair with Clinton, complete with excerpts from "love tapes" Flowers said she had recorded from phone conversations with the governor. The story was picked up by the national press, forcing Clinton and his campaign aides to defend the candidate against charges of infidelity. Clinton's campaign staff immediately drew two battle fronts: discrediting the *Star* and the sources of the story, and facing the public directly through television with an ambiguous denial. Discrediting the report presented few problems for Clinton's staff. Because of the *Star*'s status as a sensational tabloid, the legitimate press was uncomfortable about using the story at all. As a columnist for the *Washington Post* pointed out, "The mainstream press . . . feels guilty, for pushing a story that derives entirely from a trashy weekly which frequently sights Elvis."[4] Clinton attempted to discredit Flowers by pointing out that she had changed her story after specifically denying the rumors in a letter written a year earlier. "It was only when money came up, when the tabloid went down there offering people money . . . that she changed her story," Clinton said.[5] Clinton also attempted to pin the responsibility for the story on enemies in the Republican party, particularly those in Arkansas. Some campaign observers felt Clinton even benefited from the situation, by "using the crisis to reinforce his image as a credible outsider who is being victimized by discredited groups like reporters and Washington insiders."[6]

A second part of Clinton's attempt to discredit the report was to indirectly attack the media for using a story from an ethically questionable source. According to one source, Clinton's attack on the *Star* was an "effort to embarrass mainstream publications into ignoring the story."[7] Without directly going after the press, Clinton tried to shame the reporters for their determination to find the "truth" about the rumors. During his appearance on the CBS News program "60 Minutes," Clinton said, "I have told the American people more than any other candidate for president. The result of that has been everybody going to my state, and spending more time trying to play 'Gotcha.'" He also pointed out that regardless of his answer to the question of infidelity, the press would not be satisfied:

> If you deny, then you have a whole 'nother horde of people going down there offering more money trying to prove that you lied. And if you say, "Yes," . . . You have, "Oh, good. Now we can go play 'Gotcha' and find out who it is." Now no matter what I say, to pretend that the press will then let this die—we're kidding ourselves.[8]

While chastising the press for their efforts to get at the base of the rumors, Clinton was still heavily dependent on television and the press to achieve the second goal of his damage-control campaign, denial of the charges. A Clinton aide was quoted as saying, "The only way out is through television."[9] Clinton had agreed to appear on ABC's "Nightline" program the evening after the *Star* previewed the Flowers story, but travel plans forced him to cancel the appearance. Instead, he and his wife, Hillary, at that point an active partner in the campaign, appeared on an abbreviated version of the CBS program "60 Minutes" following the Super Bowl.

The Clintons' appearance on the program seemed planned to accomplish two goals. First, Clinton admitted to "wrongdoing" and to "causing pain in my marriage." However, he denied the specific charge of an extramarital affair with Flowers. When pressured to provide specifics about the admission of wrongdoing, Clinton steadfastly refused. He instead insisted that the American people already knew what the ambiguous denial meant: "I think most Americans who are watching this tonight—they'll know what we're saying, they'll get it, and they'll feel that we have been more candid."[10] The strategy appears to have been to avoid making an absolute statement of denial such as Gary Hart had made in 1988. When the press proved Hart had lied, his candidacy was over. By admitting to ambiguous "wrongdoing" while denying specific charges, Clinton avoided being trapped in details.

Despite Kruse's observation that "one cannot produce apologetic discourse for another person," Hillary Clinton played an important role in her husband's defense strategies.[11] Mrs. Clinton was a "stark contrast" to the "helpless victim" that Gary Hart's wife appeared to be.[12] From the onset of the accusations, Mrs. Clinton was involved in the defense, attacking the credibility of the *Star*. Her appearance with Clinton on "60 Minutes" underscored the "partnership" image of the Clintons' marriage, lending credibility to Clinton's claim that the couple had worked out earlier problems in their marriage. Mrs. Clinton did not seem disconcerted in talking about Gennifer Flowers; she and Clinton agreed Flowers was a "friendly acquaintance."[13] Mrs. Clinton also indicated that she was not staying with a philandering husband just for the sake of appearances: "I'm not sitting here as some little woman standing by my man. . . . I'm sitting here because I love him and I respect him and I honor what he's been through and what we've been through together."[14] It was Mrs. Clinton who first used the phrase "zone of privacy," a key aspect of the Clintons' explanation for the ambiguous nature of answers about their marital problems.

Overall, the "60 Minutes" appearance drew on the social myth of the "value of challenge," that implies that "suffering begets maturity, humility, and wisdom"—all qualities which would be considered key attributes for a presidential candidate.[15] In this case, the Clintons presented themselves as marriage partners who had come through hard times to produce a stronger union. Clinton bristled when the interviewer suggested Mrs. Clinton had accepted his infidelity in return for political rewards such as the opportunity to be First Lady. "You're looking at two people who love each other," Clinton said. "This is not an arrangement or an understanding; this is a marriage. That's a very different thing."[16] The image also served as a "bolstering" factor to help Clinton "identify himself with something viewed favorably by the audience."[17] Roberts said the strategy makers apparently hoped that "many voters, having suffered marital troubles of their own, [would] find the couple recognizable and sympathetic."[18] The Clintons several times referred to the special understanding "the American people, at least people who have been married for a long time," would have of their situation.[19]

By attempting to cast the American people rather than the press as the ultimate judges of Clinton's future in the presidential race, the appearance served as *translatio*. Throughout the interview, the Clintons redefined their judges by such statements as "We're going to do the best we can to level with people, and then we're going to let them make up their minds. I think if the American people get a chance, and if they're trusted to exercise their vote right . . . this country will be OK."[20] A final strategy present in the "60 Minutes" appearance was "identification," an attempt to "depict [one's] own goals as the goals of the [audience]."[21] Clinton attempted to shift the voters' attention from his marriage and possible indiscretions to the country's economic problems, saying, "The only way to put it behind us . . . is for all of us to agree that 'This guy has told us all we need to know . . . Let's go on and get back to the real problems of the country.' "[22]

Before polls had time to clearly reflect public reaction to the Clintons' defense strategies, a second revelation threatened to force an end to Clinton's candidacy—a question of possible draft dodging.

THE DRAFT DEFERMENT QUESTION

Perhaps because the draft-dodging charge came so quickly after the allegations of marital infidelity, the Clinton campaign used completely different strategies for dealing with the problem, strategies some observers felt were not as effective. A New Hampshire newspaper criticized the Clinton staffers for "bad handling of the furor over the draft" because "they decided, unlike with the Flowers affair, they would try to define the 22-year-old circular issue, a poor decision given the critical timetable."[23] The criticism seems valid, for unlike the womanizing issue, the draft-dodging issue continued to provide ammunition (albeit ineffective for the most part) for the Bush campaign up until the last days of the campaign.

The criticism points to a clear difference between the strategies for handling the two issues. For the Flowers accusations, Clinton used deliberately ambiguous answers to allow individual Americans to decide exactly what he and his wife meant when they said their marriage had overcome problems. For the draft-dodging question, however, Clinton faced the issue squarely and tried to explain explicitly his intentions and thoughts of twenty-two years earlier.

The draft issue, once again, had been introduced in Clinton's gubernatorial campaigns in Arkansas. During his first campaign for governor, in 1978, an aide to Clinton's Republican opponent accused Clinton of conveniently backing out of a commitment to ROTC after his danger of being drafted for Vietnam was past. At the time, Clinton explained away the questions by saying he had backed out of the agreement shortly after it was made and that he never received the deferment. However, in the 1992 presidential campaign, the issue came back to haunt Clinton in the form of a story by the *Wall Street Journal* and ABC News. ABC News obtained a copy of a letter Clinton had written in 1969 to an official in the ROTC office at the University of Arkansas. The letter thanked the official for "saving" Clinton from the draft and showed the young Clinton's concern with keeping his "political viability." This story and the letter were released only days before the New Hampshire primary, sending Clinton's standing in the polls down.

On 12 February Clinton appeared on the ABC news program "Nightline" to try to neutralize negative reactions to the letter. Throughout the program, Clinton again used two strategies. First, he attempted to portray himself as consistent, and secondly, he tried to diffuse the draft-dodging accusation as an issue.

Three times in the thirty-minute program, Clinton referred to the consistency of his responses to the draft question, even during his gubernatorial campaigns. Early in the program, Clinton said, "The *Journal* story itself confirmed what I said all along, which is that I gave up my deferment before the lottery came in . . . . I did not dodge the draft, I did not do anything wrong, and that has not been contradicted, even by people who have changed their stories over the intervening years."[24] In contrast to the fickle stories of his opponents, Clinton portrayed himself as sticking with the same story for years: "The important thing is that the letter is consistent with everything I've been saying for the last 13 years, since I was first asked about this in late 1978."[25]

Clinton seemed to realize that his candidacy depended on convincing voters of his truthfulness. As a *Newsweek* reporter said, "Polls show most people don't care if Clinton has been unfaithful, but they won't forgive him if he has lied."[26] For both the infidelity issue and the draft issue, Clinton stated he had advised others to tell the truth. The truth issue was one thing Clinton did not dispute in the "love tapes" Flowers and the *Star* released; he said he encouraged Flowers several times to "just tell the truth."[27] On "Nightline," when Koppel asked about Dan Quayle and his service in the National Guard to avoid Vietnam, Clinton said, ". . . at the time I said Dan Quayle ought to just tell the truth, get the facts out and let it go."[28] Clinton's attempt to show consistency in his answers about the draft and his insistence that bringing out the truth would solve problems show that he wanted to defuse the character weaknesses the press and the Republicans were beginning to associate with him.

A related strategy was to downplay the importance of the letter by attributing it to the emotions of a "deeply agitated 23-year-old boy, a young man."[29] While he did not abandon the principles set forth in the letter, Clinton tried to place the situation clearly in the past. He tried to show the emotions of the letter as only one aspect of his personality, which had matured over the past twenty-two years. As one reporter said, "Implicit in Clinton's public explanation of the ROTC letter was the fact that he was guilty, not of some political felony, but of a passing fever of youthful impudence."[30] Another aspect of the strategy was to disparage using the personality of the young man as a criterion for judging the current candidate. As Clinton said, "We've been talking about a letter I wrote twenty-two years ago as if it's a test of present presidential character."[31] Clinton then mentioned conflicting statements by President Bush during the State of the Union address and the New Hampshire campaign as proper tests of "presidential character." He went on to suggest his own "whole record as governor, my demonstrations of character, my fitness to lead" be compared to Bush's record.[32]

Some themes from the earlier defense did reoccur in the draft defense. Clinton once again made the American people the ultimate judge, saying, "If the people know the facts, I think they'll be all right."[33] Ironically, Clinton used military imagery while pledging to "try to give [voters] this election back, and if I can give it back to them and fight for them and fight for their future . . . I know we can go beyond here and continue to take this fight to the American people."[34]

Clinton also indirectly chastised the media again, this time for distracting the campaign from the serious issues to questions of character. He said, "For three weeks, of course, I've had some problems in the polls. All I've been asked about by the press are a woman I didn't sleep with and a draft I didn't dodge."[35] However, Clinton did not directly attack the media; it was as if he wanted subtly to shame reporters into covering issues in which he felt voters had a true and vital interest.

In some ways, Clinton's defense against the two sets of accusations brought against him during the month before the New Hampshire primary displays standard characteristics of the apologetic genre, such as the identification strategies mentioned earlier. Clinton's apologia seems to fall quite naturally into the category of "explanative" address, in which "the speaker assumes that if the audience understands his motives, actions, beliefs . . . they will be unable to condemn him."[36]

"Differentiation" seems to be an especially prominent strategy in Clinton's apologies. As Ware and Linkugel note, a speaker using differentiation techniques attempts to divide "the old context into two or more new constructions of reality" which are meant to change the meaning the audience sees in the event.[37] In the draft-dodging defense, Clinton constructed a new and different reality about the 1969 letter for the public. On the one hand, the letter appears to be a telling indication of Clinton's manipulation of the system. However, after Clinton's explanation, the letter became the "true reflection of the deep and conflicted feelings of a just-turned-23-year-old young man."[38] The same sort of strategy was used in the infidelity defense to transform a view of Clinton as a cheating husband into Clinton as a husband who has made mistakes, overcome the problems and learned from the experience—a very positive image. This differentiation contributed to the "regenerative" function of the apologias, asserting that "one is now somehow fundamentally different and worthy of increased valuation than at some previous time."[39] Clinton's differentiation of his past selves—a confused young man, a husband who was a source of pain for his wife—from his current self seems to be an attempt to convince audiences that the new Clinton is substantially different and suitable to be president.

Given the recent past history of politicians who suffered unpleasant revelations during presidential campaigns, it is unlikely, however, that any of the apologetic strategies would have been effective without another strategy Clinton and his advisors used—inoculation to prepare the public for such accusations.

USE OF INOCULATION IN APOLOGIA

Although it has been an accepted variable for study in persuasion research, the concept of inoculation has not been discussed in connection with apologetic rhetoric. Clinton's defense provides an interesting example of how inoculation may indeed be an effective accompaniment for apologia.

McGuire and Papageorgis first applied the medical concept of inoculation to psychology. They noted that a patient "might be given an inoculation of the infectious virus itself (in a weakened form) such as would stimulate, without overcoming, his defenses."[40] Applying the theory to persuasion, they concluded "prior exposure to refuted counterarguments tends to make a belief more resistant to subsequently presented strong forms."[41]

Clinton and his aides apparently realized early in the campaign that the candidate would be vulnerable to attack, particularly on the same issues that had surfaced in the gubernatorial campaigns—womanizing and draft-dodging. Learning from Gary Hart's failure to handle the womanizing issue, Clinton was quoted as saying, "I wish I could find a way to get all these stories out early so I don't have to deal with them after I'm nominated, when they can be so distracting."[42] Getting the stories to the public at any stage of the campaign did, however, pose a substantial risk, which the Clinton team offset through the use of early inoculation techniques.

In September, shortly before announcing his candidacy for the presidency, Clinton "launched a pre-emptive strike by admitting to past marital problems."[43] In a breakfast with the press, Clinton and his wife agreed their sixteen-year marriage had had problems. Clinton said, "We have been together for almost 20 years and we are committed to each other. It has not been perfect or free from problems, but we are committed to each other and that ought to be enough."[44] The strategy, just as it later was in January 1992, was to admit to problems without going into specifics, leaving audience members to guess exactly what kind of marital problems the Clintons had overcome. This inoculation of "womanizing" charges later proved to be important in Clinton's defense against the specific charges of infidelity with Gennifer Flowers. Having admitted to marital problems, Clinton could now say, "go back and listen to what I've said. . . . I have acknowledged wrongdoing, I have acknowledged causing pain in my marriage. I have said things to you tonight and to the American people from the beginning, that no American politician ever has."[45] At the same time, he could categorically deny the specific charge of an affair with Flowers, while keeping his actual marital problems nebulous. The strategy contributed to the image of truthfulness and consistency that Clinton developed while defending himself against the accusations, an image which has already been discussed as vital to his success.

Keeping the admission of "wrongdoing" ambiguous certainly would serve Clinton's purpose in inoculating the public. As McGuire and Papageorgis note, the counterarguments used to inoculate must come in a "weakened" form so as not to overpower the very beliefs the persuader hopes to strengthen. If Clinton had spelled out specific cases of adultery or even of "lust in the heart," as Jimmy Carter did, listeners would have had a specific sin to attach to Clinton's character. Instead, the terms "wrongdoing" and "causing pain" can apply to any number of acts, yet semantically are less threatening. We have all been guilty of "wrongdoing" in one form or another; we are therefore more willing to forgive "wrongdoing" than "adultery" or even "lust." Keeping the admission ambiguous allowed Clinton to appeal for forgiveness to a larger audience. While Clinton could not hope to change the minds of those most extreme in their views, his strategy would make him more appealing to that large body of people who had not yet made a decision on his character.

Throughout the campaign, Clinton followed that initial inoculation of admitting to being less than perfect with "booster shots." Shortly after the defense on the draft-dodging issue, a regular theme in Clinton's speeches for several months was, "If you're looking for someone who's perfect, you'll need to look somewhere else."[46] In June, a little over a month before he would be chosen the Democratic nominee, Clinton was asked by talk-show host Arsenio Hall to give his flaws and quipped, "We don't have enough time."[47] This strategy of self-deprecation was obviously preparation for a hard-hitting fall campaign. One well-known consultant said, "The [character] issue will be back in the fall . . . . Bush will turn the focus to family values."[48]

Why were the "booster shots" necessary? Clinton may have been familiar with two aspects of human nature. One is the "social homogeneity" which McGuire and Papageorgis said is common "even with respect to so controversial an issue as presidential preference."[49] Clinton may have realized that once people had formed an opinion about his character, they would not be likely to seek out new information about the subject. Therefore, during the period when his character was being publically discussed following his apologies, Clinton probably wanted to ensure that his version of his character was presented along with the Republicans' version and the press's version.

This strategy of "boosting" his image of the fallible but honest and consistent candidate, in conjunction with another analysis of a common human trait, almost certainly was planned to have more effect during the fall campaign than during the preconvention months when it was most prevalent. Clinton may have depended on people's resistance to seeking new information about their beliefs to keep the image he projected during the "booster shot" period as the predominant image. Secondly, he may have hoped that by admitting to mistakes himself, the public would defend him against "petty" attacks later in the campaign. After all, if a person has already admitted to not being perfect, it is redundant and mean-spirited to keep pointing out imperfections. One indication that this strategy worked came in the second presidential debate, when audience members specifically asked candidates to stop mudslinging on character and to instead focus on issues such as the deficit and the economy.

Clinton floundered in the polls for a time after the two apologies, and the "character issue" was constantly mentioned in connection with his name throughout the campaign. However, he overcame those early negative associations to become the president in a race that was not particularly close. Perhaps, just as with a physical inoculation, the apologetic inoculation caused a short-term reaction before the internal defenses took over. For a time, Clinton certainly seemed to be taking as important a gamble with his political life as the pioneers of immunization took with the lives of their patients. It remains to be seen if apologetic inoculation can work as well for other political candidates in the future.

NOTES

1. D. Maraniss and B. McAllister, "Just When He Thought the Worst Was behind Him," *Washington Post*, 24 February 1992, 14.

2. M. Collins, S. Edwards, and C. Bell, "Dem Front-Runner Had Affair with Miss America," *Star*, 28 January 1992, 25.

3. Ibid., 36.

4. Mary McGrory, "Flowers and Dirt," *Washington Post*, 28 January 1992, A2.

5. CBS News, "60 Minutes," 26 January 1992, 3.

6. Gloria Boreger and Steven V. Roberts, "Democrats' Fatal Vision," *U.S. News and World Report*, 10 February 1992, 37.

7. Steven V. Roberts, "Defusing the Bombshell," *U.S. News and World Report*, 3 February 1992, 4.

8. CBS News, "60 Minutes," 26 January 1992, 4.

9. Michael Kramer, "Moment of Truth," *Time*, 3 February 1992, 13.

10. CBS News, "60 Minutes," 26 January 1992, 4.

11. Noreen Kruse, "The Scope of Apologetic Discourse," *Southern Speech Communication Journal* (Spring 1981): 286.

12. Roberts, "Defusing the Bombshell," 31.

13. CBS News, "60 Minutes," 26 January 1992, 3.

14. Ibid., 5.

15. Charles U. Larsen, *Persuasion: Reception and Responsibility*, 218.

16. CBS News, "60 Minutes," 26 January 1992, 5.

17. B. L. Ware and Wil A. Linkugel, "They Spoke in Defense of Themselves: On the Generic Criticism of *Apologia*," *Quarterly Journal of Speech* (October 1973): 277.

18. Roberts, "Defusing the Bombshell," 31.

19. CBS News, "60 Minutes," 26 January 1992, 3.

20. Ibid., 5.

21. Noreen Kruse, "Motivational Factors in Non-denial *Apologia*," *Central States Speech Journal* (Spring 1977): 18.

22. CBS News, "60 Minutes," 26 January 1992, 4.

23. K. Landrigan, "Primary Reason Voters Indifferent: The Level of Frustration, Despair," *Nashua Sunday Telegraph*, 16 February 1992, E3.

24. ABC News, "Nightline," 12 February 1992, 4.

25. Ibid., 7.

26. Eleanor Clift, "Character Questions," *Newsweek*, 10 February 1992, 26.

27. Kramer, "Moment of Truth," 13.

28. ABC News, "Nightline," February 1992, 11.

29. Ibid., 10.

30. M. Cooper, "Clinton Something," *Village Voice*, February 1992, 33.

31. ABC News, "Nightline," 12 February 1992, 11.

32. Ibid.

33. Ibid.

34. Ibid.

35. Ibid.

36. Ware and Linkugel, "They Spoke in Defense of Themselves," 283.

37. Ibid., 278.

38. ABC News, "Nightline," 12 February 1992, 7.

39. Ware and Linkugel, "They Spoke in Defense of Themselves," 279.

40. William J. McGuire and Demetrios Papageorgis, "The Relative Efficacy of Various Types of Prior Belief-defense in Producing Immunity against Persuasion," *Journal of Abnormal and Social Psychology* (1961): 327.

41. Ibid.

42. Michael Kramer, "The Self-making of a Front-Runner," *Time*, 27 January 1992, 20.

43. Roberts, "Defusing the Bombshell," 30.

44. Dan Balz, "Wilder, Clinton Fault Harkin as Democratic Race Takes Form," *Washington Post*, 17 September 1991, A2.

45. CBS News, "60 Minutes," 26 January 1992, 3, 4.

46. CBS News, "CBS This Morning," 10 August 1992.

47. "Arsenio Hall Show," 3 June 1992.

48. Michael Kramer, "The Vulture Watch," *Time*, 10 February 1992, 27.

49. McGuire and Papageorgis, "The Relative Efficacy of Various Types of Prior Belief-defense in Producing Immunity against Persuasion," 328.

DE/RECONSTRUCTING
HILLARY

From the Retro Ashes of the Donna Reed Fantasy to a '90s View of Women and Politics

SANDRA GOODALL

To say that Hillary Clinton's experience in campaign '92 was a roller coaster ride would be a gross understatement. She went from unknown to hated to forgotten to revered and back again many times. Unlike her husband, Bill Clinton, her story was not played out primarily on CNN, "Arsenio," or "Larry King Live." Hillary Clinton's story was found in the chasm between Republicans and Democrats, between traditional "family" values and modern values, between men and women and women and women. Her story found voice around dinner tables, in offices, conference rooms, in phone calls to friends and to talk radio shows around the country, at Republican and Democrat precinct meetings, and throughout the academic discourses that permeate our lives.

Hillary's story is created from the multiple myths of campaign '92. It is a story in which she is both a willing actor and an unwilling character. In some ways it is less a story about Hillary and more about who we are as women in the nineties. The real story of campaign '92 is the elevation of a discussion central to our lives—*the role of women*—in politics, in the home, in the workplace, in relationships, as mothers, as wives, as friends, as enemies, as people, as chattel, as servants, and as the only other sex on the planet.

In this essay, I will explore how the focus of Hillary Clinton in campaign '92 also became a focus on women and women's issues. This focus gave voice to a large number of women who until then felt voiceless. Not only did campaign '92 recognize the forgotten middle class, it also acknowledged the millions of women who were left out of the women's movement and who did not fit into the traditional roles, models, or ideologies of the religious right.

One function of public discourse is to create narrative *personas* with which marginalized people can identify; that is what, for many of us, Hillary Clinton did and does. So this is, too, very much *my* story. As a Clinton-Gore campaign worker, as a woman, and as a voter, it is hard for me to separate my personal experiences from my analysis of Hillary's role in the campaign. This will be a personal story interspersed with academic citation and voice, occasionally borrowing from conversations that surrounded me during and shortly after the campaign. It is a story about *an* experience, not of *the* experience. It is not a story about truth or even representation, but of the weaving of a narrative about a thing called politics.

A VIEW FROM THE TOP OF THE ROLLER COASTER RIGHT BEFORE . . .

Until January of 1992 the public story of Hillary Clinton's life had been all about the steady climb to the top of the first hill of life's roller coaster. The Wellesley and Yale Law School graduate, member of numerous boards, successful law partner, wife of Bill, and mother of Chelsea had, with some of the bumps and lumps of life, reached the top of that hill. For a few brief months from the time her husband announced his candidacy for president until January of 1992, to most of us it seemed, she sat on the top, surveying her life and the world around her, waiting for the time to come when her life would change and the car she was riding in would leap forward.

I remember glancing at CNN during Bill Clinton's announcement that he was running for president and thinking "This is the guy Steve (Smith) told us to watch for? The one who would be president someday? This guy from Little Rock, Arkansas?" That is all I really knew, all most of us really knew, about Bill and Hillary Clinton until January.

The First Big Hill: Straight Down into the Gennifer Flowers Story

Bill Clinton was my lover for 12 years. —Gennifer Flowers

If you don't like what he stands for, then don't vote for him."
  —Hillary Clinton

In January, following Clinton's announcement, *Star* magazine published allegations by Gennifer Flowers, a nightclub singer and ex-Arkansas state employee, that she had had a twelve-year affair with Bill Clinton. The rumor was that the Republican National Committee, or some Rs in Arkansas, or that now truly famous group (thanks Ross!) the Republican dirty tricks committee, paid Flowers $175,000 to come forward and expose Bill Clinton as a philandering two-timer. In past years these types of dirty tricks had worked rather well; yet this year was different. This year, rather than remaining in the tabloids, the Flowers's bombshell exploded all over prime time. This should have marked the end of Bill and for that matter Bill and Hillary Clinton, but there was a dynamic at work that neither the Republicans nor the Democrats realized existed: Hillary Clinton and the disgust of the American people with political bedroom games.

Many of us at one time or another have walked in either Gennifer Flower's high-heeled f—— me spikes or Hillary Clinton's low no-nonsense pumps. As I sat amazed by what was unraveling on CNN, and later "60 Minutes," the support I gave Bill Clinton didn't have nearly as much to do with his qualifications to be president as it did with whom I believed and ultimately whom I identified with—Hillary or Gennifer—*at that point* in my life. I have been reading and rereading a lot of Gregory Bateson, and it seems he would have summed it up this way:

> The importance of this point can scarcely be overemphasized, when we are considering the validity of hypotheses relating to sex . . . human beings are not only reticent and dishonest, but even totally unable to achieve an objective view of their own behavior [much less] that of others.[1]

So whether or not women believed Bill had more to do with our experiences *with a* or *as a* Gennifer Flowers. It had more to do with how we perceived Flowers standing on the podium, flipping her blond-on-black hair in her flaming red suit, as well as the number of Gennifer-with-a-G Flowers we have encountered or the times we, ourselves, had been a Gennifer Flowers, than anything Bill Clinton could have said or done at that moment in the campaign. And it had more to do with the *positioning* of Hillary as a complex smart woman and loving wife than anyone yet realized.

At this point in my life I pulled for Hillary. Hillary became for some (and for me) the image of themselves as the "wronged" women and for others the image of the woman they had wronged. She garnered sympathy from both camps. Those who had been wronged supported her because they had been there too. Those who had done the wronging supported her because she gave them a way to assuage their own guilt. Yet, where was Bill in all this? Sitting on the couch looking guilty and sorry.

THE STORY FROM THE HEADLINES

> The map is not the territory, even when the physical territory is the only embodiment of the map. —Bateson

Hillary emerged as the woman who *forgave and forgot* (until Gennifer and the *Star* dredged the mess up again). If we respected Bill (which always meant Hillary *and* Bill), it was for working hard to save his (their) marriage and for keeping it together, even if we hadn't or couldn't. Hillary was touted in the national press as popular, strong, and victorious. She became

the woman who worked hard to save her marriage and her home.
—*Time*, 27 January, "Hillary Clinton:
Partner as Much as Wife"

the woman who sat firmly *beside* her man.
—*Wall Street Journal*, 31 January, "Hear Her Roar:
Hillary Clinton, Lawyer and Mother,
Drafts New Role for Wives in Presidential Politics"

the woman who took control of the ship headed for the rocks and brought it steadily, strongly back on course.
—*Wall Street Journal*, 29 January,
"Hillary Clinton Plans Media Campaign
to Bolster Husband's Presidential Bid"

Throughout this article I will refer to the headlines of major newspaper articles to illuminate the discussion. I found the headlines revealing and useful for tracking the events and sentiments that surrounded the campaign. They are shorthand terms for the complex texts and contexts that campaigns are created from and on. In many ways these headlines set the tone for what was to come next.

Watching the Clintons on "60 Minutes," I began to see the first hint that Hillary Clinton would defy definition. She did not fit the feminist mold, nor was she a traditional political housewife. Unfortunately, this dichotomy and her display of strength, calm, and faith during the interview would eventually be used against her.

SOUND BITES AND HURT FEELINGS

You know, I'm not sitting here like some little woman, standing by my man like Tammy Wynette. —Hillary Clinton

Tammy [Wynette]'s music faithfully follows the notion that country music is poor folks' psychiatry . . . a salve for the beleaguered housewife who grits her teeth as destiny dumps its slop on her head. —*Newsweek*

A few days after the "60 Minutes" interview, Tammy Wynette released a statement which said that she was watching the interview with her grandchildren when Hillary made reference to her and to one of her songs. Wynette wrote:

Mrs. Clinton, I, with no apologies, am as angry as I can be with your statement, "I'm not sitting here like some little woman, standing by my man like Tammy Wynette." . . . Mrs. Clinton, I was baby-sitting my four grandchildren last night when you made your remarks about me. My eight-year-old granddaughter said, "Mamaw, why did she say that about you?" I truly was speechless. I had no answer. I simply said, "I don't know, angel."[2]

This was Hillary's first sound-bite "mistake," and upon examination it seems humorous. "Stand by Your Man" is Wynette's signature song *and* the title of her 1979 autobiography. Tammy Wynette *is* "Stand by Your Man" and the song *is* Tammy. In an interview with *Newsweek* she said, "Basically, country people don't think about protesting . . . I have no desire to be freer than I am." A look at Wynette's marital past may shed some light on the sound bite that should *not* have stirred controversy—least of all in Tammy Wynette's mind.

Tammy married her first husband at seventeen. Euple Byrd (I'm from the South and I can't pronounce it) turned out, according to her autobiography, to be boring, lazy, and good only at fathering children. She left with their three children in 1966 and headed to Nashville. She married Don Chapel. While married to Chapel she fell in love with George Jones, famous for marrying young women (*really* young in some cases); making a lot of money which he blew on young women, booze, and coke; and showing up at shows totally trashed (something his fans seem to find endearing for some reason). The marriage to Chapel ended in 1975 after a much-liquored Jones walked in on a argument between Chapel and Wynette. Wynette writes:

> All of a sudden [George] was a tornado, wrecking my house. He looked straight at Don and said, "You don't talk to her like that." . . .
> Don stammered, "Wha-what's it to you? She's *my* wife!"
> George shot back, "That may be so, but I love her."
> He had rescued me from a husband I didn't love, just like the knight on the white charger saved the captive princess in fairy tales.

Tammy Wynette's relational history, which only shows up in political analysis because of an unconscious s/flip of the tongue, is one of standing by her man even when most of us would have walked out and then, when a better prospect comes along, of leaving anyway. Hillary, however, had not turned ignorant eyes and ears to the situation in her marriage. She knew the score and her admission of that knowledge is in both the "60 Minutes" interview and her reference to the song. Hillary said, "I am *not* sitting here like some little woman standing by my man like Tammy Wynette" (emphasis mine). The song speaks for itself.

As Hillary was defending Bill, Tammy was defending Tammy and the right to be a stand-up woman. This was the beginning of Hillary's dilemma over the media's and the nation's schizophrenic understanding of who she was.

TEA AND COOKIES

"I suppose I could have stayed at home, baked cookies and had teas . . . ," Hillary Clinton said.

". . . but what I decided was to fulfill my profession, which I entered before my husband was in public life. You know, the work that I've done as a professional, as a public advocate, has been aimed in part to assure that women can make the choices that they should make—whether it's a full-time career, full-time motherhood, some combination, depending upon what stage of life they are at—and I think that is still difficult for people to understand right now, that it is a generational change." [This is the part of the sound bite most of us missed.]

I remember listening to the report of this story on NPR and being really surprised that women found this sound bite problematic. I have spent the last two years living in a place called Six Mile, South Carolina. Six Mile is a rural, somewhat remote community nine miles from Clemson University, where my husband is developing a communication department, twelve miles from Pickens the county seat; seventeen miles from Seneca; and as far as I can tell not really six miles from anything. It was the only place where, after five trips to Clemson, we could find a house after a period of prolific hiring at the university (which was then followed by a period of prolific budget cuts).

The move meant I would give up a promising graduate career at the University of Utah, where I had been awarded a graduate fellowship in the Ph.D. program. While doing my master's work there I had *our* one and perfect child. For my child the move meant being within driving distance of his only living set of grandparents, one aunt, uncle, and cousin. It meant being near family and establishing, for our son, family relationship that my husband and I felt strongly had figured heavily into who we were.

There is no way to describe the experience of motherhood for me other than overwhelming. For me, this child brought overwhelming feelings of love, joy, fear, and most of all responsibility. Bud and I, after many hours of discussion, decided we did not want to put Nicolas in day care, full-time or otherwise. *We* did not want someone else caring for Nic six to seven hours a day. And, since Bud was the one earning the money at the time, *we* decided I would stay at home with Nic for the first two years, until we were comfortable with putting him in day care or having someone else tend him.

So here I was, sitting in Six Mile, caring for my child, making curtains and slipcovers, playing endless games of patty-cake, doing some volunteer work and listening to hours of CNN, C-SPAN, and NPR so that I didn't go brain dead, when I heard the tea and cookies thing. I was surprised and then I was confused. Was I supposed to be *hurt*? That was what NPR and CNN were telling me. Because *I* am staying home, *I* should be insulted, but I wasn't. I understood *exactly* what she was saying, yet apparently many women didn't . . . maybe because they weren't listening, maybe because the media didn't emphasize the context of the remark, choosing instead to emphasize the sound bite.

The tea and cookies comment was a reaction to an accusation by Jerry Brown that Governor Clinton had improperly "funneled money to his wife's law firm." There was a hint of suggestion that Hillary could not succeed as a lawyer if her husband didn't somehow help out. There was the implication that women and politics, more accurately, *working* women with *husbands* in politics, don't mix. Hillary's response was again taken as a slight, but this time to a group of women voters large enough to be considered important. And, the comment gave the religious right the first real ammunition they needed to begin the portion of the campaign that branded Hillary a *radical* feminist. The media tide had turned, and it turned with a vengeance. It portrayed Hillary as the

selfish yuppie.   —*Washington Post*, 10 March,
"Hillary Clinton, Trying to Have It All"

and within a ten-day period as an issue, a factor, a problem, and an ordeal.   —*Washington Post*, 17 March,
"Clinton's Wife Finds She's Become an Issue";
Washington Post, 18 March, "The Hillary Clinton
Factor"; *Washington Post* (again), 21 March,
"Hillary's Ordeal"; *New York Times*, 26 March,
"The Hillary Problem"

I talked about the comment with my husband, with friends at Clemson, with friends from graduate school, with my buddy Rita, and I still didn't get it, until I talked to another stay-at-home mom. She was angry: She felt she had been slammed and that she didn't deserve to be put down for staying home. I also found out she didn't enjoy being at home: It wasn't really her idea. She had a job she really liked, but it was hard to get up in the mornings and get the kids to the sitter; she was tired all the time; and when she got home there was so much to do she couldn't keep up. She really didn't have to work, although the extra money was nice. Who did Hillary Clinton think she was, commenting on her life? She has a cook and nannies and a private secretary. She has never had to deal with this alone . . .

I left thinking "Who is really angry with whom here? Whose fault is it that *your* life isn't what *you* want it to be? What did she mean alone? Where was what's his name through all this?"

As for me, I was still overwhelmed by the love and the joy and still mostly the responsibility, putting off my writing another few minutes to watch Nic roll over again or try to walk or to listen to him babble in pre-speak or to just sit by and watch him sleep. I suppose I could have gone on and worked on my Ph.D., taken classes, and put my child in day care, but . . .

WHAT ABOUT THE MEDIA?

What the media did consistently during campaign '92 was to report what others observed (Dole, Buchanan, Robertson, etc.) or attempted to create out of the political rabble (of Dole, Buchanan, Robertson, etc.) rather than what they were privileged to observe. The media are the eyes and ears of the American people. We obviously cannot be everywhere, all at once, discovering for ourselves the news. Instead, we must rely on a media that all too often is concerned more with careers and ratings than with quality, the big scoop rather than the impact of a sensationalist story, the sound bite rather than the context. The cookies and tea incident is a good example of this type of reporting during campaign '92. Bateson's work is informative here. Consider the following quotation as if Bateson is discussing a reporter:

> He will falsify the priorities of his utterance, indicating a high importance for a relatively trivial message or denying the importance of a message which he feels to be vital. In addition, he may code the message in a metaphoric form without indicating that such a code is being used. Even a second metaphoric code may be made to simulate an objective message about some other

subject in the real world. [He] may even make very small changes in a straightforward message, changes just sufficient to enable him to tell himself secretly that this is not his message.[3]

This quote comes from Bateson's work on schizophrenia, but it isn't too far off from what was happening in the media during the campaign. Hillary became a metaphor for women's problems, a lightning rod for everything both good and bad with the feminist movement. She became a character caught in the middle between

traditional values and modern life.	—*Washington Post*, 31 March, "Clinton Hints He'd Appoint Wife to Administration Post"
Democrats and Republicans.	—*New York Times*, 12 April, "George & Barb & Bill & Hillary"
feminists and stay-at-home moms.	—editorials in the *Los Angeles Times*, 22 March, "Goodbye to the 'Lady of the Manor': It's Time Americans Recognize That Presidential Wives Can Contribute as Much to Political Life as Their Men" and "Some Bake Cookies, Others Buy: Can't Careerists Be Comfortable with Their Choices without Putting Others Down?"

The last straw for Hillary may have been an article by Gail Sheehy in *Vanity Fair*. Shortly after its release Hillary left the national scene, retreating to the safer venue of the local press along the campaign trail she continued to hit hard for Bill. I read the Sheehy article and reread it, wondering, "What is this woman's axe?" Certain passages allude to Sheehy's agenda or at the very least a style of writing that overshadows her subject with negative undertones. Some excerpts from the article follow:

When the cameras dolly in, however, one can detect the calculation in the f-stop click of Hillary's eyes. Lips pulled back over her slightly jutting teeth, the public smile is practiced; the small frown establishes an air of superiority; her hair looks lifelessly doll like.

and . . .

If he loses, Hillary predicts, "Bill and I have great opportunities, we'll always be able to make a good living, we've got a wonderful

daughter—we'll be fine." It doesn't usually work that way, however, particularly not for two driven people whose every axon
and dendrite have been tingling for months as they crisscross the
country in matching campaign planes, eager to deliver political
redemption to the masses. If suddenly they land, SPLAT, back in
Little Rock, and they wake up to the concern that their child has
been necessarily neglected, and perhaps Hillary begins to thaw
out the small, excruciatingly painful little package in the deep
freeze labeled "Bill's Marital Mistakes," this could be a very
difficult period.[4]

It is no wonder with this kind of speculation on her personal life
that Hillary Clinton, a very private person by all accounts, took cover
in the day-to-day concerns of the campaign and left the media handling to her much-easier-going husband. It was not so much what
Sheehy wrote, but the lasting impression of her words that caused
Hillary to retreat and "[i]t follows necessarily that misunderstandings
and inconsistencies (either deliberate or accidental) regarding the con-
tingencies of interchange are likely to be profoundly traumatic,"[5] something I was about to discover myself.

HILLARY AND THE FEMINIST ISSUE: SOME PERSONAL THOUGHTS

The weekend of the South Carolina primary a close friend of mine and
Bud's brought his new wife down south for a visit. This was our friend's
first marriage. He waited later than most people do, and we were
extremely excited for him. I was excited by the prospect of intelligent
company, lively adult, political, and academic conversation, and eager
to meet this new person in our very special friend's life. I was not, however, prepared to be thrown into a debate I was only beginning to realize existed. I was not prepared for the hostility and anger I experienced
from someone who had chosen a very different path from my own. It
was not until I began my research on Hillary Clinton and read the coverage of her during the campaign that I realized the wide gulf, the
tremendous anger, that exists *not between men and women, but between women
and women*, who make different choices and choose different paths.

After dinner and putting the baby down we adjourned to the front
porch (it's a southern thing) to talk and enjoy some adult time.

Surprisingly, the conversation immediately turned to me, or in particular, my lifestyle, even more specifically stay-at-home moms and what my friend's new wife thought about us. Ultimately, as it seems to have frequently since I decided to stay at home, the question of my "status" came up, the assumption being that because I have chosen family over career I must be a right-wing Republican religious fanatic. She asked, "Are you a feminist?" As always, I found myself saying, "No, I am not a feminist. It is a label that I do not identify with and don't choose to use." What I really wanted to say was, "We're not all broken out with feminism down here like you all are up north" (to borrow a line from one of Carolina's less-enlightened political figures), but I bit my lip out of respect for Bud and our friend. My friend's wife was appalled and like clockwork the laundry list started to reel off: Do you believe in abortion? No, I believe in a woman's right to choose. Do you believe in equal pay for equal work? Yes, but I realize there are historical complications that make this an individual responsibility not a overarching reality. And the implicit question, the one that is never quite spoken but that comes through in the talk: Do you believe that all men (present company excluded, of course) are evil incarnate, mean, and out to return us to the chattel state? The explicit spoken question/accusation, "How could you do this to us? We have worked hard so that you could have a choice!"

Excuse me?

The feminist movement has taken a very serious turn, and campaign '92 helped throw the spotlight on it high bright. The movement no longer concentrates on the white, male, patriarchal system, but has found a new unassuming target—the women who don't agree with the debate, who don't find voice in the rhetoric of victimage, and who would rather *be*, rather than talk about *being*, equal. Gloria Steinem writes that "in the 1980s when women's chain reaction of truth-telling was rising to nationwide visability in incest survivor conferences and TV talk shows, most movement groups . . . were stretched to the breaking point just trying to hang on to past gains, and to defend against efforts to demonize feminism."[6]

A February 1992 *Time*/CNN poll found that 63 percent of women polled did not consider themselves feminists and half of those polled did *not* feel the women's movement reflected women's views.[7] It became less and less fashionable to be a "feminist" in the late 1980s anywhere but on college campuses. According to the survey, "in 1985, given the choice between having a job or staying at home to care for a family 51 percent of women perferred to work; by 1991 that number fell to 43 percent."[8]

Academic feminists became heavily entrenched in the "speaking bitterness" that has become language of the victim's movement and in turn the feminist movement. The feminist movement did not, at least not on the surface, possibly not even at its depths, have a lot to offer women who had not been abused by a parent or a spouse, had not been discriminated against, or had not suffered a lack of self-esteem, which was quickly becoming the feminist movement's new rallying cry.

The feminist movement had less and less to offer me. The attack by my friend's new wife confirmed for me why. Frankly, I'm tired of "feminists." That is not to say I am tired of the positive ideas that some factions of feminism attempts to represent, but I am tired of the shrill voice of radical feminist ideology that claims to represent the oppressed masses that are so ignorant they cannot be deemed responsible enough to fight for themselves. Feminists are always angry—on some level—about something. Feminists assume that all women share their victimage, their anger, and their individualized struggles. At the same time they attempt to negate or subjugate the voices of women who are not angry, not victims, not struggling, rather than hold them up for role models and mentors. And, as I write this for a presumably academic audience, I know this is an extremely unpopular position. To tell you the truth, I'm not quite sure what a feminist is anymore and neither are most of the people I know. There no longer seems to be a clear-cut feminist agenda. If there ever was one, it has been taken over by the numerous and politically different factions that call themselves feminist and often I think to the detriment of a "real" women's movement, that includes all women.

No one seemed to represent radical feminist ideology to me less than Hillary Clinton. Yet, what we began to see in campaign '92 was a heightening of the divisions of women based on a tug for or push against Hillary Clinton. The extreme levels to which women bashing women has risen caught many of us so off-guard that we found ourselves lost in the medial, halfway between feminist and traditionalist, not really accepting or accepted by either position. It is the lack of a "real" women's movement—one that supports *choice* about marriage, children, sexuality, religion, and all the other gray areas in our lives—that led to intolerance by one side or the other and that created the confusion over Hillary.

There is an old Eastern philosophy that purports you cannot be something if you cannot envision yourself as you would be. The feminist takes this one step further by envisioning all women as they would have them be, fellow feminists engaged in whatever feminist agenda they might be involved in at the time. Bateson calls this move *schismogensis*. It assumes that the individual in a symmetrical relationship with another will tend, perhaps unconsciously, to form the habit of acting as if he or she expected symmetry in further encounters with that other, and perhaps, even more widely, in future encounters with all other individuals.[9]

Unconsciously perhaps, feminists *expect* symmetry to occur *at all levels* in their encounters with *all* women and on a larger scale with all people. The problem occurs when the expected symmetry is met with unsymmetrical or disproportionate behavior in others. Gloria Steinem sees this move toward subjugation as a defining problem in the downfall of the movement itself. She writes,

> *Many feminists in academic and other traditional professions have learned to write and speak in a way that excludes the uninitiated, and sometimes condescends towards all that is experiential, emotional, or even popular.* Yet knowledge that is understood by a few can only be acted upon by a few, and excluding what doesn't fit into the professions leave most of women's experience with no place to go.[10]

As the feminist learns patterns of symmetrical behavior from other feminist, she not only comes to expect like responses from other women, but becomes defensive, hostile, and angry when she does not encounter like behavior in others.

So while feminists were claiming Hillary Rodham Clinton as a fellow feminists they were actually pushing away many of the women who should have deeply identified with Hillary Clinton the person, leaving her adrift and unable to connect with the very groups she should have represented. The women who have been displaced by the feminist movement nonradicals, and the women who did not fit the right-wing ultraconservative mold, became wary of Hillary and stayed wary throughout most of the campaign. Others began seeing her as

Satan in a suit and pumps, a threat to society and to their very way of life.

The feminist movement sets us all up. Rather than accept Hillary as a person who has worked to balance family and career and who often chooses the former over the latter, she became branded as one of *them,* alienating women who made other choices or contributed in other ways. Rather than respect her pro-family position, the media, the religious right, and feminists all saddled her with a label that is too often misunderstood and misrepresenting.

Once the religious right successfully positioned Hillary Clinton as a radical feminist, it became easy to separate her from the call for family values she has championed all her life. The right used the image of a hardened feminist to create an image of Hillary Clinton that would, as feminist rhetoric often does, divide and splinter women even further than they were. To make their case even more insulting, they used Marilyn Quayle to represent traditional family values.

As the feminist image was cast, the other side—traditional, stay-at-home moms—were seen to rally to defend the cause of, well, being traditional. And the Democrats were trying their best to control Hillary's image. At a time when issues should have been the focus, editorials around the country were discussing

Hillary's headbands.

—*Los Angeles Times,* 19 June,
"The Politics of Appearance"

Hillary bashing.

—*New York Times,* 8 June,
"Give Hillary a Break"

and, what kind of First Lady Hillary would make.

—*New York Times,* 18 May,
"Hillary Clinton as Aspiring First Lady:
Role Model, or a 'Hall Monitor' Type?"

Read Hillary Clinton's words or watch her face as she speaks about anything—her politics, her marriage, her child, her activism for children—and you do not get anger, you get passion; you do not get victimage, but someone who works for the underdog; you do not see struggle, you see hard work, responsibility, and accountability. How do I know? I read her words, her legalese, her speeches, her interviews, and I read Bill's too. I particularly liked the speech she gave at Wellesley College, her alma matter, which is excerpted below:

You know the rules are basically as follows:
If you don't get married you are abnormal.
If you get married but don't have children, you're a selfish
   yuppie.
If you get married and have children but then go outside the
   home to work, you're a bad mother.
If you get married and have children but stay home, you've
   wasted your education.
And if you don't get married but have children and work outside the home as a fictional newscaster you get in trouble
   with the vice-president.[11]

I watched them closely whenever they were on the tube. At some point
I decided I liked them, and, more important, I respected them, their
politics, their values. So, I signed on to the campaign. I became, for the
first time in my life, politically active.

A SUMMER OF POLITICS

After many unreturned phone calls, I finally connected with the
Democratic chairman for Pickens County. A serious bubba named
Barry. Barry believes in the old-time Democratic party, the one that has
lived in the South forever and has served him, his daddy, his daddy's
daddy, and so on, quite well. I was invited to attend the monthly meeting of the Pickens County Democratic party to see how I might "help."
The meeting was held at the Six Mile Community Center, a building
that with its brick facade is one step up from a metal building. It serves
the Ladies' Club, the Boys' and Girls' Scout Troops, and other groups
and as the town hall.

There were about nine or ten people in the room when I walked in,
and they immediately quieted. I sat down and smiled and tried to make
small talk. A few minutes later, with all twenty-two of us in place, the
meeting began. Barry thought it might be nice if we went around the
room and said why we were interested in working for Clinton. I was
seated about a third of the way around the room between the oldest
living Democrat in Pickens County and the former mayor of Six Mile.
After listening to another speech about "my daddy was a Democrat
and so was my daddy's daddy," I said something brief about feeling a
connectedness to the Clintons and having a child I felt deserved a

better world. The room seemed to relax, and the former mayor laid his hand on mine and said, "I've been a nervous wreck for the last ten minutes thinking I was sitting next to the next First Lady herself." I laughed; we both have blond-not-our-real-color just-below-the-chin bobbed hair, blue eyes, and unfortunately we have both been blessed with round faces that if viewed from the wrong angle (like dead on and sometimes from either side) look really chubby, but I had never thought about looking like anyone but me until then. This wasn't the last time during the election or after that I would be mistaken for Hillary Clinton.

Barry turned out to be a really bitter guy. He had been high on Harkin. He, the other Harkin supporters, and the ex-Kerry supporters (mainly the war vets) remained divided and refused to get on with the campaign throughout June and July. It became increasingly clear that this was going to be a problem. In August I met the Clinton-Gore campaign coordinator based in Greenville. David was a young Clinton enthusiast from D.C. who was sick of the county infighting and old-time politics that did not fit with this campaign. He wanted to bring in more people like me, first-time political activists, to work on the campaign. David, a slew of young political first timers, and I had a great time turning the old-time Democratic system in the upstate on its head for the next four months.

That Great Big Lovefest in July

With the Democratic National Convention days away, Hillary reemerged "softer" and made over. She was on the cover of *People*, sitting on the grass with Bill and Chelsea—a picture of the all-American family. Newspaper articles focused on

her makeover.
—*Los Angeles Times*, 19 June, "The Politics of Appearance"

her newfound friendship with Tipper Gore.
—*New York Times*, 8 July, "Mrs. Clinton Introduces Mrs. Gore at Children's Hospital Ceremony" and *Washington Post*, 16 July, "The Women with a Ticket to Ride"

and her softer, less feminist side.
—*New York Times*, 13 July, "A Softer Image for Hillary Clinton:

For days we waited—excited, petrified, nervous. What if *they*
screwed up? What if the speeches, the show, the message—the
convention—wasn't good? What if it blows up in our faces? Even those
of us at the bottom rung of the campaign ladder knew that if the convention didn't fly, if it wasn't a huge success, if it didn't unite the party
like no other convention had, we were sunk. It would be over and that
as they say would be that. We wondered about Bill's speech, what Jerry
and Jesse would do, how Hillary would come across. We spoke about
these people—the Clintons, Ron and Jerry Brown, and even Bernie
Shaw—like we had known them for years, as if this were an election
for high-school class president, rather than president of the United
States.

If you had been in my living room the first evening of the
Democratic National Convention, you would have witnessed a grazing that went from the networks to CNN and finally to C-SPAN, which
remained the channel of choice throughout the convention. The
grazing began when after only fifteen minutes or so we were no longer
satisified to hear Bernie Shaw drone on about "where's Jerry," "the
Bubba ticket," and the surface of the events that bore little relevance
to the events themselves. We wanted, and most Americans who
watched needed, to *feel* the spirit of the event itself, in its entirety, gavel
to gavel.

I watched C-SPAN, amazed, uplifted, and unencumbered by talking heads. C-SPAN gave us both that freedom and that gift. I watched,
waiting to see a glimpse of the next first family; there they were standing in Macy's, waiting for the moment when they would stroll across
a New York street carried along by the hopes of those of us watching.
I sat glued to the tube not wanting to miss a second, and I watched as
they emerged into the convention center and the crowd went crazy. I
watched until credits rolled across C-SPAN sometime around one
o'clock in the morning. I watched Hillary and Tipper hug, and I
remember telling my husband that it was as if a hand had come down
that night and touched Bill Clinton on the head and said "you will be
the next president." It was electrifying, it was amazing, and I will admit

that at some point I felt like I was going to cry (something I rarely do with a lot of people around; in fact, something I have only done when my grandfather died, when my son was born, and when I took my mother to see *Driving Miss Daisy*). And in the middle of it all was Hillary Clinton, being real, being fun, being excited for her husband, being in love with this guy who had done all the things he said he was going to do, and being Chelsea's mom. And it was good . . . until the Republicans struck.

FIRE AND BRIMSTONE IN AUGUST

You didn't have to be a Democrat or a Bill Clinton supporter to be a little frightened by what happened in Houston in August 1992. You only had to be a little this side of the religious right to feel the hatred that must have been building in these folks for years. As the cameras scanned the vast expanse of the Houston Astro Dome, what I noticed first was the huge number of vacant seats. It didn't matter that the numbers weren't as bad as they appeared. The crowd at the Astro Dome looked sparse and dead compared to the lively, young, standing-room-only crowd at Madison Square Gardens. The second thing I noticed was that the venom began to flow from the minute the first speaker walked onto the stage. Each speaker spoke with an exclusion-ary vengeance that built into a hatred for everything that wasn't Republican, white-washed, ultraconservative, and Christian.

And at the very center of the hatred was a symbol of everything that was wrong with America, everything that was bad and evil. A symbol was emerging that to the religious right represented somehow in ways only those who think like these people do could understand. It was a symbol that rolled AIDS, homosexuality, child abuse, condoms, sex outside of marriage, the decline of the white male, all into one neat package and that symbol was Hillary Clinton. I am torn at this point on who, Pat Buchanan or Marilyn Quayle, illustrates this point best. So I will let them both speak:

Pat:

> "Elect me and you get two for the price of one, Mr. Clinton says of his lawyer-spouse," Buchanan declared. "And what does Hillary believe? Well, Hillary believes that twelve-year-olds

should have the right to sue their parents, and Hillary has compared marriage and the family as institutions to slavery—and life
on an Indian reservation.

"Well, speak for yourself, Hillary," Buchanan added, pointing his finger mockingly at the television cameras. "This, my
friends, this is radical feminism."[12]

Marilyn:

> "In my generation," she said, "not everyone believed that the
> family was so oppressive that women could only thrive apart from
> it."
>
> She described unnamed-but-not-unknown liberals as angry.
> "They're disappointed because most women do not wish to be
> liberated from their essential natures as women. Most of us love
> being mothers or wives."[13]

The Republicans totally misread the chasm that had been created by
the feminist movement. The Republicans did not see the depth of
despair of those caught in the middle, that did not want to identify
with either the radical feminist or the ultraconservative traditionalist
side. We were pushed to choose and we chose. We chose: choice, not
decrees; tolerance, not hate; and a youthful future over a failed past.
We chose to remain in the chasm. By choosing Bill and ultimately
Hillary Clinton, we chose not to fall back on one side or the other. We
chose to stay in the chasm because for us that is what Hillary Clinton
had begun to represent—a middle ground, a balance.

> Rosalie, who has raised three children and has not worked
> outside her home since she married more than 40 years ago, is
> about the same age as Barbara Bush. Sixty . . . well, let's just say
> 60 and leave it at that. I can understand why she [Barbara Bush],
> as a woman of our generation, would feel as she does. The
> choices she made, which are very much like the choices I made,
> were the only ones really open to us.
>
> I don't understand why a woman would make them today,
> when it is possible to do the right thing not only for your hus-
> band and children, but also for yourself. If I had to do it over
> again—today—I would have married later so I could have com-
> pleted my education and, once my children were raised, made a
> contribution of my own to others.
>
> That's why I don't understand a young woman like Marilyn

Quayle, who seems willing to sacrifice herself to become a kind of satellite of her husband's ambition. Maybe what this is about is just the fact that she is a lousy lawyer? Maybe that's why the whole bunch of them seem to resent Hillary Clinton so much. Out of the mouths of women with traditional values . . .[14]

We are in a new place. We are seeking new and improved mentors. Women most especially are seeking new role models. The nineties have been touted as the decade of the woman and women's stories need to be heard, not overshadowed by labeling (feminist, lesbian, angry, etc.) but presented *without* prejudgment or bias. We need to wake up to the reality that the feminist movement does not define. Most of us cannot and will not have it all. And we need to accept and understand why that's OK.

WITH HILLARY COMES BALANCE

There are no more supermoms. They went the way of paneled station wagons and "Father Knows Best" reruns. Whew! What a relief. Now we can begin to create the nineties mom out of the retro ashes of the Donna Reed fantasy. Staying at home with a small child is hard work. I repeat *hard work*. It is not the same as when Kitten and Bud were growing up. We have come too far to go back to the perfectly dressed Ann answering the door at eight o'clock in the morning to find her equally perfectly dressed neighbor there waiting for a cup of coffee. We have learned too much about sex, drugs, rock n roll, the stock market, and other real-life realities to think that staying at home and wearing pearls at two o'clock in the afternoon is a desirable possibility. With all the catharting that has gone on within the feminist movement, we realize we can finally be honest and that while we would like to have it all, realistically we *can't*. Maybe, too, what we defined as having it all in the eighties wasn't what we really wanted after all.

We can't all be executives with nannies and perfectly behaved, completely balanced children, gorgeous supportive husbands, lots of interesting friends, and a beautiful, spotless house (I refer you to Zoe Baird's dilemma, if you think it is still possible). A lot of women tried it in the eighties and found out the truth: They were getting up between five-thirty and six to dress themselves, their children, and occasionally, a husband. They and their grumpy spouses and children wolfed down breakfast before leaving the house at seven so that everyone could get to day care, school, or work. Somewhere between five and six the kids would get picked up and then the round of dinner, homework, and housework would begin. By ten the last child was in bed and the parents would grab thirty minutes or so together before they fell asleep on the couch exhausted. The next morning it would begin all over again.

No wonder families fell apart in record numbers in the 1980s. No wonder parents lost touch with their children and spouses lost touch with each other. No one had the time to keep in touch. What little time was spent together as a family was spent on maintenance rather than enhancement of family life.

Yes, there *are* some women out there who have managed to balance a career and a family and have done it very well. The point is that rather than hold these examples up to us in an attempt to make some women feel guilty for not having it all or for not wanting to we should be learning from all the examples the 1980s had to offer us. There are also a number of families that didn't manage the balancing act, and, rather than continue to lose touch with their children, they decided or are in the process of deciding to make the sacrifices necessary—monetary, career, and self-esteem—to have not just a life, but a *family* life. Hillary and Bill Clinton are good examples; yet rather than being rewarded for their struggle, and sticking with it, they were impaled by those whose own role models seemed severely lacking. The religious right, who gave us Jimmy Swaggert and Jim and Tammy Faye Baker, called into question the morals of Hillary and Bill Clinton.

We live in a confusing time, probably even more than in the sixties and seventies. The role of women is even more in question. Families are no longer passé patriarchal institutions, but rather constructions that vary based on the religious, sexual, career, social, political, and gender preferences of those who create them. Slowly we are becoming aware that without some serious attention to our families the very entity that roots our moral, educational, and economic systems will decay and the nation along with it.

THE END OF THE RIDE OR IS IT?

After the triumph of the convention, a much-revitalized and redone Hillary joined the boys on the bus. She didn't just *look* different, she *was* different. There was something much more cautious, more restrained than before. Gail Sheehy, Virginia Postrel, Pat and the Gang, among others, had made her less trusting, less open, and less visible.

The sting of the Republican convention had been felt by George Bush, too. He took trips to Montana and out on the boat. He called back Jim Baker, and he refused to debate—which gave us a reason to have a party. The Pickens County Democratic Party and the Clemson Students for Clinton and Gore held a Where's George party in the lounge at the Holiday Inn in Clemson. We decorated with Clinton-Gore banners, "Where's George?", No Debate-Dodger for President posters, and more and settled in to watch the speech by Clinton given at the sight of the first, now-canceled debate. It was a huge success.

During the real debates we held our breath waiting for it to be over, praying Bill or Al wouldn't screw up. And when Admiral Stockdale spoke, we sat quietly unable to make eye contact, unable to speak it hurt so badly to watch.

BACK ON TOP AT THE AMERICAN GALA

I would like to end with the image I began with—Hillary Clinton at the top of the roller coaster. But this time she's overlooking Washington, D.C., and in many ways the whole of the United States, entering the next landmark period in her life, overseeing the inaugural festivities, and listening to the questions: Is it true she will have an office in the west wing? How will she be held accountable if she doesn't have a government appointment? To quote Lynn Martin, "It's not like the president is going to fire his own wife." Did you see that hat she wore? How much do you thing she spent on that gown? What do you think she will do about . . . and slowly the car on the roller coaster starts moving forward again.

Even as I am finishing this piece, I find myself taking frequent breaks to go and watch my little guy help the big guy wash the car for the first time. It is a Kodak moment I don't want to miss. I have made my choice. I choose a lifestyle that would make other woman (and most men) crazy. I choose a lifestyle that even my own Donna Reed, traditional stay-at-home mom does not understand. She has often said that if she could do it over she would have gotten the education I did and she would have had the career I gave up. She would have tried to have it all. The old saying the grass is always greener seems to fit the struggle between women and women all too well. The struggle between staying at home and nurturing your children or going to work and having the glamorous career is not a universal struggle but an individualized struggle which should take place within each family, and each family should feel the support and the freedom to make that choice. I thank Hillary for working to make our choices a little easier to live with.

NOTES

1. Gregory Bateson, *Sacred Unity: Further Steps toward an Ecology of Mind*, ed. Rodney E. Donaldson (New York: HarperCollins, 1991).

2. Alex Heard, "Standing by Your Men," *New Republic*, 17 February 1992.

3. Bateson, *Sacred Unity*, 117.

4. Gail Sheehy, "What Hillary Wants," *Vanity Fair*, May 1992.

5. Bateson, *Sacred Unity*, 130.

6. Gloria Steinem, "Helping Ourselves to Revolution," *Ms.*, November/ December 1992, 24.

7. Nancy Gibbs, "The War against Feminism," *Time*, 9 March 1992.

8. Ibid., 55.

9. Bateson, *Sacred Unity*, 54.

10. Steinem, "Helping Ourselves to Revolution," 26.

11. Christopher Daly, "Hillary Clinton Faults Capital's Values Lectures," *Washington Post*, 30 May 1992, A10.

12. Jack Nelson and James Gerstenzang, "Buchannan Castigates Both Clinton and His Wife, Hillary," *Los Angeles Times*, 18 August 1992, A1.

13. Ellen Goodman, "GOP Goes Too Far in the Bashing of Hillary Clinton," *Atlanta Journal Constitution*, 22 August 1992, A19.

14. Tim Rutten, "Since When Did Working Women Become the Enemy?" *Los Angeles Times*, 27 August 1992, E1.

IMAGINING THE IMAGE

Reinventing the Clintons

IRVING J. REIN

In the film *The Idolmaker,* a songwriter protagonist practices the art of transforming young Italian males into rock stars. The film, which chronicles the rock period of the sixties, finds the songwriter seeking a replacement for a protegé who now rejects him. In a restaurant scene, the songwriter and a friend strike a bet that a sixteen-year-old busboy chosen there at random can be made into a star. The busboy, who has heavy eyebrows and dark, dramatic, brooding good looks, turns out to have severely limited singing and dancing skills. During an intense period of transformation, the songwriter teaches the young man, whose character is loosely based on the singer Fabian, to walk, talk, sing—to become a star. Having effected the physical and musical transformation, the songwriter markets the ex-busboy throughout the Eastern seaboard and eventually produces a national star.

Is Bill Clinton the Fabian of the nineties? Clearly, the image makers of Bill and Hillary Clinton used many of the same techniques in the nineties that the songwriter of the sixties used to remake Fabian. More important, the dramatic and nonfiction strategies of theater and show business continue to permeate political campaigning, further threatening the public's ability to choose objectively among candidates.

If Fabian is reincarnated in Bill Clinton, a small-town politician masquerading as president, then who were the other candidates? Perhaps George Bush was closest in image to Englebert Humperdinck, an English singer with a fake German name who sings for an audience of middle-aged women. Bush was an apparent middle-of-the-roader, looking in vain for the right fork. Was Perot a political Willie Nelson? Like the singer, Perot was successful in his sector but seemingly paranoid about big government's pursuit of his private life and possessions.

THE WINNING IMAGE

Image has become the god term of the last thirty years in political campaigning, as political studio techniques have become fashionable. Upon superficial examination, image seems directly descended from the Greek term *ethos*. It is a likely association, since each term emphasizes perceptions of the audience and appears to favor personality and character over content. Aristotle's theory of ethos, in fact, had remarkably different attributes than our current understanding of image; Aristotle defined it to be a person's essential character as audiences perceived it. Aristotle argued that speakers must possess moral character, good will, and intelligence in order to possess ethos. Even more to the point, Aristotle claimed that if speakers wanted to be perceived as having ethos, they needed to have it in reality—there was no faking: Ethos could not be put on to fool the public. At its core, ethos meant projection of credibility and trust. Conversely, if you lacked ethos, audiences were unlikely to believe in your presentation; in fact, you could not communicate effectively.

The modern turn on image has more to do with imagination, theater, and putting on a show. In image making, the candidate needs to be malleable and photogenic. The marketing terms *stretch* and *reach* are crucial in creating image, because a character has to have stretch—the elasticity to change—and reach—the core attributes to do so. For example, judging from his 1988 campaign for the presidency, Sen. Bob Dole from Kansas has little stretch and no reach. Conversely, candidates such as Congressman Richard Gephardt, former Sen. Gary Hart, and Bill Clinton all are politicians who will do whatever it takes to reach a political goal: They are malleable and photogenic.

The move to prizing image over ethos is not without consequences. During the final weeks before the election, I spoke to a number of audiences about the strategies of the campaign. I would frequently ask the question, "How many of you feel that you really know the candidates?" The answers, while admittedly anecdotal, were revealing. Most listeners were reluctant to raise their hand. Only 2 or 3 percent felt they knew the three candidates in any meaningful sense. Audience members claimed to know little about the candidates' makeup and felt unsure in ascribing simple attributes. They had lots of information from television, friends, history, observed behavior, and issue discussions, but they didn't feel comfortable in saying, "Yes, I know who the candidates are and I feel confident in my selection."

The irony is that voters today appear to have more information about the candidates than at any other time in history. The '92 campaign was marked by a barrage of information passed through informal channels such as MTV, Arsenio Hall, Larry King, and Phil Donahue. Ross Perot's strategy of using half-hour "infomercials," in which he carefully and sometimes tediously explained his position on the budget deficit, also facilitated information flow. Moreover, the news media adopted the policy of evaluating political positions on a daily basis. Despite this outpouring of information, many voters were still uncertain of the character of their candidates. The voters had the information, but not the understanding.

An important reason that understanding lagged behind information is the campaign managers' and designers' skillful use of image making. There is a long history of imaging candidates in America. Abraham Lincoln, for example, benefited from the services of newspaper publisher Joseph Medill, who helped to redefine Lincoln's image and candidacy. In the early fifties, Rosser Reeves fashioned television advertising for Dwight Eisenhower, using many of the jingle strategies of consumer products —endless variations of "We like Ike" and "The Man from Abilene." Since that advent of television campaign commercials, a steady influx of advertising, public relations, and theatrical strategies have permeated the political campaign business.

The apex of the theatrical influence appeared to be the "Morning in America" commercials that the Republicans designed in the eighties. Sold to audiences as the perfect candidate, Ronald Reagan appeared to Democratic critics as perfect as a packaged box of cereal, preferably Fiber One. This packaging displayed Reagan only in favorable settings with appropriate casting and carefully selected backdrops, including an idealized relationship with his spouse. All signs and symbols were aimed at a single, understandable issue of the day.

During this period the Democrats became upset with the less-effective quality of their campaign commercials and public relations and envied the remarkable results of the Republicans in staging drama. Many Democrats felt the strategies of the Republicans were unfair, outrageous, and demeaning of the public trust. "Democrats don't do that kind of stuff," was a frequently heard claim. Yet, it was galling that the Republican strategies worked; voters were drawn to their souped-up images. The Democrats needed to reinvent their strategy.

FROM HOLLYWOOD TO WASHINGTON

The "stuff" of reinvention is the Hollywoodization of politics combined with an audience that has learned the language of theater. The Republicans did not invent the style changes, which evolved from the refinement of new technologies and from inevitable changes in audience tastes. What they accomplished was a skillful crossover of film-studio transformation and promotion techniques to presidential politics.

The first moment of truth occurred in the early twentieth century when the film industry recognized that stars, not stories, sell admissions. The search for a star began with the promotion of little-known actress Flo Lawrence into a box-office sensation and led quickly to the building of iconic figures such as Douglas Fairbanks and Mary Pickford. Studio heads dramatized stars' lives to give depth and meaning to audiences eager to hear about the stars' public and private escapades.

The need for stars led to a studio system that recruited young men and women from all walks of life. Louis B. Mayer, studio head of Metro Goldwyn Mayer (MGM), ran his operation like a baseball team manager as he polished his prospects so they could rise through the ranks.[1] The system taught aspirants how to dress, sit, walk, and talk. Newly constructed public relations staffs placed the stars in appropriate settings, and staged dates, openings, and lifestyles. Designers of image created story lines for stars to live out and to create fan interest. The studio designer changed the actors' names, invented backgrounds, controlled marriages, and created demand. The awful truth of all these transformations was that they worked. The Clark Gables, Joan Crawfords, and Rita Hayworths had become real, larger-than-life fakes—a privileged group of sheltered superstars.

The system was most adroit at keeping its stars out of trouble. They pioneered such diverse strategies as selecting a studio executive to claim that he, and not Clark Gable, was driving a car that killed a pedestrian.

The executive consequently received a one-year jail sentence, thus saving Gable's career.[2] The studios were experts in public apologies, suppressing information on personal habits, buying off witnesses, reassembling hotel rooms, and using euphemisms to redirect the media and the public. The stakes were high, and the talents assembled to write the releases, organize the film campaigns, and restructure reality were unparalleled.

The studio system died in the forties, and in its place rose agents, managers, producers, and consultants who transferred the methodology to sports, business, medicine, and politics. These sectors had image needs and, more important, the money to finance elaborate transformation campaigns.

Today, the studio system of politics is in full flower. A cadre of consultants—media, campaign, advance, public speaking, speech writing, costume, and staging—are available to redo the candidate. In fact, hiring an all-star team of political experts is a badge of credibility. The visibility of the consultant's work has created an aura of celebrity around the field. Hiring consultants such as Bob Squier, David Axelrod, Jim Carville, or Arthur Finkelstein is one measure of success and can encourage the media to take the candidate's campaign seriously.[3] Calling in a Hollywood producer to "do" the inaugural of a mayor is considered a triumph because the campaign's finance committee, having done first-rate fund-raising, can attract such talent.

THE DEMOCRATIC PROBLEM

Until now, although the Democrats equaled the Republicans in the image game at state and city levels, they lagged at the top spot. Hubert Humphrey, Walter Mondale, Jimmy Carter, and Michael Dukakis were in private largely as they appeared in public—natural, real, unvarnished, and with warts. It was the Republicans who bottled soapsuds, rode parade horses, and created images at the presidential level.

Imagine the surprise of righteous Democrats when the Clinton campaign delivered their slick reinvention of Bill and Hillary. The high point of the invention was the featured piece of the convention, the thirteen-minute film romantically entitled "The Man from Hope." Hollywood producers Harry Thomason and Linda Bloodworth-Thomason of "Designing Women" and "Evening Shade" fame reenacted the Reagan strategy in producing the cinematic type of characters that Americans love. In fact, the Democrats used the phrase "reintroducing Clinton to the American public" when they described the anticipated effect of the film.[4] In a short period, three phenomena—the film's effect, adding Sen. Albert Gore to the ticket, and Ross Perot's withdrawal from the race—propelled Clinton into a fifteen- to twenty-point lead that he held almost to the very end.

What issues compelled the Clinton campaign handlers to reinvent the Clintons? During the winter of 1992, the Clintons weathered some powerful personal attacks, including particularly troubling charges of sexual improprieties. An outbreak of media frenzy fanned Gennifer Flowers's charge of having had a long-term affair with Bill Clinton. As evidence, she produced a taped phone conversation with Clinton that suggested an intimate relationship. The issue was complicated by Clinton's earlier having used political clout to have Flowers appointed to a minor administrative position in the Arkansas state government. Clinton survived the charge, but his image suffered. The Gennifer Flowers incident lingered in the minds of many voters.

For a good stretch, the campaign seemed permanently entrenched in extinguishing Clinton gaffes: marijuana, Madison Bank, and brother Roger. The answers to the embarrassments were not as important as the Clinton style. The new position was to ignore the specifics and con-centrate on his creating a mythical character drawn from entertain-ment.[5] It was a philosophy that made the attacks difficult to sustain as Clinton became inseparable from sitcom characters. He was a star made for TV—prepared, polished, and potent.

Each of the charges whetted the appetite of the media and the pub-lic for exposé. The handling of the charges was often structured as a half-hour television program. Clinton was not unlike "The Fresh Prince of Bel Air," a likable, talented schmoozer who has an unerring ability to put his foot into his mouth and barely extract it by the time the closing credits roll. The parallel is striking even in the use of drugs and in the handling of "brothers." Clinton, of course, never inhaled; and Fresh Prince never used drugs, but he kept them in his school locker ready for an emergency, so neither ever consummated. Fresh Prince lived in his uncle's household as a relative; his symbolic "brother" was a weak, ineffective preppy cousin named Carlton, whom the cool and collected Fresh Prince always saved from himself.

Similarly, Clinton seems to pull his brother, Roger, out of the clutches of some personal or business crisis.[6] Does it make any difference that Clinton is real and Fresh Prince is a fictional character? Or do we now see both of them as sitcom characters? A little trouble was to be resolved in thirty minutes, and Clinton was no more real or imagined than the Fresh Prince.

An additional image problem was the characterization of Hillary Clinton as strident and aggressive in her appearances in the media and before live audiences. Some American voters felt a growing reluctance to accept her "new woman" role as a candidate's spouse who did not cook or do other wifely duties. Rumor indicated that Hillary was really the boss and would run the presidency. These allegations about Hillary Clinton showed up in the polls as strong negatives.

The campaign had a dilemma to resolve. A strong, cross-country wave of sentiment for change coincided with record high anti-incumbent feelings about Bush's handling of the economy and other issues. Yet, there was a reluctance to vote for Clinton, other than as the best alternative. The campaign needed to provide positive reasons for voting for Clinton or run the risk of good economic news moving Bush back into the lead. An even more compelling need was to innoculate Clinton against Republican charges by creating a positive image.

TRANSFORMING THE CLINTONS

What tools allow for change of someone's image? In a political campaign, consultants advocate a number of key elements and charge high fees for that advice. A first consideration is *who defines the candidate*. The three possible definers in campaign terminology are your opponents, the media, or your own campaign handlers. Conventional wisdom asserts that Michael Dukakis advisors allowed Bush to define Dukakis, thus losing the campaign. A related issue is in what defining moments does the public finalize a candidate's image? One defining moment for the Clintons was their appearance on "60 Minutes" to defend themselves against the allegations of Gennifer Flowers. Millions of voters watched the Clintons and formed impressions regarding what they were like, what values they held, and if they were trustworthy. Prepped mainly by Thomason and Bloodworth-Thomason, the Clintons held steady. Voters witnessed an emerging redefinition as

Hillary Clinton gazed adoringly at Bill and the two touched knowingly and seemingly spontaneously. Having dodged the big bullet, the handlers were encouraged to redefine further.

Although the Clintons survived "60 Minutes," the media and the Republicans continued to define their personas. Clearly, with the definition of Bill Clinton as a "womanizer" and a "waffler," the increasingly used phrase "Slick Willie" was cutting too close to the core. He was becoming the all-time champion collector of one-word italics, quotation marks, and exclamation points.

On the other hand, Hillary Clinton was perceived as a left-wing feminist, an aggressive surrogate for her husband. In some ways these qualities were positive: Clinton's waffling was considered pragmatic and even-handed; his wife's new-woman image was seen as progressive and appealing to younger or liberal voters. The campaign handlers, however, believing that the definitions lacked winning potential, decided to assume the power of redefinition.

Four major elements are transformation weapons in a consultant's arsenal.[7] The first is *concept generation,* which concerns finding the appropriate type or character for each of the Clintons. The second is *testing the concept* in a number of venues to see if it works. The third is *concept refinement,* which includes altering signs and symbols such as appearance, behavior, movement, and material. The fourth is *actualization* as the candidate and the concept must meld. In this final stage, a teaching strategy such as role modeling, acting, or behavior modification is used to transform the candidate into the image.

What did the handlers do? They regenerated Clinton as a down-home, exercise-loving family man. Because he was elastic in character, he was as malleable as Silly Putty. In terms of Clinton, certain changes were intentional, others fortuitous: His hair was tinted a distinguished silver[8] and he gained weight, slowing his gait. In some ways, he began to look older than Bush. His suits, bulging at the waistline, gave him the appearance of a slightly frayed family man, hardly the image of a womanizer. It was as if Clinton willed himself a pious persona. More likely, his old image as a ladies' man was allowed to wither as his handlers employed concept refinement to produce a 1950s reproduction of actor Danny Thomas in "Make Room for Daddy."

Crucial to Clinton's concept refinement was his use of language and style. His test on "60 Minutes" featured language that was intimate, informal, and emotional. The encounter had the drama of "Oprah Winfrey" or "Geraldo" as Clinton accused the media of playing a game of "gotcha." At one point he knowingly told the interviewer that Americans got the "drift" about his past. In a virtuoso performance, on cue he challenged the interviewer for insinuating the Clinton marriage was an "arrangement." He went on to mirror the late Duke of Windsor with "We intend to be together thirty or forty years from now whether I run for president or not, and I think that ought to be enough."[9] Early in the campaign, Clinton had discovered that the powerful language of the entertainment programs stirred the American public. He took that insight to the next level when he appropriated the style of television talk-show intimacy. The new Clinton was not a cynical, wayward politician, but a struggling, concerned average Joe trying to save both his unstable marriage and a wounded nation.

The changes in Hillary were even more dramatic. In a remarkably short period, her concept was remade from a strident, liberal feminist, to a soft, adoring homemaker.[10] She had a complete makeover of dress, hair, speaking style, and even speaking material. Early photographs revealed her to be unconcerned about appearance, looking in the seventies as if she had stepped out of a Clifford Odets thirties play. Martha Sherrill observed that Hillary made herself over in the eighties by adopting tailored apparel, blonde hair, and glamorous makeup.[11] The presidential campaign image change was the second makeover of Hillary. In terms of material she became a champion cookie maker, and she and her husband struck a mutual chord of family togetherness. To give the image resonance, northern-raised Hillary assumed a slight Arkansas accent, which startled the folks back home in her adopted state.[12] A further refinement was the creation for Hillary, her friends, and former classmates of venues to meet and extol her warmth and cut-up humor. She was a nineties version of Betty Crocker and all that was missing was a kid.

The sudden appearance of their daughter, Chelsea, living evidence of the commitment between Hillary and Bill, was the thread that bound this image change. It was "Leave It to Beaver," "Make Room for Daddy," and "Mayberry, RFD" all wrapped into one big package. In fact, the Thomason/Bloodworth-Thomason's sitcom "Evening Shade," a weekly prime-time program about life in a small town in Arkansas, came to virtual reality as a Clinton campaign vehicle. Many

Clinton campaign themes and travails were chronicled in the show that reached twenty-three million viewers a week.[13] Incidentally, it aired opposite "Fresh Prince."

The moment when all image elements coalesced was at the annual Democratic convention in June of 1992. That convention evening in New York was among the most orchestrated in political history. The "eventing" began with Bill and Hillary Clinton walking through the streets of New York leading to the convention site, recreating many of the same emotional strategies of the Frank Capra film, *Mr. Smith Goes to Washington*. Their march included a visit to Macy's department store and greetings to various supporters, allies, and political leaders spotted along the way. The Clinton family symbolically gathered the plain folks to march on the Establishment.

The short campaign film "The Man from Hope" created new themes about the Clintons and reinvented some others. The film itself made no mention of governing policy. In contrast, material followed a completely emotional level intended to increase the Clintons' ethos. For example, for the first time Bill Clinton's family background was introduced to the public. His deceased father was characterized as having been an alcoholic with whom Bill had almost fought physically.[14] His mother, presented as a pillar of small-town values, ostensibly held the family together. Bill himself seemed to be an Eagle Scout version of Kevin in the "Wonder Years"—hard working, a leader, and mostly pure.

At the film's culmination, President Jack Kennedy greeted young Bill, a high school student on a special leadership trip to Washington. The Kennedy clip embodied the moment in which Clinton was transformed from an Arkansas adolescent into a man destined to lead this country. This example of leadership-by-association was somewhat preposterous, as if Jack Kennedy had somehow passed the torch to Bill Clinton to lead the country thirty-two years later. Audiences raised on "I Dream of Jeannie," "Bewitched," and *Ghost* can relate to out-of-body experiences.

An example of the sitcom style of "The Man from Hope" was Hillary's description of her first meeting with Bill. While he was talking to a group of fellow students at Yale Law School about his future, his eyes met hers—there was this connection, she boldly walked over to him and said, "Well, if we're going to stare at each other I might as well introduce myself. I'm Hillary Rodham." Absolute romance! If Ron and Pat could ignite sparks, so could the Clintons.

The rest of the film emphasized their Arkansas roots, family, and contentment with each other. It was the joining of perfection and clearly it worked. Using the language and style of sitcoms, the film struck a responsive chord with the audience. The voice-overs, the music, the enactments all were drawn from half-hour television. No complicated arguments about the economy and jobs intruded: They would follow in the acceptance speech that Clinton would deliver. Using the sitcom style and the restructuring of the Clintons' behavior, movements, and dialogue, the filmmakers spoke a language that millions of Americans could relate to.

Even more telling was the further restructuring of reality. Deciding that the small town of Hope was an excellent metaphor for Clinton's life, the filmmakers portrayed him as smitten with the town. Yet, the facts of the case are different. Clinton lived in Hope until he was seven years old and then moved to Hot Springs, where he was raised. Before the reinvention, he rarely returned to Hope or mentioned it. The strategy of isolating and exaggerating a small part of the candidate's life is classic studio image making.

WHY IMAGE MAKING WORKS

Clearly, it is crucial for winning to seize the power of definition before the other candidate does. Both parties know these types of strategies. Then why did image-reinvention work for Clinton and not for Bush? Given the free marketplace and the ability to buy image services, why is it more effective for one candidate than another?

Despite the advantages of technology and the use of theatrical strategies, many candidates discover innovative ways to lose. Some candidates just can't handle change, and find redefinition onerous. To one degree or another, candidates such as Ross Perot, Sen. Paul Simon, and Paul Tsongas have resisted the change strategies of their handlers.[15]

A related problem is for a candidate to attempt a character change that is too far from the original. Voters often mistrust a free trader who suddenly advocates managed trade. In the 1988 presidential primary, Richard Gephardt suddenly became an unabashed protectionist, after a decades-long political career of pushing free trade. He became the object of fierce criticism and it took him down.

Second is the problem of de-linking. Key people often break from the candidates and their absence causes lapses in strategy. In the failed 1992 campaign of George Bush, Lee Atwater's death was crucial in that he had been a key figure in pulling together the '88 campaign.

Third, a candidate may believe in his or her own transformation and become difficult to manage. Candidates sometimes believe that the new image is their real self and forget what got them there in the first place.

Fourth, there are cycles; different styles appeal at different times. For example, in the early fifties, Dwight Eisenhower appealed to members of both parties as a former general who was organized, who possessed unquestioned integrity, and who was the hero of a post–World War II population.

Fifth are cultural limitations. Concerns about big business or environment take over in certain periods. A real concern for self and getting ahead in the business world marked the eighties. In the campaign of 1992, issues that favored Clinton, such as global economic competition and the environment, were important to his success.

Sixth is the failure to understand how the public perceives an image. It becomes hard for people working in a campaign to step outside and observe what is effective. As campaign pressures intensify, handlers sometimes don't get close enough to the audience to understand it. Ross Perot and his story of a conspiracy against his daughter and Bush and his audience's devastating questions during the second debate are both examples where the candidates seemed to lose touch with their own image, their own perception, and what the audience could possibly infer.

Why did the Clinton reinvention take hold? There are three reasons for the successful transformation. The first is the malleability of Bill Clinton, who can play different roles easily and effortlessly. The marijuana episode demonstrates this quality. By claiming he took the drug but did not inhale, in one stroke, he managed to proclaim his hip, sixties radical side, and in the same breath project himself as a square, band-member nerd who shops at Wal-Mart.

The second reason is Clinton's need to please an audience. Seemingly addicted to the smell of grease paint and the roar of the crowd, he leapt offstage into crowds suspended only by the security forces who clung to his pants belt. A born crowd pleaser will change costume to win an audience.

The third quality is Clinton's faith in political talent. He knows the campaign process better than most advisors. He understands redefinition and is willing to undergo it. Clinton's faith in political expertise is also an edge when the pressure is on and the campaign is wobbling. He is less likely to panic and permanently damage his campaign.

Significantly, the three qualities of Clinton are more similar to Reagan than to Bush. In Bush, the Republicans had a candidate who wanted to be himself. In the image-age business, Bush was no Elvis.

CONCLUSION

Entertainment has taken over politics just as it has taken over sports, business, and medicine. The reason these strategies dominate is because they work. Because of the strategies' power and persuasiveness, the media, candidates, and advisors all are playing their part to make entertainment-style politics effective.

The candidates who allow themselves to become manipulated images are not totally to blame. In most cases, the candidate recognizes that the style wins elections, and that in order to implement their agendas, the candidate must win. The problem short-term is that the voters often receive messages that are inaccurate, incomplete, or misleading. In the long-term, candidates who become elected officials frequently cannot shake their sitcom image and regain what they consider their true selves. In some cases, the campaign image makers stay on to govern as the elected official finds he or she is permanently bound to the campaign mode.

There is always Hope. There is no question that there will be countermovements. For example, Russell Feingold from Wisconsin was elected to the Senate using a cinema verité hand-held camera strategy. Feingold and other candidates such as Paul Wellstone of Minnesota fought slickness and were successful. However, in general, the carefully prepared image is still the defining characteristic of major political campaigns. In *The Idolmaker*, the songwriter, having lost control of his second transformed singer, tries to make himself into a star—just don't expect that to happen to those who handle potential candidates for office. They know the pitfalls of standing alone in the limelight.

NOTES

1. Charles Higham, *Merchant of Dreams: Louis B. Mayer, M.G.M. and the Secret Hollywood* (New York: Donald I. Fine), 105.

2. Ibid., 211.

3. The media cover the signing of celebrity consultants with the same reverence as the reporting of an NFL football coach switching teams. It was considered a triumph of the Clinton campaign to lure Carville after his successful management of the Harris Wofford senatorial campaign in Pennsylvania.

4. When the author confronted a Clinton consultant with charges of Hollywoodization, the charges were defensively and quickly countered. The consultant claimed that Clinton was unknown to the public and needed to be "reintroduced" in a formal manner. The use of "reintroduce"—a friendly and benign term—was telling.

5. Jacob Weisberg, "Southern Exposure," *New Republic,* 2 November 1992, 13–15. Weisberg documented the Thomasons' strategy of "designing a mythic backdrop for the Clintons" and developed the relationship between "Evening Shade" and the Clinton sitcom campaign.

6. Priscilla Painton, "The Burden of Being Bill's Brother," *Time,* 18 January 1993, 52–54. Painton sees Roger "cast as the suburban version of Billy Carter . . ."

7. See Irving Rein, Philip Kotler, and Martin Stoller, *High Visibility* (New York: Dodd, Mead, 1987), 194–240.

8. Jeanne Moos, "Does He or Doesn't He?" Cable News Network, 17 October 1992. Hairstylist Christopher Zerebny said, "He probably uses something like a Grecian Formula type. . . . Nobody's hair is really that color naturally."

9. Robert Shogan and David Lauter, "Clinton Seeks Brass Ring," *Los Angeles Times,* 4 June 1992, 1.

10. See Michael Kelly and Maureen Dowd, "The Company He Keeps," *New York Times Magazine,* 17 January 1993, 26–27.

11. Martha Sherrill, "The Retooling of the Political Wife," *Washington Post,* 13 January 1993, D1.

12. Charles F. Allen and Jonathan F. Portis, *The Comeback Kid: Life and Career of Bill Clinton* (New York: Birch Lane Press, 1992), 216.

13. Weisberg, "Southern Exposure," 13–15. Weisberg argues that both "Evening Shade" and Thomason/Bloodworth-Thomason's "Designing Women" emphasize New South values which are often identical to the Clinton agenda.

14. The key word in many of Clinton's accomplishments is *almost.* He almost smoked marijuana; he is almost a conservative Democrat; he is almost committed to a balanced budget; and he almost wanted to be drafted.

15. One version of the Ross Perot dropout revolved around his refusal to become more voter friendly; Paul Tsongas was urged to broaden his appeal, but stayed Paul; as a debate advisor to another Paul in 1988, Paul Simon, I can personally vouch for Simon's unwillingness to change his image.

THE NEW YORK CONVENTION

Bill Clinton and "A Place Called Hope"

LARRY D. SMITH

The quadrennial presidential nominating conventions are many things to many people. Politicians, journalists, communications technicians, public-relations specialists, and their respective entourages pursue a variety of personal and professional agendas throughout this carefully orchestrated four-night event. While lounging between shows, participants are bombarded by "special editions" of the nation's print media such as the lengthy inserts produced by the local newspapers, the host of newspapers flown in from around the country, and the detailed "convention previews" presented in the national news magazines (e.g., *Time, Newsweek, U.S. News and World Report*). Typically, these magazines feature in-depth interviews with prominent convention personalities. We open this chapter with *Time*'s Democratic National Convention preview and its interview with Arkansas governor Bill Clinton.

Governor Clinton had an extremely tough primary campaign. Few candidates for the presidency have experienced the level of personal scrutiny Clinton endured. But *no candidate* charged with marital infidelity, drug use, military draft evasion, and anti-American activities has *ever* survived the primaries and won his party's presidential nomination. Clinton did. And now his charge was to use the New York convention to transform his candidacy from a regional, individually oriented campaign to a national, party-based contest. Clinton's perspective on his task was evident in his *Time* interview:

> We live in a time when the politics of personal destruction have been proved very effective. This President [George Bush] got

there not with a vision but by first taking out his primary opponents and then taking out his general-election opponent. We also live in a time when people think pretty poorly about anybody who is in public life. So you carry that baggage with you, and winning the primary process has often been almost as much a negative as a positive. Then you've got probably the deepest disillusionment with the American political system in my lifetime, much deeper than it was at Watergate. . . . It means I've got a real job to do to demonstrate to people that I'm not part of the problem. . . . I think I'm being given a chance in effect to start again.[1]

Indeed, like over two-thirds of the nominees before him, Clinton did not travel to New York to "win" his party's presidential nomination; to the contrary, his mission involved the creation of party-wide support for his primary campaign victory. Citing the lone resolution appearing in the first presidential convention's platform (Andrew Jackson and the Democrats in 1832), Dan Nimmo and I explain this phenomenon and apply it to our study of the 1988 conventions: "Just as the first national convention of a major political party in 1832 did not 'nominate' a candidate for president, but instead cordially concurred in repeated endorsements by various state legislatures, so too in 1988 neither major party convened to nominate, but instead to legitimate endorsements by voters in statewide presidential primaries."[2] The 1992 Democrats also faced the institutional challenge that is the orchestration of "cordial concurrence." Yet, *Clinton's* candidacy required more. The themes to emerge from the New York convention had to do more than establish party unity for the fall campaign; they had to embrace the various attacks on Clinton's character as well.

This essay examines the narrative strategy Clinton and the Democrats used to respond to this situation. The following pages reveal how the 1992 Democratic National Convention (DNC) wisely opted for a convention narrative with two levels of development: the *party's* "People First: New Covenant" tale and the *presidential nominee's* "I believe in a place called Hope" story. Through such narrative tactics the DNC and Clinton achieved harmony between the party/candidate stories, articulated a fall campaign capable of deflecting the "character issue," and, in general, orchestrated a successful convention. I begin with a brief theoretical overview and follow with the specifics from 1992.

ORCHESTRATING CORDIAL CONCURRENCE:
A NARRATIVE VIEW

A consideration of convention orchestration as a narrative process necessarily begins with the assembly's institutional function. Paul T. David, Ralph M. Goldman, and Richard C. Bain offer the definitive word regarding the institutional functions presidential nominating conventions perform.[3] Through nomination, platform, campaign-rally, and governing-body activities, the parties attempt to solidify, and occasionally expand, their resources for the general election. Over the years these various activities have been allocated their own moments in the convention program: party business (e.g., seating delegations, selecting convention officers, organizing committees) is conducted early on Monday; platforms are now discussed and drafted prior to the convention and ratified on Tuesday; demonstrations and entertainment (campaign-rally enactments) appear throughout; the nominating/voting activities occur on Wednesday (for president) and Thursday (for vice-president); and the national committee members interact during the week and officially meet on Friday. These various institutional acts comprise what 1988 Republican convention manager Bill Phillips termed the convention's "shell." Phillips's executive assistant, Merri Jo Cleair, explained that once the convention's order of business (the shell) is in place, convention programmers fill in "the entertainment or speeches and the special effects and the things you do for television."[4] In other words, the convention programmers build a "show" around the convention's institutional "shell" that is designed to introduce a "keynote" theme on Monday and maintain thematic continuity throughout the four-day event.

To suggest, then, that the conventions are "extended dramas" that lend themselves to narrative critique appears to be a supportable claim.[5] Here I evaluate the narrative continuity of the 1992 DNC by way of the three-step technique I call narrative synthesis.[6] The method first involves a recognition of the narrative's function and, from that starting point, reduces the subject matter to its constituent parts (i.e., characters, values, and plots). Afterward, those raw materials are organized into a composite text that reflects the story's theoretical implications. This approach has proved useful in critiques of dialectical narratives (network television news) that attempt to separate fact from fiction for audiences, rhetorical narratives (convention oratory and party platforms) that pursue persuasive goals, and poetic narratives (Bruce Springsteen's lyrics) that involve artistic expression.[7]

I maintain convention discourse is a "rhetorical" narrative that pursues three persuasive objectives: (a) to identify the combatants (the "us" vs. "them" characterizations central to a two-party system's rhetoric); (b) to establish party values; and (c) to generate story lines that provide motives for partisan action. The following pages interpret these narrative elements as they appear in the 1992 New York convention's oratory, party platform, and video presentations.[8] The findings indicate the extent to which the Democrats successfully orchestrated "cordial concurrence" and party unity through a two-phase narrative strategy that cast their presidential ticket in terms acceptable to a diverse constituency and, correspondingly, established a narrative posture capable of withstanding the much-anticipated Republican attacks on Clinton's character. Let us begin with the "party story."

THE 1992 DEMOCRATIC NATIONAL CONVENTION: THE PARTY STORY

Losers of five of the last six presidential elections, the Democrats gathered in New York armed with the traditional "time for a change" argument. Relying on the four-session approach that requires convention participants to endure six- and seven-hour sessions, the 1992 DNC used narrative tactics that managed to ease the pain that accompanies this marathon convention style. Monday's floor-based overview of female U.S. Senate candidates and three-tier keynote (featuring Bill Bradley, Zell Miller, and Barbara Jordan), Tuesday's reasonably smooth platform ratification and its now-traditional appearance by Jesse Jackson, Wednesday's nominating and voting rituals, and Thursday's acceptance speeches unfolded in a slow but systematic fashion.

The DNC told a story of change through a "New Covenant: People First" plot that contained two parts. From Monday through Wednesday the Democrats argued for the need for change (part one) through traditional convention rhetoric based on the "us versus them" grammar of a two-party contest. Once that need had been established, the DNC followed with part two of the show and Thursday night's emphasis on the presidential ticket. Wednesday featured a transition from "the need for change" to the "agents of change" by way of a strategic appeal to party history: The DNC used a segment honoring Robert F. Kennedy to establish its ticket's political heritage, to anchor its emphasis on "people first" via a romantic construction of Kennedy's philosophy, and to issue a direct appeal to the "Reagan Democrats" to return to their party. Whereas the 1988 Democrats labored to recast their party through slogans such as "this is not your father's party" and an abridged platform, the 1992 Democrats took the opposite path. The New York Democrats directly embraced party history as they offered a "new argument," not a "new party." "The New Covenant" represented an attempt to unify traditional Democrats against a common foe (the evil elites that comprise the GOP, of course, personified in George Bush and Dan Quayle). Hence, they relished party history, described the evil qualities of Republican policies and personalities, and turned to a ticket that offered a new plan (the New Covenant) that featured values (people first) predicated on a remodeled party history. Undeclared presidential candidate Ross Perot's Thursday morning announcement that he would not run for office further enhanced the Democrats' show. After three days of arguing for "change," the Thursday night emphasis on the "agents of change" received a boost from Perot's departure as the competing agent of change removed himself from the contest.

Essential to the successful orchestration of cordial concurrence is the management of the stage production itself. The New York convention turned to Hollywood-based producer Gary Smith producer of the 1988 Atlanta DNC to orchestrate his second consecutive convention. Smith used a telegenic mixture of films, remote broadcasts, alternative forms of presentation (e.g., having the female Senate candidates address the assembly from the convention floor), and a coherent script to present the New Covenant story. Smith's creative use of the "video wall" positioned behind the rostrum facilitated the production's thematic qualities. For instance, when speakers addressed the convention the video wall featured the words *people first* softly displayed within the various murals (sketches of Clinton, scenes of Americana, etc.) and thereby constantly reinforced a single theme (the words *Responsibility, Opportunity,* and *Community* also appeared). Assuredly, the 1992 DNC was a tightly packaged affair that reflected Smith's experience with party conventions.

For additional insight into the party narrative that emerged from New York, we turn to the characters portrayed in the story. In other writings I argue that convention rhetoric often features "broad appeals to widely admired values and stories" that are given a sharp partisan edge through the characterization process.[9] Through party characterizations, the 1992 "heroes and villains" are created in an effort to "generate conflict" since "In the absence of conflict, citizens and voters have few reasons for partisanship; as a result, party characterizations may be blunt, oversimplified, and insulting." The 1992 DNC most certainly subscribed to this narrative principle.

The DNC harmonized a "party of the past vs. the party of the future" tune in which it lambasted the "Reagan-Bush years" and the economic recession Democrats attributed to the two administrations. Gov. Ann Richards (Texas) proclaimed: "We're tired of hearing about the eighties, they are over. We're tired of hearing about the Reagan era; it's over." Atlanta mayor Maynard Jackson transformed Ronald Reagan's 1984 campaign theme ("morning in America") to his rhetorical advantage: "There's mourning in America all right. There's weeping and mourning." Jackson continued: "Let us tell Bush and Quayle 'if you fool us once, shame on you. But if you fool us twice, shame on us.'" Unlike the 1988 Atlanta convention and its reluctance to directly attack Ronald Reagan, the New York Democrats did not hesitate to attack the Reagan-Bush administration.

Many attacks involved foreign and domestic issues; more focused on Bush's leadership. With regard to foreign policy, examples include Jesse Jackson's claim that it is "racist and wrong" for the Bush administration to "lock the Haitians out" and the party platform's concern for "national security" matters. Yet the bulk of the DNC's attack strategy blasted Bush's domestic policies and his leadership style. For instance, Party Chair Ron Brown labeled Bush's administration a "failed presidency" and Gov. Mario Cuomo (New York) described Bush's leadership style through a maritime metaphor. The governor lamented "the ship of state is in trouble" and argued:

> The crew knows it. The passengers know it. Only the captain of the ship, President Bush, appears not to know it. He seems to think that the ship will be saved by imperceptible undercurrents, directed by the invisible hand of some cyclical economic god,

that will gradually move the ship so that at the last moment it will miraculously glide past the rocks to safer shores.

The crux of Bush's "leadership problem"—according to Democrats— was the president's lack of political vision. Keynoter Bill Bradley attempted to lead a cheerleading session by describing Bush's reaction to the deficit, rising health-care costs, the Los Angeles riots, and the environment. The New Jersey senator said Bush "waffled and wiggled and wavered" on these crucial matters. Charleston (South Carolina) mayor Joe Riley Jr. described the Bush administration as "visionless" and "directionless"; Louisville (Kentucky) mayor Jerry Abramson announced the country could no longer wait for Bush to "rediscover America" and "get it right the second time"; Maxine Waters maintained "we can't wait around for George Bush to develop the 'vision thing,' we need Bush to get ready for the 'exit thing'"; and, Ron Brown suggested the president was helpless: "George Bush, the guy who's fallen and just can't get up."

Joining the DNC's portrayal of Bush's leadership style were relentless attacks on his economic policies and the perceived lack of compassion that inspired those decisions. Bronx borough president Fernando Ferrer said Bush had "presided over the largest dismantling of the American economy since 1929" and renamed the president "George 'what-recession?' Bush." Sen. Harris Wofford (Pennsylvania) concluded Bush "must have pushed the snooze button" when the "economic alarm" sounded. "George Bush has driven the world's most powerful economy into the ditch," declared John Martin, chairman of the National Association of State Legislators. Former presidential candidate Paul Tsongas maintained: "The Bush legacy is clear. America has become the greatest debtor nation on earth, increasingly unable to compete in world trade markets as it sinks further into debt. He has taken the treasure of ten generations and sacrificed it to false happy days political rhetoric." Another presidential hopeful, Sen. Tom Harkin (Iowa) dubbed Bush "George Herbert Hoover Bush," and—in one of the DNC's most colorful remarks—Rep. Alan Wheat (Missouri) observed that "nobody can do that voodoo better than you do."

Accompanying these attacks on economic matters were negative portrayals of the Republicans' electoral strategy and political philosophy. Cuomo labeled the GOP tactics as a "cynical political arithmetic that says you can add by subtracting, you multiply by dividing." Joe Riley noted Republicans "divide us, to pit urban against rural, city against suburb, rich against poor." Hubert Price, president of the National Association of Democratic County Officials, harmonized that Bush and the Republicans responded to cries of suffering with "a constant stream of platitudinous el toro pooh pooh." Former presidential candidate Sen. Bob Kerrey (Nebraska) offered a personal view by stating, "I'm a man who became a Democrat in 1978 because I do not believe the Republican party gives a damn about the American people." And, in an emotional speech that recounted how she and her two children had contracted the AIDS virus, Elizabeth Glaser recalled: "Exactly four years ago my daughter died of AIDS. She did not survive the Reagan administration. I am here because my son and I may not survive four more years of leaders who say they care, but do nothing."

Complementing the negative portrayals of Bush and the Republicans were predictable descriptions of the Democratic party and its nominee. The 1992 DNC portrayed itself as the party of inclusion, the party of change, and as a party that respects its political history. Throughout, DNC speakers depicted Clinton as the embodiment of these treasured principles. For example, Cuomo commended Clinton because he "believes, as we all here do, in the first principle of our commitment, the politics of inclusion," and Ron Brown claimed Clinton brought "together under one great, vibrant tent people of all races, genders, sexual orientations, classes, ethnic groups, religions, and the disabled of America." Rep. Jose Serrano (New York) said, "Bill Clinton is the embodiment of the American dream" and that the Arkansas governor had "faced difficulties and obstacles to his progress that George Bush and Dan Quayle could never imagine much less overcome." Lastly, Boston mayor Raymond Flynn identified Clinton as someone "who knows what it means to come from a family that lives from paycheck to paycheck," to which keynoter Gov. Zell Miller (Georgia) added Clinton "feels our pain, shares our hopes and will work his heart out to fulfill our dreams."

To anchor these characterizations in party tradition, the DNC revisited party history. Richard Gephardt noted that the 1992 convention had returned the party to its "historic role as agent of our enduring American revolution." Keynoter Barbara Jordan described the party's historic role as "the instrument of change in policies which impact education, human rights, civil rights, economic and social opportunity and the environment." Ron Brown forcefully affirmed, "We stand for the noble past of Roosevelt and Truman and Kennedy and Carter." And a film on the DNC platform identified the New York Democrats as the descendants of Thomas Jefferson. Moreover, the convention's tribute to Robert F. Kennedy (featuring a film and speeches by Joseph and Edward Kennedy) conveyed RFK's legendary idealism and compassion for the disadvantaged and oppressed. Correspondingly, Cuomo's nomination speech cast the Arkansas governor as a leader who "cherishes the ideals of justice, liberty, and opportunity and fairness and compassion that Robert Kennedy died for."

Joining the strategic construction of identities that establish the battle lines for the fall campaign is the articulation of party values that, in effect, provide the rationale for these "good" and "evil" characterizations. Speakers described their commitment to "compassion," for "individual prosperity," and for the proverbial "American Dream" (to name but a few of these value-laden clichés). Of course, these partisans also explain the evil qualities of the opposition by noting their detachment, their abuse of privilege, and their "insincerity." For the DNC, values such as compassion, hope (in fact, the nominee was born in Hope, Arkansas), social responsibility, and tolerance battled Republican indifference, elitism, and irresponsibility.

The most direct statements of party values are found in the respective platforms. Since these documents are the only institutionally approved statements of partisan resolve available, much debate surrounds their contents. The 1992 Democratic platform moved away from its 1988 edition (a seven-page "letter to the American people") and returned to convention tradition via a ten-thousand-word document.[10] The New York platform, entitled "A New Covenant," represented an attempt to recast the party's liberal history in more moderate terms. Thus, the *Chicago Tribune* described the document as a "self-help platform" that argues for a "new social contract" between the American people and their government.[11] With phrases such as "governments don't raise children, people do" and with attacks on "big government theory that says we can hamstring business and tax and spend our way to prosperity," the DNC platform displayed "whole sections that would have been hooted down not too many years ago."[12] After describing "the last twelve years" of "Republican irresponsibility and neglect" which has inspired "the anguish and the anger of the American people," the DNC platform calls for *A Revolution in Government*.[13] The document's preamble reflects the argument:

> To make this revolution, we seek a NEW COVENANT to repair the damaged bond between the American people and their government, that will expand OPPORTUNITY, insist upon greater individual RESPONSIBILITY in return, restore COMMUNITY and insure NATIONAL SECURITY in a profoundly new era.

The DNC platform stressed virtues such as personal responsibility, strengthening the family, and the need for military might—all values that would find a positive reception in any GOP platform. The New York platform also endorsed liberal positions such as government-paid abortions for the poor, higher taxes on the wealthy, and civil rights protection for homosexuals. This move toward the middle inspired D. Rosenbaum to write: "The platform . . . puts new conservative words to an old liberal tune in an attempt to find a middle road between the unfettered capitalism espoused by Republicans and the welfare state economics of the Democrats' past."[14] The narrative logic of the Democrats' 1992 platform was reinforced from the rostrum as well.

The Democrats countered the "government is the problem" theme used by the Republicans throughout the 1980s by portraying government, and the office of president, as powerful forces for "good." For instance, Sen. Patrick Moynihan (New York) identified Democrats as people who believe that "government can embrace great causes, do great things," and Clinton defined the president's role "as a powerful force for progress." Yet, the DNC tempered its view of government with a strong call to individual responsibility via an emphasis on individual initiative and responsibility (themes that would be welcome at any 1980s Republican convention). As we shall soon observe, Clinton used biblical imagery to label the concept: "I call this approach a New Covenant—a solemn agreement between the people and their government—based not simply on what each of us can take but on what all of us must give to our nation." Democrats consistently harmonized the New Covenant tune and the value of shared responsibility between government and the citizenry. To that end, Sen. John Breaux (Louisiana) advocated "forg[ing] a New Covenant that asks all of our citizens to give something back in return for what this country gives them" and Rep. Dave McCurdy (Oklahoma) maintained "government is not some automatic teller machine drawing on someone else's account. Anyone who receives from government has an obligation to give something back."

The DNC used a widely shared value—"People First"—to anchor its New Covenant rhetoric in party history. The words *people first* frequently appeared on the video wall behind the speakers and served as the convention's dominant value appeal. Ron Brown affirmed that Democrats know that government works best when it puts "people first." Bill Bradley challenged the party not only to win the presidential election, but "to give American men and women control over their lives once again." Tom Harkin used the theme to draw a distinction between the two major presidential candidates' economic plans: "Governor Clinton's plan puts people first, George Bush's plan puts wealthy people first." After three days of "people first" graphics, films, and speeches, Clinton's acceptance speech issued the capstone call: "Our priorities must be clear: we will put people first again."

The party's "New Covenant: People First" story emphasized three issues that supported the value of shared responsibility: jobs, health care, and education. Many statements, such as Queens borough president Claire Schulman's, addressed all three issues. Schulman stated: "[Clinton] knows that the most critical issue facing us today is the creation of meaningful and important jobs for our citizens. He believes in a national health care plan that provides quality care for all Americans. And he will be an education President who provides equal and quality education for all our children." Exploiting the predictable Republican "family values" argument, Lena Guerrero affirmed that "the most fundamental family value in America: a job." Arkansan Lottie Shackelford discussed the education issue by noting that Clinton "knows how important education can be in changing people's lives because it changed his." And Jay Rockefeller used self-deprecating humor to discuss health care, "Americans deserve health care that you don't have to be a Rockefeller to afford." To be sure, the New York convention articulated a coherent, historically grounded story that cast the characters and values of the 1992 election in a manner that inspired party unity. Furthermore, Gary Smith orchestrated the various elements of the New Covenant production in a superb fashion. That program now turned to its "star" and the New York narrative's second phase: "I believe in a place called Hope."

THE 1992 DEMOCRATIC NATIONAL CONVENTION: THE BILL CLINTON STORY

The New York production moved from the "need for change" to the "agents of change" by way of yet another appeal to party history. On Wednesday evening, after the "roll call of the states," Bill, Hillary, and Chelsea Clinton offered a telepolitical version of an act John Kennedy performed in 1960. That is, the nominee and his family appeared in the convention hall for a brief statement. The Clinton family walked through a mall adjoining Madison Square Garden (of course, accompanied by television cameras; hence, the telepolitical features of this symbolic act) as the convention hall watched on the many TV monitors in the Garden. Once on stage, Clinton stated:

> The rules of this convention preclude my acceptance tonight but thirty-two years ago another young candidate who wanted to get this country moving again came to the convention to say a simple thank you. And so I want to thank Dave McCurdy and Maxine Waters and magnificent Mario Cuomo for putting my name in nomination tonight. I want to thank you all for being here and loving your country and to tell you that tomorrow night I will be the comeback kid. Good night and God bless you all.

That the Clinton and DNC campaign staffs had carefully articulated a story that strategically cast the nominee in a romantic version of party history is clear. Such was the nature of the *party's* portion of the DNC narrative. Now that story turned in a different direction to the intensely personal introductions of the Democrats' presidential ticket.

Thursday night is always the tightest portion of the four-day show: Speaking times are closely monitored; demonstrations are rigorously regulated; and the party's share of the television networks' "prime time" carefully cultivated. Party conventions exercise considerable care in introducing their nominees, and the 1992 DNC most certainly abided by that tradition.

Thursday night opened with two tributes, one for Mo Udall and one citing prominent Democrats who have died since the 1988 convention. A series of speeches followed, featuring John Breaux, Doug Wilder, Richard Gephardt, and George Mitchell (among others). Afterward, Barbara Mikulski, Tim Wirth, and John Lewis nominated Al Gore for the vice-presidency; the DNC suspended the rules (thereby dismissing the required roll call of the states) and nominated Gore by acclamation; and a film introduced the Tennessean. Gore offered an intensely personal speech that featured few attacks and many appeals to basic values. By probing the depths of his personal life (in particular, an accident that almost killed his son) and stressing the values of his upbringing, Gore effectively set the scene for Clinton's remarks. A brief demonstration followed Gore; the convention heard from singer Jennifer Holiday; and Ann Richards introduced the Clinton film. With a sketch of Clinton displayed on the video wall, Richards explained: "Bill Clinton is not a creation of the media or of this party. He's not a cardboard cut-out candidate. He is a real human being: a son, a father, a husband and a friend. And those of us who know and respect Bill Clinton want you to know that this Democratic party has a presidential nominee that you would be proud to call your friend."

Recent introductory films have used a variety of tactics: Reagan's 1984 historical overview of his first term (narrated by the president), Mondale's (1984) and Bush's (1988) mix of personal scenes and professional histories (narrated by professional announcers), Dukakis's (1988) tour of his home town hosted by his Academy Award-winning cousin Olympia, and Bush's (1992) Robert Mitchum–narrated feature on "The Presidency." Of these approaches, Clinton followed Reagan's style   a personally narrated, intensely emotional portrait that used production techniques (soft close-ups, historical video, and light musical accompaniment) that enhanced the film's intimate tone.

The thirteen-minute, thirty-seven-second video unfolds in four parts. Part one features Clinton's, his wife's (Hillary), his mother's (Virginia Kelley), and his brother's (Roger) recollections about the nominee's formative years in Hope, Arkansas, and beyond. Part two introduces the political leaders that shaped Clinton's philosophy (John and Robert Kennedy and Martin Luther King). Part three returns to personal matters, and Part four offers a closing collage that synthesizes the previous historical events with the 1992 presidential campaign.

The film opens with a black-and-white photograph of the "Hope" train station and Clinton's narration about life in this small southern town (accompanied by "home video" and various still photos of Hope). There Clinton recalls his father's death (Bill was born three months after his father died in an automobile accident), his mother's struggle, and his grandparents' values. Of particular interest are Clinton's recollections regarding his grandparents' opposition to segregation and their progressive world view. The film continues with Hillary Clinton's thoughts about Clinton's grandparents (and how they "valued education above all else"), Virginia Kelley's memories of young Bill and a teen-age confrontation with his stepfather (Clinton's stepfather was an alcoholic prone to violence, and Kelley recounts how Clinton, then in the ninth grade, confronted his stepfather and demanded "don't you ever, ever lay your hand on my mother again"), and Roger Clinton's thoughts about life with his brother. This segment concludes with a close-up of Bill Clinton and this statement: "I was raised to believe in this country, to believe in this system, to believe that elections were good things that gave people a chance to have their say and change the course of events."

The film then moves to part two and its "political positioning" through scenes of Clinton meeting John Kennedy and video of Martin Luther King and Robert Kennedy. There brother Roger recalls young Bill reciting King's "I have a dream" speech "by heart," and Clinton contends the speech represents "the greatest political speech of my lifetime." Part three features cuts between Hillary and Bill Clinton describing how they met at Yale, how the nominee proposed marriage, and their child's birth. Of these various scenes, clearly, Clinton's opportunity to witness his child's birth is the most poignant. Clinton contrasts these experiences with his father's death in an emotional style that, in many respects, represents the film's essence. After comments by Chelsea, scenes of Bill and Chelsea playing softball, and Clinton's thoughts about his "60 Minutes" interview (regarding his marital problems) and Chelsea's response to that program, the film segues into its closing collage. As the video features a plane flying across the sky, various home-video sequences, and campaign footage, Clinton softly states:

> Sometimes late at night on the campaign plane I'll look out the window and think how far I am from that little town in Arkansas. And yet in many ways I know that all I am or ever will be came from there. A place and a time when nobody locked their doors at night, everybody showed up for a parade on main street, and kids like me could dream of being part of something bigger than themselves. I guess there'll always be a sadness in me that I never heard the sound of my father's voice or felt his hand around

mine. But all of us have sadness and disappointment in our lives and hopefully we grow stronger for it. I know every day that I'm alive I hope I'm a better person than the day before. I hope that every day from this day forward we can be a nation coming together instead of coming apart. And I hope that we as a people will always acknowledge that each child in our country is as important as our own. [several home-video scenes of Chelsea] I still believe these things are possible. I still believe in the promise of America. And I still believe in a place called Hope. [video returns to the black-and-white photo of the Hope train station]

Once the video faded to black, the Democratic nominee for president of the United States slowly walked from the shadows and waved to the crowd. The traditional "welcoming" demonstration lasted but a few minutes—Clinton wasted no time (especially network prime time) in getting to his acceptance speech.

Clinton issued a three-part acceptance speech that stressed, in his words, "who I am, what I believe, and where I want to lead America." Before venturing into the body of his remarks, Clinton first praised Al Gore, thanked Mario Cuomo, acknowledged his primary campaign rivals (allowing for applause for each), and accepted his party's nomination: "And so, in the name of all those who do the work, pay the taxes, raise the kids and play by the rules, in the name of the hard-working Americans who make up our forgotten middle class, I accept your nomination for President of the United States." Afterward, Clinton announced "we meet at a special moment in history," reviewed the end of the "Cold War," and concluded, "now that we have changed the world, it's time to change America." To reinforce that view, Clinton attacked George Bush: "The incumbent President says unemployment always goes up a little before a recovery begins. But unemployment only has to go up by one more person before a real recovery can begin. And, Mr. President, you are that man." Clinton closed his introduction by recalling the words of a New Yorker who questioned Clinton's "people first" rhetoric and asked "why should I trust you?" The remaining parts of the nominee's speech responded to that inquiry.

Part one of Clinton's acceptance—"who I am"—involved a value-laden portrait of those who had influenced his life. He gained his "fighting spirit" from his mother, his compassion from his grandfather, and his concern for "our children and our future" from his wife. Telling his mother and his wife "I love you" and placing his grandfather's wisdom above his professors' at Georgetown, Oxford, and Yale, Clinton carefully painted a self-portrait that said more about his family and its influence than himself.

The speech moved into its second section—"what I believe"—with his views about the Republicans' family-values rhetoric. Clinton declared: "Frankly, I'm fed up with politicians in Washington lecturing the rest of us about 'family values.' Our families have values. But our government doesn't." From there Clinton identified America's problems and the need for a change of leadership by contrasting his views with Bush's. Citing economic woes, image problems (i.e., the Japanese prime minister saying he felt "sympathy" for the United States), unemployment, tax inequities, and the budget deficit (and after each point closing with a "we can do better" refrain), Clinton argued:

> So if you are sick and tired of a government that doesn't work to create jobs; if you're sick and tired of a tax system that's stacked against you; if you're sick and tired of exploding debt and reduced investments in our future—or if, like the great civil rights pioneer Fannie Lou Hamer, you're just plain old sick and tired of being sick and tired—then join us, work with us, win with us. And we can make our country the country it was meant to be.

The nominee continued his Bush-Clinton comparison by addressing a variety of issues (e.g., health care, AIDS research, a balanced budget, and family farms), by assessing Bush's failure in those areas, and by closing each point with an "I can do better" refrain. To conclude this portion of his text, Clinton discussed his stance on abortion ("Hear me now: I am not pro-abortion, I am pro-choice strongly") and affirmed: "Jobs. Education. Health care. These are not just commitments from my lips. They are the work of my life."

As a segue to the speech's final section, Clinton issued his lone invitation to Ross Perot's now-abandoned followers. Clinton reiterated his "people first" argument, cited Perot's comments about a "revitalized Democratic party" (the Texan's rationale for not running), and announced "join us and together we will revitalize America." Although Clinton spent little time inviting Perot supporters to join his campaign (no doubt, the speech was prepared well in advance of Perot's

Thursday morning press conference), the various "join us" banners and posters present throughout Madison Square Garden communicated the DNC's sentiments.

Part three of Clinton's acceptance—"where I want to lead America"—contained four parts: the New Covenant argument, an attack on George Bush for his lack of vision, the value of vision, and the specifics of Clinton's New Covenant vision. After noting that "trickle down economics has sure failed," the Arkansas governor stated:

> That's why we need a new approach to government—a government that offers more empowerment and less entitlement, more choices for young people in the schools they attend, in the public schools they attend, and more choices for the elderly and for people with disabilities and the long-term care they receive—a government that is leaner, not meaner. A government that expands opportunity, not bureaucracy—a government that understands that jobs must come from growth in a vibrant and vital system of free enterprise. I call this approach a New Covenant—a solemn agreement between the people and their government—based not simply on what each of us can take but what all of us must give to our nation. We offer our people a new choice based on old values. We offer opportunity. We demand responsibility. We will build an American community again. The choice we offer is not conservative or liberal. In many ways it's not even Republican or Democratic. It's different. It's new. And it will work.

From there Clinton attacked Bush and his lack of vision: "Of all the things George Bush has ever said that I disagree with, perhaps the thing that bothers me most is how he derides and degrades the American tradition of seeing—and seeking—a better future. He mocks it as 'the vision thing.' But just remember what the Scripture says: 'Where there is no vision the people perish.'" After further establishing the value of "vision," Clinton turned to the specifics of his "New Covenant" vision and applied that argument to business, education, health care, middle-class incomes, welfare, and defense contexts. Throughout, Clinton concluded each statement with a "That's what the New Covenant is all about" refrain.

Clinton closed his discussion of the "New Covenant" vision with a "politics of inclusion" appeal. Declaring that "tonight every one of you knows deep in your heart that we are too divided," Clinton maintained "it is time to heal America." The nominee noted that those in power always blame "them" (i.e., the minorities, the liberals, the poor, the homeless, the people with disabilities, the gays, etc.) for America's problems; however: "But this is America. There is no them; there is only us. One nation, under God, indivisible, with liberty, and justice, for all. That is *our* Pledge of Allegiance, and that's what the New Covenant is all about."

Clinton concluded his acceptance speech with a brief defense of his home state and the anticipated attacks on Arkansas, a reiteration of the New Covenant vision, and a brief cheerleading segment (chanting "we can do it"). Afterward, Clinton returned to a personal tone, recalled seeing his daughter's birth, and lamented that his father had not enjoyed that privilege. Clinton then announced that "somewhere at this very moment a child is born in America" and urged his audience to "let it be our cause" to ensure "her" prosperity. Clinton stated: "Let that be our cause and our commitment and our New Covenant. My fellow Americans, I end tonight where it all began for me: I still believe in a place called Hope."

With his final words, Clinton stepped back and waved to the crowd as his wife and child joined him, and the convention hall resounded with the sounds of Fleetwood Mac's "Don't Stop (Thinkin' about Tommorow)" (the Clinton-Gore campaign song). The 1992 Democratic National Convention now settled into its concluding demonstration and, with that, adjourned until 1996.

The following day, after the required appearance before the Democratic National Committee, the Clinton and Gore families boarded a bus and took their "people first" campaign on the road. There would be no holidays, no vacations. "Our Friend" Bill Clinton took his "plan" on the road to town meetings, picnics, hayrides, and other "people first" venues. The "New Covenant: People First/I believe in Hope" story would not close until election night when Clinton stood, victorious, before his adoring followers in Little Rock, Arkansas. After much celebration and predictable oratory, the president-elect paused, looked out over the crowd, and closed his presidential campaign with these words: "And I still believe in a place called Hope."

CONCLUSION

The telepolitical age (1984–date) has seen the Democrats try very distinct approaches to presidential politics. In 1984 the party turned to a loyal partisan with direct ties to party history and a historic vice-presidential selection. In 1988 the party relied on a political technocrat unsure of his political heritage but committed to redefining the party as the "party of the future." The former took a stance (primarily on taxes) and was rejected; the latter avoided stances and was defeated by his functional equivalent. Where would the party go in 1992?

The 1992 Democrats gave the nation its first baby-boomer ticket, positioned that team in the middle of the political spectrum, and advanced a traditional challenger argument: "It's time for a change." Columnist David Broder offers this assessment of that strategy: "This is a different kind of gamble the Democrats are taking this year—a gamble on a generation that has yet to produce a political leader who inspires national confidence. In nominating the Baby Boomer ticket of Bill Clinton, 45, and Albert Gore, Jr., 44, the Democrats have certainly broken with their past. Whether they have secured their future is another question altogether."[15] The Democrats introduced their baby-boomer ticket through a strategy that did not, as Broder suggests, break with "their past" but merely recast that "past." The "New Covenant" theme allowed *the party* to embrace—not reject—its history by asserting it had a "new plan" based on an old philosophy, "people first." The DNC established the need for change, introduced the type of change it proposed, placed that argument in a historical context, and presented a presidential ticket that personified that carefully crafted position. A narrative interpretation of the New York convention reveals how the Democrats achieved these strategic objectives.

First, the Wednesday night tribute to Robert Kennedy, Clinton's post–roll call appearance on Wednesday evening, the video of young Bill Clinton meeting John Kennedy, Clinton's comments regarding Martin Luther King's "I Have a Dream" speech and his emphasis on his grandparents' progressive values, and the "New Covenant's" paraphrasing of John Kennedy's "ask not what your country can do for you . . ." philosophy all worked to maintain harmony between the party's "New Covenant" and Clinton's "I believe in Hope" stories. As

I have noted throughout this work, the New York DNC sharply contrasted its predecessor in Atlanta in its systematic application of party history and traditional principles to give a contemporary spin to an old argument. Just as Ronald Reagan and the Republicans based their 1980 and 1984 campaign rhetoric on a "proud to be an American" inclusionary grammar, Bill Clinton and the DNC told an inclusive tale designed to inspire Democrats—especially "Reagan Democrats"—to be "proud to be Democrats" once again.

This narrative tactic was complemented by Thursday night's "just plain Bill" theme (the "I believe in a place called Hope" yarn) that served as the second portion of a two-phased strategy. Both the Clinton film and his acceptance speech followed Ann Richard's lead in that they worked, in harmony, to introduce a person "you would be proud to call your friend." But Bill Clinton was to be more than a mere "friend"; he was a friend with a *plan*. Clinton and Gore's postconvention bus tour gave life to the "New Covenant: People First" *plan* in a fashion that gradually served as a deflective device. That is, when Clinton's character was attacked by the Republicans or the news media, "just plain Bill" responded—often, from his bus—that the cause and his *plan* were bigger than himself. Clearly, Bill Clinton was not the hero in his story; in fact, he was "just plain Bill." The "plan" was the hero in this tale. Moreover, throughout the general election, whenever George Bush or Dan Quayle endured personal attacks, the Clinton campaign refused to comment and, instead, emphasized the Clinton plan versus the Bush plan (or, according to Democrats, the lack thereof). Such a storytelling strategy would eventually prove to be Clinton's "narrative teflon": He would focus on his *plan* and, in doing so, transcend the "politics of personal destruction" he described in his *Time* interview. While fragments of this strategy emerged during the primaries, they crystallized during the four days of the New York convention.

These storytelling maneuvers also served the institutional task of achieving "cordial concurrence" during the nominating convention itself. From a narrative perspective, the key to convention orchestration rests with the production's continuity. Both in terms of the show's production qualities and thematic unity, the test of a convention's success or failure lies in its ability to articulate an internally consistent portrayal of party identities and values through master plots that establish the general election's strategy. The 1992 New York Democrats and the Clinton-Gore campaign most certainly achieved this level of narrative continuity.

Recent local, state, and national elections have consistently demonstrated the utility of narrative principles in *telepolitical* contests. The thematic discipline required by these ever-expanding contests is considerable. To be placed on the defensive or to vacillate between themes is assuredly a prescription for failure. Bill Clinton's successful campaign reinforces this position: From the outset his campaign stressed his "plan" (for instance, making copies available at local libraries in New Hampshire), and he continued to emphasize his plan through the convention when he added the story's "I believe in a place called Hope" dimension. Through these narrative tactics, Clinton was able both to focus on his themes (thereby remaining consistent) and to deflect the anticipated attacks on his character.

All of this points to a striking similarity between the narrative tactics evidenced in the 1980 and 1984 Reagan campaigns and Clinton's 1992 effort. In both cases, the campaign told a story that placed its leading character not in the heroic role, but as an agent of a heroic principle (a far cry from Bush's "I am that man" argument). For Reagan, "America" was his story's hero and the two-term president was merely an average "American," just like you and me. For Clinton, "the plan" was the hero and "just plain Bill" was merely an advocate of that plan and its traditional argument, "people first." Throughout his tenure in office, this strategy provided the foundation of Ronald Reagan's political "teflon" (i.e., the popular label for Reagan's ability to deflect direct criticism). The extent to which Clinton will extend this *electoral* narrative strategy to a *governing* narrative strategy may very well be an indication of his presidency's success.

NOTES

1. Henry Muller and John F. Stacks, "An Interview with Clinton: He Denounces the Politics of Personal Destruction and Says Bush Himself Is to Blame for It," *Time*, 20 July 1992, 25.

2. Larry David Smith and Dan Nimmo, *Cordial Concurrence: Orchestrating National Party Conventions in the Telepolitical Age* (New York: Praeger, 1991), 2.

3. Paul T. David, Ralph M. Goldman, and Richard C. Bain, *The Politics of National Party Conventions* (Washington: Brookings Institution, 1960).

4. Smith and Nimmo, *Cordial Concurrence*, 65.

5. Larry David Smith, "The Nominating Convention as Purveyor of Political Medicine: An Anecdotal Analysis of the Democrats and Republicans of 1984," *Central States Speech Journal* 38 (1987): 259.

6. Larry David Smith, "Convention Oratory as Institutional Discourse: A Narrative Synthesis of the Democrats and Republicans of 1988," *Communications Studies* 41 (1990): 19–34.

7. For insights regarding dialectical narratives, see Larry David Smith, "Narrative Styles in Network Coverage of the 1984 Nominating Conventions," *Western Journal of Speech Communication* 52 (1988): 63–74; and Larry David Smith, "How the Dialectical Imperative Shapes Network News Content: The Case of CNN vs. the Entertainment Networks," *Communication Quarterly* 40 (1992): 338–49. With regard to rhetorical narratives, see Smith, "The Nominating Convention as Purveyor of Political Medicine"; Larry David Smith, "A Narrative Analysis of the Party Platforms: The Democrats and Republicans of 1984," *Communication Quarterly* 37 (1989): 91–99; Smith, "Convention Oratory as Institutional Discourse"; and Smith, "The Party Platforms as Institutional Discourse," *Presidential Studies Quarterly* 22 (1992): 531–44. For the poetical, see Michael Hemphill and Larry David Smith, "The Working American's Elegy: The Rhetoric of Bruce Springsteen," in Robert Savage and Dan Nimmo, eds., *Politics in Familiar Contexts: Projecting Politics through Popular Media* (Norwood, N.J.: Ablex, 1990), 199–213.

8. The remarks attributed to speakers appearing before the Democratic National Convention are taken from the broadcasts of the conventions by the C-SPAN television network.

9. Smith, "Convention Oratory as Institutional Discourse," 24.

10. See Smith, "The Party Platforms as Institutional Discourse."

11. "Democrats Pass a Self-Help Platform," *Chicago Tribune*, 13 July 1992, 12.

12. D. Rosenbaum, "Democratic Platform Shows Shift in Party's Roots," *New York Times*, 14 July 1992, A9.

13. "Excerpts from the Platform: A 'New Covenant' with Americans," *New York Times*, 15 July 1992, A10.

14. D. Rosenbaum, "Party's Quest for a Middle Road: A Liberal Stance in Business Suits," *New York Times*, 15 July 1992, 1, A10.

15. David Broder, "Can Clinton and Gore Generate Trust from Their Own Generation?" *Chicago Tribune*, 16 July 1992, 13.

THE INTERTEXTUALITY OF "THE MAN FROM HOPE"

Bill Clinton as Person, as Persona, as Star?

THOMAS ROSTECK

The evening of 16 July 1992, Madison Square Garden, New York City, the Democratic National Convention: The house lights dim and music comes up on the loudspeakers. On the screen, a black-and-white photograph of a street, apparently in a small town, clearly from the mid-1940s. A slow pan left reveals the wooden train depot—the word HOPE painted in block letters on the side nearest the tracks. Then, the voice of the candidate: "I was born in a little town called Hope, Arkansas, three months after my father died."

Beginning there and for the next thirteen minutes, the delegates to the Democratic National Convention and members of the television audience are invited to enjoy a depiction of presidential nominee William Jefferson Clinton quite unlike any they had seen before.[1] The story is one of Clinton's broken childhood home, of pulling himself up by the sweat of his brow, of his deep religious faith, and the film wastes no time in sounding these main themes. As the camera pulls back from the railway station, Clinton begins his account of growing up in his grandparents' two-story house and of their deep belief in education. Casually dressed in a blue shirt open at the neck and a blazer, the candidate speaks directly into the camera when not providing a voice-over. The film mentions that he was born into a home with an outhouse in the back and dwells on the family's financial struggles after the death of Clinton's father. In one emotional moment, his mother, Virginia

Kelley, recalls the night thirteen-year-old Bill intervened to prevent his stepfather from mistreating her.

Clinton's stepbrother talks about how "Bill took over the leadership role in our family when he was just a kid," and his mother describes the nominee as someone destined for government service "in one form or another." We see a young Clinton shaking hands with President John F. Kennedy at a Rose Garden ceremony in 1963, and then, describing his wonder at a country where "somebody like me who came from a little town in Arkansas who had no money, no political position or anything would be given the opportunity to meet the president." Clinton's political lineage is drawn to include Dr. Martin Luther King Jr. and Robert F. Kennedy, whose assassinations he refers to as two of the most tragic and pivotal events of his generation. The candidate discusses the interview where, sitting beside his wife, he answered questions about allegations of an extramarital affair. Later the couple watches the program with their daughter. "It was pretty painful, you know, to have your child watch that," he admits. As for what his daughter thought, Clinton says: "She said, 'I think I'm glad you're my parents,' and after that, I knew whatever happened, it would be all right."

But the film is not without lighter moments. In a set of cross-cut interviews the candidate and his wife describe their first meeting, subsequent marriage, and first home. Later, Hillary Clinton tells how her husband once called her into a bedroom to watch their then-three-month-old daughter. "He yelled, 'Look at this! She rolls over to the edge of the bed and then she rolls back. She must understand gravity.'" "About twenty minutes later," Hillary Clinton says, "I hear this plunk, as my daughter 'unlearns' gravity."

In its final sequence, the film returns to Hope, Arkansas, which is both a "time and a place far away" for the candidate. Yet he describes it as a place "where kids like me could dream of being part of something bigger than themselves." "All I am or ever will be came from there," Clinton says. "I still believe in the promise of America," he affirms, as we watch slow-motion images of his wife, his daughter, himself on the campaign trail, "I still believe in a place called Hope."

Reactions to this Clinton campaign film, which has come to be called "The Man from Hope," have been almost universally positive.

Indeed, concluded one critic, the film is "a masterpiece, perhaps the masterpiece, of political advertising." "So powerful [is] the film" that it stands as a "triumph of suggestive compression."[2] Most commentators mention the emotional portrait it presents. As one says, the image is not of a political candidate, but "a fine, decent American, manly but sensitive, firm in his ideas of right and wrong yet compassionate, a devoted husband and doting father, a man who has had his share of troubles in life but prefers to talk about the troubles of others. Bill Clinton, the film seems to say, represents the best that small-town America can produce."[3] The film's power, said another, comes from "its recurrent subliminal message: here is a man who has nothing to hide, who can look Americans straight in the eye and bare his soul."[4]

Democratic responses were, predictably, even more enthusiastic. The film "won the heart of every delegate" at the convention.[5] And Clinton campaign chairman Mickey Kantor called the film "probably the best ever in the history of either party."[6] Reacting to the portrayal of the close-knit Clinton family, one Democratic viewer concluded, "this is real life."[7]

The opposition party and even those within President George Bush's campaign staff were reportedly "wowed" by the film's emotive power.[8] Some made comparison to earlier candidate films and admitted "The Man from Hope" "created a set of images and cultural symbols that, like Ronald Reagan's 'Morning in America' ads, struck a resonant chord with the voting public." The film, said one partisan, showed Democrats that "it's they, not the Republicans, who are the real Rockwellians, the ones truly rooted to American values."[9]

Given such enthusiastic comment, it seems clear that "The Man from Hope" is a document of uncommon effect. But beyond questions of immediate reaction, the film is a complex and interesting communication artifact: one that seems to operate on several interrelated planes of symbolic action. It is made up of historical documentation such as still photographs, home movies, interviews, and news film footage. But it also utilizes other symbolic strategies including the biographical narrativizing of the candidate's life. Further, it deploys mythologizing strategies such as the construction of a heroic persona, an iconography of reverence and a moral concern for personal sacrifice and altruistic service. Given this complexity, "The Man from

Hope" obviously invites speculations that bring us squarely in touch with questions of depiction in political documentary films. In this case, we may frame the issue thusly: How may Bill Clinton the historical person be transformed into "Bill Clinton the true believer from Hope, Arkansas?"[10] Essaying an answer to this question invokes concern with visual argument, political persuasion, and nonfiction film.

But in considering such issues, we must not lose sight of "The Man from Hope" for what it is: a carefully crafted text that uses symbolic strategies to influence, and more specifically, that was designed to deal with a specific set of campaign problems suffered by candidate Bill Clinton in the summer of 1992. I will argue that "The Man from Hope" invites its audience to reconstruct its central figure and thus attempts to deal with his "image problems" by depicting presidential candidate Bill Clinton as a historical person (an agent of social activity) within a narrative field as a character and within a mythic or contemplative field as an icon or symbol (an idealized and heroic embodiment of shared values and attitudes). That is, "The Man from Hope" simultaneously invites its audience to contemplate "three Bill Clintons"—historical person, narrative character, and exemplary persona.[11] Moreover, I suggest that each of these three intertextual dimensions—history, narrative, myth—are necessary for a reading which retains the potential to reconstitute Bill Clinton as "presidential" and to prompt its audience to support a Clinton candidacy.

Thus, we shall keep two questions before us as we go. First, in what way does "The Man from Hope" solicit our judgment of William Jefferson Clinton and seek to deal with the "image problems" that threaten his candidacy? Second, what is the relationship of political image, narrative, and nonfiction film? I will contend that these questions arc part-and-parcel and that the film uses our foreknowledge of the conventions of documentary referentiality, conventions of narrative reading, and conventions of what we may call the "American success myth" or the "Horatio Alger myth" to attempt a shift in our perception of the character of Bill Clinton.[12] To address how "The Man from Hope" invites such an intertextual reading, I will first set the film within its context and discuss its production, then analyze its dynamic textuality.

CANDIDATE BIOGRAPHY FILM AND MAKING "THE MAN FROM HOPE"

The political campaign film is not a genre of especially recent vintage.[13] In practice, these films serve several ends. First, they introduce the candidate, often taking the place of the traditional convention speech. In this way, the films help establish the themes of the campaign and visualize the ideas the party will feature in the upcoming general election campaign. Often, segments from these visual presentations arc uscd for other campaign purposes such as spot advertisements or special telecasts.[14] Also, the campaign film serves as a way to unify the party—giving supporters a chance to rally behind their own nominee.[15] In part this may be because such films are visualizations of the traditional emphases of each party and the elements of their rhetorical history. Jeanne Morreale accounts for the wide appeal of such visualizations by describing the campaign film as a contemporary form of epideictic rhetoric which chiefly "serves to celebrate values."[16] As we shall see, the directors of the Clinton campaign sought to use "The Man from Hope" in each of these ways to elevate and simultaneously to redefine their candidate.

Problems of the Candidate from Hope

Coming into the July convention, presumptive nominee Bill Clinton faced a difficult and unique situation: a three-way general election campaign against a once-popular incumbent Republican president and the unpredictable yet influential third-party candidacy of a billionaire businessman. The challenge was complicated because Clinton also faced recurring questions on the so-called "character issue." The nominee was dogged throughout the primary campaign by questions about his personal life including fidelity to his marriage, his draft status, his use of marijuana, his image as an "intellectual" out of touch with real people, and a perception as a "tax-and-spend" liberal Democrat who, Republicans alleged, raised taxes forty-three times in his eleven years as governor of Arkansas. According to Clinton's own camp, "too many Americans [saw] the nominee as a 'rich kid' who won a Rhodes Scholarship and was privileged to spend time in London smoking marijuana and avoiding the draft."[17]

Reflecting the seriousness of this issue, Clinton came into Madison Square Garden carrying extraordinarily low approval ratings—as low as 16 percent in one national poll in late June—and high negative ratings—consistently at 40 percent in polls taken from April through June. These numbers and Clinton's primary season performance left even core Democratic constituencies uneasy.[18] In short, many Democrats no doubt feared that in the general election the Republicans would, in the words of primary campaign rival Sen. Bob Kerrey, "crack Clinton open like a ripe peanut" on these character issues.

The problem that the Clinton campaign faced may be generally understood as having to do with the "image" of the candidate. Students of political communication have long understood that "image" is perhaps the most potent ingredient in contemporary electoral politics, prompting a favorable or unfavorable impression of the candidate and thus securing voter support.[19] Some have suggested that candidates who succeed are those most able to present a highly wrought and consistent image—one that fits with the dramatic demands of a current political scene.[20] Others have argued that since campaigning itself is a character-centered activity, then the portrayal or the image of the candidate is crucial for election to office because it goes to the very heart of voter decision making.[21]

To meet these critically important "image issues," the Clinton campaign needed a strategy that would replace reports of the candidate's supposed indiscretions with a new image more appealing to a majority of potential voters. "Clinton's goal [must be] to redefine himself," said one political analyst at the time. "He has to change the way people see him and make himself into someone Americans can like."[22]

Thus, the strategy of the July Democratic convention was to "reinvent Bill Clinton" and to make the candidate into "a new, less damaged and more interesting nominee."[23] Recognizing that their candidate came into Madison Square Garden with "a second chance to explain who he is," the Clinton campaign wanted to give a fuller picture of Clinton's character "after the beating it took in the primary season and the pummeling Republicans were sure to give it in the fall."[24] As Clinton advisor Rep. Mike Espy described it, the New York convention was "to be spent on Bill Clinton's *story*."[25] And the recasting of Clinton's image was to be accomplished, Espy continued, through the telling of the "whole *story* of his life"[26] [my italics]. As his advisors conceived it, then, "The Man from Hope" was to be consciously designed to recast the candidate and "to retool [his] image."[27]

Following this advice, Clinton turned to family friend, Linda Bloodworth-Thomason to produce for the convention "the film that would reintroduce the family to the country."[28] Bloodworth-Thomason, a fellow Arkansan and creator, writer, and producer of the popular CBS television series "Designing Women" and "Evening Shade," said Clinton gave her free rein to work, with little input from campaign advisors—he "just said: 'Show the American people who we are.'" In planning for the film, Bloodworth-Thomason recognized that "there was [to be] nothing slick about it . . . you put a camera two inches from a man's face, and you ask him about the most painful and happiest moments of his life, he has nowhere to go, and nowhere to hide. He just has to be exactly who he is."[29]

Facing some disagreement within the campaign over the specific content and shape of the final version of the film, Bloodworth-Thomason argued for personalizing the story of the nominee. Clinton's media consultants, Mandy Grunwald and Frank Greer, wanted the film to meld Clinton's personal story with his political one, but Bloodworth-Thomason fought this interference and kept the focus upon "a pure human-interest drama."[30] Grunwald, however, won another battle, keeping the Vietnam issue, which Bloodworth-Thomason wanted to include, out of the film.[31] Nevertheless, "The Man from Hope," all agreed, would not be designed to gloss over the candidate's shortcomings. Instead, it intentionally presented the Clintons as "real people, with all the warts," not dream-like family Americana.[32]

After these preplanning decisions, production time was necessarily compressed to a few weeks and Bloodworth-Thomason searched through photographic collections and archives for pictures of Clinton, his family, and the town he grew up in. The producers also quickly filmed a series of interviews with Clinton, wife Hillary, daughter Chelsea, stepbrother Roger, and mother Virginia Kelley.[33]

Finally, by the end of the second week in July, the film was complete and ready for national telecast where it was scheduled to precede Clinton's acceptance speech at the convention.[34] Speaking to reporters the day of the broadcast, Bloodworth-Thomason warned that the film "is powerful stuff. I'll be happy if people are lying face down on the carpets, sobbing . . . it's good television."[35]

READING "THE MAN FROM HOPE" INTERTEXTUALLY

To account for "The Man from Hope" as "powerful stuff" is to investigate the way the film invites its audience to apply certain interpretive paradigms for understanding. One way of explicating the paradigms of interpretation we bring to this film is grouped under the critical rubric of "intertextuality." The theory of intertextuality proposes that any one text is necessarily read in relationship to others and that a range of knowledge is brought to bear upon it. These intertextual knowledges pre-orient the reader to exploit the text by activating it in certain ways; that is, by making some meanings rather than others.[36] According to Roland Barthes, these sorts of textual relations are so pervasive that our culture consists of a complex web of intertextuality, in which all texts finally refer only to each other.[37]

Given the striking and complex textual action of "The Man from Hope" and its symbolic construction, my contention is that any audience seeking to make sense out of "The Man from Hope" is likely to do so by actively reading it as part of three dominant intertextual relationships: text and history, text and narrative, text and myth. These intertextual relationships are simultaneous within the film, and any segment may potentially "mean" within more than one of the relationships at a time. But for now and for purposes of explication, I will consider each intertextual level separately.[38]

Intertextuality of History: Bill Clinton as Person

Bill Clinton, the historical person, the social agent located in history, enters this text initially as onscreen and voice-over narrator. "The Man from Hope," as all nonfiction documentary texts, stands in a peculiar relationship to the "historically real" and thus to conventions of interpretation. As genre, documentary provides its audience with a way to grasp the world; indeed, this has been one of the senses of "documentary" since its inception—providing a "record" of the real.[39] But this reference to the world also forces limitations on the documentary audience. First, documentary is shackled to "brute facts"; because it is constructed from series of photographic images, documentary necessarily indexes events which are verifiable independent of the imagination.[40] Second, documentary is limited by convention. Viewers have expectations about formal features of the nonfiction film and can be expected to decode a work according to those assumptions unless they are overtly invited or required to do otherwise.[41] In short, the documentary form activates conventions that prepare us to expect a privileged status for the indexical link between sign and referent, and any reader's tacit acknowledgment of this link anchors the documentary image in the specificity of history. What is most important for understanding "The Man from Hope," however, is the way our agreement to the reality of what we see in the nonfiction domain is essential preparation for the symbolic levels of narrative and of myth.

This crucial historical intertext of "The Man from Hope" is built from still photographs, home movies, the testimony of friends, news footage of events, and an interview with the candidate himself. Clinton and others—his wife, brother, mother, and mother-in-law—talk about events in the early and mid life of the candidate. This talk is illustrated by a series of visual images, which work together with the verbal dimension and serve as collaboration or verification for the past events described.

The first one-third of the film consists chiefly of still photographs that shift from images of the town of Hope, to the train depot, to Clinton's grandfather. But by far the biggest number of these are photos of the young Bill Clinton. Taken together, they trace the arc of his life: photos of a newborn, of a young man in bow tie and jacket, a smiling young man standing before a front porch; Clinton with his brother Roger, holding his hand; the two brothers, Bibles under their arms, apparently leaving for Sunday services. Indeed, the sense conveyed is of photos from a family album: the single-parent family, the town where the candidate was born. But beyond that, a second-level of connotation is that these photographs are "history."

The family photographs are signified as historical "data" in a further way by the marker of color—its presence or absence. The photographs we see in the first half of "The Man from Hope" are black-and-white stills and thus carry the suggestive connotation of archival value. As the film unfolds, the blacks-and-whites in the early photos give way to color photos (albeit with a "faded" and overly greenish palette), then to moving film and then to videotape. Finally, near its conclusion "The Man from Hope" incorporates newsreel footage of Bill Clinton the candidate on the campaign trail, speaking on the stump, shaking hands, surrounded by a shower of confetti. Thus, the use of the archival photographs and materials traces the movement of time and the temporal development of the story of Bill Clinton from long-ago past to near past to present.

Most important, this temporal development reveals a past for which there is ample artifactual evidence. "The Man from Hope" draws upon our ready, indeed almost automatic, acknowledgment that what we see and hear is not an imaginative fabrication, but rather a rendering, however clouded by memory, of a time and a place that has a concrete and palpable existence. Indeed, the archival photographs (and later the film/video footage) ask our assent to the referentiality of the discourse—that what we see and hear indeed happened as it is described.[42] The photographs give evidence for the events described in the narration, offering an indexical sign that verifies the veracity of the events spoken.[43]

This narration too serves to establish the "truthfulness" of its account of history. One striking element of this accounting in "The Man from Hope" is the intercutting of the interview segments to present the historical event. This tactic occurs at numerous places in the film. For instance, early on, Clinton and his mother recount the story of the night young Bill stood between his mother and an abusive stepfather. We see both in medium close shot.

> *Clinton:* I was in the ninth grade. He kinda, he got violent with my mother one night and I bulled through the door and told him he wasn't going to do that anymore. I just said . . .
> *Virginia Kelley:* Stand up. I have something to say to you. And obviously he couldn't stand up. And so he got in his face and he said, "Daddy, if you're not able to stand up I'll help you. You must stand to hear what I have to say." And some way or other, he stood. And Bill told him then, "Don't you ever, ever lay your hand on my mother again."

The sharing of the responsibility of the telling of the tale is an interesting tactic that acknowledges the subjectivity of observation but also reveals that the multiple narrators share exactly the same remembrance of the event. This adds to the developing sense of the "truthfulness" or the fidelity of the accounting to the event in history. In the same way that jurists look to corroborating eyewitness testimony to build credibility, "The Man from Hope" builds its own credibility in the way that it presents both "archival photographic evidence" and more than one "eyewitness" to corroborate the account given by Bill Clinton.[44]

Thus the focus upon the same historical event unites the multiple tellings, allowing them to resonate and to provide confirmation for one another. This same tactic of intercutting interviews happens at several other points in "The Man from Hope" with slightly different effect. For instance, Bill and Hillary seem to complete each other's accounts of their first meeting.

> *Hillary Clinton:* . . . he was watching me because I was watching him because I was in the law library at this long table studying. And I finally thought, you know, that this was kind of silly.
>
> *Bill Clinton:* And finally she just put down the book she was reading and got up and walked the entire length of the law library and she walked up to me and she said . . .
>
> *Hillary Clinton:* If you are going to keep looking at me and I'm going to keep looking back, we ought to at least know one another. I'm Hillary Rodham.
>
> *Bill Clinton:* And what's your name? Well, I couldn't remember my name.

This sequence has the dual effect of not only corroborating the story but also of providing demonstrative evidence for Dorothy Rodham's following comment, that the two Clintons show a sort of "synergy" in their relationship.

Thus, in its presentation of action and event drawn from history, "The Man from Hope" offers multiple testimony and archival photographic evidence—each proofs of a sort that the events depicted in the film are verifiable in history. To shift judgment of its central figure, "The Man from Hope" must enrich and magnify specific historical moments and give to them a potential for greater meaning; and it will do so through the relationships of text/narrative and text/myth. But this transubstantiation into the imagery of narrative and the ideological or mythic requires our assent to the "reality" of the historical. Our willingness to grant a faithfulness or fidelity to the historical is the crucial element in the potential success of the textual argument of "The Man from Hope."

In a sense, what the film does in referring to our sense of the conventions of documentary referentiality is to build a foundation that supports the superstructure of the rest. The visual substance of the historical person of Bill Clinton provides the semiotic substance for narrative character and mythic persona. But the historical intertext provides evidence more than argument; argument, we shall see, operates more within the narrative and mythic levels.[45]

Intertextuality of Narrative: Bill Clinton as Character

"I was born," the hero says, "in a little town called Hope, Arkansas, three months after my father died . . . It was a wonderful little small town, you know, where it seemed that everybody knew everybody else." As story, the film begins conventionally. We see still black-and-white photos of an older gentleman behind the counter of a general store, a fade to another image, this of a parade—high-school band and tractor-drawn float.

"The Man from Hope" presents a biography—the "life" of Bill Clinton. But biography by design counters the errant movements of a life with the smooth curve of narrative form. As story, the closure and unity of biographical narrative stand at odds to the open-endedness and incoherence of life as it is lived, and thus every biography is an attempt to impress reality with meaning and significance.[46] Like all documentary, this film operates in the crease between life as lived and life as symbolized and represented, and the potential for meaning in "The Man from Hope" depends upon this relationship. "The Man from Hope" turns to the constructing of a narrative and character for an answer of how to suggest an interpretation that gives meaning to the events of a single life.[47] Thus the story of "The Man from Hope" draws upon an audience's familiarity with the romance stories found in other "coming of age" films or film biographies.

For instance, we hear of the value of education early in the hero's life and learn that our main character "was able to read at a really young age." After the father's death, the young single-parent family was of narrow means, and the concern over money motivates a separation of mother and son that leads to one of the hero's "most vivid memories of childhood." His mother "went back to New Orleans to finish her nursing education . . . And during this time she was away, one time my grandmother and I went down on a train to visit her and I remember we pulled out of the station and my mother kneeled at the side of the track and cried." This is, we are assured, not a person "born wealthy" with "all the privileges you could imagine."

As "The Man from Hope" develops we encounter the familiar deep structure of the *Bildungsroman:* The adolescent Clinton confronts his stepfather, then takes over the "leadership" role in the family. He comes to appreciate "religion." He goes to the courthouse and graciously has his last name changed to the "same" as his younger brother. He evinces an interest in "human events," and, in one of the most celebrated sequences in the film, he meets and shakes the hand of a romanticized and doomed president. The young man goes to college. It is the turbulent sixties, and he volunteers to take supplies "down into the burned-out part of the city." He meets his wife while at Law School. They marry, return to Arkansas, have a child in one of "the great experiences of his life."

Recasting Bill Clinton as the main character in the familiar narrative form of the biography grants to the text several potential advantages important for the action the film solicits from its audience. First, it bestows order to the events of a life, and second, it tenders an implicit meaning or significance to that life. Moreover, these advantages arise for the most part from the narrative form itself.

In general, narrativity is complex and multilayered, depending for meaning on the shared knowledge of narratee and audience.[48] Further, scholars of narrative have concluded that narratives work as communication devices to create interpretive contexts for social action. By rounding out an action, a story not only focuses attention and judgment, but also offers an explanation about the significance of those actions. In short, narratives take events from the historical context and provide them with a structure and an interpretation that makes the events meaningful.[49] Hayden White describes how this might happen: Whenever events are temporally ordered as in a narrative, the ordering gives to the events a "natural" meaning because it is "like" the world we know. As White says, narrative gives to randomized historical events the form of story.[50] History is thus revealed as possessing a structure and an order of meaning it does not possess as mere sequence.

So, the conventions of narrative structure we have learned by way of prior experience with such narrative texts—conventions such as closure, consistency, character, temporal development—provide a way for us to experience the life of Bill Clinton within a familiar form. This has the potential to reconfigure subject, audience, and immediate time and space, thereby presenting a diegetic world of clearer, simpler meanings in contrast to the randomness of reality. The "biography of Bill Clinton" presents its argument for "who Bill Clinton is" under cover of the familiar and simple structure of the narrative form and so suggests that this life has an order and hence a potential for "meaning."

One of the orders of meaning in "The Man from Hope" is an interpretation common to the genre of the biography. Just as narrativity elides order with meaning, so too in the biography does the temporal ordering of the events of a life give rise to the assumption that the events are causally connected and that a character in the present is a result of events and influences in the past. That is, in "The Man from Hope," the narrative form invites an interpretation of Clinton as the product of the small-town upbringing and as embodying attitudes expected in someone raised without "money or position." Even though explicitly acknowledged at the end of the film ("all I am or ever will be comes from [Hope]"), the meaning is carried implicitly in the narrative form of the biography throughout. We are invited to read the youthful experiences of our main character as indicative of the man: that Bill Clinton is product and representative of the experiences of his life—a life indexed to connotations of small-town values and the common man. Thus, even more than structuring the life of Bill Clinton as a recognizable story and allowing it to be more readily understood, the narrative also has an element of moralizing.[51] Not only does this narrative arise out of the desire to have historical events of Clinton's life display the order of narration, but it also seeks to endow those events with a significance they do not possess as mere sequence.

In this way, I suggest, narrative level takes the raw materials of history and seeks to reshape these, to give them a familiar structure and hence a potential for meaning. Biography is, as White again explains it, the desire to represent the moral under the cover of the aesthetic.[52] And it is, I suggest, by inviting its audience to "read" Bill as a hero within a familiar narrative form—a structure drawn from fiction as well as from biography—that "The Man from Hope" seeks to reconstitute its real central figure as one both "destined"—perhaps for the presidency—and as one embodying certain beliefs and values.

The desire for moralizing significance is never far from the surface of "The Man from Hope," and another way that this film seeks to refigure the image of Bill Clinton is by allegorizing the biographical story of Clinton to the level of myth. Thus, "Hope" rests at the intersection of another set of familiar texts, and the film draws upon one of the most venerable and potent of American cultural myths.

The theme of "rags-to-riches" runs "like a thread through American folklore," and the story of the self-made man advancing on his own efforts is one of the "most influential" of our cultural myths.[53] While there are, of course, many examples of real-life self-made men, the American success myth appeared originally and in its most rarified form in the series of novels published in the 1880s and 1890s by Horatio Alger Jr. As artworks, the novels were remarkably similar in plot and characterization.

The hero is always an American young man, independent, eager to work hard, and to make his own way to success.[54] Typically, the Alger protagonist is the "son of a widow" who finds himself "living on narrow means." He "exercises strict economy," often times taking menial labor to help make ends meet as he and his widow mother struggle financially. Despite being on one of the lower rungs of the economic ladder, the Alger hero maintains a personal code of morals and conduct that is always quite high, even exemplary.[55] Through it all, he maintains a "pleasant expression" and a "bright, resolute outlook." Characteristically, the Alger hero has a "warm heart" and a "clear intellect," and "in spite of his poverty achieves one aspect of American success: becoming the most popular boy" in town.[56] Inevitably, the young hero, associating himself with benevolent benefactors and role models, struggles upward from his boyhood of privation and self-denial into a youth and manhood of prosperity and honor. While in every Alger novel, there was "some luck about it," the hero is "indebted for most of his good fortune solely to his good qualities."[57] In this, its prototypical form—the Horatio Alger story—the rags-to-riches, self-made man celebrates aggressive individual initiative, individual virtue, and individual goals.[58]

Drawing upon this potent American cultural myth, "The Man from Hope" constructs Bill Clinton as iconic persona and embodiment of this success myth. We have already noted in some detail how the program constructs his childhood as one of deprivation and one in which education was the way that one worked out of lower rungs of society and how this exemplifies his irreproachable qualities. Since the filmmakers can count on their audience's prior experience with the text of the rags-to-riches myth, it invites us to see Bill Clinton enacting the virtues that would, given the mythic pattern, inevitably foretell the success he seeks.

The account of the confrontation with his alcoholic stepfather is one such incident. Here the young man makes the alcoholic and abusive stepfather "stand up" in order that he can deal with him. And after it was over, Clinton says "I never stopped loving my stepfather or thinking he was really a good person." Thus, the film plays it two ways: Clinton as someone who will stand up for what he believes in and stand up to a bully, and Clinton as someone who shares a feeling for other people. Thus, the hero embodies the Alger hero's values of individualistic conviction and altruistic compassion and enacts them both in the encounter with his stepfather.[59]

As the film develops Bill Clinton further takes on the sets of values and virtues that cast him as the bearer of qualities necessary for the myth of success—equality, education, hard work, religious fervor, fair-mindedness. Finally, by the end, Clinton's ethos and the "myth of American success" come to be nearly identical.

The relationship between myth and text are important for understanding how "The Man from Hope" might work upon its audience. In his study of the role of communication in the political process, Lance Bennett argues that myth is the most important part of the campaign process.[60] For Bennett, the display of personality is an important defining characteristic of the presidential election ritual and the focus on mythic conflict is the way in which private life concerns are translated into shared public images and formulations. To Bennett, the struggle of candidates Clinton, Bush and Perot becomes the struggle between groups, or the battle of good and evil, or the representation of such life concerns as economic security or social harmony.[61] This suggests that "Hope" with its conventional plotline, symbolic or mythic story, and personifications is reflected in other popular culture texts.[62] The form and story line of "Hope" is harmonious with forms of the American myth of success as represented in the Alger series, in adventure stories and westerns.[63]

In sum, an auditor is invited to read "The Man from Hope" in terms of its archetypal mythic frames, and so the documentary layers a signification drawn from conventions of "story" or "myth" over the nonfiction archival evidence of Clinton's life. Indeed, we may say that Hope represents a blending of rhetorical forms and conventions. It imposes an order on the real that is a function of alternation between conventions of the nonfiction "reality" and a symbolic reading that promises a resolution paralleling that of other stories.

The text represents an intersection of two sorts of signifying codes: the one, based on our assent to the indexical relation of image and world; an acknowledgment of the ontological potency of the nonfiction text. The other, based on the mythic and narrative, drawn from a cultural stock of characters and soliciting us to read the biography as myth, as the acting out of an allegory or parable. Thus, for the reader of "The Man from Hope," the manner of realization is a distinctly fictional configuration, while the message is not.[64]

But in saying this, I am not saying that this documentary text is read like a "fictional" discourse. On the contrary, the reader is constantly pulled back by the "stickiness of the indexical image" to the notion that this is a real person, in a real situation. It is this difference in the imaginary and the indexical that separates the nonfiction discourse from the "mythical" or "fictional." As Bill Nichols has said, the ground of documentary resides in the relation between character and social agent; a person acts as an agent in history, not a narrative, no matter how much we give meaning to the former by way of the latter.[65] Yet it is also this confluence of symbolic forms that suggests the potential of "The Man from Hope" to elicit audience reaction.

"THE MAN FROM HOPE" AND THE CAMPAIGN FOR THE PRESIDENCY

So far we have seen that "The Man from Hope" is a sophisticated text that effectively blends art and ideology. According to this reading, the text constructs "Bill Clinton" as a sign simultaneously depicted as a historical person, as a character, and within a mythic field as an icon or symbol. But we cannot forget that the film would be a failure if it did not retain the potential to shift sensibilities in the historical world. That is, for all its artifice, "The Man from Hope" is a campaign document designed to secure for Bill Clinton votes in an upcoming national election. But how does the film solicit action? How does it invite a viewer to bridge the gap between text and world, between the realms of the symbolic and the real?

Let us set the issue by turning to the conclusion of the film. Here, the "story" of Bill Clinton leaves off in a rather symbolically unsatisfactory way, and the biography of Bill Clinton as narrativized is incomplete. For example, the concluding sequences of "The Man from Hope" turn from the telling of the Clinton biography and show instead candidate Clinton on the campaign trail and speaking from the podium in newsreel footage. Thus, temporally we are returned from the narrativized past to the present time of the campaign. And here, seeming in *medias res,* the narrative abruptly winds up with a voice-over peroration about the future of the nation as taken from the candidate's standard campaign stump speech. Yet, this abrupt and fore-shortened ending, far from weakening the emotional and cognitive effect of the text is the masterstroke that offers an invitation for partisan political support. In short, "The Man from Hope" solicits historical action in the service of symbolic satisfaction.

To explain, consider the nature of narrative itself and of the combined action of the intertextual domains of history, narrative, and myth. Already we have seen how the text draws upon expectations and conventions of narrative that an auditor might have gained from prior experience to assist in making sense of the life story of Bill Clinton. One of the most important of these conventions is what is called narrative closure.[66] Closure refers to the necessity of "believable narratives" to round out their action in a way satisfying to the reader and to provide a sense of completeness to the telling of the story. To be accepted as plausible accounts, "good" narratives must "tie up loose ends" by offering an explanation for the actions of characters and event by projecting a denouement that is consistent with the symbolic "world" of the story. As Bill Nichols puts it, "narrative, as a closed system, gives the appearance of resolution to conflicts that remain unresolved in the historical domain."[67]

It is, I suggest, this function of narrative closure that best explains the rhetorical action of "The Man from Hope" and can best account for the way it demands a response as political document. This demand is keyed to the symbolic or narrative expectations and conventions of the story. As a reader "knows" the paradigm myth which structures the Clinton persona in the text, and likely also knows from prior experiences "how" narratives that interpret this cultural myth "should" end, the reader has the symbolic prerequisites to complete the narrative of "The Man from Hope" for themselves—to "help" the "hero" achieve his goal.

But the story of Bill Clinton is yet to be resolved as in the paradigm: Bill Clinton, social agent, is not yet president and the version of his story that enacts the success myth is thus narratively open and incomplete. To symbolically round out the myth and the narrative that parallels it, the text implicitly offers the chance to satisfy narrative closure and to do so only by action in the world in support of the real Clinton candidacy. Drawing upon and crossing intertextual reading levels, completion and closure of the biographical narrative of the character "Bill Clinton" must take place not in the space of the text but in history.

I suggest that in this way, the invitation for audience action is implicit in the symbolic action of "The Man from Hope." The text trades upon our own conventional sense of the lack of closure of the finished narrative as the means to transfer action from text to world. Put another way, the interaction of myth and narrative prompt action in history by asking its audience to complete the symbolic structure of "The Man from Hope" in and through cognitive restructuring and subsequent action. The closure of the narrative provides a mechanism to satisfy viewer involvement even as this mechanism also leads to the recognition that full symbolic satisfaction requires additional action in the historical world to which the film constantly and simultaneously refers.[68]

INTERTEXTUALITY AND "THE MAN FROM HOPE"

My interpretation of "The Man from Hope" has argued that this campaign documentary attempts to solve the local and short-range problems of recasting the image of Bill Clinton through the "telling of the whole story of his life" and that it does this by drawing upon three intertextual relationships: text and history, text and narrative, text and myth. Moreover, these three intertextual dimensions are each necessary, I suggest, for a reading which reconstitutes Bill Clinton as "presidential."

These three axes reveal Bill Clinton taking on the attributes of character (here clustered around the journey as biographical odyssey and the ritual of self-discovery) and of icon (here associated with qualities of conviction and compassion) but also remaining situated as a historical agent to which the film's indexical sounds and images continue to return.[69] It is this dynamic rhetorical action that defines "The Man from Hope" and that possibly redefines its central figure. And it may well be that a reader's final recovery of "The Man from Hope" is in large measure determined by which of these discursive relationships are privileged.

But it is also this ambiguity of reading levels—these "leaky" intertextual relationships that retains for "The Man from Hope" a potential to succeed as a discrete, exigent, persuasive argument. More precisely, our reaction is solicited to the candidate we "meet" as historical person, as narrative character, and as iconic persona of the American myth of the "self-made man." These permeable reading levels may well account for the potential persuasive potency of the documentary argument, for it offers the potential of being read across any of those levels without letting go of the documentary promise that the images which frame the discourse are ultimately tied to the "real."

Thus several conclusions seem warranted. First, questions about how the nonfiction film structures or represents a specific person in such a way that this historical person may be seen as exhibiting a certain significance of image and action is a pivotal one in the study of the documentary film.[70] Nichols has framed this concern in this way: "documentary film raises in acute form the persistent question of what to do with people . . . in what ways can an individual be represented in documentary? by means of what conceptual framework can we imbue the body—its appearance and actions—with significance?"[71] We have found that in "The Man from Hope" the text operates simultaneously along the three axes: the secular trinity of Bill Clinton—person, persona, character—requires the substance of the historical person to provide substantiation for the narrative character and the mythic persona. Drawing upon our knowledge of the conventions of myth and narrative, "The Man from Hope" solicits our political action in history to complete the symbolic action of the mythic biography instantiated in the text.

A second conclusion concerns the relationship between intertextuality and the discrete text. On this question, intertextuality is argued as a clear break with formalism and the notion of the self-contained text that opens to close analysis.[72] That is, when the point of critical engagement with the text becomes its relationship with other texts, then the notion of the artifact as a self-contained, discrete artistic whole is exploded.

But my analysis of "The Man from Hope" suggests that the decisions a critic must make about intertextual readings is not a simply stated dichotomy: either the polysemic, diffuse "intertext" or the discrete text of traditional criticism. Rather it suggests that in the nonfiction documentary discourse at least, the text itself blurs if not erases this simplistic bifurcation. For what we have seen is that the documentary text claims a privileged link to the historical situation; it uses our experience of understanding and decoding narrative; it engages our foreknowledge of the signifying power of myth and spectacle—it is, in short, quintessentially intertextual. But at the very same moment, "The Man from Hope" exploits these potential levels of intertextuality to assist in the rather local project of transforming exigence and solving the problem facing the Clinton campaign. And we may be warranted then in concluding that however we may want to distinguish between the discrete text and the intertextual "text," in this case, the intertextual relationships may well account for the function of the discrete text as a discourse set in a specific time and place.

Finally, a last conclusion touches upon the relationship between what we may call historical and imaginary discourses. "The Man from Hope" exploits three intertextual domains with the potential result that identification with a character and a sense of narrative agency impinge on the sense of poetic structure made from historical material. The narrative structure has an underlying reference to the ethical and to a moral purpose outside the narrative discourse itself, and narrativity is a way to make the real have an order of meaning that is appropriate to the imaginary.[73] We have in "The Man from Hope" a discourse that disguises its moral—that Bill Clinton is a product of a consistent set of moral strictures—by the imbrication of an aesthetic structure belonging to the area of the imaginary.

Thus, "The Man from Hope" invites its audience to see its central figure quite differently; it positions Bill Clinton as an agent in history, yet then reconstitutes him in a filmic representation that introduces axes of narrative and myth, while all the while holding to its indexical reference.[74] Bill Clinton becomes both simultaneously real and symbolic, while "The Man from Hope" prompts our response through the use of symbolic tactics more commonly associated with narrative or fictional film than nonfiction. By allowing the real to be read through the aesthetic and the mythic, "The Man from Hope" provides a frame to transform Bill Clinton and invites its readers to take action in history prompted by a knowledge of narrative and mythic convention. It is this dynamic action that sustains investigation of "The Man from Hope" far beyond the campaign that gave it rise.

NOTES

1. The three big networks (ABC, CBS, and NBC) along with CNN (Cable News Network) cut away from the video during its presentation at the Democratic convention; C-SPAN and PBS ran the film in its entirety. Stuart Elliott, "Clinton Video Now an Infomercial," *New York Times*, 24 August 1992, late ed.: D7 and Brian Donlon, "Networks Dash Bloodworth-Thomason's 'Hope'" *USA Today*, 16 July 1992, first ed.: 3D.

2. Jonathan Raban, "Bill Clinton, Simplified: How a Complex Candidate Learned the Dick and Jane Language of Presidential Politics and Became a Contender," *Los Angeles Times Magazine*, 30 August 1992, home ed.: 12.

3. William Grimes, "The Democratic Ticket—Big-Screen Salute," *New York Times*, 17 July 1992, late ed.: A11.

4. Ibid.

5. Ibid.

6. Diane Haithman, "Designing Presidential Politics," *Los Angeles Times*, 25 July 1992, home ed.: F1.

7. George Jordan, "A Video Portrait 'With All the Warts,'" *Newsday*, 17 July 1992, city ed.: 28.

8. Margaret Carlson, "Bill's Big Bash," *Time*, 27 July 1992, 34.

9. Jacob Weisberg, "Southern Exposure: Clinton as Sitcom," *New Republic*, 2 November 1992, 13.

10. Similar issues are a recurrent concern in film theory; see Andre Bazin, "The Stalin Myth in Soviet Cinema," in *Movies and Methods*, vol. 2, ed. Bill Nichols (Berkeley: University of California Press, 1985), 29–40.

11. These levels are adapted from those suggested by Bill Nichols, "Questions of Magnitude," in *Documentary and the Mass Media*, ed. John Corner (Baltimore, Md.: Edward Arnold, 1986), 107–22. Also, see Nichols, "History, Myth, and Narrative in Documentary," *Film Quarterly* 41 (Fall 1987): 9–20.

12. Nichols, "History, Myth and Narrative," 10.

13. Morreale dates the beginning of the candidate films to the 1952 campaign when both major parties used such presentations at their conventions, but what has changed over time is the supposed influence of these films in the current era of the "televisual campaign." It is now assumed that the campaign film, directed primarily to the

television audience rather than to convention delegates, is one of a political party's most effective persuasive resources. See Jeanne Morreale, "The Political Campaign Film: Epideictic Rhetoric in a Documentary Frame," *Television and Political Advertising*, vol. 2: *Signs, Codes, and Images,* ed. Frank Biocca (Hillsdale, N.Y.: Lawrence Erlbaum, 1991); for other work on the campaign film, see Charles H. Fant, "Televising Presidential Conventions, 1952–1980," *Journal of Communication* 30:4 (1980): 132; Bob Donath, "If You Liked the Convention, You'll Love the Ads," *Advertising Age*, 19 July 1976, 65; Herbert W. Simons, Don J. Stewart, and David Harvey, "Effects of Network Treatments on Perceptions of a Political Campaign Film: Can Rhetorical Criticism Make a Difference?" *Communication Quarterly* 37 (1989): 184–98; Susan B. Mackey, "The Eighteen-Minute Celluloid 'Vision' of Reagan's America," paper presented to the Eastern Communication Association Convention, Baltimore, Md., May 1988. The best overall history of presidential campaign advertising is Kathleen Hall Jamieson, *Packaging the Presidency* (New York: Oxford University Press, 1984). However, Jamieson does not concentrate specifically upon the genre of the campaign film, focusing instead upon the general advertising spots and strategies.

14. Michael F. Smith, "The Ensemble Cast Versus the Star Machine: Narrative Casting Differences in the 1984 Presidential Candidate Films," paper presented at the 1992 Speech Communication Association Meeting, Chicago, Ill., November 1992, n.p.

15. Ibid.

16. Morreale, "The Political Campaign Film," 188.

17. Juan Williams, "Clinton's Reinvention Convention: Can the Candidate—and Party—Get a Fresh Start?" *Washington Post*, 12 July 1992, final ed., C1.

18. Ibid.

19. See W. Lance Bennett, "Assessing Presidential Character: Degradation Rituals in Political Campaigns," *Quarterly Journal of Speech* 67 (1981): 310–21; Bill O. Kjeldahl, Carl W. Carmichael, and Robert J. Mertz, "Factors in a Presidential Candidate's Image," *Speech Monographs* 38 (1971): 129–31; Richard F. Vatz, "Public Opinion and Presidential Ethos," *Western Journal of Speech Communication* 40 (1976): 196–206.

20. See Dan Nimmo and James E. Combs, *Mediated Political Realities*, 2d ed. (New York: Longman, 1993), chapter 2.

21. Bruce Gronbeck, "Negative Narrative in 1988 Presidential Campaign Ads," *Quarterly Journal of Speech* 78 (1992): 295.

22. Larry Sabato, professor of political science, University of Virginia, quoted in Williams, C1.

23. Williams, C1.

24. Carlson, "Bill's Big Bash," 34.

25. Williams, "Clinton's Reinvention Convention."

26. David M. Timmerman, "Competing Recipes for American's Future: A Narrative Analysis of the 1992 Presidential Candidate Videos," paper presented to the Speech Communication Association Meeting, Chicago, Ill., November 1992: n.p.

27. Steve Proffitt, "Los Angeles Times Interview: Linda Bloodworth-Thomason," 22 November 1992, home ed.: M3.

28. Margaret Carlson, "Just a Couple of Hicks with 40 Million Viewers," *Time*, 18 January 1993, 27

29. Haithman, "Designing Presidential Politics," F1.

30. Weisberg, "Southern Exposure," 13.

31. Both Grunwald and Bloodworth-Thomason have claimed credit for finding the bit of archival footage acclaimed as a highlight of "The Man from Hope": the 1963 film clip showing John Kennedy shaking hands in the Rose Garden with the sixteen-year-old Clinton, a clip found at the Kennedy Library; see Carlson, "Bill's Big Bash," 34; also see Weisberg, "Southern Exposure," 13.

32. Jordan, "A Video Portrait 'with All the Warts,'" 28.

33. Ibid.

34. "The Man from Hope" was subsequently used in different ways by the Clinton campaign. It ran later in the campaign as a television infomercial, a program-length commercial with program-style content, which the Clinton camp ran on national cable networks and superstations. Typically, during these infomercials, the film ran twice during a thirty-minute segment and was accompanied by a telephone number viewers could call to obtain a copy of Clinton's economic plan. "It's a nice way to build up viewership"; said Grunwald, "we decided not enough people had seen" the biography during the convention; quoted in Elliott, "Clinton Video Now an Infomercial," D7. "The Man from Hope" was also used again on the eve of election day. Coupled with the regular thirty-second commercials throughout the day, the Clinton campaign hit all three major networks with half-hour ads during prime-time. The programs featured a slightly reedited version of the "The Man from Hope" film biography combined with a pastiche of images from Clinton's bus tour through the country. The half-hour showed the "story" of Bill Clinton but updated it with the postconvention bus trip scenes—including "nuns squeezing Clinton's cheeks, farmers stringing home-made signs from their combines in the summer heat"; see John Hanchette, "Clinton, Perot Buy Election Eve Half-Hour TV Ads," *Gannett News Service*, 2 November 1992.

35. Donlon, "Networks Dash Bloodworth-Thomason's 'Hope,'" 3D.

36. John Fiske, *Television Culture* (New York: Methuen, 1987), 108.

37. Ibid., 115.

38. As Roland Barthes has argued, "everything signifies ceaselessly and several times, but without being delegated to a final great ensemble." See Barthes, *S/Z* (New York: Hill and Wang, 1974), 12.

39. John Grierson, *On Documentary*, ed. Forsyth Hardy (New York: Praeger, 1966).

40. While I do not want to imply here that the documentary text presents an "innocent" and "objective" image of the real, it does seem clear that the documentary text has its grounding in ontology of the photographic image. See Andre Bazin, "Ontology of the Photographic Image," *What Is Cinema?* vol. 1, trans. Hugh Gray (Berkeley: University of California Press, 1967), 9–14.

41. Peter Rabinowitz, *Before Reading: Narrative Conventions and the Politics of Interpretation* (Ithaca, N.Y.: Cornell University Press, 1987), 24.

42. Nichols, "Questions of Magnitude," 107.

43. For instance, when we reach the present time in the film, we have family video-tapes of Bill and Chelsea Clinton dancing, the daughter in a fancy party dress; or we have images of the father and daughter skipping stones over a pond or the daughter curtseying and that these images have the time-date stamp encoded by the video-recorder.

44. L. Bennett and M. Feldman, *Reconstructing Reality in the Courtroom: Justice and Judgment in American Culture* (New Brunswick, N.J.: Rutgers University Press, 1981).

45. Bill Nichols, *Representing Reality: Issues and Concepts in Documentary* (Bloomington: Indiana University Press, 1991), 251.

46. Nichols, "History, Myth and Narrative."

47. Nichols, "Questions of Magnitude," 114.

48. W. R. Fisher, "Narration as a Human Communication Paradigm: The Case of Public Moral Argument," *Communication Monographs* 51 (1984): 1–22; W. R. Fisher, "The Narrative Paradigm: An Elaboration," *Communication Monographs* 52 (1985): 347 67; H. White, "The Value of Narrativity in the Representation of Reality," in W. J. T. Mitchell, ed., *On Narrative* (Chicago: University of Chicago Press, 1981), 1–25.

49. Bennett and Feldman, *Reconstructing Reality in the Courtroom.*

50. White, "The Value of Narrativity," 4.

51. Ibid., p. 14.

52. Ibid.

53. Richard Morris, "Rags-to-Riches: Myth and Reality," *Saturday Review,* 21 November 1953, 15.

54. J. O. Robertson, "Horatio Alger, Andrew Carnegie, Abraham Lincoln and the Cowboy," *Midwest Quarterly* 20 (1979): 244.

55. Madonna Marsden, "The American Myth of Success: Visions and Revisions," in Jack Nachbar, Deborah Weiser, and John L. Wright (Eds.), *The Popular Culture Reader* (Bowling Green, Ohio: Popular Press, 1978), 42.

56. Robertson, "Horatio Alger, Andrew Carnegie, Abraham Lincoln and the Cowboy," 245.

57. Ibid., 246.

58. Marsden, "The American Myth of Success," 45.

59. Timmerman, "Competing Recipes for America's Future."

60. W. Lance Bennett, "Myth, Ritual, and Political Control," *Journal of Communication* 30:4 (1980): 170–71.

61. Ibid., 178.

62. Hal Himmelstein, *TV Myth and the American Mind* (New York: Praeger, 1984), ix–xvi.

63. Walter R. Fisher, "Rhetorical Fiction and the Presidency," *Quarterly Journal of Speech* 66 (1980): 124–25.

64. Charles Affron has suggested that once this sort of alternation occurs, the "nonfiction becomes more or less informed with presentations essential to dramatic texts, and its veracity becomes more or less a function of artistry and expressivity."

See "Reading the Fiction of Non-Fiction: William Wyler's 'Memphis Belle,'" *Quarterly Review of Film Studies* 7 (1982): 54.

65. Nichols, "Questions of Magnitude," 121.

66. It should be said that this characteristic of fidelity is one of the most important elements of narrative rationality. See Fisher, "Narration as a Human Communication Paradigm," 1–22, and "The Narrative Paradigm: An Elaboration," 347–67; also John Louis Lucaites and Celeste Michelle Condit, "Reconstructing Narrative Theory: A Functional Debate," *Journal of Communication* 35 (Autumn 1985): 90–108.

67. Nichols, "History, Myth and Narrative," 13.

68. Ibid., 9.

69. Ibid., 18.

70. I have suggested one way that this may happen, through the figure of synecdoche where a historical person comes to be seen as the representative of both myth and of a class of persons. See Thomas Rosteck, "Synecdoche and Audience in Television Documentary: the 'Case of Milo Radulovich,'" *Southern Communication Journal* 57 (1992): 229–40.

71. Nichols, "History, Myth and Narrative," 9–10.

72. This is a common point of contrast in theory: see Rabinowitz; Roland Barthes, "From Work to Text," *Image-Music-Text*, trans. Stephen Heath (New York: Hill and Wang, 1977), 155–64; this point is stated in the literature of speech communications, most recently in Beverly Whitaker Long and Mary Susan Strine, "Reading Intertextually: Multiple Mediations and Critical Practice," *Quarterly Journal of Speech* 75 (1989): 473.

73. White, "The Value of Narrativity," 13–14.

74. Nichols, "Questions of Magnitude," 118.

PRESIDENTIAL DEBATE AS POLITICAL RITUAL

Clinton vs. Bush vs. Perot

DALE A. HERBECK

It has become increasingly fashionable of late to lament at the sorry state of democracy in the United States. While much has been written, many commentators seem willing to blame the media for corrupting the American system of government.[1] The popular press, for example, is routinely blamed for focusing on questions of personality at the expense of substantive issues, for simplifying or even trivializing the discussion of complex policy questions, and for reducing political discourse to an endless series of easily digested sound bites.

Against this backdrop, political debates seem to offer candidates a unique opportunity to take their unedited message over the media directly to the people. In an article appearing in the *Chicago Tribune*, Newton Minow and Clifford Sloan affirmed this reasoning by stressing:

> For all of their flaws, presidential debates represent an extraordinary opportunity for millions of Americans to see and hear the presidential candidates for an extended period of time. It allows the public to observe the candidates—to be exposed to their patterns of thought and expression—without the immediate filter of sound bites, pundits and 30-second ads. Despite the problems with presidential debates—and the debates can certainly be improved—they far surpass the existing alternatives as a tool of civic discourse.[2]

Kathleen Hall Jamieson and David S. Birdsell concurred in this judgment in their book *Presidential Debates*, suggesting that "the debates offer the longest, most intense view of the candidates available to the electorate. Uninterrupted by ads, uncontaminated by the devices programmers use to ensnare and hold prime-time attention, the debates offer sustained and serious encounters with candidates."[3]

Unfortunately, the potential implicit in debates among the presidential candidates has gone largely unrealized. Instead of affording the viewer a rich discussion of the major issues facing our leaders, David Zarefsky, among others, has lamented that we have "debased" presidential debates into political spectacles virtually devoid of substance.[4] Candidates have skillfully negotiated formats which allow them to routinely avoid answering important questions, to recite memorized or scripted passages, and to avoid any meaningful discussion of troublesome topics. The media has played an equally dubious role, often reducing the debate to a memorable line appearing later in the news while using dubious measures to declare winners and losers.

Not surprisingly, we tend to remember presidential debates of recent history more for egregious errors than for well-crafted arguments. Michael Dukakis, the Democrat's candidate in 1988, is notable for his clinical and detached response to an emotionally charged hypothetical question regarding the rape of his wife; President Ronald Reagan ended the second debate with a closing statement that featured a disjointed trip down a California highway in 1984; President Jimmy Carter was ridiculed for admitting that he discussed nuclear doctrine with his daughter in 1980; and President Gerald Ford is still remembered for emphatically stating that there was no Soviet domination of Eastern Europe in 1976.[5] The 1960 debate between Nixon and Kennedy, while devoid of major gaffes, stills brings back images of a youthful John Kennedy confronting a sweaty Richard Nixon whose face bore a suspicious five o'clock shadow.

Against this backdrop of potential and disappointment, Bill Clinton brought a fundamentally different approach to presidential debates. Candidate Clinton's approach to the 1992 presidential debates was unique, largely because it attempted to transcend the spectacle by directly engaging the viewer as a participant. This occurred, most obviously, in the second presidential debate which featured a format Clinton devised that involved the audience in directly questioning the candidates. The effort to engage the public was also evident, however, in Clinton's negotiating strategy prior to the debates, in his performance during the debates, and in discourse from his campaign regarding the debates.

In the pages that follow, this chapter assesses the success of Clinton's effort by analyzing the extended negotiations between the parties regarding the number and nature of the debates, briefly characterizing the three debates among the major candidates, considering some inferences that can be drawn from the 1992 presidential debates, and by suggesting that such contests are best understood as political rituals. Ultimately, it will be argued that Clinton "won" the debates, not because he was the better debater, but rather because of his unique vision of the role that debate plays in a democratic system of government.

THE PRESIDENTIAL DEBATES OF 1992

As a result of a Twentieth-Century Fund Report, "For Great Debates," a bipartisan Commission on Presidential Debates was created for the purpose of guaranteeing future presidential debates. After the debates between Kennedy and Nixon in 1960, there were no presidential debates in 1964, 1968, and 1972. The debates that occurred in 1976, 1980, 1984, and 1988 were preceded by intense battling over rules and procedures. The idea behind the commission, which originated with Newton Minow and Clifford Sloan, was to negotiate the logistics before the heat of the fall campaign in an effort to minimize the incentive for partisan politicking for strategic advantage.

The original commission plan for presidential debates in 1992 called for three presidential debates and a single exchange between the vice-presidential candidates.[6] In response to frustration with the panel approach used in previous presidential debates, the commission proposed using a single moderator who would address questions to the candidates. Paul Kirk, former Democratic National Committee chairman and co-chair of the commission, explained that "we want to have the most spontaneous, free exchange between the candidates and not have time taken up by panels of three or four."[7] The commission believed that a single moderator format would promote such interaction by encouraging more follow-up questions while simultaneously creating the possibility for more direct confrontation between the candidates.[8]

From the outset, Bill Clinton expressed a willingness to debate President Bush. He readily accepted the scheme proposed by the commission, which included agreement on the number of debates, the dates, and the format.[9] Clinton also embraced the concept of a nonpartisan commission negotiating the rules instead of direct negotiations between the campaigns. In marked contrast, the Bush campaign summarily rejected the commission's lone moderator format, apparently fearing that it would work to Clinton's advantage since it would likely produce a more spontaneous exchange on a relatively limited number of topics. White House Chief of Staff James Baker, many felt, also believed that agreeing to debates early on would freeze any momentum toward Bush. Since Clinton held a commanding lead in virtually all of the polls, some speculated that Baker was intentionally delaying the debates until Bush had a chance to narrow the gap.[10] Whatever the motivation, White House spokesman Marlin Fitzwater defended the decision by noting that "when you're running, you tend to take a very narrow view of your own interests."[11]

As an alternative to the commission's scheme, the Bush campaign proposed a series of two debates using the traditional format which had the candidates responding to questions from an approved panel of journalists with little opportunity for follow-up questions or direct confrontations.[12] The Bush campaign apparently believed that this would produce a wide-ranging discussion on a variety of topics, allowing the president to address his foreign-policy successes while limiting the amount of time spent discussing the economy. Not surprisingly, the Clinton campaign rejected the Bush proposal, arguing that the candidates should debate according to the original commission plan. While some worried that "the dispute over debates has already resulted in scrapping one debate . . . and there is no guarantee of any further debates,"[13] others were less concerned. The *New York Times*, for example, rationalized that "the maneuvering for advantage over seemingly technical details is with good reason: debates can decide elections."[14]

The inability to agree on a format forced the cancellation of the first debate scheduled at Michigan State University on 22 September 1992.[15] Clinton charged that Bush was trying to avoid debating, and he emphasized his willingness to debate the president by campaigning in East Lansing on the night of the proposed exchange. Soon, demonstrators clad in chicken costumes were appearing at Bush rallies, calling attention to the president's unwillingness to debate. David Letterman, appearing on his "Late Night" show, offered a satirical list containing "Top Ten Debate Conditions Demanded by George Bush."[16] This sort of criticism, which clearly annoyed Bush, led him to push his advisors to arrange for debates.[17] No doubt, Bush's inability to narrow the gap in the polls and the recognition that the public apparently wanted presidential debates, also led the Republicans to rethink their hard-line strategy.

The Bush team responded with an aggressive new proposal that called for four debates, one occurring every Sunday beginning on 11 October 1992. This scheme, which initially seemed to catch Clinton off-guard, allowed Bush to briefly occupy the high ground on the debate over the debates. In fact, Bush went on the offensive, charging that "Gov. Clinton has responded to my challenge the same way his response (sic) to issues, like free trade, fuel efficiency standards, and middle-class taxes—he waffles. I can't find him. He's missing in action."[18]

At this moment, the debate about the debates became the single most important issue of the campaign, effectively precluding meaningful discussion of any other topic. Clinton, fearing the public might conclude that he was afraid to debate, immediately reconsidered his decision not to negotiate directly with the Bush campaign. After consulting with the bipartisan Commission on Presidential Debates, Clinton agreed to meetings and Mickey Kantor immediately met with Bush campaign chairman Robert Teeter. As a result of this dialogue, the campaigns agreed to a series of four debates utilizing a combination of formats to be held over nine days shortly before the election. Ross Perot, who lurked on the edge of candidacy during the debate about the debates, was invited to participate, but he seems to have played little part in determining the format.

Given this sordid history, it is not surprising that the 1992 presidential debates reflected a series of compromises.[19] The first presidential debate, using a format that Bush favored, was moderated by Jim Lehrer of PBS with questions from a panel composed of three reporters (Ann Compton of ABC News, John Mashek of the *Boston Globe*, and freelance journalist Sander Vanocur). The candidates took turns answering questions with the primary respondent receiving two minutes with a minute for rebuttal by the other candidates. The second presidential debate, using a format proposed by Clinton, employed Carole Simpson as moderator with questions from undecided members of the studio audience. The final presidential debate employed elements of both the first and second debate, with Jim Lehrer of PBS serving as moderator for the first half of the debate and questions from a three-reporter panel (Susan Rook of CNN, Gene Gibbons of Reuters, and Helen Thomas of the United Press International) during the second half.[20] A separate debate for the vice-presidential candidates was held between the first and second presidential debates. This exchange featured a single moderator (Hal Bruno of ABC News), asking questions of Al Gore, Dan Quayle, and James Stockdale.

The First Presidential Debate at St. Louis

In the days immediately prior to the first debate, both Clinton and Bush spent a good deal of time trying to shape expectations. Bush was quick to note that "I'm not an Oxford-trained debater," making reference to Clinton's education as a Rhode scholar in Britain.[21] Clinton retorted that Bush, given his participation in debates in 1980, 1984, and 1988, "is the most experienced debater since Abraham Lincoln."[22] Instead of focusing on the relative skills of the debaters, the media spent time theorizing about what the candidates would need to do to win the debates. Most believed that Clinton, leading in the polls, could win by appearing presidential while avoiding a major gaffe. Since President Bush was trailing badly in the polls on the eve of the debates, the same commentators held that "the man who must gamble it all on an aggressive, go-for-broke strategy is Bush, whose need for a knockout blow means that a draw is a loss."[23]

The first presidential debate, which was held on the campus of Washington University, in St. Louis, Missouri, on Sunday, 10 October 1992, demonstrated that all three candidates possessed formidable advocacy skills. Moderator Jim Lehrer and the three-reporter panel directed seventeen questions to the candidates, most dealing with domestic concerns. By most accounts, Ross Perot gave the most impressive performance in the first debate. Perot offered an assortment of memorable lines, including a warning that "we are sitting on a ticking time bomb"[24] and a blunt statement that "if you hate people, I don't want your vote." When discussing the economy, Perot noted

> Well, they've got a point. I don't have any experience in running up a
> $4 trillion debt. I don't have any experience in gridlock government,
> where nobody takes responsibility for anything and everybody blames

everybody else. I don't have any experience in creating the worst public school system in the industrialized world, the most violent crime-ridden society in the industrialized world. But I do have a lot of experience in getting things done.

When the debate turned to the equity of certain types of taxes, Perot uttered his famed "If there's a fairer way, I'm all ears" response. He also promised that the lobbyists, "those guys in $1,000 suits and alligator shoes," would "be over there in the Smithsonian" Institution if he came to power.

Clinton pursued a fairly predictable strategy in the first debate. He began by denouncing Bush's commitment to "trickle down economics." "Tonight I have to say to the President," Clinton said, turning to face Bush, "Mr. Bush, for twelve years you've had it your way. You've had your chance and it didn't work. It's time to change. I want to bring change to the American people, but we must all decide first: Do we have the courage to change for hope in a better tomorrow?" Clinton reiterated this theme throughout the debate, arguing "We need a new approach" because "we're living in a new world after the cold war and what works in this new world is not trickle-down, not government for the benefit of the privileged few, not tax and spend, but a commitment to invest in American jobs and American education, controlling American health-care costs and bringing the American people together."

Since the bulk of the questions concerned economic issues, Bush was forced to spend a disproportionate amount of time defending his domestic policy. Brief references to Bosnia, Somalia, and China, hardly allowed Bush to establish his credentials as the foreign policy president. Bush did, however, counter Clinton's charge that the country is "coming apart at the seams." According to Bush, "I would hate to be running for president and think that the only way I could win would be to convince everybody how horrible things are. Yes, there are big problems, and yes, people are hurting, but I believe that this agenda for American renewal I have is the answer to it." Later in the debate, however, Bush announced that he would make James Baker a domestic policy czar if reelected. While clearly appealing to Baker's success as Secretary of State managing America's foreign affairs, this proposed change in leadership seemed to undercut the credibility of Bush's claim that the economy was already on the road to recovery.

The most dramatic exchange in the debate occurred after Bush criticized Clinton for participating in the demonstrations during the Vietnam war while a student at Oxford. The key piece of evidence supporting this accusation, popularized by conservative Congressman Robert Dornan of California, was Clinton's visit to Moscow during his Christmas break in 1969–70. This charge was not unexpected, as the Bush campaign had spent several days before the debate raising questions about Clinton's behavior. "It's not a question of patriotism," Bush charged. "It's a question of character and judgment." In a pointed rebuke, Clinton turned to face Bush while invoking the memory of Sen. Prescott Bush's courageous decision to support a motion to censure Sen. Joe McCarthy. In a stinging rebuke that made the highlight films on the late evening newscasts, Clinton charged:

> You have questioned my patriotism. You even brought some right-wing Congressmen into the White House to plot how to attack me for going to Russia in 1969–1970 when over 50,000 other Americans did. Now I honor your service in World War II. I honor Mr. Perot's service in uniform and the service of every man and woman who ever served, including Admiral Crowe who was your Chairman of the Joint Chiefs and who is supporting me. But when Joe McCarthy went around this country attacking people's patriotism, he was wrong. He was wrong. And a Senator from Connecticut stood up to him named Prescott Bush. Your father was right to stand up to Joe McCarthy; you were wrong to attack my patriotism. I was opposed to the war, but I love my country and we need a President who will bring this country together, not divide it. We've got enough division. I want to lead a unified country.

Since Clinton was the last to answer the original question, President Bush did not have an opportunity to respond to Clinton's reference to his father.

In many respects, Ross Perot won the first round. His presence on the stage with the candidates of the Democratic and Republican parties clearly legitimated his unconventional candidacy. His no-nonsense philosophy clearly connected with the audience, and at times his personality dominated the contest. At the same time, Bill Clinton offered a strong performance and undoubtedly solidified his hold on the front-runner's mantle. Indeed, at least one of the instant opinion polls declared Clinton the winner.[25] The clear loser in St. Louis was George Bush. While one poll found that 94 percent of Bush supporters thought that Bush had won,[26] the president failed to reach beyond his constituency, and in the process, he squandered a precious opportunity to begin narrowing the gap between himself and Clinton.

Republican hopes were lifted, however, by a surprisingly strong showing by Vice-President Dan Quayle in the vice-presidential debate two days later on 13 October 1992. While Al Gore appeared stiff or even wooden, Quayle aggressively attacked Clinton, and Gore was slow to leap to the defense. On numerous occasions, Quayle accused Gore of "pulling a Clinton," or waffling on the issues.[27] James Bond Stockdale, Ross Perot's number-two man and a genuine Vietnam war hero, seemed strangely out of place and many openly wondered afterward whether he would be able to assume the presidency. Stockdale began his opening statement by asking, "Who am I? Why am I here?" At the end of the debate, the viewer was left with no good answer to either question. Any forward momentum that Perot may have gained from the first debate was abruptly halted by Stockdale's showing, while Quayle's performance so exceeded expectations that Republican spirits, dampened by Bush's tepid effort in St. Louis, were lifted.

The Second Presidential Debate at Richmond

The second debate, held on 15 October 1992, in Richmond, Virginia, featured questions from the audience and produced the most detailed discussion of policy options of the three debates. Moderator Carole Simpson began by encouraging the audience to address the issues and it was clear from the outset that the 209 uncommitted voters present were truly concerned with substantive considerations. One of the first questioners complained that "the amount of time the candidates have spent in this campaign trashing their opponents' character and programs is depressingly large."[28] The next questioner extended the thought by asking: "Can we focus on the issues and not the personalities and the mud?" Not surprisingly, the citizen questioners ignored the character issues associated with Clinton's draft record and his antiwar activities in Europe which had been such a large part of the first debate. In the process, the questioners prevented Bush from pursuing the aggressive attack initiated two days earlier by Quayle.

Although some critics complained that the audience's questions were "self-interested,"[29] "very parochial,"[30] and "as dull as C-SPAN at midnight,"[31] other commentators reported that "the voters blew the whistle on mud wrestling and had a civilizing effect on the often feral 1992 campaign."[32] The questioners asked about jobs, health care, and deficit reduction. The most poignant moment of the debate occurred when a young black women asked, "How can you honestly find a cure for the economic problems of the common people if you have no experience in what's ailing them?" After Perot explained his personal experience as a businessman, Bush tried to respond but could do no better than explaining that "the national debt affects everybody. Obviously it has a lot to do with interest rates." When pushed by Simpson to explain how the economic problems had affected him personally, Bush was seemingly unable to formulate a cogent response. His third attempt, which came the closest to answering, spoke in general terms about economic misery and suggested that he could empathize because "I don't think it's fair to say, you haven't had cancer, therefore you don't know what it's like." Bush continued, "I don't think it's fair to say, you know, whatever it is, that if you haven't been hit by it personally—but everybody's affected by the debt because of the tremendous interest that goes into paying on that debt, everything's more expensive." When his turn came, Clinton established direct eye contact with the questioner, empathized by suggesting that the questioner had known "people who've lost their jobs and lost their homes," and then he explained that as governor of tiny Arkansas, "When people lose their jobs, there's a good chance I'll know them by their names. When a factory closes, I know the people who ran it."

Clinton was clearly the most at home with the format as he repeatedly moved toward the questioner as queries were directed to him. He spoke with empathy and he worked the crowd in a way that projected sincerity. Even when the other candidates spoke, Clinton's facial expressions held the attention of the audience. Jeff Greenfield of ABC News reported that "Governor Clinton commanded the atmospherics."[33] By the mid-point of the debate, George Bush was checking his watch to either plan his strategy or to determine how much longer the questioning would continue. He looked at his watch three times, an action prominently highlighted in accounts of the debate, and he finished the evening by offering a closing statement delivered from behind his stool. Ross Perot alternated between standing awkwardly before a stool that was clearly too tall and half-sitting, while dispensing his famed one-liners ("If you want to have a high-risk experience comparable to bungee-jumping, go into the Congress").

Media accounts quickly declared Clinton the winner. More than either Bush or Perot, Clinton had been in control of the event. Not only did he answer the questions most directly, but he commanded the entire stage. Not surprisingly, a CBS poll conducted immediately after the debate found that 54 percent thought Clinton won, 25 percent though Bush won, and 20 percent thought Perot was the winner.[34]

The Third Presidential Debate at East Lansing

By the eve of the third debate, it was evident that the race was Clinton's to lose. As the candidates squared off in East Lansing on 19 October 1992, an ABC poll showed Clinton with a commanding eighteen-point lead and a network map showed Clinton leading in thirty-one states with 368 electoral votes.[35] A growing number of political commentators declared that Bush must score big in the third debate if he was to have any chance of winning the election. While Bush responded with his best performance to date, he was still chastised for not being able to deliver "a decisive knockout punch."[36]

George Bush, deviating little from his campaign strategy, clearly entered the final contest with an aggressive plan to attack Clinton on taxes and trust. Early on, in response to a question about mistakes Clinton might have made but was unwilling to acknowledge, Bush directly criticized Clinton's performance as governor:

> Well, the record in Arkansas. I mean look at it. And that's what we're asking America to have. Now look, he says Arkansas is a poor state. They are. But in almost every category they're lagging. I'll give you an example. He talks about all the jobs he created in one or two years. Over the last 10 years since he's been Governor, they're 30 percent behind—30 percent—they're 30 percent of the national average, on pay for teachers, on all of these categories Arkansas is right near the very bottom.[37]

In the summary at the end of his answer, Bush claimed that "Arkansas is doing very, very badly against any standard—environment, support for police officers, whatever it is."

In addition to directly challenging Clinton's record in Arkansas, Bush invoked the grim specter of America with both a Democratic president and a Democratic Congress. In a direct reference to the Carter administration, Bush noted that "interest rates were 20 percent. Inflation was 15 percent. The misery index—unemployment and inflation together—it was invented by the Democrats—went right through the roof."

Bush and his advisors also anticipated that Clinton might address the Bush promise in the first debate to name James Baker as a domestic policy czar. Bush was ready when Clinton announced that "the person responsible for domestic economic policy in my administration will be Bill Clinton. I'm going to make those decisions." In his most memorable line of the debates, Bush quickly retorted, "That's what worries me. That he's going to be responsible. He's going to do—he would do—and he would do for the United States what he's done for Arkansas."

Finally, in his closing statement, Bush returned to the trust issue. He summarily dismissed Clinton's effort to distinguish between the character of the president and the character of the presidency. He went on to approvingly note that "Horace Greeley said the only thing that endures is character. And I think it was Justice Black who talked about great nations like great men must keep their word." The unstated conclusion to this argument, of course, was that Bush alone possessed the requisite qualities to safeguard the interest of the United States.

Although the third debate was Bush's best performance, it was far from perfect. Bush admitted to several "mistakes" during the previous four years. The most obvious one, in Bush's mind, was his decision to go along with the Democrats and raise taxes, which forced him to abandon the famed "Read my lips" pledge made during the 1988 campaign. Later in the debate, Bush admitted he erred in seeking closer relations with Iraq prior to Saddam Hussein's invasion of Kuwait. Bush also floundered when answering a question about the number of women in his inner circle. He praised Rose Zamaria, a White House administrator, for being "about as tough as a boot." Sensing the thrust of the question, he continued to add "Jim Baker's a man. Yeah, I plead guilty to that." Bush also misspoke at times, referring to "trickle-down government" instead of "trickle-down economics" and he referred to "90/90 hindsight." While these may be small errors, in retrospect, each of these answers helps to explain the failure of the Bush presidency.

Almost without exception, the commentators were quick to report that the debate would probably have little impact on the election's outcome. While most admitted that Bush had given his best performance to date, the media was also quick to note the absence of a "knockout blow." At best, Bush had scored well in this round, even though it appeared he would probably lose the bout. Worse yet, the public had been unimpressed by Bush's confrontational tactics. An instant poll by ABC News found 39 percent of Americans thought Clinton won the debate, 25 percent said Ross Perot won, and 19 percent said George Bush won.[38]

While the debates were entertaining, a close reading of the texts some months after the fact reveals that the candidates broke little new ground. Although there were some notable lines, all three contenders were content to rely on their larger campaign themes. Clinton, for the most part, tried to direct the debate toward the failure of George Bush's economic policy. Bush responded by attempting to shift the campaign away from the economy, most often, by trying to cast the election as question of which candidate could be trusted. Ross Perot, understandably, represented his candidacy as a challenge to a failed political system. Yet, it would be a serious error to claim that the debaters avoided issues of substance. On numerous occasions, Clinton was pressed to prove that his economic plan was viable without far-ranging tax increases. President Bush was repeatedly forced to defend his economic policy and to answer questions about Iraq that he would probably have preferred to avoid. Ross Perot, despite his engaging persona, was hard pressed to explain just exactly how he would break the gridlock or achieve so many of his promises.

REFLECTIONS ON THE 1992 PRESIDENTIAL DEBATES

In retrospect, it is easy to downplay the importance of the 1992 presidential debates. Bill Clinton entered the debates as the front-runner; he offered strong performances in each of the three contests, and he went on to win the presidency by a comfortable margin. It is equally easy to explain Bush's defeat on either the sorry state of the economy or his inability to offer a cogent domestic agenda.[39] Whatever the explanation, no political commentator to date has seriously suggested that the presidential debates contributed to Bush's defeat. The prevailing political opinions suggest, at most, that Bush failed to exploit whatever opportunity the debates might have provided for him to salvage a disastrous candidacy.

Such thinking, it should be added, is consistent with the existing research on presidential debates.[40] Although there are reports linking presidential debates to election results,[41] there is precious little empirical support for the claim that presidential debates are decisive in deciding the outcome of presidential elections.[42] This does not mean, however, that it is impossible to draw any meaningful lessons from the presidential debates between Clinton, Bush, and Perot. In fact, some important insights can be formulated about the 1992 presidential debates by examining several aspects unique to them concerning their frequency of occurrence, their utilization of various formats, their coverage by the media, and their inclusion of three participants.

Frequency

The four debates held in a nine-day period, for example, seemed to dramatically constrain the media's ability to shape public understanding of what happened.[43] In previous years, a candidate's performance could be dissected over a period of days or even weeks. The intervening time period allowed ample time for the media to interpret events and shape public understanding. So, for example, many who watched the debate between Ford and Carter in 1980 rated it as a draw immediately after the debate. Ford's refusal to admit he had erred in denying Soviet domination of Poland, coupled with the media accounts which emphasized the significance of this error, quickly created the impression that Carter had actually won the debate.[44] This sort of reworking was not possible in 1992, simply because there was insufficient time for analysis. The debates occurred literally every other day, meaning the last debate was instantly old news with everyone focusing on the next round. Even if one of the candidates had made a major error, there would have been another debate within forty-eight hours providing them with an opportunity to clarify or elaborate on their position.

Further, each debate was only part of the larger series. Instead of assessing the debates as discrete events, we were left with a play divided into four smaller acts. While the audience formed an impression of each act, they reserved judgment on the whole performance until it was complete. Some even likened the debate to a television mini-series,[45] although it would surely have been a series plagued by disconnected episodes. By the culmination of the third presidential debate, it was apparent to everyone that Bush was the loser simply because he had failed to win a decisive victory that would turn the momentum in his favor.

Format

Much of the traditional criticism of recent presidential debates is also applicable to the 1992 debates. The press conference format, in which a panel of journalists takes turns posing questions to the candidates, continued to disappoint. By design, this format makes the questioners into celebrities and encourages them to phrase elaborate questions to demonstrate their own knowledge of the issues. Not surprisingly, each of the journalists is so preoccupied with asking their own question that they frequently neglect to ask damning follow-up questions. Aware of this limitation, the candidates are able to dance around difficult questions.

These limitations of the panel approach were evident throughout the 1992 presidential debates. In the first debate, Clinton's one-minute attack on Bush for questioning his patriotism fell at the end of the questioning cycle, precluding Bush from responding. Therefore, the audience had to wait until the second debate for Bush to address Clinton's charge that Bush's own father would be ashamed of his use of "McCarthyism." Bush responded to Clinton's allegation:

> I remember something my dad told me. I was 18 years old, going to Penn Station to go into the Navy and he said, "Write your mother"—which I faithfully did—he said, "Serve your country"— my father was an honor, duty and country man—and he said, "Tell the truth." And I've tried to do that in public life, all through it. And that says something about character.
>
> My argument with Governor Clinton—you can call it mud wrestling but I think it's fair to put in focus—is I am deeply troubled by someone who demonstrates and organizes demonstration in a foreign land when his country's at war.

While a very appropriate response, surely some of its force was lost because it was uttered four days later without the benefit of context. One can only imagine how much more powerful this reply would have been if Bush had been able to respond immediately after Clinton spoke.

Another problem was that the abbreviated format allowed candidates to either avoid answering difficult questions or, if they had been inclined to answer them, it made it impossible for the candidates to offer sufficiently detailed responses. In the famed Lincoln-Douglas debates of 1858, the two candidates each had ninety minutes to address a single issue. In contrast, in the first debate in 1992, the first candidate had only two minutes to answer a question, followed by the other candidates giving a one-minute rebuttal. This would have been barely sufficient had the candidates addressed one or two themes for the entire debate, but the opening questions invited candidates to define the "single most important separating issue of this campaign," to outline how their personal experiences distinguish them from the other candidates, and to identify issues of character which distinguish the individual candidates. Rather than remaining on any single topic, the next questioner always ventured off in another direction. So, the first debate continued to discuss tax increases, defense cuts, a gasoline tax, defense conversion, and job creation. All of these themes were addressed in successive questions. The result was a series of shallow exchanges by the candidates on a wide-ranging set of topics. While this may have highlighted some of the differences in the candidates' respective positions, it failed to produce much genuine argumentative clash. It was precisely this sort of problem which led Kathleen Jamieson and David Birdsell to lament that "rather than eliciting depth, the (panel) format invites sloganeering. Brief answers on a shower of topics create an informational blur. The press panel asks questions designed to elicit news headlines, not information of use to voters. The superficial is rewarded, the substantive, spurned."[46]

Despite the novelty of the citizen-as-questioner format, it suffered from many of the same limitations. While the citizens demonstrated that they were well informed about the issues and were as fully capable of framing questions as the media, the second debate also lurched from theme to theme with vague answers and no meaningful follow-up questions. In contrast, the lone moderator format used for the vice-presidential debate and the first half of the third debate, clearly demonstrated that a single interlocutor with a more flexible time limit was more capable of initiating a series of questions and inciting direct confrontation of the candidates. Regrettably, the experience with the lone moderator format in 1992 may make candidates less likely to agree to such a format in future debates. The very spontaneity which makes this format interesting creates the uncertainty that all candidates prefer to avoid.

Media Coverage

The way in which the 1992 debates was covered by the media was also disappointing. Almost immediately after each of the contests, the media was quick to declare a winner. Such judgments were frequently based on one or two memorable lines or on the results of an instant opinion poll. Watching late-night coverage of the debates was much akin to viewing sports highlights, as a commentator tried to reduce a ninety-minute exchange to two or three decisive moments which could be completely captured in brief film clips. In 1992 the first debate was memorable for one or two witty lines from Perot and Clinton's reference to Prescott Bush to defend his patriotism; the second debate featured Clinton's emphatic response to how unemployment had touched him while George Bush studied his watch; and the third debate will be remembered for Bush's expressed worry that Clinton truly would be responsible for American economic policy. Media coverage frequently flattered Perot, in large part, because of his penchant for speaking in short sentences that became easy sound bites. In contrast, George Bush's rambling syntax offered more of a challenge to editors, meaning that he probably received less-flattering coverage.

Such coverage, more than anything else, probably reinforces the conception that the debates failed to address the substantive concerns. While the debates might have have featured a more-detailed discussion of the issues, it would be misleading to claim that the debates were devoid of serious argumentative clash. Reducing the debates to one or two notable film clips, which makes for a concise story, eliminates any appreciation of the larger context by removing any reference to the issues that were discussed. Regrettably, such coverage may be more important than what actually transpired in the debates. As Jamieson and Birdsell have observed, "a growing body of data suggests that the voters' shifting perception of the candidate's success in a debate is shaped not by actual debate performance but by the media call of who won or lost."[47]

The presence of three debaters also constrained the exchanges. While Dukakis was free to speak directly to Bush, the presence of a third candidate in 1992 prevented the thrust and parry sometimes seen in presidential debates. It is difficult, for example, to imagine a 1992 equivalent of Lloyd Bentsen's disparaging comparison between John Kennedy and Dan Quayle. The presence of a third debater transformed the debates into an occasionally spirited question-answer session among the contenders, as opposed to a dynamic confrontation between two advocates.[48]

So too, the unique nature of Perot's candidacy further constrained the interaction. Both the Clinton and Bush camps were genuinely interested in appealing to Perot's constituency, so neither of the leading candidates was willing to risk aggressively attacking Perot. While Perot's strong showing in the first debate might have changed this strategy, Stockdale's poor showing in the vice-presidential debate marginalized the threat enough so that both Clinton and Bush were content to spend most of their time talking to each other. As a result, there was comparatively little criticism of anything that Perot said and we might expect the same treatment for third-party candidates in future debates.

Finally, the presence of Perot undoubtedly worked to the Democrat's advantage. Since Perot's candidacy was grounded primarily in the failure of American economic policy, he spent the bulk of his time in the debates relentlessly hammering on economic themes. This focus not only called attention to Bush's failure, but it deflected attention away from the trust issue that Bush wanted so badly to address. The one time Perot did address the question of character occurred in the first debate when he summarily dismissed the issue by noting

> I think it's very important to measure when and where things occurred. Did they occur when you were a young person in your formative years? Or did they occur while you were a senior official in the Federal Government? When you're a senior official in the Federal Government spending billions of taxpayers' money and you're a mature individual and you make a mistake, then that was on your ticket. If you make it as a young man, time passes.

Even if discounting Bush's charge, Perot brought the debate back to federal spending. By highlighting the economic issues on top of the

Democrat's agenda, Perot's presence undoubtedly helped focus the debate to Clinton's advantage.

PRESIDENTIAL DEBATES AS POLITICAL RITUALS

What then are we to conclude from this review of the 1992 presidential debates? If the debates had no decisive impact on the election results, why are they worthy of our study? Can we do more than frame a limited set of conclusions based on the frequency of the debates or the differences between the formats employed? Even though the debates may not have been a deciding factor in Bill Clinton's election, they nonetheless served an important political function. It is unfortunate that the media's obsession with winners and losers, exemplified by their reliance on instant polls and immediate discussion of a debate's political ramifications, has created the erroneous impression that debates have value solely because they might influence the outcome of the election. While this possibility cannot be dismissed, presidential debates have intrinsic value because they constitute an important political ritual.

A democratic government, in a very fundamental way, draws its legitimacy from the people through elections. In a pragmatic way, elections are necessary to select leaders. But in a more fundamental way, elections are necessary to legitimate leadership. Debates, featuring an open exchange among the candidates, are an important part of the presidential legitimation ritual. Jamieson and Birdsell suggest that:

> The belief that our system entails democratic choice is evident
> in the presence of two or more candidates whose task is to
> demonstrate that one would better represent the country than
> the others. Throughout the debates, the candidates will agree
> that the problems facing the country are solvable, that its insti-
> tutions are functional, and that the people rule.[49]

Given all this, it is not surprising that presidential debates have become an important political ritual in a relatively short period of time. Just like presidential press conferences, which originated in the Kennedy administration and are now commonplace, voters now expect the presidential candidates to submit themselves through public argument for critical scrutiny.

When Clinton, Bush, and Perot consented to debate last fall, they overtly affirmed their faith in the power of the people. By submitting their respective candidacies to the public through a discussion of the issues, the nominees also demonstrated their belief that informed discussion is the best way to make government policy. In 1992, by most accounts, at least 100 million Americans watched one of the three presidential debates.[50] Through this simple act of participation, the public revealed their commitment to a democratic system of government and their belief that presidential elections are important.

If the debates are understood as a political ritual, much of the common criticism of them can be dismissed. While we might lament the lack of substance, the very presence of the presidential candidates in a forum where they are questioned by a moderator, panelists, or citizens suggests that our cherished democracy is viable. Although we might wish for a format that allowed for a more-substantive interaction between the candidates or a more-detailed discussion of policy options, presidential debates remain a spontaneous public exchange of viewpoints among candidates for office. Despite the instant opinion polls and all of the professional commentary, an individual citizen is still free to form an opinion, to express that opinion widely, and to cast his or her vote accordingly.

Bill Clinton clearly recognized from the outset that presidential debates are an important political ritual. This was immediately evident in his willingness to debate George Bush. When Bush declined, Clinton was quick to travel to East Lansing on the night of the canceled debate to demonstrate his desire to come before the people. Moreover, it was Clinton who consistently argued for debates according to the presumably objective guidelines formulated by the nonpartisan Commission on Presidential Debates. When Bush suggested an alternative format, it was Clinton who compromised, surrendered the original commission plan, and agreed to begin direct negotiations.

It is not surprising that Clinton was willing to debate, for his entire candidacy reflected a willingness to appeal directly to the public. His troubled campaign survived early questions through appeals that reached beyond the media to take his side of the story to the American people. Clinton then took the unprecedented step of appearing on "60 Minutes" on Super Bowl Sunday, along with his wife, Hillary, to discuss their marriage and charges of infidelity. Later, he played his saxophone on the "Arsenio Hall Show." He laughed at himself on MTV. He was a regular on the morning talk shows, and he staged numerous televised town meetings. Through each of these unique forums, Clinton was able to take his case directly to the voters without the filtering influence of the mass media. While many have denigrated these appeals, such efforts represent an effort to "regenerate democracy" by inviting the public to participate directly in the political process.[51]

Given his desire to reach the people, it is not surprising that Clinton argued for the unique citizen-as-questioner format used in the second debate. While this format may not have produced a superior discussion, citizen participation served an important symbolic purpose. In a very real way, the candidates came before the people in Richmond that October evening. While Clinton clearly excelled in this setting, it is important to remember that citizen participation was consistent with his view of the political process. Campaign Chairman Mickey Kantor said the campaign liked the format because "it gets over the filter that people in the media and, frankly, people in politics get into—the questions are more substantive."[52] While George Bush was seen on national television glancing at his watch as he stood before the public, Bill Clinton was forging a unique rapport with the studio audience and, symbolically, with the viewing public.

The public responded to the Clinton message by electing him president of the United States. While it is impossible to argue that the debates were responsible for Clinton's victory, it is clear that Clinton understood presidential debates were an important political ritual. To the extent that anyone "won" the 1992 presidential debates, a case could be made that it was Bill Clinton. He clearly faired the best in the polls conducted by the networks and in the judgment of the political commentators. But in a more fundamental sense, he "won" because he understood that the debates were a ritual through which an aspiring candidate could legitimate his candidacy to the voting public.

NOTES

1. See, for example, David L. Swanson, "The Political-Media Complex," *Communication Monographs* 59 (December 1992): 397–400; Larry J. Sabato, *Feeding Frenzy: How Attack Journalism Has Transformed American Politics* (New York: Free Press, 1991); Douglas Kellner, *Television and the Crisis of Democracy* (Boulder, Colo.: Westview, 1990); Robert

M. Entman, *Democracy without Citizens: Media and the Decay of American Politics* (New York: Oxford University Press, 1989); Neil Postman, *Amusing Ourselves to Death: Public Discourse in the Age of Show Business* (New York: Viking, 1985).

2. Newton M. Minow and Clifford M. Sloan, "End the Debate over Debates," *Chicago Tribune*, 22 September 1992, 21. Newton Minow was co-chair of the League of Women Voters' Presidential Debates Steering Committee in 1976 and 1980. Clifford Sloan was director of the Twentieth-Century Fund's Presidential Debates Project. Sloan and Minow co-authored the fund's 1987 report, "For Great Debates."

3. Kathleen Hall Jamieson and David S. Birdsell, *Presidential Debates: The Challenge of Creating an Informed Electorate* (New York: Oxford University Press, 1988), 126.

4. David Zarefsky, "Spectator Politics and the Revival of Public Argument," *Communication Monographs* 59 (December 1992): 412–13.

5. For a more extensive listing of gaffes, see ibid., 412; Walter Shapiro, "What Debates Don't Tell Us," *Time*, 19 October 1992, 32–33; Richard L. Berke, "The Debate: Candidates Cram for First Debate," *New York Times*, 11 October 1992, A1.

6. "Criteria for Upcoming Presidential Debates Determined," CNN Inside Politics, 11 June 1992, Transcript #86–4, np.

7. Ibid.

8. For a more elaborate discussion of the history of the commission, refer to Minow and Sloan, "End the Debate over Debates," 1.

9. Thomas Oliphant, "Baker Moves to Make the Debates More Comfy for Bush," *Boston Globe*, 30 August 1992, 67.

10. See, for example, Myron Waldman, "Wild West Show: Aides Debating Rules of Debate," *Newsday*, 14 September 1992, 17, and Sidney Blumenthal, "Why Am I Here? A Debate Round Up?" *New Republic*, 9 November 1992, 16.

11. Marlin Fitzwater, "Regular White House Briefing," Reuter Transcript Record, 16 September 1992, np.

12. Richard L. Berke, "The Debates; First TV Debate Canceled as Bush Sticks to Objections over Format," *New York Times*, 17 September 1992, A1.

13. Minow and Sloan, "End the debate over Debates," 21.

14. Berke, "The Debates; First TV Debate Canceled as Bush Sticks to Objections over Format," A1.

15. In addition to the debate in East Lansing, the Commission proposed presidential debates on 4 October at the University of San Diego and on 15 October at the University of Richmond. The vice-presidential debate was tentatively scheduled for 29 September in Louisville. See B. Drummond Ayres Jr., "The Debates; Bush Rejects Panel's Plan for Three Debates," *New York Times*, 4 September 1992, A13.

16. This list, which aired on 24 September, was presented in descending order. The demands included: "10. Bush shirts, Clinton skins. 9. After Bush speaks, moderator must add, "he's right, you know." 8. Swimsuit competition counts for at least 30 percent. 7. After debate Clinton can't do "Arsenio" for two weeks. 6. At all times Clinton must be referred to as "Mule Boy." 5. No questions about the last four years. 4. Adopt "Family Feud" format. 3. Bush: fancy cedar podium. Clinton: paper hat and milk crate. 2. Clinton must be in full hillbilly regalia. 1. Answers must be in the form of a

question." Doug Camilli, "Donny Osmond in Toronto: Canadian Dollar Slides," *The* (Montreal) *Gazette,* 6 October 1992, B7.

17. "A Silver Bullet," *Newsweek,* November/December 1992, 85.

18. George Bush, quoted on CNN Inside Politics, 30 September 1992, transcript #178. See also Adam Nagourney, "Issue Number 1: Debates, Debates, Debates," *USA Today,* 1 October 1992, 12A.

19. For a discussion of earlier formats, see Sidney Kraus, *Televised Presidential Debates and Public Policy* (Hillsdale, N.J.: Erlbaum, 1988), 29–71.

20. The different formats are described more completely in Howard Rosenberg, "The Debates: Throw Away the Score Card," *Los Angeles Times,* 9 October 1992, F1; Richard L. Berke, "The 1992 Campaign: Political Memo; Which Debate System Worked Best? It's a Debate," *New York Times,* 21 October 1992, A19.

21. Thomas B. Rosentiel, "Pundits and Polls May Pick Debate Winner," *Los Angeles Times,* 11 October 1992, A1.

22. Ibid.

23. James P. Gannon, "Advice to Debaters: Challenge, but Keep Your Cool," *Gannett News Service,* 11 October 1992.

24. All references to the first debate are drawn from "Transcript of First TV Debate among Bush, Clinton and Perot," *New York Times,* 12 October 1992, A14+.

25. The instant *Newsweek* and CBS polls declared Bush the winner, while an ABC poll found in Clinton's favor. See Howard Kurtz, "Ringside Scorers and Spiners: Pundits, Press Favor Pugilistic Metaphors in Analyzing Debate," *Washington Post,* 13 October 1993, A10.

26. Ibid.

27. All references to the vice presidential debate are drawn from "Transcript of the Vice-Presidential Debate (Part I)," *Washington Post,* 14 October 1992, A15+.

28. All references to the second debate are drawn from "Transcript of Second TV Debate between Bush, Clinton and Perot," *New York Times,* 16 October 1992, A11+.

29. Howard Kurtz, "'People's Debate' Produced Relentlessly Substantive Exchange," *Washington Post,* 17 October 1992, A11.

30. Ibid.

31. Michael Kelly, "The Surrounding Scene; It Seemed like Donohue, but with Bush, Clinton and Perot, It Wasn't," *New York Times,* 16 October 1992, A9.

32. Maureen Dowd, "The 1992 Campaign: News Analysis; A No-Nonsense Sort of Talk Show," *New York Times,* 16 October 1992, A1.

33. Tom Shales, "The Debate Goes On . . . and On and On," *Washington Post,* 16 October 1992, D1.

34. David S. Broder, "Clinton, Bush, Perot Stick to Issues in Debate," *Washington Post,* 16 October 1992, A1.

35. Howard Kurtz, "Has Bush Been Written Off? In the Eyes of News Media, Last Night was President's 'Last Chance,'" *Washington Post,* 20 October 1992, A21.

36. "Before a Full House," *New York Times,* 20 October 1992, A26. See also Richard Cohen, "Throw in the Towel," *Washington Post,* 21 October 1992, A19.

37. All references to the third debate are drawn from "Transcript of 3rd TV Debate between Bush, Clinton, and Perot," *New York Times*, 20 October 1992, A20.

38. Howard Kurtz, "Has Bush Been Written Off?" A21.

39. See, for example, Anna Quindlen, "Public and Private; A Place Called Hope," *New York Times*, 4 November 1882, A31.

40. Howard Kurtz, "Campaign Debates: A Contest of Styles with Just a Few Defining Moments; They May Not Sway Votes, but Often Help Crystallize the Choice," *Washington Post*, 9 October 1992, A16.

41. See, for example, David J. Lanoue, "One That Made a Difference: Cognitive Consistency, Political Knowledge, and the 1980 Presidential Debate," *Public Opinion Quarterly* 56 (Summer 1992): 168–84.

42. A review of previous research is well beyond the scope of this article. For a general overview of this line of research, refer to Judith S. Trent and Robert V. Friedenberg, *Political Campaign Communication: Principles and Practices* (New York: Praeger, 1983), 265–67.

43. See, for example, Robert D. Deutsch and Selden Biggs, "Primer for a Debate Orgy; Tactics Change in Three-Man Clash," *Atlanta Journal and Constitution*, 11 October 1992, G1.

44. Kathleen Hall Jamieson, *Eloquence in an Electronic Age: The Transformation of Political Speechmaking* (New York: Oxford University Press, 1988), 113.

45. Kathleen Hall Jamieson, for example, suggested that "the four debates might come to function as a single event, as a mini-series." See Richard L. Berke, "The Debate: Candidates Cram for First Debate," 1; and Sharon D. Moshavi, "Elections Enter New Television Age," *Broadcasting*, 2 November 1992, 12.

46. Jamieson and Birdsell, *Presidential Debates*, 118–19.

47. Ibid., 171.

48. One commentary likened a three person debate to a "beauty pageant." See Deutsch and Biggs, "Primer for a Debate Orgy; Tactics Change in Three-Man Clash," G1.

49. Jamieson and Birdsell, *Presidential Debates*, 10.

50. "Bush, Clinton and Perot drew spectacular audiences during their nine-day series of debates—a total of more than 100 million watched at least one of the four, with more than 90 million tuning in to see last Thursday's encounter in Richmond and more than 91 million watching the finale in East Lansing, Mich., on Monday night." Dan Balz, "Voter Anger Doesn't Equal Voter Apathy," *Washington Post*, 21 October 1992, A1.

51. Michael Gurevitch and Anandam P. Kavoori, "Television Spectacles as Politics," *Communication Monographs* 59 (December 1992): 420.

52. Berke, "The 1992 Campaign: Political Memo; Which Debate System Worked Best?" A19.

RIDING THE ROLLER COASTER

Bill Clinton and the News Media

PHILIP SEIB

George Bush is unbeatable.

In 1991 that was the premise on which the great majority of politicians and journalists based their appraisals of the upcoming presidential campaign.

Post–Gulf War opinion polls showed that Bush had parlayed resolute jingoism into apparently unassailable popularity. Potential Democratic challengers—such as Al Gore, Jay Rockefeller, and Mario Cuomo—were content to let their ambitions simmer. Running against Dan Quayle in 1996 seemed a much less daunting prospect than did taking on a popular incumbent.

This timidity created a vacuum that had to be filled. The Democrats, after all, would have to nominate *somebody*. So, spurred by prescience or egotism or some combination of the two, candidates emerged. As portrayed to the public by the news media, it was an uninspiring array.

Some were painted in drab tones, some in garish hues. All looked flawed. Tom Harkin seemed too liberal; Bob Kerrey too unfocused; Jerry Brown too weird; Paul Tsongas too dour. Their credentials as officeholders and party leaders were unexceptional.

Contrasted with this field, Bill Clinton stood out. He was a long-term governor with a reputation for innovation about issues such as public education. He had chaired the Democratic Leadership Council, which was dedicated to moving the party rightward into the ideological mainstream.

At first, journalists watched Clinton with some skepticism. Without fail, stories about him mentioned his tedious speech nominating

Michael Dukakis in 1988. This was an example of reporters' overrating insider politics. Few voters remembered or cared about that speech.

While reporters chuckled about Clinton's penchant for using ten sentences where one would do, the candidate himself was addressing more important matters. He was raising money, hiring skilled campaign professionals (such as master strategist James Carville and thoughtful pollster Stan Greenberg), and proclaiming a moderate philosophy that avoided the extreme liberalism that so often had wrecked campaigns of fellow Democrats. Most significant, Clinton began to position himself as a caring antithesis to George Bush—a potential president who would concentrate on domestic issues, especially economic inequities.

THE FIRST HONEYMOON

The weakness of the Democratic field plus Clinton's own work ethic paid off. By late 1991 articles were appearing with such headlines as "Bill Clinton Breaks Free of the Pack"[1] and "Bill Clinton: Front-Runner by Default."[2]

Such news coverage can become self-perpetuating. Contributors see it and decide to get on board with a likely winner. A candidate's picture plus a "front-runner" headline on the cover of a news magazine early in a campaign is an unparalleled fund-raising tool.

Voters also are influenced by this early journalistic handicapping of the presidential horse race. Many people have neither the time nor the inclination to scrutinize every candidate in a crowded field. They're likely to start at the top—the purported front-runner—and move down the list only as far as they need to go to find someone they consider worth voting for. By virtue of heading the list, Clinton had first opportunity to display his wares. The news stories that hailed him as leader of the pack also presented capsule biography and summarized his record as Arkansas governor. All major candidates get this treatment, but the front-runner gets more of it.

Early in the campaign, examinations of candidates' records tend to be fairly gentle. For example, in an early *Time* cover story about Clinton (27 January 1992), the section on his governorship began this way: "Clinton has shown a rare talent for sniffing out issues and acting on them at a state level before they become hot nationally." The passage continued with a favorable review of his education reforms. This early in the campaign, such articles often don't include much criticism from political opponents or journalists themselves. That comes later, but in the meantime the front-runner fortifies his position.

Not all is sweetness and light. Instinctively, journalists take potshots at front-runners. Cautionary notes could be found in the tone and substance of stories that for the most part could be considered boosterish.

Journalists acknowledge their own influence. For instance, a largely favorable *Time* story contained this debunking of the front-runner mystique: "Before a single caucus or primary ballot has been cast anywhere, the national press and television have anointed Bill Clinton" as the candidate to beat.[3] And, a bit later in the same article: "Perhaps the most distressing aspect of the Clinton boom is a suspicion that it is largely an artificial creation by the press. Journalistic pundits are constitutionally incapable of confessing that they have no idea what will happen in a presidential race; they are irresistibly driven to impose some sort of structure on the most shapeless contest."[4]

But enthusiasm for Clinton had its limits. Warning signals went up early: "The political press corps . . . has gone into a deep swoon over his candidacy, from which it will sooner or later recover."[5] The way it would "recover" was foreshadowed by continuing mention of "rumors about Clinton's alleged extramarital affairs."[6]

GENNIFER

The news media giveth, and the news media taketh away.

From front-runner to damaged goods. The transformation doesn't take long. Just ask Gary Hart.

Or Bill Clinton.

The front-runner label was becoming firmly affixed, other contenders' campaigns were bogged down, and an upset Democratic victory in a Pennsylvania Senate election was seen as evidence that George Bush might be vulnerable. All was right with Bill Clinton's world.

Then the *Star*, a sensationalist tabloid most easily found in supermarket check-out lines, printed Gennifer Flowers's allegations that she and Clinton had had a long-running affair. "For 12 years I was his girlfriend," she said, "and now he tells me to deny it."

Considering Ms. Flowers's choice of forums, the knowledge that she had been paid for her tale, the absence of supporting evidence and the presence of obvious inaccuracies, plus Clinton's assertions that "the story is just not true," many news organizations at first approached the story gingerly. But this is the kind of topic that is a magnet for public curiosity and reportorial fervor.

The Flowers charges soon were being covered by virtually every news organization, no matter the heights from which they looked down upon the *Star*. For good measure, some tossed in other Clinton womanizing rumors that had even less corroboration than did Flowers's claims. Some reports—such as in *Newsweek*—pointedly listed the factual errors and contradictions in Flowers's rendition of events. But many news consumers simply studied the big photos of Bill and Gennifer and sometimes Hillary, "the wronged wife," and treated this as soap opera.

By the time the Clintons appeared on the post-Super Bowl broadcast of "60 Minutes" (estimated audience: 100 million), the Flowers story had pushed aside all other campaign news. This television appearance epitomized the mess: CBS News, for so long the paragon of high journalistic standards, was following the *Star* in an exercise in mass voyeurism.

Clinton was threatened from several sides. Presumably, a certain number of voters would not support him if they suspected him of adultery. But probably a far larger number would turn away from him if they thought he was lying. And worst of all, if he became known to voters as solely "the candidate with the woman problem," he'd lose his standing as a serious contender for the White House. He'd be seen as nothing more than the new incarnation of Gary Hart.

In hindsight, Clinton's two principal strategic decisions seem wise. By going on "60 Minutes," he could state his case for himself and let the public judge him while he did so. With Hillary at his side, he could talk about a marriage that had had problems and still seem reasonable when he refused to allow press and public to snoop around in every corner of his personal life.

The second decision was to try to force press and public attention back to *his* agenda. He realized that while the Flowers story fascinated some voters, it was a passing fascination. At ballot-casting time, more substantive matters—principally the economy—would determine how people voted. Clinton understood—perhaps better than many journalists did—the dichotomy between the news media's interests and the public's interests.

He survived, but he was damaged. His credibility and his front-runner status now were shaky. The "character issue" loomed large, and soon was to grow larger still.

SLICK WILLIE AND VIETNAM

A smart guy. Fast on his feet. Always has an answer. Tells people what they want to hear. Glib. Slick.

Slick Willie. The uncomplimentary nickname wasn't a creation of the national press corps. It was bestowed by a newspaper editor in Pine Bluff, Arkansas, who thought his governor tended to be too quick to shift positions and embrace or abandon issues based solely on political self-interest.

In itself, being slick isn't politically fatal. Ronald Reagan, for example, retained his teflon coating for most of his eight years in the White House. But if the news media make an issue of slickness, if they draw the public's attention to the slip-slide of inconsistencies . . . then it's a problem.

Clinton survived the Gennifer Flowers episode because he told voters at least as much as most of them wanted to know. They didn't care to learn every sordid detail; it would be embarrassing just to hear any more about it. Also, the purported scandal didn't seem to have much to do with how Clinton might run the country. Besides, Hillary was sticking with him. So let it go.

Vietnam was another matter. Just to mention it was to tear a bandage off a still-festering wound. Today's specifics don't matter as much as do hazy memories of yesterday.

Clinton's efforts to avoid service during the war were far from unique. Many of his contemporaries tried their best to avoid combat. By 1969, when Clinton was writing his draft board from Oxford, the war clearly was a bloody, unwinnable mess.

So, it wasn't merely what Clinton had done that attracted the critical attention of press and public. His main problem arose from how he handled the issue in mid-campaign, releasing "all the facts" one day, then changing or supplementing them the next. When reporters see their quarry zigging and zagging this way, bloodlust rises and the pursuit is on.

The issue isn't simple; its legalistic and moral complexities are familiar to any American male who was college age in the late 1960s and early 1970s. Clinton as an undergraduate at Georgetown University had a student deferment from the draft. This was available to any full-time college student. In order to continue to protect himself from the draft while he went to Oxford as a Rhodes Scholar, Clinton told his draft board that he would enroll in an ROTC program. This would extend his deferment. But while in England, Clinton decided not to enter ROTC and instead took his chances with the draft. In the first draft lottery, in 1970, his birthdate was assigned a high, safe number.

Through all this, he worked the system cleverly and legally. But two decades after the fact, some people—especially his political foes—saw something unsavory in his maneuvering, while many others saw it as irrelevant, particularly given their concerns about current economic issues.

Clinton had already been wounded by the Gennifer Flowers controversy. His explanations about it might have been finally accepted, but they weren't totally believed. Now came a string of slightly contradictory versions of how he had secured the ROTC placement. Was this further evidence of a significant character flaw?

That's the question news coverage addressed. As the New Hampshire primary neared, Clinton was badgered by queries about his background while his chief rival, Paul Tsongas, was able to stick to his economic message.

Clinton, however, was lucky. New Hampshire's economy was in such shambles that most voters were not distracted by ancient history, no matter how assiduously the news media pursued the story. For example, on the morning after a "Nightline" appearance devoted to discussion of the draft issue—a morning when Clinton's 1969 behavior dominated news coverage—the candidate found himself answering questions from New Hampshire voters about taxes, day care, and education.[7] As with the Flowers allegations, the press's priorities were not necessarily the public's priorities.

Of course, Clinton's political opponents—Democrats in the primaries and Republicans later—did their best to keep the controversy bubbling. Shortly before the November election, the Bush campaign made new charges about Clinton's patriotism and judgment, resulting in headlines such as "Clinton, Oxford and the Draft."[8]

Could Clinton have handled the news media better and limited the damage this issue did to him? He aroused reporters' suspicions by adding to and revising his story. In hindsight, he might have been better off had he unloaded all information immediately. Perhaps then the controversy would have burned out because of lack of fuel.

On the other hand, Clinton probably was trying to stop the story quickly by downplaying the topic and not providing an exhaustive recapitulation of all he had done. He hoped that journalists' news judgment would lead them away from the draft and back to topics of current importance.

Not all reporters were guilty of piling on. Tom Griffith, news anchor of WMUR, New Hampshire's most highly regarded television station, said of the draft story: "Any of us that grew up in that era understands that a student deferment by itself shouldn't be a liability, so I'm going to drop this."[9]

Griffith was not alone. Writing in *Columbia Journalism Review*, William Broyles—former editor of *Texas Monthly* and *Newsweek*, and a Vietnam veteran—noted that reporting of the draft issue was "generationally tone deaf. The implication was that avoiding the draft during Vietnam was the moral equivalent of turning your back on America after Pearl Harbor, and not the accepted practice of an entire generation of college students." Further, wrote Broyles: "Reading all this coverage I found myself wondering if the press is too blunt an instrument to probe such sensitive psychological terrain. How well would we journalists answer shouted questions about what we did twenty-five years ago?"[10]

The principal lesson politicians might derive from the episode is this: Don't appear to be evasive. Clinton may have been hurt less by his 1969 behavior than by his apparent lack of candor in 1992. The Flowers and draft controversies planted doubts about his honesty that lingered throughout the campaign.

THE DEPTHS

Through all his tough times early in the campaign, Clinton maintained one advantage over which he had little control: the absence of a "heavy-hitter" Democratic opponent. While he was most vulnerable, a Mario

Cuomo or Bill Bradley might have been able to use Clinton's tarnished credibility as reason for entering the race. Without well-funded and well-recognized challengers, Clinton was able to plod onward, locking up the nomination with a round of primary victories in June, including a win over Jerry Brown in California.

Journalists, however, appeared far from impressed by Clinton's prowess. On 4 May the *New Republic*'s cover headline was, "Why Clinton Can't Win." And *Time* magazine ran this caption with a photo of the presumptive nominee: "He prevails: Clinton finally locks up the Democratic nomination—and no one notices."[11]

The tone of *Time*'s story about Clinton that week after he'd been assured of having a majority of convention delegates reflected the press's growing skepticism about his voter appeal and increasing interest in Ross Perot's prospects:

> The challenge facing Clinton is both simple and serious: How does he reintroduce himself to voters enraptured with the mystique of Ross Perot? For years, Clinton had been carefully prepping for a race where he would be the agent of change, the only alternative to the do-nothing status quo of George Bush. Now it is Perot who embodies this anti-Establishment anger, while the Democratic challenger is suddenly relegated to an uncomfortable me-too role as the candidate offering change for the timid voters still loyal to the orthodoxies of two-party politics. . . . Epic change is in the air: Perot could transform the two-party system in as dramatic a fashion as the fall of communism altered geopolitics. All too often, however, Clinton still acts like an old-line Democratic candidate."[12]

Opinion polls reflected such sentiments. Perot moved into first place in some, with minimal enthusiasm found for Clinton or Bush. And as press reports of Perot's surge—such as his "victory" in California primary exit polling—took precedence over stories about Clinton, the momentum Clinton hoped to have going into his party's national convention dissolved.

But just as Clinton had survived the Gennifer Flowers and draft controversies, he proved his resilience. Several shrewd uses of the media paid off.

In an appearance before Jesse Jackson's Rainbow Coalition, Clinton criticized rap singer Sister Souljah for what he called "racist" comments. Jackson was obviously displeased, but Clinton got what he wanted: news stories portraying him as willing to stand up to Jackson. This was in clear contrast to other Democrats, such as Walter Mondale and Michael Dukakis, who had seemed intimidated by Jackson.

This renewed Clinton's credibility as being more centrist than liberal, and reinforced his claim of being a "different kind of Democrat." Such coverage helped offset stories such as *Time*'s referring to him as "old-line."

Also, Clinton appeared on the "Arsenio Hall Show," complete with saxophone and dark glasses. His musical talent may have been debatable, but his relaxed, self-deprecating humor made him appear less "slick"—not such a bad guy, after all. He came across as "Bubba," unpretentious and not too far removed from the average American.

Although the viewing audience for the show was relatively small, news coverage was extensive, especially pictures of Clinton wailing through "Heartbreak Hotel."

Through such strategic ploys, Clinton reasserted control over how he was depicted by the media and how the public saw him. This helped keep his party's regulars in line behind him. Even if they weren't certain about the extent of Clinton's strength or Perot's appeal, they knew by now that George Bush was weak, perhaps fatally so.

Clinton entered July rejuvenated, negative news coverage mostly behind him, at least for the moment.

THE SECOND HONEYMOON

For Bill Clinton and the Democrats, July 1992 was a wonderful month.

A *Time*-CNN poll taken on 16 July found Clinton leading Bush 49 percent to 29 percent. This came on the heels of a Democratic National Convention that gave Clinton ample opportunity to redefine himself for public consumption. Also, Ross Perot—for reasons stated and unstated—suddenly announced that he would not be a candidate.

This gave Clinton a much better chance to recapture the blue-collar base so essential to Democrats seeking the presidency. Although many had voted for Reagan and Bush, their unhappiness about the economy and the status quo generally set them adrift. Now, without the allure of Perot, Clinton wouldn't have to worry about their vote being split between two non-incumbents.

News coverage helped fortify Clinton's apparently commanding position as front-runner. Notably absent in reports coming from the convention were tales of chaos and genuflection to special interest constituencies. A typical press description came from Michael Kramer in *Time*: "It was like a Republican Convention. Everything worked. The words were good. The television was good. The propaganda, especially, was good . . ."[13]

The touch of reportorial cynicism in that passage does not obscure the basic story line: The convention was a success. Clinton's firm control plus the absence of significant negatives gave him and his party the appearance of winners.

Democrats knew they were dealing with a public that was at least vaguely dissatisfied with the Bush administration. Positive news reports reinforced images gleaned from live nightly convention coverage. Also, news stories were especially important in 1992 because the three biggest networks had reduced their live coverage and viewership had shrunk. Combined ratings for ABC, CBS, and NBC averaged 17.3 percent of the audience for each of the four evenings of the convention, compared with 20.8 percent in 1988.[14]

As those ratings diminished, the importance of news accounts grew. Voters who did not see the convention themselves were more likely to pay attention to the press's version of events and to accept more readily journalists' judgments about what was important. When columnists such as *Time*'s Hugh Sidey wrote that the convention was "the grandest Democratic political spectacle in 32 years,"[15] presumably, a fair number of voters took note.

The convention and its coverage certainly helped Clinton, giving him the "bounce" in the polls that he wanted. But nothing in the convention coverage could match the favorable impact of news stories soon to come.

From New York, Bill Clinton and vice-presidential nominee Al Gore embarked on their national campaign in seemingly archaic fashion. They traveled by bus.

But far from being a misuse of their time, this turned out to be one of the most brilliant strokes of their campaign. As they wended their way across the country, the numbers of people they encountered were not as large as those they would have reached had they used chartered jets and visited only the largest cities. The real value of their trip was found once again in *indirect* voter contact. News reports—most of which in this case ranged from merely positive to unabashedly adulatory—sustained the Clinton-Gore strategy: "to show off a youthful, energetic ticket eager to engage Americans up close."[16]

Local TV stations went so far as to preempt programs such as "Family Feud" and "The Price Is Right" to provide live coverage as the Clinton-Gore caravan rolled through town.

During the six-day trip immediately after the convention and in other excursions later in the campaign, the Democrats enjoyed headlines such as "Clinton-Gore Caravan Refuels with Spirit from Adoring Crowds."[17]

This trip, wrote *Newsweek*'s Joe Klein, "seemed to tap into a primordial public yearning; it touched the same vein Ronald Reagan, steeped as he was in 1930s Hollywood fantasy visions of America, had always worked effortlessly (and which George Bush, uncomfortable with visions, has ignored at his peril)."[18]

This similarity to Reagan's idyllic version of America was no accident. These were real people in real small towns, not the invention of advertising wizards. Nevertheless, to influence the look and tone of news stories, "the buscapade was carefully 'advanced' to resonate with nostalgic symbols of mainstream American life: flags and balloons, front porches and town squares."[19]

The second bus tour in August was another hit, especially with local media. For example, in Eau Claire, Wisconsin, the *Leader-Telegram*'s front-page headline was: "Bus Tour Drawing Accolades: Rural Areas Get Rare View." This was accompanied with color photographs covering much of the page. The next day, the headline was "Clinton Says Voters Need 'Courage.'" And on yet the next day, the same paper included seven articles about the candidates' visit, plus a full page of photos.[20]

During a general-election campaign, presidential candidates are infrequent visitors to small cities and towns. Local journalists there usually watch the campaign from a distance; they're just as removed from the day-to-day politicking as their audiences are. Having the opportunity actually to cover a campaign, to talk with the candidates, and to be caught up in the glamor of presidential politics is enough to transport many local reporters into journalistic ecstasy. Add Bill Clinton's carefully measured personal charm to the mix, and odds are that coverage is going to be favorable.

As the bus tours proceeded, even some members of the national press corps remained impressed. Joe Klein wrote about "the emotional connection [between candidates and public] that mocked and then demolished the industrial-strength cynicism of the 150 journalists tagging along."[21]

The upbeat mood of the politicians on these trips, coupled with the relatively informal and open access to Clinton, nurtured pro-Clinton sentiment among some reporters. This spirit was mocked in numerous episodes of "Doonesbury" during the campaign, as cartoonist Gary Trudeau satirized the press corps's sometimes uncritical enthusiasm for Clinton.

This tendency toward boosterism did not happen by accident. Clinton's savvy aides fully understood the value of friendly news coverage. The staff, so appealingly young and intelligent, cultivated reporters, preaching the Clintonian gospel of the virtues of generational change. Many reporters—not as cold-bloodedly objective as they pretend to be—were won over.

The bus tours were "retail" politics—meeting voters, rather than just reaching them wholesale via television. But it was also wholesale in the sense that "the campaign knows that from each passing visit with each roadside crowd it derives a benefit far out of proportion to the number of voters present."[22] That's because news reports brought the bus tour via their pages or air waves to a vastly larger audience. "Isolated on buses, exposed to mile after mile and hour after hour of cheering Clinton supporters, even the national reporters tend to respond with positive stories."[23]

Those stories helped Clinton sustain momentum provided by the convention. With roughly three months to go before the election, the Democrats were chipping away at the calendar. Each day dominated by upbeat news reports brought Clinton a bit closer to the White House.

THE FRONT-RUNNER

By late summer 1992, journalists' opinions of the presidential contest's probable outcome were far different than they had been less than a year before.

Clinton's lead in the polls had surged to close to thirty points immediately after the convention, then had dropped some, but remained comfortably in double digits. The economy showed no signs of rebounding dramatically enough to restore voter confidence in Bush. The Republicans seemed dazed as they searched for issues and identity.

Republicans got plenty of exposure during their national convention in Houston. Speeches by Pat Buchanan, Marilyn Quayle, and others were bitterly negative, but this approach helped Bush in the polls (at least short-term) and laid groundwork for continued attacks by portraying Clinton as soft on tax increases and "family values."

The Democrats, however, considered the Republican Convention to have done the GOP more harm than good. Clinton strategists contended that the Bush forces hadn't convincingly addressed economic issues and had alienated many moderate voters by going overboard, for example, in their attacks on Hillary Clinton.

In the precarious position of front-runner, Clinton faced news coverage that seemed based on expectations that he would slip and the race would narrow. For example, on the Sunday after the Republican Convention ended, a 23 August *New York Times* story was headlined, "Clinton Dismisses His Drop in Polls," with a subhead, "Clinton Goes in Search of New Momentum." But by the following week, the *Times* ran a headline stating, "Bush's Gains from Convention Nearly Evaporate in Latest Poll."

Rather than rely solely on the networks and major publications to deliver their message, the Democrats continued to use a variety of local media and "infotainment" vehicles, such as the Oprah Winfrey and Larry King shows. And by scheduling town meetings, bus tours, and the like, the Clinton campaign was employing "what might be called the 'field of dreams' media strategy: If you stage it, they will come."[24]

By the week of 7 September, Bush began seriously grappling with the economy as a principal campaign issue. Also, the Republican attack on Clinton finally achieved some coherence. Using the networks' morning news-chat shows, Bush's surrogates warned that a Clinton presidency would mean across-the-board tax increases.

Meanwhile, journalists continued to prod Clinton about his Vietnam War draft status. Apparently frustrated by attacks from Bush and from the press, Clinton lashed out. An 8 September *New York Times* story headlined "Clinton Accuses Reporters of Bias" told of the Democratic nominee's claims that the press was ignoring new allegations about Bush's involvement in the Iran-contra scandal. Clinton said reporters instead kept pestering him about what he considered trivial matters concerning his lack of military service: "You've got a feeding frenzy on about something that even if it's true, doesn't amount to a hill of beans."

To some extent, the public seemed to agree with Clinton's assessment of this issue. A *Time*-CNN poll conducted in late September asked, "Has too much attention been paid to Clinton's draft record?" Sixty-two percent answered "Yes."[25]

With little more than a month to go in the campaign, most polls showed Clinton holding on to a solid lead. But Ross Perot's 1 October announcement of candidacy made predicting the outcome even more perilous.

Journalists, like most politicians, have grown comfortable with the standard format and pace of presidential campaigns. Reporters and pols slog together through the confusing and crowded primaries, participate together—some grudgingly, some delightedly—in the national party conventions, and then some run and others handicap the final stretch of the two-horse race. Perot's spectral and then real presence disrupted all this.

News stories about potential Perot impact reflected journalists' unhappiness about enormous changes at the last minute. Typical was this comment: "Like an avid amateur playing with professional athletes, Perot has nothing at stake but his prodigious ego."[26]

The day-to-day struggle between Clinton and Bush was briefly pushed into the background as journalists tried to decide how Perot would affect the November vote. Would he capture blue-collar "Reagan Democrats" who had been drifting toward Clinton because of the economy? Would he target his nemesis, George Bush, by making his main effort in the states that Bush most needed to win? Would he be embraced by voters as a populist savior or dismissed as a rich kook?

For reporters, such guessing games fuel many a news story and many a barroom bull session. Perot further complicated matters with his aloof style: His public appearances were infrequent, and his contacts with the press even more rare. With his enormous bankroll, he could ignore conventional campaign method and rely on paid media—thirty-minute "infomercials" as well as traditional thirty-second spots. And to replace daily give-and-take with the political press corps, he used the friendly formats and softer questions of "Larry King Live" and similar programs.

Clinton, like Bush, was relatively gentle in his treatment of Perot. Neither of the two major party candidates wanted to alienate Perot supporters who might come back into the conventional fold on election day.

This mildness was evident as the presidential debates began. Perot impressed voters with his crisp can-do promises and his folksy zingers, but Clinton and Bush focused principally on each other, relying on established themes. In the first debate, for instance, Clinton's most memorable line was: "Mr. Bush, for twelve years you have had it your way; you've had your chance and it didn't work. It's time to change."

News analyses of the candidates' performances were generated in great volume and were consistently positive about Clinton, uncertainly so about Perot, and lukewarm about Bush. Those news consumers just skimming the print coverage of the debates got this same tepid impression of Bush's performance. Headlines reinforced the image of Clinton as the dominant force in the campaign.

Here is a sampling of headlines after the first debate: in the *Washington Post*, "Clinton, Perot Hit President on Economy" and "A Big Win Eludes Bush in Debate"; in the *New York Times*, "Bush Didn't Score the Needed Knockout."

After the second debate: in the *Dallas Morning News*, "49% in Poll See Clinton as Debate Winner."

During the final debate on 19 October, Bush seemed to have rekindled some of his fire, but Clinton's on-stage demeanor—and the press's appraisal of it—made the Democratic challenger look at least as presidential as the incumbent did. After this debate, too, Bush got little help from headline writers: in the *New York Times*, "Bush Pushes Hard in 3d Debate but Foes Put Him on Defensive."

Clinton also benefited from journalists' tough approach to GOP insinuations that Clinton was unpatriotic because he had participated in peace demonstrations and traveled to the Soviet Union while studying in England. During the first debate, Clinton reminded the president of the stance against red-baiting that his father, Connecticut senator Prescott Bush, had taken during the 1950s: "Your father was right to stand up to Joe McCarthy. You were wrong to attack my patriotism." Bush had no effective response.

Press coverage about this helped Clinton. It was typified by the headline on a 19 October *Time* story: "Anatomy of a Smear." Another story in that same issue of *Time* said that in resorting to "destructive tactics," Bush had "wandered over the line of decency."[27]

THE FINAL DAYS

Bush's relentlessly negative campaign was having its desired effect. The "trust and taxes" theme loosened Clinton's hold on some of his support. The Democrat's poll lead shrank from double digits to five points in one survey and just one point in another. Many voters seemed ready to rely on a "stick with the devil you know" theory when they went to the ballot box. Perot's support continued to grow, reaching the level at which Clinton's strategists feared he would hurt their man more than Bush.

The best horse race is a close horse race. From journalists' standpoint, nothing is better than a photo finish. One question pervaded late coverage: "Can Bush do it; can he come from behind and win?" Daily reports of various polls provided the quantitative measure of the run down the home stretch.

Press speculation can become a self-fulfilling prophecy. The more credible the portrayal of a candidacy, the more likely voters will be to consider supporting that candidate. The more doubt the press casts on the outcome, the less likely voters are to be caught up in a front-runner's bandwagon effect.

Some press-reinforced sense of inevitability clung to Clinton. For instance, *Business Week* featured this headline a week before the election: "The View from the Corner Office: Bush Is a Goner" (with a story about CEOs expecting a Clinton win). The *New York Times* on 18 October offered these headlines: "Democrats' Hopes Soar, Republicans' Grow Heavy," and "Leading in the Homestretch, Clinton's Campaign Grows More Confident."

Within a few days, however, the tone of political stories changed. Now the message to voters was, "Don't go away folks; this race isn't over." A new suspense permeated coverage. Consider this drumbeat of preelection headlines:

"Inroads by Perot Concern Clinton Camp"

—*New York Times,* 22 October

"Presidential Race Looks Tighter" —*Washington Post,* 25 October

"Contest Tightens as Perot Resurges and Clinton Slips"
—*New York Times,* 25 October

"Bush, Buoyed by Polls, Scrambles to Rebuild Winning Coalition," and "Clinton Is Abandoning His Emphasis on Issues for the Attack Strategy of an Underdog" —*New York Times,* 30 October

"Clinton Pushes toward Finish Line Shadowed by Stubborn Rival" —*Washington Post,* 1 November

"Bush Surges in Ohio, His Big Battleground State"
—*New York Times,* 2 November

And then, finally, votes instead of speculation:

"Clinton Triumphs" —*Dallas Morning News,* 3 November

LESSONS

News coverage of Bill Clinton's candidacy and of the overall 1992 campaign taught some lessons worth pondering before the next presidential election. Among the most important are these:

1. Understand voters' real interests. Jobs and the deficit, not Gennifer and the draft, were voting issues in 1992. "It's the economy, stupid!"
2. Respect the complexity of issues. For instance, economic plans advanced by Clinton, Bush, and Perot all deserved more thorough independent scrutiny by news organizations. Voters should be offered informed analyses of such hard-to-understand matters.
3. Resist the temptation to overcover trivia, such as Clinton's appearance on the "Arsenio Hall Show" and Dan Quayle's comments about Murphy Brown. These merited some coverage, but not the journalistic orgies they precipitated.
4. Beware of front-runner fever. Early front-runner status may be just artificially created by the press, proclaimed rather than earned. Continued coverage makes this status self-perpetuating. The press should not present voters with faits accomplis.
5. Define "character" in terms of what voters need to know about a potential president. Germaneness should be the test; how

might a candidate's purported strengths and weaknesses of character affect the ability to govern? Also, hypocrisy and fabrication should be reported. Overall, newsworthiness, not voyeuristic curiosity should determine what gets covered.

6. Be skeptical about the honesty of candidates who release "the whole story" in bits and pieces, as Clinton did with information about his draft status. Candidates will be best served if they're forthright from the start. Otherwise, they'll keep negative stories alive.

7. Be ready for unconventional candidacies. Once Ross Perot showed strength in the polls, he should have been covered aggressively, even if Bush and Clinton didn't seem to know how to deal with him.

8. Don't let politicians avoid the news media by relying on alternatives such as paid media and "new news" talk shows. Keep demanding access, and let voters know that the candidates are ducking hard questions.

9. Understand the machinations of media-savvy campaign staff members who carefully cultivate reporters. These courtships— especially if not recognized as fundamental exercises in persuasion—can lead to slanted coverage.

10. Identify the most important facet of a story and make sure the public understands its importance. For example, in the Moscow visit story, Bush's tactics were at least as newsworthy as Clinton's having taken the trip.

11. Resist the temptation to make the horse race seem tighter than it really is just to sustain public interest in coverage.

This is not a foolproof prescription for perfect campaign coverage, but it's a start.

NOTES

1. Margaret Carlson, "Lexington: Bill Clinton Breaks Free of the Pack," *The Economist*, 14 December 1991, 32.

2. Margaret Carlson, "Bill Clinton: Front-runner by Default," *Time*, 30 December 1991, 19.

3. George C. Church, "Is Bill Clinton for Real?" *Time*, 27 January 1992, 15.

4. Ibid.

5. Carlson, "Bill Clinton: Front-runner by Default."

6. Ibid.

7. Lance Morrow, "The Long Shadow of Vietnam," *Time*, 24 February 1992, 20.

8. Steven V. Roberts, "Clinton, Oxford and the Draft," *U.S. News and World Report*, 19 October 1992, 36.

9. D. D. Guttenplan, "Tracking the Campaign," *Columbia Journalism Review*, November/December 1992, 26.

10. William Broyles Jr., "Campaign Issues: Draft," *Columbia Journalism Review*, November/December 1992, 42–43.

11. "The Week," *Time*, 15 June 1992, 20.

12. Walter Shapiro, "Clinton Plays It Cool," *Time*, 15 June 1992, 33.

13. Michael Kramer, "Front and Center," *Time*, 27 July 1992, 28.

14. Marvin Kalb, "Too Much Talk and Not Enough Action," *Washington Journalism Review*, September 1992, 34.

15. Hugh Sidey, "What Defines Character?" *Time*, 27 July 1992, 46.

16. Howard Fineman, "Keeping the Big Mo Rolling," *Newsweek*, 3 August 1992, 27.

17. Gwen Ifill, "Clinton-Gore Caravan Refuels with Spirit from Adoring Crowds," *New York Times*, 19 July 1992, A20.

18. Joe Klein, "On the Road Again," *Newsweek*, 17 August 1992, 33.

19. Fineman, "Keeping the Big Mo Rolling."

20. Richard L. Berke, "Clinton Bus Tour Woos and Wows Local Press," *New York Times*, 9 August 1992, 30.

21. Klein, "On the Road Again."

22. Michael Kelly, "Democrats' Road Tour: Selling the Ticket Retail," *New York Times*, 7 August 1992, A14.

23. Ibid.

24. Kenneth T. Walsh, Michael Barone, and Matthew Cooper, "The Media Battle," *U.S. News and World Report*, 31 August 1992, 49.

25. Laurence I. Barrett, "Three's a Crowd," *Time*, 5 October 1992, 30.

26. Ibid.

27. Michael Kramer, "It's Clinton's to Lose," *Time*, 19 October 1992, 30.

EASY ACCESS
TO SLOPPY TRUTHS

The '92 Presidential Media Campaign

RITA KIRK WHILLOCK

> *I said in my acceptance speech at Atlanta that the 1988 election
> was not about ideology but about competence. I was wrong. It
> was about phraseology . . . And going negative . . . I made a
> lot of mistakes in the '88 campaign. But none was as dam-
> aging as my failure to understand this phenomenon, and the
> need to respond immediately and effectively to distortions of
> one's record and one's positions.* —Michael Dukakis

In order to understand the dynamics of the 1992 presidential media
campaign, we must first recognize that this election was not limited to
events unfolding during this particular election cycle. Democratic candidates had been scalded by their opponents in the last three races.
There was a history of hard feelings and ethics charges between the
ideological camps. There was also a strong perception that no matter
who the Democrats nominated, Bush would carry the election in 1992.

Democratic contenders entering the race were presumed to be running for the purpose of testing the political waters and setting up a
national organization that could mount a serious challenge in the '96
race. Yet in order to be a contender in '96, the Democratic nominee
could not afford to be labeled a loser. In the long term, the strategy for
a Democrat in this election cycle was to win the party nomination and
then control the perceptions of losing to Bush in the general election.

Within the Clinton campaign, the task of controlling perceptions was paramount. Beginning where the '88 campaign left off (and perhaps using Dukakis's statement as a credo), Clinton operatives began the 1992 season with a distinctly aggressive strategy. Insiders agreed early in the process that no charge would go unanswered. That included previous defeats which left fearful images about Democratic control in the American psyche.

On day one, Clinton confronted the Republican party and the Bush camp for its previous sins, including Willie Horton and the defeat of the Democratic bloc in the South. Understanding the advantage of playing to inherent strengths, the mythic positioning of a southerner seeking victory from the ashes of defeat did not escape the notice of Clinton handlers.

Clinton addressed the crowd on the steps of the Old Statehouse in Arkansas, the site of two secessionist conventions that led to the state's withdrawal from the Union in 1861. "Here in the shadow of this great building," Clinton engaged in battle. "We know all about race-baiting. They've used that old tool on us for decades now. And I want to tell you one thing: I understand this tactic, and I will not let them get away with it in 1992." Thus, Clinton began to carve out a unique relationship with the public and a distinct image that would run throughout the campaign, offering himself as the defender of voters, rather than a suitor for votes. Through word and symbol, Clinton positioned himself and the Democratic party he represented as the champion of the defeated, and in the America of 1992, there were a lot of us.

THE OPENING ROUND OF THE MEDIA CAMPAIGN

The media campaign began later than usual in the 1992 election season. In part, the absence of better-known Democrats like Dick Gebhardt and Lloyd Bentsen and the uncertainty of a Cuomo candidacy resulted in low financial support for the field. As a result, the media phase began some three months after the candidates surfaced.

Early in the election cycle, Clinton was perceived as the front-runner in a pack of also-rans whose sole purpose in this election was to prepare for a more viable chance in '96. Front-runner status typically means that the candidate's favorable name recognition is higher than those of opponents, and it often results in more free media coverage. Using the perks of front-runner status as a vehicle for establishing

Clinton's credentials, the Clinton campaign experimented with traditional advertising strategies. Unlike Tsongas, who used traditional identification-building strategies as the first candidate to take his campaign to the air, the Clinton campaign opened with a direct response ad, urging interested voters to call in for Clinton's "Plan for America's Future." The Clinton team then produced a series of written documents covering issues from health care to education, which he offered to those who requested them.

The strategy was atypical. Campaigns usually begin with high-image ads that seek to define a candidate's essential character. Once positioned, campaigns carve out positions on more substantive issues. The fact that Clinton emerged with an agenda rather than an image seemed appropriate for a campaign devoted to addressing the issues more deliberatively. It seemed to play to Clinton's strength as a scholar and helped build a perception of him as a thoughtful leader.

The strategy had other implications as well. First, the importance of having voters initiate contact with the campaign should not be underestimated. Rather than blanketing towns with documents no one would read, Clinton asked voters to become involved. Voters were asked to make a call in a subtle demonstration of their genuine interest in the subject and commitment to making a reasoned choice. Second, the ad reinforced the notion that Clinton was the defender of the American voter with a plan for change, not just a suitor courting emotional favor with abstract platitudes. His plans for renewal served as proof of his sincerity and attempted to perceptually fill the void left by the vague political ads proffered by his opponents. The strategy proved effective. According to Frank Greer, senior member of Clinton's advertising firm, fifteen thousand New Hampshire viewers requested a copy.[1]

While the ad had strategic value, it did not establish voter familiarity with the candidate nor clarify Clinton's values or character. This deficiency magnified the effects created by the emerging Gennifer Flowers' story. While accounts of infidelity had floated around in Arkansas politics for some time to no avail, the blond-bombshell story as covered by national news media reeked of a Gary Hart escapade. The womanizing image could not be permitted to stand. As a result, the campaign faced its first response challenge before it had secured a strong, positive public image for the man himself.

Rather than attempt to rebut the charges through traditional advertising methods, Clinton's use of alternative media (in this case "60 Minutes") saved the media budget for an attempt to refocus the campaign. Two factors are significant. First, the Clinton campaign recognized the importance of responding to all charges, particularly those like the infidelity issue that had potential fallout for the election. Second, the campaign team responded to the attacks but reserved the budget for ads that would "quickly preempt news developments and 'push past' whatever may be on the press's dirty little minds at the moment—Gennifer Flowers, the draft, golf at a lily-white club."[2] This approach was particularly important since media budgets are severely restricted in the early stages of the election as donors await the emergence of a supportable contender. Further, the strategy permitted wise use of available funds, recognizing that fund-raising would be difficult while the candidate was under siege. An inability to raise money when the campaign needs it most has destroyed many candidacies before they have a chance to begin in earnest.

Using "60 Minutes" and other news vehicles to respond to the infidelity issue, the Clinton team backtracked with advertisements to establish and bolster Clinton's identity. In a particularly effective ad called "Hope," Clinton bombarded the airways with imagery. This was a critical campaign move. In it, the story unfolded of Clinton, the poor boy who turned leader of men. The closing shot of a young Clinton shaking hands with John F. Kennedy was as definitive in this campaign as the shot of Bush being rescued from the ocean during World War II was in the '88 campaign. The juxtaposition between Clinton and Bush, two leaders from different generations with differing values, served not only to begin crystallizing choices for November, but established Clinton as a child of Camelot. Given Kennedy's own habits of infidelity, the symbolic association may have helped reduce the impact of the Flowers episode by reducing its relevance to leadership. Without condoning Clinton's supposed affair, voters seemed more interested in traits that might affect Clinton's leadership abilities. The issue that would challenge that trait would be the draft.

Close on the heels of the infidelity issue came the draft. Again, the issue was not new to people in Clinton's home state. It had been a topic during several of Clinton's gubernatorial elections in Arkansas without much avail. The difference was again a matter of juxtaposition with Bush. Bush's one unilaterally noted strength was his foreign-policy experience. His own service in World War II was as commendable as his leadership in several international crises since assuming the presidency. Most Democratic contenders in the early primary stages stuck to the one cluster of concerns where Bush was weak: domestic issues. The significance of the draft issue for a candidate who had to face Bush in the November election was frightening. It seemed to provide evidence that the leading Democratic contender was another sure loser. The New Hampshire primary proved otherwise.

The results of the New Hampshire primary should have served as a wake-up call to those who believed that military and foreign-policy credentials would be valued over a strong domestic agenda. The Kerry media strategy helped underscore this point. In an attempt to take advantage of Clinton's misfortunes, Kerry shifted from issue spots on health care and trade to push his biographical ad. The timing is notable. In the wake of the Clinton draft story, Kerry defined himself as a Vietnam veteran who lost his right leg in battle and earned his country's Medal of Honor. The Kerry campaign was hoping to poise itself for the fallout over the draft issue and to offer Kerry as the acceptable alternative to Clinton. Despite the fact that Kerry outspent the Democratic field and made a strong argument based on his military leadership credentials, the issue foremost on voters' minds was the economy.[3] The New Hampshire primary offered hope that the Democrats and their domestic reform agendas could take them to the White House.

Clinton's success in weathering the barrage of charges that surfaced in the opening round of the campaign is due to Clinton's persistence in working to overcome a deficiency and to the campaign's ability to place all available media resources at his disposal. While the advertisements pushed the issue themes and the press pursued the latest scoop on personal behavior, the media strategy employed what some within the campaign called the "Arsenio strategy." This was an effort designed to bypass the press and speak directly to the people. The development of this strategy and Clinton's successful handling of the format proved influential. Starting with New Hampshire, Clinton took advantage of direct contact with the voters. The more familiar he became to them, the more they liked him. His success in the use of these alternative formats helped to push past the political booby traps that seemed to assault his campaign.

In the first election battle of the campaign, Clinton had been badly bruised but still managed to come in second behind Tsongas. Clinton called himself the "Comeback Kid" on primary night. In the political world, he certainly was. Few candidates can expect to survive the kinds of serious attacks that caused Clinton to drop in the polls thirteen points in four days. The New Hampshire primary proved he was a survivor.

The future, however, was still in question. Jerry Brown, once thought to be the least-threatening opponent, was neck and neck with Clinton in polls released just prior to the Connecticut and New York primaries. In Colorado and Maryland, the Clinton camp had to contend with the Tsongas surge. But Clinton was no more damaged than his November opponent, George Bush.

On the other side of the ballot George Bush was being tested by two controversial figures: Pat Buchanan and David Duke. Both claimed Bush was selling out conservative interests and betraying the trust of the American people. With the relative merits of the Buchanan-Duke candidacies at issue as well as the growing protest movement by conservatives who felt betrayed, Bush was unable to reap the benefits from the Democrats' squabbling or Clinton's misfortunes.

The Bush campaign, besieged by disorganization, failed to hire Roger Ailes, the architect of his '88 media campaign. Meanwhile, Robert Teeter, Bush's '88 pollster, was appointed as campaign director. While Bush was organizing, Buchanan was taking aim. In fact, Bush did not begin buying media time until the third week in January when polls were already detecting a Buchanan foothold.

Buchanan hit hard with an attack on the "read my lips" pledge, claiming that America could not afford four more years of Bush. The Bush team ignored the Buchanan challenge. Instead, Bush appealed to popular frustration with government gridlock in an ad asking voters to help him throw out the Democratic Congress. Not only did the campaign fail to provide a reasonable response to the substance of Buchanan's claim, the response ad created symbolic disparities that seemed to support the "actions speak louder than words" charge. The disparate message was derived from the visual text, which featured Bush speaking to the public from the Oval Office. The tone of the ad served to perceptually (and negatively) distance Bush from the pack of candidates who were in the field pressing flesh to get the vote. Speaking from a power position in the White House rather than from the fields of New Hampshire, the ad served to perpetuate the notion that Bush was out of touch with the ordinary citizen.

For Bush, two problems were readily apparent. First, the Bush campaign was too disorganized to mount a coherent response or to recognize significant charges. Second, the ad campaign failed to define Bush in such a way as to unify core constituents.

The impact of the combined attacks from Buchanan and Duke on the right and the Democratic pack on the left should have served to position Bush as the centrist candidate. Yet the Bush team was unable to make that claim and was left without a strong base of support. Results of the New Hampshire primary showed Bush making the weakest showing of an incumbent president (53 percent) since Johnson in 1968 (50 percent). That election resulted in Johnson's withdrawal from the presidential contest.

THE BATTLE OF THE WOUNDED

Two issues defined the primary battles that led to the nominations of Clinton and Bush. The first was the recognition by the Clinton team that in their effort to run damage control, they had left New Hampshire voters frustrated. The one issue voters cared most about, the economy, received only secondary attention. The upcoming Democratic primary battles were clearly dependent on how well the campaigns got their economic messages across to the voters. The issue Bush faced was the inability of the Republican party to exert control over the arguments and tactics of its far-right wing. In a throwback to Clinton's prediction at his announcement address, the Republican campaigns seemed vitriolic and isolationist. A disorganized Bush campaign seemed incapable of defining the party's ideological agenda.

Bill Clinton and the Democratic Opposition

Before the first primary vote was cast, numerous pundits had declared on varying occasions that the Clinton campaign was over. Columnists Rowland Evans and Robert Novak reported that Clinton was "one of the walking dead who sooner or later will keel over."

Damaged but not yet defeated, Clinton managed to hang on, making a respectable second-place showing in the first primary. Yet Clinton had lost his front-runner status, a loss that actually helped the campaign since front-runners face increased scrutiny by the media. Fortunately, the party now had three viable contenders, each having won enough support to merit media attention. Paul Tsongas, a rather dry persona with a fighting spirit, won the New Hampshire primary and scored high in the public opinion polls. Jerry Brown, a wild card no one had previously suspected of having much of a chance after his fifth-place finish in New Hampshire, placed second in the Maine caucuses and began developing a strong protest vote.

Clinton received two advantages from this twist of fate. First, having been scrutinized already by the press, he got a brief respite while the media turned their guns on the other contenders. Second, by losing his front-runner status he was free to go on the attack.

The campaign had a brief window of opportunity to turn itself around. In order to do so, the media strategy needed to achieve three specific tasks: define the opposition, maintain a clear and consistent message, and utilize every available media outlet.

All three Democratic candidates clustered around the economic issue, routinely spouting plans and approaches to whomever would listen. Perceptually, voters needed to be able to distinguish the difference among these leaders, their positions, and their approaches to governing.

The use of attack ads helped serve that purpose. In races where there are numerous candidates, the trick is to avoid attacking one opponent in such a way so as to repel voters and leave them for another candidate to court. This process is usually accomplished by establishing perceptual definitions of opponents such that your candidate is in the middle ground of the debate. The Clinton team took the opportunity to stake out their turf.

Jerry Brown was defined as someone far-left of center. This was not difficult to do. He was still remembered by many as "Governor Moonbeam" some ten years after his term as governor of California. In the 1992 election he refused campaign contributions of more than one hundred dollars and staked his fund-raising on a 1-800 phone drive. Both actions seemed to deny conventional campaign success formulas and were described as "flaky" approaches to campaign finance. Yet Brown made a surprisingly strong showing in the early stages of the election. In keeping with the character issue, the one premise best suited for attack was not a specific action, but Brown's judgment skills.

In a typical "flip-flop" ad, Brown was pictured on the right side of the screen, then on the left in a sequence of visuals that left the impression he was on both sides of issues. The announcer argued that while Jerry Brown says "he'll fight for the people," the "question is . . . which people?" As an example, the ad suggests that Brown claims to support working families but then proposes a flat tax that favors the wealthy.

Meanwhile, the Clinton team attempted to position Tsongas on the far right, at least economically. Tsongas might be more accurately described as a "card-carrying liberal,"[4] but his economic position was strongly conservative. But Tsongas was difficult to understand. His "national industrial policy" was more confusing than trickle-down economics, a factor that permitted the Clinton team to define his policy for him.

Tsongas's position was defined in a comparative ad that began with the question, "Paul Tsongas or Bill Clinton?" Then, using *Time* magazine as a source, the announcer contended that "much of what Tsongas proposes smacks of trickle-down economics." The ad cites a capitol-gains tax cut, a cut in the cost-of-living adjustment for Social Security recipients, and a gas tax as example of his policies. Then the ad argues that Clinton's plan is different, including a policy that would make "the rich pay their fair share."

Equal to the descriptions these ads provided of Brown and Tsongas are the defining characteristics on which Clinton maligned his Democratic opposition. Based on information that emerged from polls and focus groups, both attacks sought to define the opposition relative to their stance on the economy. Other issues were subservient to that theme.

At the same time, Clinton developed strong argument ads designed to demonstrate how his value-centered leadership would affect the handling of issues he would face as president. Depicting Tsongas's plan as another version of "Reaganomics" and Brown as "Liberalism" incarnate, Clinton nestled into a moderate position, stressing "people first" in a series of issue ads. Slowly, the Clinton campaign began to hone their message to voters. The paid media strategy had limited success. The main benefit was in demonstrating the campaign's ability to control a clear and consistent message. Campaign insiders, however, were also aware that the paid media were not advancing the campaign. Many believed that the campaign survived only because of Clinton's sheer tenacity in redoubling his efforts each time problems arose.

The one almost indisputable success for the media strategists was their use of free media. In the free-for-all contest that followed Clinton's weak New Hampshire showing, the use of alternative media became more important than the paid advertising. In the background of the Democratic contest, Ross Perot emerged onto the political stage from, of all unexpected places, the "Larry King Live" show. From "Donahue" to MTV and the network morning news shows, the airwaves resonated with political discussion. Even radio, a medium that had taken a backseat in presidential elections since 1952, became a tool for getting messages across to targeted voting audiences. By some expert accounts, Jerry Brown's use of radio call-in shows was a key factor in his win in Connecticut.[5]

The free media were also instrumental in helping the campaign get through "the dark days of May." Despite the fact that Clinton wrapped up the nomination long before the convention, the campaign looked like a loser. With Perot now in the race, Clinton ranked third with only 25 percent of the vote. Money was tight. Although people knew more about Clinton's positions, they still failed to get a good sense of who Clinton was as a person, a factor that left him vulnerable to future attacks. At the urging of media strategist Mandy Grunwald, the Clinton campaign experimented with another media outlet: "The Arsenio Hall Show." The "Arsenio" strategy had been brewing for some time. Clinton was successful virtually each time he appeared on the talk-show circuit. Appearing on "Arsenio" seemed like a good move. The added twist for this particular appearance was that Clinton would play the sax as he had for the "Tonight Show" four years earlier.

Clinton's Arsenio appearance worked in two ways. First, it put him back in the news with front-page coverage. Second, it showed a side of Clinton that voters had rarely seen. He was "friendly, relaxed and engaging."[6]

The other event that helped reestablish the campaign's momentum was a news event where Clinton attacked rap singer Sister Souljah during a speech to the Rainbow coalition. In almost open defiance of Jesse Jackson, Clinton argued that Souljah had made racist statements. Jackson lashed out, claiming that Clinton's remarks were designed to appeal to white conservatives. Clearly, the action was politically calculated to precipitate free news coverage and position Clinton as a moderate. Perceptually, it demonstrated that Clinton was willing to stand tough against Jackson and the left wing of the party. Clinton made headlines again.

Significantly, the 1992 general election was just ahead. With Perot, a strong independent candidate who was changing the traditional two-party scenario, a "politics as usual" media strategy was out of the question. A new design that incorporated a carefully targeted and effective media strategy became paramount. Consequently, the Clinton campaign reorganized in June to attempt to resolve, among other things, the media problem. Although Greer, Margolis, Grunwald and Associates, the media firm that had seen the campaign through the primaries, was retained, new insight was needed. The campaign hired additional political consultants (Squier-Eskew-Knapp-Ochs Communications and Michael Donilon from Doak and Shrum), creative talent (including Donny Deutsch, Linda Kaplan Thaler, Ken Gilbert, Paul Spencer and David Angelo), and the services of a firm specializing in communications to black audiences (Valerie Graves, senior vice-president of Uniworld Group). The team, publicly announced on 4 July, had only a couple of weeks of preparation time before Perot announced his withdrawal from the race. In hindsight, the fact that a strong team was assembled before the withdrawal may have been a lucky break. A two-person race might not have provided the incentive for the Clinton campaign to hire this many well-known and successful consultants.

While the ad team began formulating its strategies, the campaign provided relief for the media team by using the talents of Clinton's long-time supporters Harry Thomason and Linda Bloodworth-Thomason, producers of the prime-time television series "Designing Women" and "Hearts Afire." Their thirteen-minute biography entitled "A Man from Hope," coupled with the campaign organization's skills in controlling the images of the convention, allowed the ad team to focus on designing strategic messages for the general-election campaign.

The success of the media during the Democratic convention cannot be understated. The Thomasons' video biography coupled with well-crafted convention speeches strategically shored up a weak Clinton image. Focus group reports and polling data revealed that people had conflicting images about Clinton. Many, for example, assumed that since Clinton had an Ivy-League education, he must be from a wealthy family. They knew little or nothing about his background. Although the video was considered simple and emotional, it worked. Additionally, Grunwald's media team provided delegates with "talking points" each day of the convention to make sure everyone knew how to advance the party's message of the day. Clinton's boost out of the convention put him in first place among the three presidential contenders for the first time in the race. The ad team had momentum to build on. The question was, could it?

The Disorganization of Bush

One of Clinton's major breaks was the Republican party's infighting. Bush's media campaign was slow to emerge in the primary season and even slower to respond to Buchanan's challenge. Although Buchanan only got 37 percent of the vote in New Hampshire, it was a stronger showing against an incumbent president than anyone had expected. As the campaign began its southern swing, Buchanan's attacks became more terse and his focus became more narrow. The Bush campaign was forced to respond.

Significantly, the racist themes Clinton denounced as Republican tactics in his announcement speech were clearly evidenced throughout the primary period by Bush's opponents. Duke's baggage as the former Grand Wizard of the Ku Klux Klan and member of the Nazi party made his promotion of Christian morality appear as thinly veiled messages of hate. Similarly, Buchanan's positions on immigration, policies toward Israel, and the quota system struck racist chords.

Perhaps the most talked about and blatant ad was designed by the Buchanan campaign as an appeal to social conservatives. The ad attacked the Bush administration for supporting "pornographic and blasphemous art." The video, a clip from the PBS documentary about gays, showed men dancing in leather harnesses. The fact that Bush quickly fired John Frohnmayer, the Chair of the National Endowment of the Arts, revealed Bush's concern that he was losing his conservative base and demonstrated his willingness to align himself with Buchanan and the ultra-right in an effort to hold on to the coalition Reagan had galvanized. The response from southern Democrats, already primed from the racially charged Helms-Gantt Senate race, was that the Republicans had now placed Willie Horton and the race card squarely back on the table.

Although Buchanan never seriously threatened a Bush nomination, his messages permanently damaged Bush for the general election. First, Buchanan kept the Bush campaign off balance through much of the campaign. The preferred course for an incumbent is to appear "presidential." Instead, Bush was forced to get into the trenches and slug it out. Second, Buchanan tested themes that would later be used by Clinton. The "you can't trust Bush to do what he promises" theme was tested in Buchanan's ads long before the Clinton team launched similar successful attacks. Third, Buchanan robbed Bush of the ability to set the party's agenda. His barrage of attacks, coupled with the Bush campaign's inability to effectively respond, pulled the Republican base away from a moderate-conservative position to the far right, leaving the party agenda narrowly defined and exclusionary.

The handling of the media campaign provides compelling evidence of the Bush campaign's general mishandling of the election. While Perot and the Democrats experimented with a newly found populism characterized by media appearances on a variety of talk-show and commercial formats, Bush confined his appearances to those which made him look "presidential." Noting that talk shows were "weird" and that appearances on programs like MTV were difficult since he was "no teeny-bopper," Bush virtually conceded those audiences to Perot and Clinton. Bush eventually began to experiment with these formats, but he never seemed fully comfortable with them. Moreover, the Bush campaign's inability to capitalize on the free media coverage these outlets provided placed even greater importance on the effectiveness of the paid media.

The paid media, however, were problematic. Only weeks after Quayle assailed the media as culturally elite and condemned their mocking of family values, the November Company (Bush's media team) announced that it would use "good taste" and "moral values" as criteria for determining where they would buy time slots for the Bush ads.[7] Further, the November Company attempted to shift the responsibility to the networks for determining which shows "were in good taste" and "reflective of the moral values of the President."[8] That request, of course, was rejected. While it is not unusual within the field of product advertising for sponsors to request information on program content, the November Company seemed to misunderstand the nature of political campaigns, particularly ones that need to reach large segments of the voting public. Not only did this strategy deprive the campaign of slots where the largest number of voters could be reached, it also inadvertently attempted to force the networks into becoming political participants through its selection of appropriate shows. The networks' rebuke of the request demonstrated the media group's political ineptitude.[9] The fact that the request was made at all demonstrated how far Bush was willing to go to appease the party's right wing.

Throughout the campaign, the media group had repeatedly misfired. At no time was this more apparent than in August. The Bush team had a unique opportunity to position Bush as a strong contender and to reestablish his own agenda before the convention. Incredibly, the campaign had a reserve of some $8 million to advance those themes, money that had to be spent before the convention.[10] The strength of this position was magnified by the fact that Clinton emerged from the Democratic convention some $2.5 million in debt. While political experts questioned the wisdom of holding onto the money so long,[11] the action created a golden opportunity to blow the election open. When the Bush campaign finally began airing spots, however, the topics included the economy and the environment. Both issues were considered among the president's more vulnerable positions,[12] particularly in light of weak signs of economic improvement and Bush's cavalier treatment of environmental issues at June's Earth Summit in Brazil. Moreover, the economy ad actually endorsed "change," a message that is difficult for audiences to use as a reason to vote for an incumbent.

Additionally, the ad team misfired on at least two other occasions. First, the team broke federal laws by illegally using the presidential seal in a political advertisement. The ads had to be pulled and reedited. Second, they circulated scripts of endorsement ads by Kevin Costner and James S. Brady, both of whom rejected the campaign's requests to appear. The combined effect was to "fuel speculation that personnel changes [were] forthcoming."[13]

Deprived of the wide Reagan base, Bush staggered into his party's convention weak and unprepared. The themes and messages were "not part of a coordinated message coming from the White House," failed to provide strong arguments in favor of Bush, and were "choppy and hard to follow."[14] Further, the convention was overshadowed by the announcement of the North American Free Trade Agreement (NAFTA) in Washington one day and news that the United States was provoking another showdown with Iraq on another.

The only coordinated message during the convention came from the Democrats who used paid ads to dispute Republican claims. Two fifteen-second ads, which compared George Bush's handling of economic issues with Bill Clinton's, concluded "those are the facts, back to the show." But this was only one way the Clinton camp upstaged Bush during his own show.

Clinton also drew media attention through billboards placed near the Astrodome. Under a drawing of a large pair of lips, was the text "Read My Lips: No New Taxes. George Bush, August 18, 1988, New Orleans, La." Clearly, the Clinton campaign was having fun goading Bush into a response. The Bush camp quickly called a press conference to release the scripts of three ads that had yet to be produced. While they were able to generate some coverage, the scripts did not generate the same coverage as those which had actually been broadcast.

Tactically, the Clinton ads served two purposes. First, they added an element of conflict to the convention coverage, resulting in free media exposure for Clinton. CNN and the three major networks, for example, each rebroadcast ads as part of their news coverage of the race.[15] The significance of this is that the campaigns began targeting ads specifically to the media, not to the voters. These efforts to generate news coverage, while not new, were certainly more blatant. Clinton media consultant Frank Greer confirmed the strategic use of the ad, when he noted: "It's a simple fact that the real message of a convention comes from the press corps."[16] The use of the ads had a secondary function as well: They permitted Clinton to respond to Republican challenges to his record that emerged during the convention. Using the lessons from recent Democratic failures, responding immediately and effectively was a key element of the Clinton strategy.

The Bush campaign's disorganization and the Clinton media assault were discouraging to Republican loyalists. Rather than providing a much-needed boost, the Republican convention left Bush at a disadvantage. To further complicate the scenario, three days into the convention, Perot intimated he might reenter the race. Campaign strategists began scurrying to restructure their plans.

COUNTDOWN TO VICTORY

The fall media campaign drew a considerable amount of public interest. This was due, at least in part, to Ross Perot's tacit reentry into the election.

The Perot Factor

Perot was successful as an innovator in media development. His thirty-minute infomercials proved that voters would listen to an extended message about a subject they cared about. Perot's first infomercial, for example, placed thirty-second in the Nielsen ratings, drawing 11.2 million households. Even a repeat of the show garnered 8.4 million households.

Further, Perot's media campaign demonstrated that advertising strength does not reside solely among politicos or the Madison Avenue crowd. His media team, lead by Dallas-area advertising specialists Murphy Martin and Dennis McClain, produced not only the infomercials but a series of unique ads as well.

Perot's challenge, however, was to stake out ground in the election contest. Polls demonstrated that he was so weakened by the time of his reentry that he was viable only as a spoiler in the race that lay ahead. The result was that despite Perot's attempts to nestle into the middle ground through ads that positioned him both as a patriot and a person with a strong economic agenda he was largely ignored by both Bush and Clinton. Neither of the other candidates responded directly to Perot's challenges, and neither attacked Perot's positions. His one notable contribution was to focus the election on the economy; a factor that was responsible in no small measure for Bush's defeat.

Lessons on Defeating an Incumbent

As the campaign entered its final phase, it was the Clinton team who maintained control over the media agenda. Four attributes characterize Clinton's fall media campaign. First, the campaign inoculated the public against the impending attacks from George Bush. Second, the campaign took the offensive in reducing Bush's credibility. Third, the campaign forced the economy to the top of the issues agenda. Finally, the media team developed a quick-response strategy that defended Clinton's record and raised the stakes for Bush each time he attacked Clinton. Note how each of these contributed to a negative public image for Bush.

The inoculation strategy began during the Republican convention. Despite Bush's "kinder, gentler" pledge in 1988, the Republican convention speakers blasted Clinton and took aim at Hillary. The Democrats responded by dropping Willie Horton's name as often as possible. For example, Clinton defended Hillary's honor, saying that the Republicans were "basically trying to make it kind of a Willie Horton-like thing against all independent, working women, trying to run against them in a way that I think is really lamentable." Other Democrats remarked about the "Hortonization" of diverse groups such as gays, pro-choice groups, or rap artists. According to Lyn Nofziger, former advisor to Reagan, the strategy was designed to "plant an idea that the Republicans are going to play dirty politics."[17] The public had been warned about dirty tricks, told the Republicans would be unethical, and were left with the clear impression that they should expect unethical smear tactics in the future. The effect of this inoculation strategy was to downplay the significance of the attacks when they came.

The second characteristic of the strategy was its use of proof regarding the issues of trust and character. This was critical in order to downplay the Bush attacks on Clinton's trustworthiness and character. One of the strongest forms of proof was created by turning George Bush against himself. In at least six different attack ads, the Clinton team juxtaposed clippings of Bush speeches against government statistics demonstrating his failure to produce the promised results. The impact of seeing Bush make the statements is compelling and far stronger than a mere assertion that he made them. It further reduces the chances of Clinton being accused of using gutter tactics himself. Using another person's words against them is far more credible than the typical mudslinging that occurs through use of implication and innuendo. In using this tactic, Clinton managed to take the moral high ground and still engage in an effective attack against his opponent.

Another type of proof is also prevalent in the ads. The Clinton team provided source citations for almost every claim they made, both those in favor of Clinton as well as those that demonstrated Bush's failure. There was no doubt Clinton had a credibility problem with some segments of the voting population. The use of seemingly unbiased sources to support the arguments aided in establishing credibility for his claims.

Finally, the campaign used anecdotal proof derived from voters' own personal experiences. The Clinton team was aware that many Americans were not confident about Bush's handling of the economy. People simply did not feel as if the country was making economic progress. The proof resulting from personal experience is almost impossible to refute. Consequently, the Bush campaign would have difficulty convincing people they were doing better than they felt they were doing.

To understand the way these proofs worked together, consider the Clinton ad that used a clip from Bush's 1988 ad where he says, "If you elect me President, you will be better off than you are today." After citing government sources showing family income down, health care costs up, and a hefty tax increase to boot, the ad concludes, "Well, it's four years later. How ya doin'?" The combination of these various forms of proof made a compelling argument.

The third characteristic of the Clinton campaign was a dogged determination to stake the election on economic issues. Unlike the primaries where Clinton sought to have a better economic position than the other contenders, the campaign saw the economy as a hands-down issue that could swing the election in Clinton's favor. The question was whether they could establish the economy as the issue of the campaign. Two things helped stake that position. First, the rumbling that Perot would reenter the race accelerated after the Republican convention, culminating in Perot's decision to run on 18 September. The Perot candidacy was established almost entirely on the need for economic reform. Thus, Perot's reentry into the race helped raise the ante on the economic issue. Second, shortly after the Republican convention, the Bush campaign yielded to the Clinton attacks and by the magnitude of responses conceded the importance of the issue. Using the now-established 1-800 response number, Bush unveiled his "Agenda for American Renewal." The response was designed to "counter the impression many Americans seem to have that the President simply has no economic agenda."[18] No doubt, the Bush campaign was trying to put the economic agenda behind them early in the fall campaign so they could move to more favorable issues. Unfortunately, they not only raised the visibility of the issue but did so with a weakly constructed plan. Unlike Tsongas's eighty-six-page economic agenda that helped him win the New Hampshire primary, Bush's twenty-nine-page plan was loaded with sound bites but weak on substance. Bush tried, but he failed to give the impression that he had developed an economic agenda that would stave off defections by Reagan Democrats.

The fourth, and perhaps most impressive, characteristic of the

Clinton media campaign was its quick-response capability. On at least four occasions, the Clinton campaign was able to respond to Bush's attacks in a way that damaged Bush's credibility. For example, on 2 October, Bush aired an attack on Clinton's economic plan. The ad featured voters from various occupations and listed the amount of tax increase they could expect to pay under the Clinton plan. Less than twenty-four hours later, the Clinton team placed a response ad in twenty states. Establishing proof from outside sources once again, the Clinton ad quoted a *Washington Post* article that said the ad was "misleading" and the *Wall Street Journal* that said Clinton's tax cuts were for the kind of people featured in the Bush ad. Not only did the campaign refute Bush's claims, it attempted to explain Bush's motive. The announcer asks, "Why is he doing it?" then answers "because George Bush has the worst economic record of any President in fifty years." Claiming that Bush is "trying to scare you," the ad concludes that "nothing could be more frightening than four more years." The ad was effective in staving off the Bush attack. Moreover, it was impressive in that the response was made so quickly. The *New York Times* noted that "it was the sort of hair-trigger counterpunch that is not uncommon in state and local politics but is almost unheard of in the layered, cautious bureaucracy of Presidential campaigning."[19]

The strategy worked. In a poll conducted among voters who had seen presidential commercials during this particular round of attacks, 68 percent of the voters said they believed Bush's ads were not truthful as compared to 35 percent who believed Clinton's ads were not truthful.[20] Despite the fact that neither was believed by everyone, Clinton clearly made headway by gutting the Bush challenge.

The effect of the ensuing attack/counterattack phase of the campaign was to raise the negative rating of both Bush and Clinton. In fact, Bush got such negative feedback that for a period of time, he virtually disappeared as a figure in his own ads. Instead, Bush used person-in-the-street formats that permitted others to do the attacking for him. This attempt to distance himself from the negative attacks is noteworthy. The strategy is designed to distance the candidate from attack politics and the resulting negative associations it produces with voters. It also allows the ads to be based more easily on innuendo and opinion. The attacks generated from the citizenry presumably reflect personal opinions and as such require no proof or validity.

By contrast, the Clinton campaign maintained its strategy of provable attacks. The contrast was marked. A Bush ad depicts the "two faces of Clinton" claiming that Clinton had taken contradictory positions on the Gulf War, term limits, and his military record. No source citations were offered. The same day, Clinton launched a "read my lips" attack showing Bush making his infamous promise, then cited Congressional Budget Office records disclosing that the Bush tax increase was the second biggest tax increase in American history. Both ads attempted to challenge the other's reliability. Clinton's attack was simply more credible.

As successful as Clinton was in responding to Bush's attacks, the Bush campaign continued to harm itself by making mistakes and unsupported assertions that drew a media response. Beginning in September, the November Company produced an ad claiming that Bush would fight for U.S. export opportunities but failed to notice the ship was owned by a Taiwanese firm. On 12 October, a Bush ad featured the cover of *Time* magazine with the headline "Why Voters Don't Trust Bill Clinton." *Time* took the Bush campaign to federal court in an effort to force them to pull the ad. Similarly, the Bush campaign ran a vitriolic attack on 29 October that showed gloomy scenes of a wasteland supposedly created by Clinton in Arkansas. The ad ended with a shot of a buzzard perched atop a lifeless tree. The ad not only enraged Arkansans, it provoked responses from news agencies that the Clinton campaign used in its response ad: "CBS, CNN and newspapers across the country call George Bush's ads misleading and wrong." The total effect of Clinton's counterattacks and the media's coverage of Bush blunders made the Bush campaign appear unorganized, incoherent, and errant.

Clinton's ability to control the media agenda in the fall campaign contributed to his victory over George Bush. The campaign's coordinated effort to shape the economy as the major voting issue was crucial. That message positioned George Bush as ineffectual in achieving his own stated goals as the leader of this nation.

By contrast, Bush's failure to exert control over the issues resulted in his interment of the one issue that provided the most strength: foreign policy. It is notable that the Bush campaign was not able to develop its "commander in chief" series of ads sooner. The series began airing only ten days out from the election. By then, the significance of the issue itself was in question.

Outside of helping to establish the agenda for the campaign, the advertisements themselves were not effective in persuading voters, despite the fact that the ads cost approximately $100 million. Despite the amount invested in the effort, a *Times*-CBS poll indicates that "the commercials this season have reinforced peoples' attitudes about candidates but have done little to sway their votes."[21] Thus, the lesson here is to take note of the way media campaigns can be coordinated to magnify key themes and messages and to help establish the national issue agenda.

SUMMARY

If there are any lessons to be derived from the use of media in the 1992 election, we must consider how this campaign served as a reverse image of the 1988 race. Clinton borrowed the formula for bringing ad talent together that Reagan and Bush utilized successfully in the three previous presidential elections: Hire politicos and creative talent and give them direction. Bush, in a throwback to Dukakis's failed ad strategy, hired Madison Avenue ad executives with little political expertise and failed to give them guidance.

Consultants who specialize in handling political races may have proven that they are no longer second-class citizens in the world of advertising. The last four elections have demonstrated that developing relationships between candidates and their constituencies is different than promoting products. Creative talent counts. Innovation counts. However, understanding relationship building and management is critical.

Further, consultants should note that politics has unique demands from product advertising. Whereas executives may take four months to develop ads for commercial product launches, political ads are confined to short turnaround periods on highly volatile subjects. Understanding the political process is critical. Product ads can be tested and retested; the timing of political ads often requires marketers to act on hunches and best available evidence. Money is tight in most elections. While a product ad may easily command a $250,000 budget, a run-of-the-mill spot for a presidential contest is typically around $40,000. Finally, political ads are subject to intense scrutiny by the press, the public, and the opposition. Mistakes cannot be covered, at least not for long.

Numerous accounts have appeared in the last few elections of the frustrations of the Madison Avenue crowd with politics. The fact that so much consensus building is required in the development and production of advertising messages is a daunting task for many. Perhaps the common advice they would offer a campaign is control the message, make sure you have direct access to the candidate, and learn to be a player in developing the election strategy.

Those strategies paid off for the media campaign of Bill Clinton. A test of its replicability awaits us in 1996.

NOTES

1. Greer in Edwin Diamond, "Selling Clinton," *New York*, 6 April 1992, 37.

2. Ibid.

3. "Voter Woes Make the Economy the Unavoidable Issue," *Dallas Morning News*, 9 February 1992.

4. Steven W. Colford, "A Marketing Guide to the '92 Primaries," *Advertising Age*, 13 January 1992, 12.

5. "Talk Radio a Player in Presidential Campaign," *Broadcasting*, 15 June 1992, 14.

6. George J. Church, "The Long Road," *Time*, 2 November 1992, 37.

7. Stuart Elliott, "Bush's Ads Will Avoid Some Television Shows," *New York Times*, 14 July 1992, Sec. D, 2.

8. Ibid.

9. Joe Mandese, "Bush Buy Becomes Morality Play at CBS," *Advertising Age*, 13 July 1992, 1.

10. Steven W. Colford, "Bush Forces Prepare Volley of TV Ads," *Advertising Age*, 20 July 1992, 42.

11. Richard L. Berke, "Bush Ads Disappoint Many in GOP," *New York Times*, 16 August 1992, 26.

12. Colford, "Bush Forces," 42.

13. Steven W. Colford, "Bush Team Slips Up Big in First TV Commercials," *Advertising Age*, 10 August 1992, 1.

14. Berke, "Bush Ads," 42.

15. Steven W. Colford, "Clinton Forces Score with 'Tactical' Use of Ads," *Advertising Age*, 24 August 1992, 3.

16. Greer in Colford, "Clinton Forces," 3.

17. Nofziger in Richard L. Berke, "In 1992, Willie Horton Is Democrats' Weapon," *New York Times*, 25 August 1992, 18.

18. Elizabeth Kolbert, "Bush's Toll-Free Number: Good Politics or Political 911?" *New York Times*, 12 September 1992, 6.

19. Michael Wines, "Clinton Squad Snaps Back Quickly at Bush Ad," *New York Times*, 3 October 1992, 8.

20. Debra Gersh, "Media Exposure Not Always Helpful," *Editor and Publisher*, 17 October 1992, 19.

21. Richard L. Berke, "Volleys of Data Replace Blatant Attacks of 1988," *New York Times*, 29 October 1992, 24.

ACKNOWLEDGMENTS

The author wishes to acknowledge C-SPAN for providing grant support for this project and also Shannon Lindsey for assisting in research.

THE FIRST E-MAIL ELECTION

Electronic Networking and the Clinton Campaign

THOMAS W. BENSON

Where and what, literally, is a presidential campaign? In a sense a political campaign is and always has been the organized collective of persons working on behalf of the election of a particular candidate, some "professionally" and a larger group as "volunteers." From the perspective of a voter, a campaign is a loose collection of communicative episodes transmitted by the mass media, public oratory, and various forms of interpersonal contact. The interactions of the campaign-as-production and the campaign-as-reception are extraordinarily complex and volatile.

A campaign may be idealized as a candidate giving a public speech to a group of potential voters. But, in fact, until this century, it was not common for presidential candidates to campaign extensively, if at all, on their own behalf. Even when they began to do so, they could not reach directly to a majority of voters isolated in time and space. And even though candidates in recent decades have fallen into a campaign routine that includes the delivery of a great many speeches, most of those speeches have been almost totally inaccessible to the public at large, either through direct attendance or as texts or audio visual recordings.[1] Other modes of communication—parades, rallies, newspapers and magazines, then radio and television, have supplemented the campaign-as-public-speaking. But closer inspection reveals that "supplement" may be too mild a term to describe the relation of the mass media to the campaign. To an important degree, as many scholars have argued, the television campaign *is* the modern presidential campaign, both in the sense that voters get most of their information about politics from television (and to a lesser extent from radio and newspapers) and in the sense that campaigns themselves are increasingly designed as television. Modern campaigns stage the theater of traditional campaigning—from visits to New Hampshire factory gates to convention acceptance addresses to a campaign speech at a nursing home or day-care center—in order to secure television news coverage. A large proportion of national campaign funds are used to produce and broadcast thirty-second campaign advertisements. A formal speech is conveyed to most voters, if at all, as a film clip, a sixty-second commentary by a TV reporter, and a ten-second sound bite from the candidate. Television news coverage and the thirty-second television political spot have made our presidential campaigns more visible, but have virtually destroyed the campaign as a meaningful occasion for extended discourse by the candidate and have at the same time contributed to a diminishment of the public space where voters may talk to one another about politics.[2]

But in 1992 both the campaign as discourse and voter interaction in the public sphere were experimentally refreshed in an unexpected domain—the Internet, a huge, worldwide network of computers.[3] In everyday use, the Internet is accessible to faculty members and students at colleges and universities and to many employees of major corporations, as well as to subscribers to commercial computer networks such as CompuServe, which, for a fee, can send and receive electronic messages through "gateways" to the Internet. Sitting at a personal computer in one's home, office, or a college computer lab, a person with an Internet connection can send a private electronic mail note or a long file of text, graphics, or computer programs to any other user on the system; can subscribe to or edit an electronic publication that is automatically distributed to a large audience; can read and respond to ongoing discussions on a wide variety of specialized computer "bulletin boards"; can interactively search through vast storehouses of files on remote mainframe computers; or can interactively search the catalogs of major university libraries. These and other related services, delivered interactively and, for most users, without any charge for ongoing or individual connections, have become a commonplace of academic and corporate life in the 1980s.

In 1992 the United States presidential campaign came to the Internet. In the account that follows, I will describe some of the primary actors in the Internet campaign, the major domains and forms of communicative activity, and the implications of the 1992 e-mail campaign for communication and politics. Our story can be only a partial one, as the e-mail campaign was a widely distributed and in many ways nonhierarchical movement, the history of which is somewhat obscured by contentions over control and credit.

This description of the Clinton e-mail campaign is based on dozens of interviews (many of them conducted by electronic mail) with participants in the e-mail campaign and on a review of hundreds of pages of archived campaign documents, electronic bulletin board postings, and e-mail messages. My approach is generally conceived as historical and critical, attempting to reconstruct the history of the e-mail campaign and to assess its implications for democratic political communication.

Public political e-mail is going to evolve rapidly, and there are likely to be at least several academic accounts of the 1992 e-mail campaign. My own survey of the campaign, based on participation at the time and several months of trying to reconstruct and reassess it after the election, points to several key communicative and rhetorical features of the e-mail campaign. What stands out especially vividly in my own rereading of the campaign and of the recollections of key participants is that the e-mail campaign reasserted the importance of discursive rhetoric and of interactive participation as elements of the democratic communicative situation. But these themes emerged in practice, and not as a clearly articulated set of themes at the outset of the campaign.

THE CLINTON CAMPAIGN IN THE VIRTUAL SPACE OF THE INTERNET

The use of electronic networking in the campaign occurred in a variety of domains on the widely dispersed Internet and on commercial networks. In all accounts of the origins of the electronic mail campaign, it appears to have developed spontaneously at several sites outside the campaign itself and to have proceeded in a loosely organized fashion that was made effective by the willingness of the campaign itself to reach out to the world of electronic networking. There was no fixed hierarchy, and although many people assumed roles of leadership, sometimes in coordination with one another, what developed was a fairly open system—in fact, "the electronic campaign" was so open that it would be misleading to call it "the" electronic campaign.

JOCK GILL AND THE COMPUSERVE CONNECTION

Jock Gill was a friend of Bill Clinton's through his wife, who had been a roommate of Hillary Rodham Clinton's in college. According to Gill, he was between jobs because of the collapse of a start-up company in the spring of 1992 when he volunteered to put his account on CompuServe at the service of the Clinton campaign. Working at first as a volunteer from his home in Vermont, then later (by some reports it was as late as October) from the campaign headquarters in Little Rock, Gill worked to organize users of electronic networks as Clinton volunteers, and to disseminate Clinton campaign materials over the networks. Gill reported to Jeff Eller, who coordinated media relations and who reported to George Stephanopolous, director of communications, who reported to James Carville, the campaign manager.[4] Gill says that when he began his operation, he was told to do all he could to get the message out, but to express no opinions of his own. He was not required to clear any of his correspondence with the hierarchy of the campaign, though he was encouraged to refer incoming e-mail to relevant campaign workers. He says that he sent some seven thousand messages during the campaign—from the convention to the election.

According to Gill, there were three separate e-mail operations connected to the Clinton campaign—(1) an internal campaign communication system that connected Bill Clinton, Al Gore, and their staffs through a UNIX-based system called "Office Power"; (2) an e-mail connection to various state headquarters and to buses and airplanes on which the campaign traveled; and (3) the public access e-mail campaign run by Jock Gill. These systems were administratively and apparently technically separate from each other—Gill's 286 computer was not connected by e-mail to the campaign's other two e-mail systems. According to some observers, the internal campaign e-mail was a venture in which until 1992 the Democrats were behind the Republicans—it is said that the Mondale and Dukakis campaigns were hampered by their relative lack of internal campaign technology compared to the Reagan and Bush campaigns. But in the area of public e-mail, the Democrats in 1992 had the field virtually to themselves. Gill claims that the Clinton campaign used information far more effectively and faster than the Bush campaign. "Prompt and efficient use of information was a key" to Clinton's victory, says Gill. Part of this promptness was accomplished in the "Rapid Response" effort of the Clinton campaign, which monitored the Bush campaign closely and saw to it that refutations of Bush claims were sent immediately to media outlets. The Rapid Response operation was both a considerable technical accomplishment and a deliberate rhetorical strategy that tried to avoid what was seen as Michael Dukakis's mistake of not responding until too late to the Bush campaign's initiatives in 1988.

Gill had a CompuServe account and inside access to the campaign, but in the beginning he appears to have had little sense of the larger world of the Internet and an unclear idea of the technical and conceptual problems he would face. Nevertheless, he provided an organizing focus and the magic of contact with the actual campaign in Little Rock. The first task was to find a way to distribute Clinton speeches and campaign documents to the widest possible audience. At this point, he met, electronically, Mary Jacobs and other Clinton supporters who had Internet experience. In addition, he made contact with volunteers at the Artificial Intelligence Lab at MIT.

Mary Jacobs, working from a University of Illinois computer, was an essential link, especially early in the campaign. She received electronic copies of Clinton campaign speeches and other documents, usually in WordPerfect format from a personal computer, and reformatted them to travel over the Internet, targeting them to various campaign-related discussion lists and bulletin boards and also sending to various special-topic groups on the network any campaign documents that related to their particular interests.

On CompuServe itself, and on Prodigy and America Online, the two other major commercial electronic mail providers, campaign documents were made available to subscribers. These commercial networks had the advantage that anyone with a computer and a modem could connect to them, even if they were unable to gain full Internet access through a university or other agency with an Internet account. CompuServe provided a window to the Internet for sending and receiving electronic mail, but a CompuServe user was not able to reach out to Internet bulletin boards and had to pay a fee for each electronic mail message entering and leaving the CompuServe domain for the larger Internet. At one point in the campaign, the Prodigy network hosted question-and-answer sessions between its subscribers and candidates Clinton and Bush.

THE MIT GROUP AND CAMPAIGN92.ORG

Not long after the Democratic convention, a group of graduate students in the Artificial Intelligence Lab at Massachusetts Institute of Technology began to organize computer communications on behalf of the Clinton campaign. Early and leading participants in this process at MIT were Amit Thakur, Eric Loeb, and John Mallery. Later in the summer, Thakur dropped out when members of his family were injured in an automobile accident, at which point Loeb, Mallery, and others were the primary MIT organizers.

The MIT organizers, at least some of whom were apparently using their efforts both as political action and as possible dissertation topics, proposed to develop automated mailing systems to facilitate the e-mail campaign. They set up a forwarding address that would send mail among a group of e-mail volunteers around the country. In addition, they worked to develop a semi-automated mail exploder and automatic poster that would send documents of various sorts and on various topics to individual subscribers and to various Internet bulletin boards.

The MIT effort, which coalesced organizationally only during the summer of 1992, when the campaign was already underway, is perhaps best thought of as an experiment, since it was not, evidently, fully operational until October, and even then there were a variety of interruptions and difficulties. In addition, there appear to have been a number of human and organizational difficulties.

At least as early as 14 August, Jock Gill was suggesting to volunteers that they "coordinate with Amit Thakur, who is running Clinton-Gore.Org on Internet for us."[5] No later than the end of August, Eric Loeb announced to various Internet groups the availability of the two-way automatic mail server at MIT, which would sort mail upward to the campaign and downward from the campaign.[6]

CLINTON@MARIST

Lee Sakkas is a forty-nine-year-old programmer analyst in the computer center of Marist College, Poughkeepsie, New York. She had attended the same high school as Bill Clinton, Hot Springs High School in Arkansas, but "unfortunately I was three years ahead of him and never met him."[7] Sakkas had some previous experience in political organizing and as a computer worker reached for a tool that was immediately at hand. She initiated a computer discussion forum about the Clinton campaign that would be available to anyone with access to the Internet.

The name "Clinton@Marist" is the address, pronounced "Clinton at Marist," of the Clinton forum on the Bitnet network—an extensive academic computer network with more or less invisible (to the user) access to the Internet. Clinton@Marist is sometimes called the "Clinton list" in accordance with networking terminology, since it is run through a software program called Listserv, an automated mailing program that automatically forwards mail sent to Clinton@Marist to anyone subscribed to the list. As of 1993, there are more than 3,750 Listserv groups available on the networks.

Lee Sakkas, who had some previous political volunteer experience but who had not ever engaged in political organizing through electronic networking, requested permission from Harry Williams, in charge of Marist Listserv operations, to initiate Clinton@Marist, Bush@Marist, and Perot@Marist on 13 July 1992. Permission was eventually granted, and the lists began operation on 8 August 1992, as news of their existence was announced over the electronic networks. According to Sakkas, she asked for the initiation of all three lists to avoid trouble:

> I deliberately requested permission to start all three lists from the beginning. I wanted to put CLINTON up but I wanted to do it in a way that was (1) fair and (2) was not likely to call down the wrath of the "higher powers" onto my poor head or onto Marist. I was delighted that I had two likely candidates to own the other lists, BUSH—Martha McConaghy, and PEROT—Charles Murphy, and that they agreed immediately when I recruited them.[8]

By 11 August, Clinton@Marist had 178 subscribers; within weeks it was up to 300, with a peak of as many as 700. As an open forum, the Clinton list carried a wide variety of messages, which began flowing into subscribers' electronic mailboxes at a high rate. Between 11 August and 31 August, the Clinton list carried the equivalent of some 855 single-spaced pages of electronic mail messages, and the volume appears to have increased up until the election in November. Within the first few days of operations, so many messages were being sent through the Clinton list that some people, unable to keep up, or finding their computer mailboxes overloaded and jammed, dropped out.

People who were working in other domains of the widespread e-mail campaign made themselves known to Clinton@Marist in short order. On 13 August, Mary Jacobs sent the full text of the 3 June 1992 appearance of Bill Clinton on the "Arsenio Hall Show." Two hours later, Eric Loeb from MIT sent a long message with the addresses and phone numbers of various state Clinton headquarters, urging readers to volunteer. Loeb also informed Clinton list readers that they could reach the Little Rock national campaign headquarters through 75300.3115@compuserve.com or the national e-mail campaign at the address clinton@ai.mit.edu—his own operation at MIT Artificial Intelligence Lab.

The largest number of messages to Clinton@Marist appeared to come from college- or university-affiliated people—students or professors—who used the list to engage in ongoing discussions of various issues of the day—economics, health care, gun control, abortion, the state of politics, their views of various political leaders (especially Bill Clinton and George Bush). As various issues popped up in the campaign, or in the general news of the day, someone would state a view or ask a question, and a line of discussion would be born. All of this flowed into mailboxes of subscribers, from perhaps forty to one hundred messages a day—too much for almost anyone to read and, if not attended to and discarded promptly, too much to hold in storage on most computer systems. Nevertheless, a largely silent core group of subscribers stayed with the list, using it as a window on the campaign. A smaller group of active subscribers pitched with glee into the debates, often responding several times a day to several different lines of discussion.

An e-mail note on the Internet begins with a fairly standard message header that can save some time in sorting through the day's mail, listing sender, date, and subject, so that it is possible to delete an unwanted message fairly quickly. An incoming message might, for example, display a header like the following:

Date:	Sun, 28 March 1993 16:53:02 EST
From:	Tom Benson <t3b@psuvm>
Subject:	Re: Clinton E-Mail research
In-Reply-To:	Message of Sun, 28 March 1993 16:01:33
	from <LLDSB@UTXDP>

In this sample message header, the "Re:" in the "Subject" line indicates that my message was created by hitting the "reply" key to a message from LLDSB@UTXDP, and that the subject line of that person's message was "Clinton E-Mail research." Hence, it is possible to maintain a relatively stable subject heading for a line of discussion on a particular topic that generates a series of responses. If the message is created directly as a note to the Clinton list, without being in reply to a former message, then it is the responsibility of the sender to type in an appropriate "Subject" line.

In the midst of the outpouring of documents, the most distinctive feature of the Clinton list was the way in which it enacted political discussion. In many ways our channels of communication appear, during a presidential campaign, to be saturated with political talk. But the impression is misleading. Even during a political campaign, most Americans do not have a "space" in which to discuss major issues of the day in a public and explicitly political context. Such talk is not appropriate at our places of work and, though we might talk about politics with family, or even with small groups of friends, such talk lacks the variety and challenge of openly accessible public debate and discussion. The civic society that rhetorical theorists celebrate is in many ways an idealization of a situation that has never been realized in practice, but that continues to act as a standard for democratic discourse.

Clinton@Marist provided an implicit—and sometimes explicit—model of such public discussion. Reading over the exchange of correspondence on the list, one is struck by the groping for a sense of what it might mean to participate in such a public forum. Although the conversation on CLINTON often grew heated, confirming one's generalized sense that the chief mood of an election campaign is anger at one's opponent, CLINTON participants, with occasional interventions from organizer Lee Sakkas, patrolled their own discussion to enforce a reasonable degree of civility and, all things considered, a remarkable level of informed and substantive discussion.

In some ways, early expectations were overly ambitious, including the expectation that if one wrote a question to the list about some policy position of the Clinton campaign, the campaign itself would answer a question or respond to advice from a constituent sent by e-mail. Still, the sense of participation seemed novel and magnetic. On 19 August, Mary Jacobs posted a note saying that it was Bill Clinton's birthday, and that birthday greetings could be sent to clinton@ai.mit.edu. On 20 August, Clinton@Marist carried a message from Bill Clinton:[9]

>Date: 20 August 1992 11:20:35 EDT
>From: Clinton for President <75300.3115@compuserve.com
>Subject: Note from Gov. Clinton
>
>Thanks for all the birthday greetings! It's great to hear from computer
>users throughout the world.
>
>I look forward to taking my Putting People First message throughout
>the country as we head through the final phase of the campaign.
>
>Thanks again for the greetings and all your help.
>
>I look forward to hearing from you!
>
>Bill Clinton

An electronic discussion can create a extraordinary sense of participation and immediacy. But in fact the campaign headquarters did not and could not monitor the Clinton list closely, either to answer questions or to accept advice, nor could the political discussions held on the list themselves resolve anything. On 19 August, one disappointed correspondent wrote to the Clinton list that

I sent mail to the campaign's Compuserve address [which had been posted to the Clinton list] regarding Clinton and Gore's views on the War on Drugs in general, and more specifically civil forfeiture, drug related penalties, and decriminalization or legalization of marijuana, but did not receive what I thought to be a full answer.

Does anyone on the list know the candidates' views on these issues? I know that Clinton would have inhaled and Gore smoked marijuana in college and graduate school: perhaps their views are a bit more realistic than the current administration's.

Also, any reader's ideas would be appreciated!

This correspondent's questions are reasonable ones for a citizen to ask of a contemporary political campaign, but ones that anyone familiar with contemporary political campaigning would not expect a presidential campaign to have the staff to spend much time answering beyond, at most, sending out a prepared handout on the general issue.

In mid-August, a suggestion, apparently from somewhere from within the campaign, and seemingly from the group around Jock Gill, floated on the Clinton list the idea that there might be an "electronic bus tour" in which Bill Clinton would "appear" electronically to answer questions on one or more Internet lists. Eventually, the idea was tried on a commercial network, Prodigy, but did not make it to the larger Internet.

AN INTERNET BULLETIN BOARD: ALT.POLITICS.CLINTON

The Internet supports a system of "bulletin board" functions, on which messages sent from any connected node worldwide will appear on a menu of messages of which a copy is held on a single computer at the node. The bulletin board software called Netnews (on CMS mainframes) and USENET (on UNIX computer systems) supports over two thousand active newsgroups, on any one of which there may be as many as several hundred messages at any one time. For each group, depending on its level of activity, local node administrators can set an expiration time, so that older messages are automatically erased from the system periodically as they are replaced by new ones. From the user's point of view, Netnews differs from Listserv lists in that instead of having the messages arrive in one's personal e-mail mailbox, the Netnews messages are held on the main computer to which one is connected and where the nested menus of groups and messages may be accessed, read, and replied to, to create an ongoing conversation.

On a typical day, a user might log on to the mainframe computer at her university, invoke the command "Netnews" (or "Usenet"), and be presented with a list of the two thousand or more active newsgroups.

The user can then page down to alt.folklore.urban, or rec.bicycles.tech, or soc.culture.italian, or alt.politics.clinton (which, after the election, became alt.president.clinton). On any day at the height of the campaign season in 1992, there were typically more than eight hundred messages in alt.politics.clinton, rotating out of circulation at a high rate, so that the typical message was held only for a week or so. Most of the messages on alt.politics.clinton were in the form of fairly heated discussion of the candidates and issues, seemingly coming from young, computer-oriented American college students. Alt.politics.clinton also received copies of the official Clinton releases originating from Jock Gill's CompuServe account. As on Clinton@Marist, a line of discussion on any given issue could continue over the course of several days or weeks, involving a high level of interaction, and there were always several subjects in play each day.

On open discussion lists such as Clinton@Marist or alt.politics.clinton, there seemed to be an implicit search for what it meant to talk politics in this domain. From time to time, discussion would become so heated that there were insulting or abusive remarks about a candidate or about a participant in the discussion. The escalation of emotional tone in e-mail open forums is a well-known phenomenon, so common that it has a recognized name among e-mail users— "flaming." It is hard to determine, in reading the long exchanges of angry notes on alt.politics.clinton, whether the tone is simply an instance of a generic computer flame war, or whether it reflects the youth and inexperience in political discourse of partisan but disconnected college students. Both of these explanations have some appeal, as does the notion that the bulletin board discussions were often heated restatements of the accusations being poured forth by negative advertising and sound-bite television news. But for many the open discussions seemed an exercise in democracy.

CRTNET@PSUVM

CRTNET (Communication Research and Theory Network) is an electronic publication founded by the author in 1985 at Penn State University. CRTNET was founded primarily as an experiment in serving the communicative interests of the academic disciplines studying human communication in higher education, especially in college and university departments of speech, rhetoric, and communication(s). It is one of the oldest, some say *the* oldest, of electronic publications in the humanities and social sciences not devoted primarily to computer-related topics. From the start, CRTNET has also welcomed nonacademic subscribers and participants and has tried to cultivate an international audience. Over the course of several years, CRTNET has averaged about one hundred issues a year, or about two issues every week. In the summer of 1992, as the American presidential campaign moved past the primary season, CRTNET was being mailed electronically to nearly one thousand addresses around the world (some of these addresses were local bulletin board systems, so it is difficult to estimate the precise number of readers; in addition, readers often forward particular copies to colleagues). CRTNET carries various professional announcements, job listings, calls for papers, research queries, and other such newsletter items. In addition, it tries to carry documents likely to be salient to subscribers with an interest in human communication, and it encourages the use of CRTNET as a forum, with active, ongoing discussion among its members on communication-related topics.

During the Gulf War, CRTNET carried a series of e-mail diaries written from Israel by Robert Werman, Bernard Spolsky, and Judy Koren, describing daily life under the Scud missile. CRTNET carried news of the August 1991 coup in the Soviet Union, published the speeches of Boris Yeltsin and Mikhail Gorbachev at the funeral of those who died defending the White House in Moscow, and in December 1991 published an edition of CRTNET from Moscow itself, where the editor was on a visit to help cultivate electronic mail connections with humanists and social scientists in Russia. After the San Francisco earthquake in October 1989, CRTNET carried reports from the scene and considered the effects of media coverage of the devastation. During the riots in Los Angeles following the 1992 not-guilty verdict in the first trial of police charged with beating Rodney King, CRTNET members reported on the communicative dimensions of life in the riot zone, and published addresses to which donations for relief and rebuilding could be sent. Open discussions have run for days, and sometimes weeks, over issues such as the communicative politics of gender, cognitive approaches to communication studies, the ethics of academic hiring practices, sexual harassment, media effects, free speech, campus speech codes, a proposed Constitutional amendment to ban flag burning, the merits of textbooks in various areas of study, and a myriad of other topics.

In 1992 CRTNET developed plans to transcribe speeches and documents relevant to the U.S. presidential campaign. Working on a summer research assistantship for the editor of CRTNET, doctoral student Anne Gravel transcribed Bill Clinton's 16 July 1992 acceptance speech to the Democratic National Convention, delivered in Madison Square Garden. CRTNET published the transcript in its issue number 599, published on 13 August 1992, which was coincidentally the same week that Clinton@Marist began operation, and in which word began to circulate along the networks that the Clinton campaign itself had a network address and would make documents available. Many CRTNET subscribers teach a variety of courses on public discourse, and immediately saw the utility of taking the Clinton acceptance speech, and the other texts that CRTNET promised to hunt down, to their classes. The next day, 14 August, CRTNET published Mario Cuomo's 15 July nomination of Bill Clinton and announced the availability of texts, for those with access, to files of campaign documents on a publically accessible electronic archive. In the next few days, CRTNET published convention speeches by Jesse Jackson and Al Gore, and the May 1992 Wellesley College commencement speech of Hillary Rodham Clinton. Throughout the rest of the campaign, CRTNET frequently published speeches by Bill Clinton.

Republican speeches were harder to come by, since for some reason the Bush presidential campaign did not catch on to the possible importance of making presidential campaign documents widely accessible. Nevertheless, starting with the week of the Republican National Convention in Houston, CRTNET published its own re-typed transcripts of speeches by Marilyn Quayle, Dan Quayle, Pat Buchanan, Pat Robertson, Mary Fisher, William Bennett, Phil Gramm, Ronald Reagan, Barbara Bush, and George Bush. In addition, CRTNET published texts of Harry Truman's "Truman Doctrine" speech of 12 March 1947, and his acceptance speech at the 1948 Democratic convention in 1948.

The speech texts published in CRTNET found their way into college and high-school classrooms around the country, powerfully altering, for those with access to the texts, the face of the whole campaign. Several American subscribers working abroad wrote in to say that these texts were their most direct connection to the presidential campaign.

FILESERVERS

One of the most useful informational resources of the Internet is its capacity to link users to remote databases of documents and software, including the catalogs of major research libraries. During the 1992 campaign, a number of electronic archives made it possible to retrieve documents of the campaign. Not all those who can send and receive electronic mail on the Internet also have the capacity to retrieve remote documents using remote log-in by a process called anonymous FTP (logging in to a remote computer using "File Transfer Protocol" as an anonymous user) and other search-and-retrieve mechanisms such as the University of Minnesota's Gopher software.

For those with FTP access, it was possible to log in to WORLD.STD. COM or NPTN (National Public Telecomputing Network at network address nptn.org), obtain an index of holdings, move to a list of files associated with one of the presidential campaigns, and request copies of individual documents from the list. The Clinton campaign made available a long list of speeches, press releases, position papers, and other materials. The Bush campaign, in contrast, made available primarily a comparatively small number of brief position papers on a variety of topics. A notable feature of the Clinton collection was the fast and aggressive production and circulation of responses to the Bush campaign as part of its "rapid response" program.

THE ELECTRONIC CAMPAIGN IN USE: CONTENTIONS AND RECOLLECTIONS

In near retrospect, the e-mail campaign of 1992 appears, from examination of documents from the campaign and from recollections of dozens of participants, to have been an overwhelmingly successful experience, though there are some bad memories as well. Though the history will certainly be rewritten as various participants set down their own versions for the public record, making this report necessarily partial and incomplete, it seems worthwhile to set down the strongest recollections of some of the participants who have been willing to share with this researcher their views of the e-mail campaign. One of the advantages of doing this shortly after the campaign is that the rapid evolution of the electronic networks will soon make it difficult to recall the conditions that governed information access and public discussion in 1992.

ACCESS TO INFORMATION

The electronic campaign made possible access to campaign information on a scale and through channels that were unprecedented. A large number of campaign volunteers who were active in the electronic side of the campaign were able to download speeches and position papers, print them out, and distribute them elsewhere in the campaign. At Ball State University in Muncie, Indiana, junior Rob Harrington, a member of the University Democrats, distributed campaign documents to "the rest of the members of UDs. In addition, I've been taking the information and transferring it to Macintosh to make copies for the general public."[10] Many e-mail volunteers reported that they were the chief source of Clinton campaign speeches and position papers for their local Democratic campaign headquarters, which had great difficulty in getting such materials directly from the campaign, which was evidently concentrating most of its efforts on the national media. Betty Lee Dowlin downloaded Clinton materials for the campaign in Centre County, Pennsylvania. Travis Raybold, a twenty-year-old computer science major at Texas A&M University, passed along documents to the Aggie Democrats, "trying to gain recognition here at A&M, an overpoweringly conservative university." Bruce Brown, an active Democrat since he worked in the McCarthy campaign of 1968, downloaded texts for his campaign headquarters in California: "The office watched the debates on TV. Then I would get almost real time texts and commentary. People would stand around my terminal as if it were TV. . . . People would ask, what does Arkansas have to say. (That was my cue to go on line.) They regarded the electronic messages as accurate information. It didn't go through a lot of different hands. (This information had not been edited. It was the *TRUE STORY* :-)."[11] Other volunteers reported that when they showed up at local campaign headquarters with a sheaf of printouts from the electronic campaign, they were at first met with suspicion, then with gratitude.

Among the most eager and grateful clients of the electronic campaign were librarians, several of whom reported that the electronic networks were their chief means of access to campaign documents. Diane Bradley, a librarian at Auburn University, collected documents during the campaign, and she reports that the heaviest use during the campaign was by faculty, some of whom were working as volunteers in local campaigns; after the election, students began to use what she had collected.

Anthony Anderson, a government documents librarian at the University of Southern California, reports that according to his own investigations, "few libraries were availing themselves" of electronic documents.[12] But Anderson was so enthusiastic about the information revolution created by the e-mail campaign that during the last months of the campaign he devoted most of his time to making documents from the electronic campaign available at his university library. He downloaded campaign documents, printed them, and compiled them in large notebooks that were available to library patrons. Anderson credits his supervisor for having the vision to allow him to spend his time on the campaign documents and comments that lack of time was the major reason other libraries seemed not to handle the material as he did. As with the e-mail volunteers who brought documents to campaign headquarters around the country, Anderson achieved a measure of local fame for being able to make so much campaign information available to USC library patrons.

Charles Fishman of the State University of New York College at Farmingdale, who was in close electronic contact with Mary Jacobs in Illinois, took the initiative to prepare "The Essential Clinton," a series of documents summarizing the Clinton campaign's positions on various issues, which he sent out to the Internet the first week in October.

COMPLAINTS

As in all campaigns, there were contentions for influence and rewards, and this has left some bitter memories even for some of those with generally positive evaluations of the e-mail campaign. Two sorts of complaints have arisen during the course of this research on the electronic mail campaign. They center on the issues of credit and of access to the decision-making process. Mary Jacobs and Charles Fishman, two leading volunteers in the Clinton e-mail campaign, are among a small number of activists who charge that they were locked out of decision making at various points in the campaign, and that, after the campaign, they were denied a proper measure of credit in the scramble for official recognition by the Clinton administration, despite their energetic participation throughout the campaign. They complain that those who gained the chief credit—Jeff Eller and Jock Gill, and to a smaller extent the MIT group—were positioning themselves for jobs in the administration. Another set of complaints is leveled at the MIT group by volunteers who report that they responded in good faith to requests to participate and then were condescended to and pushed aside when they offered technical advice that, in their view, the beginners at MIT badly needed, but which was neglected, they charge, out of mixed motives, arrogance, and, in at least three reported cases, sexism. It is difficult to evaluate these complaints. They all have a ring of narrative credibility, especially since they are mutually confirming and since they are consistent with what often happens in the power scramble of a political campaign. Defenders of the MIT group respond to these complaints by pointing out that they themselves were overworked volunteers, often without political or "human" skills, and that although their eventual computer systems were fairly simple and not up to the full load of the network—and in many ways replicated software that was readily available on other systems—they did eventually come into use and performed reasonably well.[13]

THE PUBLIC SPHERE

Although the e-mail campaign of 1992 was a remarkable enactment of democratic rhetoric in an age often deplored for the current degradation of the public dialogue, it was not a fully shaped embodiment of the conditions of the public sphere, as posited by Jurgen Habermas, his admirers, and critics. According to Craig Calhoun, we should be mindful of Habermas's "constitution of the category of the public sphere as simultaneously about the quality or form of rational-critical discourse and the quantity of, or openness to, popular participation."[14] Access to the electronic campaign was restricted to those with the money to use a commercial service or the status to tap into the Internet through a university or corporation.

Even among those who had access, there were familiar distortions of discourse on bulletin boards and discussion lists, where a well-recognized form of energetic and aggressive speech tended to drive other modes out of the discussion.[15] Most Americans never had any access whatever to what was happening on the computer bulletin boards, though by the next campaign this will have changed somewhat.

On the other hand, though those who had access to the 1992 e-mail campaign were privileged, they were not in direct, two-way touch with those who were running the campaign and competing for power. They were members of a large academic-technical-managerial sub-elite that seemed to feel itself not only entitled to have an opinion but, in a sense, required to have an opinion, a condition that, whatever their level of criticism, makes them, as a class, in the view of Jacques Ellul, particularly willing subjects of propaganda.[16] Their influence as a public may be minimal, even if considered only as a problem in information overload. It is virtually impossible for a government to carry out its traditional functions and at the same time increase by several orders of magnitude its interactions with the public. In discussing experiments in public-access e-mail, Hiltz and Turoff cite Varley's work on Santa Monica's Public Electronic Network: "Most of the politicians do not participate directly—even Santa Monica's 'guru of participatory democracy,' State Assemblyman Tom Hayden, insists that he and his staff don't have time for PEN.'"[17] Implicit in the computerized campaign, but usually unspoken and unrecognized, were a series of power structures that structured power unequally. Decisions about the issues and about the campaign, and decisions about the spoils of the campaign, were not in fact merely the rational outcome of a public debate among all the "participants."

IMPLICATIONS AND PROSPECTS

Jock Gill speculates that on the model of fractal mathematics, the working structures modeled in the 1992 e-mail campaign could be repeated on the largest scale, encompassing a wholly new mode of interaction between the people and their government. After the election, in January 1993, Gill was appointed to a White House staff job, as Director of Electronic Publishing and Public Access Email, again reporting to Jeff Eller.[18] Already, through his office at the White House, presidential documents are being made routinely available to the Internet community. The White House has further announced the creation of direct presidential and vice-presidential Internet addresses, and the intention to open other agencies of government to direct, two-way electronic mail access. Vice-President Al Gore, continuing the interest in the "information highway" that he helped to promote as a senator, argues that high-speed data networks will have both economic and political benefits for the country. In June 1993 Bill Clinton and Al Gore released an electronic mail announcement to the networks:

THE WHITE HOUSE
Office of Presidential Correspondence
For Immediate Release   June 1, 1993

LETTER FROM THE PRESIDENT AND VICE PRESIDENT IN ANNOUNCEMENT OF WHITE HOUSE ELECTRONIC MAIL ACCESS

Dear Friends:

Part of our commitment to change is to keep the White House in step with today's changing technology. As we move ahead into the twenty-first century, we must have a government that can show the way and lead by example. Today, we are pleased to announce that for the first time in history, the White House will be connected to you by electronic mail. Electronic mail will bring the Presidency and this Administration closer and make it more accessible to the people.

The White House will be connected to the Internet as well as several on-line commercial vendors, thus making us more accessible and more in touch with people across this country. We will not be alone in this venture. Congress is also getting involved, and an exciting announcement regarding electronic mail is expected to come from the House of Representatives tomorrow.

Various government agencies also will be taking part in the near future. Americans Communicating Electronically is a project developed by several government agencies to coordinate and improve access to the nation's educational and information assets and resources. This will be done through interactive communications such as electronic mail, and brought to people who do not have ready access to a computer.

However, we must be realistic about the limitations and expectations of the White House electronic mail system. This experiment is the first-ever e-mail project done on such a large scale. As we work to reinvent government and streamline our processes, the e-mail project can help to put us on the leading edge of progress.

Initially, your e-mail message will be read and receipt immediately acknowledged. A careful count will be taken on the number received as well as the subject of each message. However, the White House is not yet capable of sending back a tailored response via electronic mail. We are hoping that will happen by the end of the year.

A number of response-based programs which allow technology to help us read your message more effectively, and, eventually respond to you electronically in a timely fashion will be tried out as well. These programs will change periodically as we experiment with the best way to handle electronic mail from the public. Since this has never been tried before, it is important to allow for some flexibility in the system in these first stages. We welcome your suggestions.

This is an historic moment in the White House and we look forward to your participation and enthusiasm for this milestone event. We eagerly anticipate the day when electronic mail from the public is an integral and normal part of the White House communications system.

President Clinton
PRESIDENT@WHITEHOUSE.GOV

Vice President Gore
VICE.PRESIDENT@WHITEHOUSE.GOV

Not long after the Clinton-Gore letter on White House electronic mail was sent out over the networks, it was announced that a congressional e-mail address had been established at CONGRESS@HR. HOUSE.GOV.

Electronic mail systems are at the very least likely to improve the level of citizen access to government information. They may also provide a somewhat streamlined means by which citizens can send mail to the White House to register their opinions on issues. But information systems are inherently unstable, subject to interaction not only with a variety of economic and technical forces, but responsive also to the strategic and competitive adaptations of groups and individuals using them to gain advantage. Speculation about the future of technologies helps us to shape those technologies to our ends, but it can also be a distraction, fostering an awe of hardware and technique that postpones difficult issues of access and use. Against the longing evident in the organizers and participants in the electronic campaign for the liberating potential of networking to transform, or at least restore, democratic discourse, one must set the recollection that the introduction of other communicative agencies has often sparked quite similar expectations—which have typically been diminished by events. Brian Winston has called this feature of technological transformation "the law of the suppression of radical potential."[19]

In conversation with the author, Jock Gill described his admiration for the notion of the "learning society," and the "learning organization," variations of which have also been promoted by Bill Clinton and Al Gore. According to the theorists of the "learning society," the American economy depends on the education of workers cognitively adapted to the technologized workplace and the information society. Gill proposes that the American economy can leapfrog to the adoption of the learning organization as its developmental model, and he sees the White House e-mail operation as an instance of this model. Writers such as Shoshana Zuboff (*In the Age of the Smart Machine*) and Peter M. Senge (*The Fifth Discipline: The Art and Practice of the Learning Organization*) argue that the postindustrial economy depends on continuous learning of technological and information-processing skills. But some, such as Douglas D. Noble, point to a darker side. Zuboff, writes Noble, calls the skills involved in this new "mind work" of corporate employees— office workers, managers, professionals and factory workers alike— "intellective skills," "abstract" skills that involve strategic planning, procedural reasoning, data processing, trouble-shooting, and technical problem solving. Zuboff's book has been highly acclaimed as the clearest expression of how new corporate information technologies, rather than deskilling or displacing masses of workers, can instead create entirely new opportunities, available to more workers than ever before, for intellectual participation in the workplace.[20]

Against the optimistic vision of Zuboff, Noble argues that the primary model and motivation for the introduction of computers and information technology into schools and workplace have been military research, with its requirements for the control of "advanced military weapons systems," and its willing dependents, chiefly "cognitive researchers' need for laboratories and legitimation, and . . . new 'intellective' requirements of corporate capital in a militarized information economy."[21] It is too early to tell whether the electronic networking of American politics will herald an era of increased citizen access to government information and an improved version of democratic self-governance, or whether, on the other hand, it will represent an increased measure of direct social control through governmental communication, an increased fragmentation of public opinion registered through keyboard plebiscites filtered by smart machines and self-interested politicians, and discussion-as-distraction on computer bulletin boards.

In 1992 the participants in the electronic campaign, and especially the Clinton side of the campaign, appeared to feel that they were participating in an activity of historic importance. Study of the e-mail campaign indicates that several forces converged to generate this optimism—making it difficult to sort out the contribution of any one of them: the sense that participants were the first users of a revolutionary technological innovation that would soon make important changes in democratic communication; the sense that a means had been found to participate in a renewal of civic discourse; the sense of having a window into the "real" campaign that was denied those without access to the Internet; the sense that their candidate had a chance to win after twelve years of Republican administrations; the sense, renewed daily in the distribution of Clinton speeches and messages, that their candidate was engaged in thoughtful consideration of issues that went beyond sound-bite solutions and negative ads, and that he wanted to use the government to do something. Accurate or not, these impressions were widely shared by participants in the electronic campaign.

As we consider the electronic campaign of 1992, which may have been of relatively little importance to the actual outcome of the campaign, and which may or may not prove to be a model that can be vastly expanded without distortion, we should also, I think, pause to notice how strongly, for its participants, the 1992 e-mail campaign revived the image of a democratic republic, a discursive space where leaders offered not merely slogans but extended and reasoned arguments, where partisans could engage in mutually coordinated volunteer efforts on behalf of national candidates, where citizens could engage in self-regulated debate on the uses and limits of a government that belongs to them. These ideals were never entirely realized in the 1992 e-mail campaign, even for the relative handful of people who were part of it, but they were everywhere manifest as the shared ideal of what participants were engaged in constructing. However inadequate our technologies and our practices, the idea of a public sphere and the longing for democracy structure our hopes and urge us to keep bending imperfection back toward those hopes and ideals.

NOTES

1. At one time, it was common for major public orations to be widely distributed in print, in edited versions, after the event—a practice that has diminished in recent decades, as the pace of speaking has increased. For a discussion of the widespread circulation of the Lincoln-Douglas debates of 1858, see especially Harold Holzer, ed., *The Lincoln-Douglas Debates* (New York: HarperCollins, 1993), 1-39; see also Paul M. Angle, ed., *Created Equal? The Complete Lincoln-Douglas Debates of 1858* (Chicago: University of Chicago Press, 1958); Robert W. Johannsen, ed., *The Lincoln-Douglas Debates of 1858* (New York: Oxford University Press, 1965); David Zarefsky, *Lincoln, Douglas, and Slavery: In the Crucible of Public Debate* (Chicago: University of Chicago Press, 1990). On the increasing frequency of presidential speaking, see Roderick P. Hart, *The Sound of Leadership: Presidential Communication in the Modern Age* (Chicago: University of Chicago Press, 1987). Texts of presidential speeches, including campaign speeches, are available in the *Weekly Compilation of Presidential Documents* and later in the series of *Public Papers of the Presidents*, but the campaign speeches of non-incumbents are not thus recorded, much less available in a timely fashion to the public during the campaign.

2. For introductions to the interaction of television and politics, see, for example, Kathleen Hall Jamieson, *Dirty Politics: Deception, Distraction, and Democracy* (New York: Oxford University Press, 1992); Kathleen Hall Jamieson, *Packaging the Presidency: A History and Criticism of Presidential Campaign Advertising*, 2d ed. (New York: Oxford University Press, 1992); W. Lance Bennett, *News: The Politics of Illusion*, 2d ed. (New York: Longman, 1988); Sidney Blumenthal, *The Permanent Campaign* (Boston: Beacon Press, 1980).

3. The Internet is a network of computers and a loose organization of computing facilities that have evolved from the ARPAnet, a network of computers formerly funded by the United States Defense Department. The core computing and communication facilities of the Internet are supported by the National Science Foundation and have adopted a common standard for passing data through a high-speed network of dedicated lines. But in everyday conversational practice, the term "Internet" is also used to refer to the whole worldwide array of computer networks that can interact with the formal "Internet." See Ed Krol, *The Whole Internet: User's Guide and Catalog* (Sebastopol, Calif.: O'Reilly and Associates, 1992), 11–13; and "Communications, Computers, and Networks," a special issue of *Scientific American* (September 1991). For additional background on the development of computer networks, see Roxanne Starr Hiltz and Murray Turoff, *The Network Nation: Human Communication via Computer*, rev. ed. (Cambridge, Mass.: MIT Press, 1993); Clifford Stoll, *The Cuckoo's Egg: Tracking a Spy through the Maze of Computer Espionage* (New York: Doubleday, 1989); Gladys D. Ganley, *The Exploding Political Power of Personal Media* (Norwood, N.J.: Ablex, 1992).

4. Gill says that within the Clinton campaign, "Jeff Eller was the father of all this. In the spring of 1992 he began trying to get the message out. He got the electronic mail operation going, and then passed it off to me." Jock Gill, telephone interview with author, 6 January 1993.

5. Jock Gill, e-mail letter to author, 14 August 1992.

6. Eric Loeb, e-mail letter to Clinton@Marist, 30 August 1992.

7. Lee Sakkas, e-mail letter to Clinton@Marist, 13 August 1992.

8. Lee Sakkas, e-mail letter to author, 10 March 1993. For a fuller account of Clinton@Marist, see also Lee Sakkas, "Politics on the Internet," *Interpersonal Computing and Technology: An Electronic Journal for the 21st Century* 1.2 (April 1993) (archived as SAKKAS IPCTV1N2 on LISTSERV@GUVM.GEORGETOWN.EDU).

9. The angle brackets at the left margin of the quoted note are a common electronic mail device to indicate that a message is being forwarded or quoted; in this case, Clinton's message was forwarded to the Clinton list by Bert Smith at MIT.

10. Rob Harrington, e-mail letter to the author, 21 February 1993.

11. Betty Lee Dowlin, e-mail letter to author, 27 February 1993; Travis Raybold, e-mail letter to author, 25 February 1993; Bruce Brown, e-mail letter to author, 28 February 1993. The punctuation at the end of Brown's letter is an icon in common use in electronic correspondence, known as a "smiley face" :-); there are a number of variations designed to convey the tone of a message.

12. Anthony Anderson, e-mail letter to author, 26 February 1993.

13. Correspondents who shared their complaints with me typically asked to remain anonymous; in honoring these requests, I have attempted to report no complaint that was not confirmed by other independent observers. My own attempts to obtain more details of the MIT operation were frustrated—after initially offering full access to their databases, the MIT group offered the condition that they be allowed an opportunity to review and comment on references to their operation, then indicated that they were preparing their own report on the campaign, and then stopped answering inquiries. Access to the databases never materialized, nor was anything beyond the most rudimentary background information supplied. Documentation of the MIT work is drawn primarily from the public record, including logs of public electronic mail during the campaign. This problem of access is a normal outcome of a political campaign, in which the winners gain the spoils and attempt to control the release of information and in which losers—and those of the winners who are frustrated—may be more forthcoming for the record. But though it is a normal occurrence, it may distort the accounts we are able to fashion of the events we are trying to reconstruct and evaluate.

14. Craig Calhoun, "Introduction: Habermas and the Public Sphere," in Craig Calhoun, ed., *Habermas and the Public Sphere* (Cambridge, Mass.: MIT Press, 1992), 4. See also Jurgen Habermas, *The Structural Transformation of the Public Sphere: An Inquiry into a Category of Bourgeois Society*, trans. Thomas Burger with the assistance of Frederick Lawrence (Cambridge, Mass.: MIT Press, 1989).

15. The mode of speech common on computer discussion lists is sometimes explicitly identified as that of hyper-rational and aggressive young white males. Several writers on network interaction have noted that women have been driven from some discussions by gender baiting. On gender issues in electronic discussion groups, see Susan C. Herring, "Gender and Democracy in Computer-Mediated Communication," *Electronic Journal of Communication* 3.2 (April 1993); Ruth Perry and Lisa Greber, "Women and Computers: An Introduction," *Signs: Journal of Women in Culture and Society* 16 (1990): 74–101; Paul N. Edwards, "The Army and the Microworld: Computers and the Politics of Gender Identity," *Signs* 16 (1990): 102–27; Sherry Turkle and Seymour Papert, "Epistemological Pluralism: Styles and Voices within the Computer Culture," *Signs* 16 (1990): 128–57; Pamela E. Kramer and Sheila Lehman, "Mismeasuring Women: A Critique of Research on Computer Ability and Avoidance," *Signs* 16 (1990): 158–72.

16. Jacques Ellul, *Propaganda*, trans. Konrad Kellen and Jean Lerner (New York: Vintage Books, 1973), 113: "The greater a person's knowledge of political and economic facts, the more sensitive and vulnerable is his judgment. Intellectuals are most easily reached by propaganda, particularly if it employs ambiguity."

17. Hiltz and Turoff, *Network Nation*, 484, quoting Pamela Varley, "Electronic Democracy," *Technology Review* (November/December 1991): 50. Information overload is a common problem for Internet users. Several volunteers reported to me that they volunteered to monitor network discussion lists and to send summaries to Little Rock through Jock Gill, but that when they heard nothing back, most of them gave up this exercise. Nevertheless, despite what seemed to many a lack of two-way interaction with Little Rock, probably denoting inattentiveness, Jeff Eller sent a message to the Clinton volunteers on the MIT list on 15 September: "FYI to the team: David Kuznet, chief speech writer and mastermind of the Notre Dame Speech, says the info he gets from e-mail is great! Keep it up!" (e-mail letter from Clinton for President 75300.3115@ compuserve.com to Clinton Team clinton-org@ai.mit.edu, 15 September 1993).

18. Jock Gill, e-mail letter to author, 14 January 1993.

19. Brian Winston, *Misunderstanding Media* (Cambridge, Mass.: Harvard University Press, 1986), 23.

20. Douglas D. Noble, *The Classroom Arsenal: Military Research, Information Technology, and Public Education* (London: Falmer Press, 1991), 192. See also Shoshana Zuboff, *In the Age of the Smart Machine: The Future of Work and Power* (New York: Basic Books, 1988); Peter M. Senge, *The Fifth Discipline: The Art and Practice of the Learning Organization* (New York: Doubleday, 1990); Lee Sproull and Sara Kiesler, *Connections: New Ways of Working in the Networked Organization* (Cambridge, Mass.: MIT Press, 1991); Charles Dunlop and Rob Kling, eds., *Computerization and Controversy: Value Conflicts and Social Choices* (Boston: Academic Press, 1991).

21. Noble, *The Classroom Arsenal*, 192. Among the chief beneficiaries of the military-cognitivist-corporate complex, argues Noble, is the Artificial Intelligence Lab at MIT. The software models for the Clinton campaign's electronic networking were developed at the MIT lab.

CLINTON GOES
TO TOWN HALL

JANETTE KENNER MUIR

Many political scholars will undoubtedly agree that the 1992 presidential election ushered in an era of campaigning which will dramatically shape elections into the next century. The context alone was compelling. An incumbent president riding the coattails of victory in a Middle East war, a lackluster field of Democratic candidates willing to challenge the incumbent, and a third-party candidate who just happened to be a billionaire all set the scene for a political campaign that would transform the way we think about the mediated process of selecting a president. One of the most significant changes in presidential campaigning was the increase in available channels for communication. Talk shows, call-in programs, computer networks, and even fax machines provided new ways of communicating directly with the public, opening up new channels and expanding the scope of media outlets. Representing a generation raised on television, exposed to computer technology, and aware of increasingly advanced and sophisticated media, it is easy to see why Bill Clinton would adapt so well to these new forms of mediation in communicating his message to the American public.

The medium which blended Clinton's direct style of engaging audiences with the potentials of new technology was the town-hall meeting. While reflecting a variety of formats, the electronic town meeting provided a way for Clinton to get his message out to as many audiences as possible, in what at least appeared to be a participatory framework. In addition to relaying a message directly to the people, he was able to further enhance the perception that people were providing input into the campaign process.

Recognizing that the electronic town hall provides a unique medium for Clinton's campaign style, this chapter considers the rhetorical impact of the town meeting from the standpoint of the specific strategies Clinton chooses in getting his message across and the perceptions that this form of participation has for the audiences involved. Three areas will be considered: the evolution of town meetings, Clinton's rhetorical strategies, and the implications of this format for the political process.

THE EVOLUTION OF TOWN MEETINGS

The earliest American form of a town meeting was developed in seventeenth-century New England and Virginia, where citizens of villages or towns would cluster around a meeting house to engage in local self-governing. "The town meeting," historian Carl N. Degler explains, "was one of the most democratic features of seventeenth-century life, a representative framework for the political forms which Americans had evolved in the wilderness."[1] Similar to the ancient Greek city-states where oratory was central to the functioning of society, the town meeting provided the opportunity for every voting member to speak in defense of his or her own actions or to argue for changes in policies. After preliminary discussion, an issue would be put to a vote, and thus, the business affairs of the society would be conducted.[2]

With the advent of television, the town meeting evolved into a framework that allowed the political candidate to directly respond to voters' questions. In 1968 Roger Ailes set up the "Ask Richard Nixon" programs in which the Republican candidate answered questions from studio audiences.[3] In 1977 Walter Cronkite hosted Jimmy Carter in a two-hour radio town-hall CBS broadcast where the former president took questions by telephone from people in twenty-six states.[4] The "Ask President Carter" program was not repeated because, according to Jody Powell, the show generated more calls than the White House phone system could handle. Carter used some other forms of town meetings in his campaign and as president;[5] however, few town-hall formats have attracted as much attention as those held in 1992.

Town Halls and Public Participation

As politics evolved into the 1980s and 1990s, public participation in the process steadily declined. Increased cynicism about leadership due to greater focus on image and style left many voters feeling disconnected from the process.[6] In his 1991 book, *Why Americans Hate Politics*, E. J. Dionne describes this disconnection well when he writes:

> Over the last few decades the faith of the American people in their democratic institutions has declined, and Americans have begun to doubt their ability to improve the world through politics. At a time when the people of Poland, Hungary, and Czechoslovakia are experiencing the excitement of self-government, Americans view politics with boredom and detachment. . . . Election campaigns generate less excitement than ever and are dominated by television commercials, direct mail, polling, and other approaches that treat individual voters not as citizens deciding their nation's fate, but as mere collections of impulses to be stroked and soothed.[7]

Dionne attributes public detachment to the nature of political campaigning and the reliance on style over substance. Some critics read this detachment as apathy. Others, however, believe that many people are angry about the ways they have been left out of the political process.[8] David Matthews, president of the Kettering Foundation, observes that:

> People are angry and that anger is deeper, more pervasive and filled with more opportunities and more dangers than ever imagined. . . . [P]eople haven't turned their back on civic duty. They want to be involved in the conduct of politics and in communities across America they are trying to find their way back.[9]

In an effort to reconnect people with the political process, and to encourage input on decisions that affect their daily lives, political researchers have developed programs to respond to these needs. In various parts of the United States, models have been established to solicit support and ideas from American voters.

The potential for town meetings to become vehicles for public participation is significant, especially given recent advances in telecommunication technology. Just over a decade ago futurists such as Alvin Toffler and John Naisbitt talked about a society where citizens could eventually decide matters for themselves, rather than surrendering the decision-making power to their elected representatives. While this form of governance may seem unlikely in our current condition, the point they make is not that far from reality. As electronic media further develop, so does the capacity to reach many more people, and in turn, to increase public participation.

Considering the potential impact new technologies can have on political behavior, Dale Bertelson urges political communication scholars to "anticipate that changes in political participation and government form will reflect emerging communication technologies."[10] While Bertelson notes the limitations of participation through electronic media, Christopher Arterton predicts that *teledemocracy*, "the use of communications technology to facilitate transmission of political information and opinion between citizens and their public leaders," will have a significant impact on the political behavior of American citizens.[11]

Advancements in technology have directly enabled researchers to develop models of public participation around the country. Christa Slaton identifies a series of experiments called *Televote*, which employ a mix of modern technology "to serve a mediational role between citizens and their representatives and to increase citizen awareness, knowledge on issues, lateral citizen interaction, and direct public participation in governance."[12] Over a dozen experiments have been conducted in California, Hawaii, and New Zealand that may offer new guides to conducting town halls in a meaningful manner. These experiments include several criteria: (1) clear information is provided to respondents (undisputed facts, pro and con arguments); (2) respondents are encouraged to discuss facts, opinions, and issues with others; (3) time is allowed for deliberation before respondents reply; and finally, (4) discussion works in concert with electronic town meetings.[13]

Arterton describes teledemocracy projects that attempt to expand the direct role citizens play in policy making by placing them in direct contact with government officials. For example, Alaska's Legislative Teleconferencing Network (LTN) receives legislative testimony from citizens and allows legislators to listen to and cross-examine witnesses as though they were in a hearing room.[14] This type of project involves citizens in ways that will improve the quality of political agenda setting and decision making; researchers conducting various experiments conclude that these projects have been successful.[15]

Slaton and Arterton both describe the ideal type of electronic town meeting as an exchange of opinions and ideas between citizens, followed by a way to gauge opinion at the end of the discussion. Town-hall meetings in 1992 were limited by the technology which was available at the time. Many meetings, however, were noted for their ability to allow audience members opportunities to directly question political candidates through satellite hook-ups.

One format that has been popularized by C-SPAN is the call-in program, where viewers are frequently given the opportunity to speak individually with their representatives via the telephone line. Many politicians have appeared on C-SPAN call-ins to answer questions and to talk directly to the audience about issues. Another call-in program that became a centerpiece during the 1992 campaign was "Larry King Live," which featured all three major candidates. Given the success of these programs, major networks followed suit by programming candidate interviews on early morning television.

1992 Town Meetings

Although Ross Perot has been credited with originating the town-hall concept as a way to get public input in the process, Bill Clinton began to use town-hall meetings early in his bid for the presidency. For example, when Clinton was in New Hampshire and the controversy surrounding his draft status arose, a town-hall meeting was a useful way to avoid the press and still get his message out to those who would listen.[16] Perot's first televised town meeting, simultaneously aired at six rallies via satellite, was similar to rallies held by both Clinton and Jerry Brown.[17] It followed Clinton's electronic town hall to four California cities by two weeks.[18]

Perot's vision of the electronic town hall varied somewhat from Clinton's idea of town meetings. Perot coined the term to encompass his belief that Americans could discuss relevant issues with a political leader via television, decide what to do about the issues, and then let members of Congress know their decision by taking an instant vote.[19] Perot's idea comes much closer to Arterton and Slaton's description of participatory democracy, because he calls for an exchange of ideas much like the early seventeenth-century town meetings. However, Arterton argues that the town-hall process envisioned by Perot would not necessarily be a unifying force, because "a town hall is where voters come together and debate on issues and cooperate with each other. Lateral and sideways communication is crucial."[20] The town meeting that Arterton imagines would not include the presence of a candidate trying to garner the participants' votes. Its potency would lie in the interactive nature of the audience.

The town meetings held in 1992 were as varied as the people who participated in these gatherings. Absent the feasibility of a system which Perot and Arterton envisioned, the meetings held by Clinton in particular ranged from computer bulletin boards[21] to the second presidential debate held in Richmond, Virginia. What essentially came to be known as televised town meetings were political programs which included a live studio audience with satellite connections to other locations, some in state, and some linked to surrounding states.

One important feature of the town-hall meeting was its reliance on local broadcast stations to produce the programs. Most of the Clinton town meetings were led by local media personalities, with C-SPAN coverage to the national audience. This provided opportunities for local stations to get attention from a nationwide audience. It also provided Clinton with the opportunity to bypass the larger and more costly major networks and to present his unfiltered message to the audience.

The remainder of this analysis looks specifically at five of the nine town-hall meetings Clinton held during his presidential campaign, including the presidential debate held in Richmond, Virginia.[22] Each meeting was coded for the types of questions asked by the audience members, the issues discussed, and the recurring rhetorical strategies used by Bill Clinton in this format. Major focus was placed on the methods of identification used and the nonverbal stylistic features evident in the meetings.

An interesting aspect of the town hall was the nature of the participants involved. Audiences consisted of undecided voters, occasional contest winners, and randomly chosen citizens. In some instances, audience members identified themselves by name and occupation; in other cases, they were merely identified as questioners. Both Clinton and the moderators claimed that he had no prior knowledge of the kinds of questions that would be asked; though, of course, general patterns emerged in the issues discussed by most people.

In the meetings analyzed for this chapter, the major issue identified was the national economy and Clinton's plans for decreasing the deficit. Of the one hundred and eight questions identified, almost one-fourth of the questions dealt with the economy and jobs. The next highest category of issues included crime and violence, with close to 12 percent of the questions dealing with gun control, neighborhood violence, and the increase in nationwide crime. Another significant area of questions dealt with minority issues. Ten percent of the questions focused on Clinton's plans to combat racism and to further minority issues. Other prominent topics included health care, education, AIDS, and international relations. With these issues in mind, several rhetorical strategies emerge, which contribute to Clinton's effectiveness in the town-hall arena. These strategies are dealt with in the following section.

CLINTON'S RHETORICAL STRATEGIES

As became most evident in the second presidential debate, Bill Clinton appeared to be quite comfortable in dealing with audiences in town meetings. While each town hall provided its own unique format, several patterns of interaction were apparent in Clinton's manner of handling the questions. Three areas will frame this discussion: organizational structure, rhetorical appeals, and stylistic elements.

Organizational Structure

In her book *Eloquence in an Electronic Age*, Kathleen Jamieson discusses the evolution of political rhetoric in the age of television. The politician who can crystallize major ideas into brief sound bites is the one who will successfully relay his or her message to the American public. She writes:

> A talent for digesting a speech into a memorable phrase is a characteristic of eloquent persons. In our age of television where political speakers are more likely to be heard in news clips than in any other environment, the value of this talent is magnified. The person who can synopsize an issue in a clear, concise, dramatic statement that takes less than thirty-five seconds to deliver is more likely to be seen and heard on broadcast news than those who lack that talent.[23]

George Bush's "a kinder, gentler nation" and "a new world order" were phrases which attempted to encapsulate his vision for America. John F. Kennedy's famous "ask not what your country can do for you . . ." has evolved into a synecdochic representation of Kennedy's era as president. These phrases, or small units of discourse, Jamieson argues, can come to stand for an entire presidency or period of history.[24]

Clinton's limited ability to turn a phrase into a memorable one that could stay with the public provided an important rationale to get his message out through nontraditional media forms. Identified by many reporters and pundits as a "policy wonk," Clinton's rhetorical style was the antithesis of the traditional ten-second sound bite, which, prior to 1992, had come to dominate campaign rhetoric. Given his understanding of issues and his interest in clearly communicating his plans to the voters, Clinton was never very good at encapsulating his ideas into brief phrases that would work on the nightly news. It is understandable then that town meetings would provide useful formats for the governor to clearly outline his policies for the American public.

One of the most effective ways Clinton was able to get his message across was through good organizational skills. Rather than rambling through answers to questions, he would present his position with three or four clear points to define his plan. For example, in a town-hall meeting aired in Texas, Clinton provides a lengthy response to a question on entitlement programs and his plans for health care. He then goes on to succinctly outline three areas to deal with the problem:

> What's the answer? Control health care costs. That's more important than anything else. Provide a basic system of health care to everybody. Number two, pursue policies that will reduce the poverty rate. Tax the income of the working poor less. Move people from welfare to work, as we have in Arkansas. Reduce poverty. And number three, ask upper-income senior citizens to subject more of their benefits to taxation under Social Security or pay more for Medicare benefits.[25]

Presenting plans in a numbered manner helped Clinton to deliver his message in a more thoughtful and organized manner. This was especially significant when contrasted to Perot and Bush in the Richmond debate. Of the thirteen questions asked by the audience, six of Clinton's responses were structured with three or more major plans he wanted to institute once in office. Bush and Perot, on the other hand, never provided this kind of structure to their positions. Campaign advisor Betsey Wright claimed during the campaign that Clinton's numbering of major arguments had been dramatically reduced from his usual pattern of outlining ten to twelve major points and overwhelming audiences with his level of information about issues. Crystallizing his major ideas with three-point plans illustrated Clinton's understanding of issues, or at the very least, his ability to reduce issue complexity to three or four clear solutions for the subject being discussed.

In line with the organizational structure of his arguments, Clinton also tended to answer questions with a problem-solution format. When asked a question about the economy during the Kentuckiana town meeting, Clinton summarizes the problem and then provides his solution:

> What has happened to you is that you're part of . . . a country where the economy is shrinking, where we're losing ground to other countries. Keep in mind, it is literally true that more than two-thirds of the American work force is working a longer work week today for lower wages than they were making 10 years ago. What I offer you is a real plan to invest in America, to invest in our jobs, in our education, in our productivity growth, in competing with other countries. I've outlined a plan to put $50 billion back into job-generating activities and to give real incentives in the private sector to create jobs and have incomes growing.[26]

By defining the problem and providing his solution, Clinton is able to bring the meeting to his areas of expertise. He takes a question posed by an audience member, frames the problem that it is addressing, relates and personalizes that problem for the audience, and then refers to his specific plan to solve the problem.

These organizational strategies fall in line with Trent and Friedenberg's discussion of the speech modules most candidates construct about the ten to twenty issues on which they frequently speak. Each module is an independent, single unit of speech that can be delivered in three to seven minutes, varied by the length and number of examples that might be given. It contains an attention-getting device, a discussion of the problem, then the specific policies the candidate has in mind to solve the problem. If time allows, the candidate might also visualize for the audience what would happen if the policies could be carried out.[27]

While most political candidates utilize speech modules in delivering their messages on the stump, Clinton regularly used modules in his town meetings. In this way, he could represent his answer in a conversational, spontaneous manner, while at the same time, clearly get his message across on a variety of issues. Being well organized helped him to achieve these goals.

Rhetorical Appeals

Throughout the town meetings, Clinton wove personal narratives, audience identification, and the Arkansas model into his solutions for the nation's problems. In this way he was able to establish credibility by illustrating that he shared common values and experiences with his audiences, that he recognized their hard work and sacrifices as they dealt with the nation's problems, and that his experience as governor of Arkansas had adequately prepared him to be president.

Identification strategies. Kenneth Burke notes that the ability to identify with one's audience is perhaps the most important element in establishing common ground, overcoming differences, and ultimately persuading the audience to one's side. He explains that:

> As for the relation between "identification" and "persuasion": we might well keep it in mind that a speaker persuades an audience by the use of stylistic identifications; his act of persuasion may be for the purpose of causing the audience to identify itself with the speaker's interests; and the speaker draws on identification of interests to establish rapport between himself and his audience.[28]

At its simplest level, identification can be conscious; that is, as when a political candidate goes to Iowa and talks about growing up on a farm, slopping pigs, milking cows, and working from dawn to dusk. Identification can also happen through antithesis, by identifying a common enemy. Clinton's ability to relate to his audiences mainly took place by building a common understanding of the similarities in ways that people were suffering, which involved both identification by commonalities and by antithesis.

Clinton attempts to build common bonds with his audience in three ways. First, he uses personal narratives of his family and his youth to illustrate why he has come to certain policy conclusions. For example, in responding to a question on family values and the role the president should play in their promotion, Clinton states:

> You may know that I was born into a single-parent family. My father was killed three months before I was born. My mother has been widowed three times. I was raised, in large measure, with grandparents, my great uncles and great aunts, but I had a lot of family values.[29]

After sharing this story, Clinton moves on to define his version of family values and what the president's role should be in their promotion. "The President," he argues, "should pursue policies which help us to rear the strongest children in the world and to keep families together and help them succeed. . . ."[30] Having first told his own story, Clinton is able both to identify with others who have struggled with nontraditional families and to stir the audience's emotions with regard to his ability to beat the odds and finally run for president.

Another example Clinton uses occurs in response to a question about his support of the Brady Bill and the necessity to deal with crime and violence in society. He shares his own story as evidence for why gun control is necessary:

> Now, you know, I know what it's like to be a victim of crime. Twenty years ago, I was robbed twice within a two-year period, and I lost everything I owned. I was really mad about it. This world is a lot more violent now than it was then. You've got more and more young people, more and more people with guns in their hands. There's a lot that needs to be done on crime. But we ought to start with the Brady bill.[31]

Whether it was the sharing of narratives about his personal experiences, his brother's problems with drugs, about Chelsea wanting to one day work with the space program, or Hillary's achievements with education in Arkansas, these brief anecdotes helped to personalize the issues in ways the audiences could readily associate with.

A second way Clinton was able to identify with his audiences was through his inclusive use of language. He frequently reminded people that everyone was included in his plans and that America could not afford to discriminate or waste anyone's energy.[32] Through inclusive phrases such as "we can do this together" and "we can do better," Clinton invites the audiences to join him in his crusade to bring dramatic change to America.

Another way that Clinton establishes identification with his audience is through the use of antithesis, or the construction of a common enemy which people could unite against. In this case, the common enemy was the status quo, and more specifically, the economy. Throughout his meetings, Clinton interwove the current problems and fears about the future:

As I traveled across America for eight months during the primary season, I found that most people felt in all the states the way the people in my home state feel. They feel anger and frustration and disappointment about the way their government's let them down. They feel genuine worry about the future.[33]

By framing the government as the problem and blaming the present system for the anxieties people hold about their economic future, Clinton was able to contrast his hope for change with the frustration over an uncaring and insolent administration. Hence, identification by antithesis became an important way to bring people together against a common enemy.

Acknowledgment strategies. In an attempt to build emotional support for his policies and to enhance his credibility as a caring president, Clinton frequently acknowledged audience members in ways which showed his understanding of their problems and his appreciation for their individual accomplishments. In some town meetings, audience members listed their names and occupations before asking their specific questions to Clinton. Frequently, they would identify themselves, provide a statement relevant to the work they did, and then explain their special problems or concerns.

On several occasions when audience members identified themselves and their specific concerns, Clinton would respond with a very personal acknowledgment of their effort. For example, when a family physician working in the Fort Worth area with HIV-infected individuals admitted that she, too, had become HIV-infected following an occupational exposure, Clinton thanked her for having the courage to be present at the meeting and then talked about his personal interest in solving the AIDS epidemic.[34] Acknowledging the expertise of a police officer when he asked about Clinton's plan to stop the national escalation of violence, the governor replied:

> I'll answer the question, Lieutenant, if you will when I'm finished
> . . . because you may have a better answer than I do. This is a
> tough issue and one we've been grappling with in our state.[35]

Clinton responded in a similar way to a uniformed Jacksonville sheriff who asked a question about juvenile crime. As Clinton answered the question, he also acknowledged the officer's efforts: "Society needs more police officers like yourself willing to risk their lives for the protection of others."[36]

One of the clearest acknowledgment strategies occurred during the Richmond debate when the woman asked the question about how the national debt had affected each of the presidential candidates. Perot talked about how he joined the race because of the economy and how disruptive his running has been to his private life. Confused by the question, Bush asked for clarification, mentioned attending a black church and reading about teen pregnancy, and ultimately concluded that the national debt affects everyone. When Clinton responded, he directly answered the woman, indicating that he had met people all around the country who shared her plight and who were personally affected by the recession. This kind of acknowledgment was instrumental in demonstrating Clinton's concerns for the American people and his understanding and appreciation for this woman's specific situation.[37]

The Arkansas model. When Ronald Reagan first ran for president in 1980 he claimed that his experience as governor of the state of California directly prepared him to be president of the United States. A governor had to balance a budget, deal with competing factions and ideologies, and please a variety of constituencies. A successful governor could claim, as did Reagan, that his or her state was a model for other states to emulate. If one could successfully tackle a state's deficit and elevate his state to prominence in some area of excellence, then the claim could be made that the governor running for president would do the same for the United States.

In 1988 Michael Dukakis attempted a similar strategy, arguing that under his governance the state of Massachusetts was thriving economically and leading in technological advancements. His claim that his state served as a model to be emulated were visually refuted when the Bush campaign ran the infamous "Prison Furlough" and "Boston Harbor" ads, which attempted to instill a fear that Dukakis probably *would* do for America what he had done for Massachusetts.[38]

As governor of the small state of Arkansas for twelve years, Bill Clinton had to overcome the perceptions of many Americans that the state was too small to be a model for anything and to contextualize the state's dismal rankings in education, unemployment, and environmental clean-up with consideration for how the state had improved during his time in office. The town-hall meeting provided a useful way for Clinton to emphasize his gubernatorial experiences. On several occasions, Clinton answered questions by talking about his successes in Arkansas. With regard to education and school choice, the governor noted that his state was the second in the country to give parents and their children more choice on the schools they attend.[39] On the issue of abortion, he identified the specific actions he had taken in his state, such as signing into law that abortions would be illegal in the third trimester and that a parent should be notified if a minor wants to have an abortion.[40] Through these examples, Clinton was able to illustrate his commitment to a woman's freedom of choice, while at the same time clarifying what he viewed as reasonable limitations which could be established by states.

Finally, Clinton was able to use his state as evidence for his commitment to the needs of senior citizens. In response to a question on the Older Americans Act and specific aid for senior citizens, Clinton notes:

> Let me tell you, I come from a state that has the second or third highest percentage of people over 65 in the United States. So I've had a lot of experience with this. . . . [I]n my own state. . . we raised the cigarette tax a little bit and put all the money into transportation for people to get to senior citizen centers, because we believe in them so strongly. . . . We have an experimental program in my state now called Elder Choices, where we take money that used to go to nursing homes, and we let older people decide how they want to use it. Over 2,000 of them are now staying in their own homes. They're much happier, and they're saving the other taxpayers money. That's the kind of system I want for all of America.[41]

It is certainly not surprising that Clinton would draw on his experiences as governor to argue for his ability to be president. However, it is interesting to note the ways he attempts to draw on the successes of a small, rural, southern state, and overcome the perceptual barriers which some voters had about Arkansas. Some of the perceptions were stereotypical assumptions; others were grounded in evidence presented by the Bush and Perot camps. Hence, Clinton's ability to establish his credibility was predicated on surmounting these barriers and gaining ground by stressing expertise as a political leader and Arkansas's success as a model state.

Stylistic Elements

Bill Clinton's ease in dealing with the town-meeting audiences was evident in his style of delivery. Through direct eye contact and comfortable body movement, the governor was able to establish a good rapport with his audiences. This was particularly apparent in the Richmond debate when Perot and Bush were both present.

Eye contact. One of the most effective ways that Clinton reached out to his audiences was through eye contact. Any basic public speaking teacher will attest to the importance of good eye contact, of the positive impressions to be gained when a speaker can look his or her audience straight in the eye and make sensible arguments. Clinton illustrated a good understanding of how to engage audiences through this nonverbal mechanism.

While many politicians naturally take advantage of television cameras to reach out to the larger television audience when answering a question at a town meeting, Clinton complemented his verbal support of the audience with direct eye contact. When asked a question, he would fix his gaze directly on the questioner and provide an answer; rarely did he draw in the other audience members as he answered. For the questioners, this gave the impression that Clinton was intensely interested in communicating specifically with them, rather than to the television camera. Even when the questioner was linked via satellite, Clinton would still look at the satellite picture while responding. For the television audience, this gave the impression that Clinton was truly interested in the individual rather than in the impression that might be made on an unidentified audience.

Clinton continued with the same direct style of eye contact during the Richmond debate. While both Perot and Bush would include most of the audience members and the television audience as they answered questions, Clinton maintained the same direct relationship with the individual questioners.

Body movement. Another way that Bill Clinton was able to draw audience members to him was through his use of body movement and gestures. Though sometimes forced to remain seated, when he could stand up and move around he appeared to be much more comfortable.

His relaxed movement was evident during the Richmond debate where not only would he engage the audience member with good eye contact, but he would also get as close as was physically possible to the questioner. By decreasing the physical distance as much as the cameras would allow, he could, in effect, decrease the psychological distance with the audience member.

An interesting example of adaptation with his body movement was during Clinton's appearance at a Florida town meeting. When a wheelchair-bound audience member asked a question, Clinton sat down in his chair, almost eye-level with the man. His overall ease with himself in this situation and his attempt to meet the man on his own level was readily apparent. This comfortable movement, coupled with emphatic gestures, complemented his verbal messages of concern about the audiences' problems.

Bill Clinton's organizational structure, rhetorical strategies, and delivery style all worked together to create an image of a candidate who could deal with a variety of issues and work in different technological configurations and to establish a give-and-take rapport with the audience. Given his ease in dealing with the town-meeting format, it is easy to understand why he would want to continue these kinds of gatherings during his presidency. If town meetings are to become a natural staple of the Clinton presidency, it is important to consider the implications for this format and to suggest directions for the future.

IMPLICATIONS FOR THE FUTURE

In looking back at the town meetings held during the 1992 campaign and at the other forms of new technology used by the candidates, it is clear that political campaign communication will never be the same again. We should therefore carefully consider Bill Clinton's role in fostering public participation and assess some of the strengths and weaknesses of the town-hall format.

Bill Clinton was the perfect candidate to usher in the new media age. He represented a generation that possibly understood how to compete in an evolving political arena and how to restore hope in the weakened economy. Clinton's ability to take his message to the public by whatever means necessary illustrates his understanding of the evolving nature of campaigning and of public expectations. Media critic Douglas Davis observes that

The "leader" in the interactive age must at least offer to consult his/her acute electorate, not merely lead it. . . . Bill Clinton's numbers began to rise late last spring only when he deserted the stump and opened himself up to interaction, political and cultural. He braved the "CBS Morning News" over and over to answer questions and faxes. He charged into the midst of MTV'S 18-to-24 year old army, tooted his sax, and imitated Elvis Presley on the eve of the New York primary. He engaged our diverse culture on a number of levels, while George Bush refused it.[42]

Bill Clinton succeeded in these forums because he understood the importance of directly reaching out to the audience and because he recognized the public's desire to participate in the political process. By saturating the media channels he was able to keep his message in the forefront and enhance his credibility with the audience.

A major factor in presenting his message was the ability to bypass traditional forms of media and choose forums that would personally reach more people. Clinton acknowledged that this strategy was an effective one: "What we are finding is, the more we are communicating directly with the people, the better I do. . . . The things I stand for . . . get out there when I do it directly."[43] While delivering his message, Clinton was able to avoid the tough questions that mostly come from journalists, while at the same time further establish his ethos with the audience.

This illustrates the first of several problems inherent in the modified town-hall process, the type of questioning that takes place in a town meeting. Despite the public popularity of the Richmond debate, many commentators criticized the lack of tough questions coming from the audience members. The questions most journalists noted as newsworthy were those dealing with requests to avoid negative attacks and to explain how the national debt had personally affected the candidates. Other questions tended to be polite and reverential.

This was also true in other town meetings. On only a few occasions did questioners directly challenge Bill Clinton. One question came from a former campaign chairman for Ross Perot; another came from Dan Quayle.[44] In both of these instances, Clinton handled the issues with humor and logical arguments.

The town-hall format does not, for the most part, provide for audience follow-up questions for the candidate. In any given town-hall meeting, Clinton could only answer twelve to fifteen questions, and time constraints limited the length of his responses. Therefore, little interaction could take place between the individual audience member and the candidate. Follow-up questions were usually provided only by the moderator, as points of clarification or as ways to redirect the topic areas.

The lack of follow-up questions enabled the candidate to merely express his viewpoint without much challenge. While audience members tended to ask good questions about issues, they were inclined to be more polite, less confrontative, and more general than specific. Therefore, while new media forms appear to be less elitist and more democratic, they lack the journalistic investigative edge often necessary for thorough discussion of issues.[45] Everett Dennis notes that the changes in media have "drawn more people into the national conversation about the election," but that the downside of these changes is that it "somehow denigrates the news process and deceives the public, as candidates are allowed open access time to be actors . . . without the benefit of intervention by serious journalists."[46]

Another inherent problem in the town-hall format is the nature of the participation. Besides the interaction between the questioner and the candidate, Clinton very rarely solicited audience input beyond the questioning process. In fact, one of the few moments where the audience did participate beyond merely asking a question was when Al Gore was present at the Kentuckiana Town Meeting. Occurring during the peak of their Midwest bus tour, Clinton and Gore seemed comfortable and energized in front of this audience, and it was Gore who at times asked the audience for a show of hands on how they had been affected by various issues. Other than these scattered moments, little involvement in the forms of idea generation, proactive policy formation, or even a nonverbal showing of hands took place during the meetings.

This lack of interaction illustrates a major concern about the format of town-hall meetings. Bertelson argues that electronic communication technologies "encourage the active participation of individuals in selective levels of the political arena," while at the same time discouraging full participation by excluding many from the formation of political issues.[47] Individuals may be participating, but the depth of involvement is shallow, limited to asking a question or making a statement. The impact of this observation is that we must realize how new technologies can be co-opted by those who are skilled in political manipulation and how public acquiescence can occur when an illusion of participation is constructed. Merely being present at a meeting with a candidate does not equal the level of participation necessary for a truly representative democracy.

There are inherent problems in the current configuration of town-hall meetings, but, combined with other forms of public participation, in 1992 an atmosphere of campaign interest developed that will undoubtedly change the way we look at politics in the future. Town meetings, increased involvement from young people, "Larry King Live," a presidential debate that allowed citizens to ask questions, and the election of 122 new members of Congress, energized Americans, and, in turn, will hold lawmakers more accountable for their actions.[48] This kind of public reaction has dramatically increased the amount of input by citizens. For example, in the first eight days of the 1993 legislative session, 1,650,143 calls were logged on the Capitol switchboard, compared to 710,465 calls only a year before. Thousands more calls and fax transmissions were placed directly to senatorial and congressional offices.[49] With Perot reminding Americans to hold lawmakers responsible for reducing the deficit and with the Clinton administration soliciting citizen input via phone calls, letters, and electronic mail, it seems certain that a new momentum in public involvement is dramatically building.

With this momentum comes a new vision of how citizens will get political information in the future. Davis predicts that the public will no longer settle for limited access to information, which will, in turn, directly affect the future of traditional mass communication forms. He writes that:

> The mass media, in brief—and the inert public that allegedly adores it—are dead. The very word "mass," as beloved here as in Marxist rhetoric, feeds American hubris. For more than a century we prospered on the techniques of "mass production" . . . We are increasingly contradictory, our minds and tastes honed by an unprecedented variety of ideas, products, and experiences. Perhaps it is better to think of us, as the Greeks thought of their citizens, and Thomas Jefferson thought of his young nation, as an assemblage of "publics" . . . a body of equals.[50]

Knowing that a host of interactive technologies exist, voters will now expect some form of direct access to Congress and the White House. The expectation is to be heard, to be able to shape and react to policy decisions: "Now the citizen, not the media, is the medium. The 'silent majority' courted by past presidents is now an outspoken minority, entwined in a net of other, equally vigorous voices."[51]

The town-hall meeting will be, by its very nature, an important rhetorical strategy for political candidates in the future. It symbolizes the moral high ground of reaching out directly to the people without the filter of a major network's interpretation. For Bill Clinton, the town meeting embodied the change that was the substance of his message, and it directly challenged the public to actively participate in the process. As campaigning evolves into the twenty-first century, it seems clear that the candidate who can combine substantive messages with this type of participatory communication channel will have a greater chance in relaying his or her message to the American public.

There are many ways that the town-hall format can be improved to better encourage the important side-way communication Arterton identified and to provide the kind of decision-making input that Perot envisioned. Recognizing his success in the 1992 campaign, one can easily see why Clinton would want continue to use this forum to explain his policies to the American public. Steve Lohr underscores Clinton's intention to use town meetings during his presidency. He reports that:

> The use of modern technology to speed reaction times and deal with the public directly, whether in televised town meetings or a program for electronically distributing White House statements nationally, is a central tenet of the Clinton Administration. As much as possible, the President wants his message delivered as he presents it, not filtered, or analyzed, by the news media. The catch phrase, used by White House officials, is that Mr. Clinton intends to speak "to people" instead of speaking "through people."[52]

Given the fact that Clinton, on occasion, continues to use these formats during his presidency, it is prudent to explore more direct ways that audience members can contribute to the process. As technology continues to advance, the administration should identify ways to solicit greater input, to continue the momentum that began to build during the campaign year. Allowing more direct interaction among audience members, establishing a way for audiences to "vote" at the conclusion of a town meeting, and providing time for good follow-up questions may begin to address those concerns expressed by scholars who study political participation.

Yet, we must be wary of some of the potential teledemocracy has to shape the nature of participation in our society. On an NPR Morning Edition program, *Rolling Stone* writer John Katz considered the impact that new technologies could have on future presidential decision making:

> It certainly would be possible for Clinton to wire the presidency into American homes through phone lines and interactive television technology. He could seek instant guidance and input on complicated social issues that now take months to ooze their way through journalistic filters and political processes. As a candidate, Clinton adroitly embraced new media technology and the culture it represented, an instinct repeatedly cited as a key factor in his victory. He says he will do the same thing as president. If he does, the very notion of what reporters do will change. Tourists may have to go to the Smithsonian to see old tapes of White House press conferences rerun on screens down the hall from the fading gowns of former first ladies.[53]

While it's unlikely that American journalism will ever reach this stage of extinction, it is certainly important to remember that there is vast potential for the future of public participation, as well as potential for excessive manipulation. In this tension lies the greatest concern for Bill Clinton and future political candidates—and one of the greatest challenges for political communication scholars.

NOTES

1. Carl M. Degler, *Out of Our Past: The Forces That Shaped America*, rev. ed. (New York: Harper and Row, 1970), 25–26.

2. Ibid., 26.

3. Jerry Roberts, "Infomercials, Talk Shows: Revolution in Coverage of Presidential Campaigns," *San Francisco Chronicle*, 2 November 1992, Sec. A., Final ed.

4. Dennis Cauchon, "Campaign Turns to Television for a 'Town Meeting,'" *USA Today*, 27 May 1992, Sec. A., Final ed.

5. Ibid., 5A.

6. Edward J. Dionne Jr., *Why Americans Hate Politics* (New York: Simon and Schuster, 1991), 3.

7. Ibid., 10.

8. Dan Balz, "Voter Anger Doesn't Equal Voter Apathy," *Washington Post*, 21 October 1992, Sec. A., Final ed.

9. David Matthews as quoted by William Raspberry, "Reconnecting People and Politics," *Washington Post*, 29 June 1992, Sec. A., Final ed.

10. Dale A. Bertelson, "Media Form and Government: Democracy as an Archetypal Image in the Electronic Age," *Communication Quarterly* 40 (Fall 1992): 332.

11. F. Christopher Arterton, *Teledemocracy: Can Technology Protect Democracy?* (Newberry Park, Calif.: Sage Library of Social Science Research, 1986), 14.

12. Christa D. Slaton, *Televote: Expanding Citizen Participation in the Quantum Age* (New York: Praeger, 1992), 2.

13. Ibid., 26.

14. Arterton, *Teledemocracy*, 105.

15. Slaton, *Televote*, 104.

16. Roberts, "Infomercials, Talk Shows."

17. Steven A. Holmes, "The 1992 Campaign: Undeclared Candidate, Perot, Using Satellite, Addresses Rallies in Six States," *New York Times*, 30 May 1992, Sec. A.

18. Cauchon, "Campaign Turns to Television."

19. Ian Brodie, "US Election: Both Sides Learn Lessons from a 'Screwy and Ugly' Campaign," *Daily Telegraph*, 3 November 1992.

20. Christopher Arterton as quoted by Bill Turque, "Wiring Up the Age of Technopolitics," *Newsweek*, 15 June 1992, 25.

21. Another type of town-hall format, which is dealt with by Tom Benson elsewhere in this volume, is done via home computers. Those who could afford Prodigy or CompuServe had the privilege of electronic access to both Bill Clinton and George Bush. According to the PR Newswire Service, the presidential campaigns set out their positions electronically and by answering online questions. The candidates' statements and answers were then posted on an electronic bulletin board on the Prodigy service. In 1992 electronic mail became a viable way for personal computer users to talk with the candidates. See "Campaign Goes Online, and the People Respond," *PR Newswire*, 4 September 1992.

22. The five town halls discussed here include meetings held in Kentucky, Florida, Michigan, Texas, and Virginia. Transcripts were available for the meetings held in Kentucky, Florida, and Texas. All town meetings are provided through C-SPAN and the Public Affairs Video Archives at Purdue University, Lafayette, Indiana.

23. Kathleen Hall Jamieson, *Eloquence in an Electronic Age* (New York: Oxford University Press, 1988), 90–91.

24. Ibid., 91.

25. Bill Clinton, "Clinton Campaign Town Meeting," KDFV-TV, Dallas, Texas. Transcript and Videotape, Public Affairs Video Archives, Purdue University, West Lafayette, Indiana. ID: 31534 (25 August 1992): 26.

26. Bill Clinton, "Kentuckiana Town Meeting," WHAS-TV, Louisville, Kentucky. Transcript and Videotape, Public Affairs Archives, Purdue University, Lafayette, Indiana. ID: 27235 (20 July 1992), 10.

27. Judith S. Trent and Robert V. Friedenberg, *Political Campaign Communication: Principles and Practices*, 2d ed. (New York: Praeger, 1990), 172–73.

28. Kenneth Burke, *On Symbols and Society*, ed. Joseph R. Gusfield (Chicago: University of Chicago Press, 1989), 191. (Gender use in original.)

29. Clinton, *Dallas Town Meeting*, 21.

30. Ibid., 22.

31. Clinton, *Pittsburgh Town Meeting*, 2.

32. Clinton, *Kentuckiana Town Meeting*, 21.

33. Bill Clinton, "Town Meeting," WQED-TV, Pittsburgh, Pennsylvania. Transcript and Videotape, Public Affairs Video Archives, Lafayette, Indiana. ID: 26556 (12 June 1992): 1.

34. Clinton, *Dallas Town Meeting*, 27.

35. Ibid., 28.

36. Bill Clinton, "Clinton Town Meeting," Florida News Network. Videotape, Public Affairs Video Archives, Purdue University, Lafayette, Indiana. ID: 32073 (9 September 1992).

37. Second Presidential Debate, Richmond, Virginia, 15 October 1992. C-SPAN Videotape.

38. Much has been written about these two ads in particular. For a close analysis of the ad campaign of 1988, see Kathleen Hall Jamieson's *Dirty Politics: Deception, Distraction and Democracy* (New York: Oxford University Press, 1992).

39. Clinton, *Pittsburgh Town Meeting*, 1.

40. Clinton, *Dallas Town Meeting*, 20.

41. Ibid., 24.

42. Douglas Davis, "The American Voter Mounts the Stage," *Newsday*, 3 January 1993, Nassau Ed.

43. Bill Clinton as quoted by Chris Black, "Clinton Woos Undecided Voters via TV," *Boston Globe*, 13 June 1992, Sec. A, City Ed.

44. Clinton, *Kentuckiana Town Meeting*.

45. Jonathan Alter, "Why the Old Media's Losing Control," *Newsweek*, 8 June 1992, 28.

46. Everett Dennis as quoted by Jerry Roberts, "Infomercials, Talk Shows," *San Francisco Chronicle*, 2 November 1992, Sec. A., Final Ed.

47. Bertelson, "Media Form and Government," 333.

48. Kevin Merida, Helen Dewar, and *Washington Post* Staff Writers, "Energized by Pulpit or Passion, the Public Is Calling," *Washington Post*, 1 February 1993, Sec. A, Final Ed.

49. Ibid.

50. Davis, "The American Voter Mounts the Stage," Sec. 1.

51. Ibid.

52. Steve Lohr, "White House: A Computer Nerdville," *New York Times*, 20 February 1993, Sec. 1, Final Ed.

53. John Katz, "Morning Edition," *National Public Radio*, 11 November 1992.

LIVING IN THE ROCK N ROLL CAMPAIGN, OR MYSTERY, MEDIA, AND THE AMERICAN PUBLIC IMAGINATION

An Intertextual Quest

H. L. GOODALL JR.

> This is not just a campaign for the presidency.
> This is a crusade for change.
>
> —Bill Clinton[1]

The world is no longer driven by power, but fascination, no longer by production, but seduction. . . . The discourses held by both the 'strategists' of mass desire . . . and the 'analysts' of their strategies . . . are as vacuous as the political space itself. The simply refract the emptiness of that about which they speak.

—Jean Baudrillard[2]

The attributes of liminality or of liminal *personae* ('threshold people') are necessarily ambiguous, since this condition and these persons elude or slip through the network of classifications that normally locate states or positions in cultural space. Liminal entities are neither here nor there; they are betwixt and between the positions assigned and arrayed by law, custom, convention, and ceremony.

—Victor Turner[3]

THE MYSTERY TRAIN

At the Democratic National Convention in 1988, Gov. Bill Clinton delivered a very long and very boring televised speech to a mostly disinterested, certainly disenchanted, live public audience. So disenchanted was the audience, they cheered and applauded most loudly when the governor announced that he was nearing the end of his speech.

Clinton was surely surprised and probably deeply saddened by the response. He had come forth on the podium that night not to be publicly chagrined, but publicly imagined. To be imagined as *the next one,* the one after Dukakis. He had come into this night filled with hope, but not yet cognizant that the truer source of his personal and political mystery was in being from a place called Hope. He was, put simply, not yet worthy; that is, not yet worthy of the powers of mediated public imagination.

However, if you watch a videotape of that performance you also see that he was transformed by it. There is a single solitary moment, a moment created through a broken space between the spoken words, a space that occurs just as the audience is most ingracious and the speaker appears most defeated, when *something happens;* in that moment, if you watch carefully the expression on his face, Bill Clinton *arrives.*

This is not an arrival that signals coming to a destination; it is instead an *arrival by reversal,* a sudden coming into a place for one's self where one *discovers* one's self, and it is achieved primarily through a sudden and unexpected surrender to a deeper, personal mystery. At that time, nobody but Bill Clinton knew exactly which self—indeed what deeper mystery—he had arrived for and was surrendering to.

> We no longer exist as playwrights
> or actors, but as terminals of
> multiple networks.
> —Jean Baudrillard[4]

What that mystery self was may have been uncertain, but where it was manifested was not. He was on television—*live,* on television. He was connected via electronic images and speech to multiple millions of American homes. This convention speech, this brief failure on these vast circuits of change, was not a loss, but an opportunity. It was an opportunity *to become,* to define himself in the mediated imaginations of a new generation of American voters, to climb aboard an electronic mystery train whose velocity depended on video tracks and whose power was derived from the collective memories of rock n roll.

So it was that Bill Clinton, Boy Governor of Arkansas and distant presidential hopeful, died that night, live, and on television.

| Where does rock n roll begin? | It begins in the blues, in the cultural politics of the Delta blues; before that in the rhythmic ditties and rhyming dirges that poke fun at the rich, the powerful, and the beautiful, from the perspective of the materially damned; before that it was slave songs and spirituals serving as places called hope in otherwise hopeless places. | Have you ever stopped to wonder why, Rock n roll will never die? |

ELVIS LIVES!

The following evening Bill Clinton was publicly resurrected, appearing live on television again, this time as a guest on Johnny Carson's "Tonight Show," joking with the host of the nation's longest-running talk show about the already widely circulated stories about Clinton's tragic death, the victim of a suicide speaking performance at the convention. He was oddly at ease for a dead man, poised there in the guest's chair, a handsome, bashful, bouyant son of Arkansas, making self-depreciating, at times comic public apologies for the delivery of a bad speech that was also, poetically, an analogic public appeal. It was a public appeal for a second chance—a second chance to be imagined, a second chance to complete the ritual process he had prepared a lifetime for, that he felt destined to satisfy. What he learned that night was that he would have to understand and use the power of television if he were ever to capture the public's attention.

Four years hence he got a second chance. Both his television performance and a mythic life-story video at the 1992 Democratic convention, as well as his frequent, unprecedented appearances on talk shows would play vital roles. So, too, would his singular ability to resurrect himself from widely, prematurely circulated stories of his certain political death. So, too, would something else—something unusual, deeply personal, mysterious, ineffable. On television, it would look like a saxophone solo performed by a man in a suit wearing dark shades. To see it this way would be to hear him play an old Elvis tune. But to see it this way, to hear it this way, would be to miss the point. It would be to fail to see this moment as the powerful working of mystery within and on the public imagination. It would be to fail to see the train entirely for the obvious presence of its tracks, and this is a train song here, a big soulful train song, the mystery train song arriving full speed and on time at the terminal intersections of the imagination, the popular imagination of our common video station.

Viewed this way, heard this way, Bill Clinton's choice of music is vitally important. Elvis lives! He's found a new place to dwell . . . Down at the end of Pennsylvania Avenue, at the Heartbreak Hotel.

But this election isn't just about music, nor is it just about choices of songs. It is about rock n roll as a way of organizing the public imagination, rock n roll as a forum for expressing personal resistance to institutional domination, rock n roll as how we live our lives passionately, most fully, through the often-contradictory lyrics of our most popular songs: love songs that speak also of heartbreak, chapel songs that whisper betrayal, fun songs we take seriously, and serious songs we make funny.

To live rock n roll is to embrace your own contradictions, even to celebrate them. Not to understand rock n roll as a force greater than its music, as, in this particular case, an explanatory bandwidth fully capable of accounting for the 1992 Clinton-Gore presidential campaign's success, is more than merely a mistake; it is to fail to hear in the music itself the powerful forces of change.

THIS TRAIN DON'T CARRY NO STRANGERS, THIS TRAIN . . .

On 3 October 1991, Gov. Bill Clinton, standing in front of the Arkansas State House, announces his bid for the presidency of the United States. The announcement was carried by all major networks. Speculation proceeds about his chances against unannounced super-media candidate Gov. Mario Cuomo.

Hillary Rodham Clinton stands confidently by her husband's side. This is not reported or commented upon.

The governor of Arkansas is surrounded by a surprisingly broad array of friends, well-wishers, and, most importantly, a staff of young, energetic strategists. This news also goes unreported.

Sometimes, the important truths reside in the margins. And what happens out there in the margins ultimately defines the meanings—and the outcomes—of it all.

Perhaps it is symbolic that the media coverage of American presidential elections begins with the images of cold snow and gray skies in New Hampshire primaries. Men and women in heavy overcoats huddle against the news or try to make it. Candidates without a chance of the numbers adding up to something in their favor act as if they do, those with a chance act happily surprised, as if they don't understand the calculations—wouldn't believe them—but *maybe* could be persuaded by them. Commentators position themselves as merely the messengers of daily events and statements, weather forecasts, and economic forecasts. Impossible truths and probable deceptions match the images, the mood, of white snow turning dirty in the frozen streets of old towns where mostly forgotten citizens—this year, mostly forgotten, *unemployed* citizens—tell it like it is for candidates who promise to do what they can. *If* elected.

Are you better off than you were four years ago? Ronald Reagan's seminal political question in 1980 is the silent partner to every interview, every image, every promise. It is the unspoken companion to this election, the ghost definition of political victory from years past, the bottomest of lines. Weary faces talk about lost jobs and lost homes, broken families, a failure of education that leaks through the screen as a failure of hope and a deep sense of injustice. Things are getting worse, not better. Sanity is the painful realization that your life, framed consistently in the cameras as midlife, is about as unhappy as your neighbors'.

Nobody says: *Hey, you guys running for Prez'dent, whatcha gonna do for me? Huh? Whatcha gonna do to make this country good again?* Nobody has to. It is as obvious, as inevitable, as snow in January in New Hampshire.

Against this backdrop a woman suddenly appears on the screen and says she has had a twelve-year affair with Bill Clinton. Her name is Gennifer Flowers, which is just too precious. And Gennifer is spelled wrong, or if not wrong exactly, then at least unfortunately. Too cutesy. Country sugarfied. A vain attempt by somebody to carve some high rarity and fawn uniqueness—some cultural capital—out of the singularly personal, an attempt in the everyday to shape a memorable event out of the spelling of one's name.

What do we see in this frame? Is Gennifer Flowers a mediated metaphor for life down in Arkansas with Bill Clinton or is this ironic public confession simply the defining moment for mediated sexual politics in this campaign? Or can this infotainment itself serve as an electronic, symbolic mechanism for the likely commingling of both broad frames, a weaving of meanings that ask not just what this man has done with this woman and whether any of *that* should influence this election, as much as what this event can do for the daily political Arbitrons of the public imagination? Pardon me, Stanley Fish, but is there a text in this crass?

She wears, for what seems like days, a scarlet dress with black lacey trim; she sports the Southern big hair, bottle blonde, and is no stranger to hair spray. She seems to think the whole world should pay attention to her, to her telling of this event, to her telling of this event over and over again in cold flat tones that reveal nothing more than the alleged facts, ma'am, and those allegations without so much as a breath of heat, a cliffhanger of smoldering intensity, or even simple human passion. If Saddam Hussein's response to the coalition forces was the Mother of All Wars, this surely must be the *Dragnet* of All Affairs. So I felt sorry for Bill Clinton before I felt sorry for Hillary Clinton, whom I later admired more than any of them for her handling of the terse fabric—and fabrications—of these media-laden narratives. I felt sorry for Bill as a *guy*, as a fellow *male*. Fallen from marital grace or not, this blonde tattler looked and sounded like the Nightmare of All Lovers. Even when we are dogs—and we are dogs, almost all of us—our downright doggitude shouldn't publicly suffer the further indignities of a badly told bedtime tale.

But badly told tales *are* also part of the carnival parcel of popular culture. For "Enquiring" minds only, this story had broken into prose earlier in a supermarket tabloid loosely referred to as a "scandal sheet"; for the tactically inclined, Ms. Flowers herself wrote and produced an illegally recorded tape of a phone conversation with the candidate; for those political buffs who desire prickly historical parallels, Gary Hart is resurrected on "Larry King Live," but to his credit refuses, politely, to speculate about any of *that*. Is asked again and refuses again, less politely. There is some small talk. And again. *No*. What we see and hear in the silences but is never said: And *"fuck* you, too."

Where there is the presence of an absence in public narratives, the absence of said presence further opens the public text. Narratives within narratives appear and are circulated. The spin is on. The SIN Spin. Popular speculation passes for public opinion. Odd correlations are associated with causes and effects of widely dissimilar phenomena because words contain nested contexts for interpretations of meanings. Like this:

S   I   N

Is Bill's hair dyed?
If yes, then surely he is
an *adulterer*. If not, then
how do you explain the
way it changes color?
Hey, any man who colors
his hair . . . Huh?

Why would Gennifer
Flowers *lie*? Well, you
know perfectly well why.
Hell hath no fury like a
woman . . . heh, heh,
fucked and chucked, as
we say. Hey, aren't we
assuming a lot here?
Maybe not. For years
down in Arkansas there
have been rumors
about Bill *polling* his
constituents . . .

P   i

Bill Clinton's ranking in
the public opinion polls
drops *thirteen* points.

The Sin Spin: (N; vernacular) (1) A mediated accumulation, speculation, and
circulation of multiple meanings and vicarious pleasures accomplished by the

narrative attribution of possible or probable sexual misconduct by presiden-
tial candidates; (2) denials, silences, explanations, excuses, outrage, counter-
charges, speeches of apologia, public tears and sorrow (and occasional
withdrawal from public life) performed as responses to the mediated circula-
tion; (3) testimony of experts on sexual misconduct (victims, perpetrators,
clergy, therapists, best-selling scandal authors) about the causes and conse-
quences of these events and narratives.

The media go on a poorly imagined, overtly ambiguous, speculative history of presidential and candidate infidelities, with the appropriate nineties middling Christian moral attitude of resigned disgust combined with obvious titillating pleasure in the near-telling. *They are really into this.* They have expected it, prepared for it, if maybe not the good-looking Boy Guv'nor from Arkansas, then surely someone else. They look backward over their own destruction of Gary Hart. Then Jack Kennedy, who escaped allegations and was summarily assassinated, for god's sake. Then there was Eisenhower. Maybe. Hey, do you think maybe George Bush . . . ? Background work has been done, sneakily, not too secretively, but mostly it doesn't surface, doesn't get spoken by those who get paid to speak it. America has played the fool for sex for so long that this year this story just isn't cutting it; there are Real Issues in this election, such as the ECONOMY, remember, STUPID?

Spin Control. Narrative ends. Ghosts remain.

Besides, in a nation where, according to a *Cosmo* poll, most of the adult voters claim to have either had or seriously contemplated having an affair, who among us is likely to cast the first stone? Or, looked at a little differently, maybe this charge is having a reverse effect: We *identify* with Clinton—the Clinton*s*—on this one. We've been there, most of us. We live here, in this house where haunted hearts break. Gennifer Flowers, by contrast—even if this charge is true—comes off as the Little Rock tattler, scandaler of sheets. Or worse. She was *paid,* it is rumored—by the state Republican officials—for her story. How much was she paid? I heard it was $175,000.

Still later I would read that the hotel she claimed for the date and time of the affair hadn't been built until two years after that.

And still later I would hear that anyone close to Bill Clinton knew his attention span for women during his troubled period never lasted very long, and certainly not twelve years.

Bill and Hillary Clinton appear on "60 Minutes" to answer the charges of his "marital infidelity," although the announced reason is to answer the charges raised by Gennifer Flowers. Bill says he "has caused pain in his marriage."

Hillary defends her husband and says she "is not some little Tammy Wynette here, standin' by her man."

They look scared, frankly. But they also look like a couple who has worked through something a long time ago that is unfortunately being brought up again, which means that they have to relive it again.

Gennifer Flowers plays the tape she claims she made when talking to Bill Clinton. It sounds friendly, not intimate. Unfortunately, it also has Bill saying something about Mario Cuomo being a mafioso.

Governor Cuomo appears on "Larry King Live" and says he regrets hearing Governor Clinton saying such a thing about him.

Tammy Wynette is widely reported as being offended by Hillary's comments. At the time, Tammy has a song at Number 11 on the charts.

A correlation study reports that people who listen to country music often commit suicide.

American politics, media carnival style. The pollsters reported that Clinton's name recognition with voters nationally increased from less than 5 percent before the Gennifer Flowers tale to nearly 90 percent following the Clintons' appearance on "60 Minutes." Opinion about whether he is telling the truth fluxuates, or perhaps coincides, with the diminishing media exposure Flowers receives in the coming days.

Later, in another "Larry King Live" appearance, Clinton suggests that Mario Cuomo is the kind of person he would consider for an appointment to the Supreme Court.

On 3 November, the day after Bill Clinton was elected president of the United States, Gennifer Flowers was asked to comment. "I know he still misses me," she says.

We sense in them the Savonarola, who would exercise his own vanities by burning a fire of other people's vanities.

—Kenneth Burke[5]

Objectivity, then, is achieved through a coalition of subjectivities.

—Kenneth Gergen[6]

Do I contradict myself? Very well, I contradict myself. America is large enough . . .

—Walt Whitman[7]

Social systems and especially large-scale societies are inescapably caught in a very fundamental dilemma. On the one hand, they can only live by a system of institutionalized values, to which the members must be seriously committed and to which they must adhere in their actions. On the other hand, they must be able to accept compromises and accommodations, tolerating many actions which from the point of view of their own dominant values are wrong. . . . In this paradox lies a principal source of strain and instability in social systems, and many of the most important seeds of social change.

—Talcott Parsons and Edward Shils[8]

On 12 February, Clinton appeared on "Nightline" to answer charges that he had evaded the draft to avoid serving in Vietnam. Earlier that day he had called a press conference in the hangar of the Manchester airport to read a copy of the letter that would be read again on "Nightline" that evening. The letter, written by then-Rhodes scholar Clinton, expressed his agony over the war and his concern about the draft. As I listened to it, I felt a kinship with his statements, his questions, his fears, and his mixed emotions. But I could see it opening up the whole damned deep angst of my generation again, the unsettled tomb of a war that had divided the country and was still dividing us with its unvanquished ghosts.

The principal content of American psychology is developmental psychology: what happened to you earlier is the cause of what happened to you later. That's the basic theory: our history is causality. We don't even separate history as a story from history as cause. So you have to go back to childhood to get at why you are the way you are. . . .

No other culture would do that. If you are out of your mind in another culture or quite disturbed or impotent or anorexic, you look at what you've been eating, who's been casting spells on you, what taboo you've crossed, what you haven't done right, when you last missed reverence for the Gods or didn't take part in the dance, broke some tribal custom. Whatever. It could be thousands of other things—the plants, the water, the curses, the demons, the Gods, being out of touch with the Great Spirit. It would never, never be what happened

to you with your mother and father forty years ago. Only our culture uses that
model, that myth.
                                                            —James Hillman[9]

It's how you remember, not
what actually happened.
                        —Sigmund Freud[10]

Our culture prizes the manifest destiny of personal continuity despite the fact that our histories as a nation are written out of discontinuities, breaks in the frame, blind spots in the rearview mirrors of time, space, and memory. The general issue of Bill Clinton's character is hereby media-constructed under the spell of mythic cultural deconstruction, rendered as an inward entity out of outward raw and rawer materials: the draft, Vietnam, war protesting in England, photographs, letters, words he might have said to roommates, ideas he might have had, his dead father, his relationship with his mother, his stepfather. It is the past that is carried into the present, not whole cloth but in shredded threads, not contextualized but in fragments.

I wonder how many of us could withstand similar scrutiny.

As an ethnographer charged with observing and commenting on the use of media and communication strategies in this campaign, I see something else as well. *"Betwixt and between, betwixt and between . . ."* These words seemed to define Clinton's semiotic position in the campaign and to the American voters. He is living for us only as a series of captured, sometimes tortured, images in the hurricane eye liminal zone of the media, and I—along with millions of others— am watching those images catch breath and dance. No, that isn't accurate. We don't watch the news, we *read into it,* circulate it among our friends and families, enlarge and expand upon it. Now, however, those of us doing the reading, the circulating, the enlarging, are divided into multiple camps, symbolically charged warring factions, defined by our historical fictions, our cultural and political interests, our experiences, the languages of our stories, the *aegis* of our ages, the meta-theories of our endangered economics, and, increasingly, our tolerance for—and interpretation of—*ambiguity.*

Clinton's earlier strategic use of ambiguity (e.g., "I have caused pain in my marriage") was the statement of a person who knew very well that fine tension that borders between saying too much and too little, and who could live with that tension. With his equally ambiguous statements about his confusion over the Vietnam draft—maintaining that he was "opposed to the war" and "loved his country"—he managed to simultaneously further *unite* and further *divide* voters and the media to/from him. For those seeking absolute answers, whose tolerance for ambiguity was low, Clinton was simply not credible, his "character" was flawed; for those who understood that the age of absolute answers had passed, perhaps with Vietnam, perhaps with a mythically blissful marriage, Clinton appeared refreshingly honest, sufficiently complex, and politically savvy enough to warrant further attention.

> Every decoding is another encoding.
>
> —Morris Zapp[11]

Not only do the technologies of social saturation fashion "the individual without character," but at the same time, they furnish *invitations to incoherence.*
    —Kenneth Gergen[12]

Identities are highly complex, tension filled, contradictory, and inconsistent entities. Only the one who claims to have a simple, definite, and clear-cut identity has an identity problem.
    —Sami Ma'ari[13]

When he finished second in New Hampshire with only 25 percent of the vote and proclaimed himself "The Comeback Kid," he did it again. No doubt his "comeback" from the Flowers and Vietnam scandals was well earned and appropriately named, but finishing *second* in American politics had never before been considered a victory. Until now.

Between New Hampshire and June the story of the Democratic primaries is one of victory and attrition. As Clinton's momentum surged through the Midwest in addition to the South, there was little doubt that he would become the party's nominee. One by one the other candidates withdrew, leaving only former California governor Jerry Brown to challenge Clinton until the end.

On the Republican side, George Bush easily won over Pat Buchanan; although Buchanan demonstrated that he appealed to a large, vehemently conservative segment of the nation. Just how large, and how vehemently conservative, this group was would not surface until the convention in August.

But the "real" news of this political season was away from these primaries, and squarely on camera. On 20 February, Ross Perot explains to callers on "Larry King Live" that if they want him to run for president, he'll do it. This annoucement not only provided the first major evidence that alternative media could be used to bypass the institutional structures typically dedicated to managing the political process, it also underscored the role that televised talk shows might have on public opinion in a presidential race. The next stage in the ritual process would be an oddly mediated one.

SAX, PEROT, AND ROCK N ROLL

The horizon of drugs is the same as that of literature: they share the same line, depending on similar technologies and sometimes suffering analogous crackdowns before the law. *They shoot up fictions, disjuncting a whole regime of consciousness.*

—Avital Ronell[14]

The dream of technology is to reconstruct human beings from images.

—Paul Virilio[15]

What do we hold against the drug addict? . . . that he cuts himself off from the world, in exile from reality, far from objective reality and the real life of the city and the community; that he escapes into a world of simulacrum and fiction . . .

—Jacques Derrida[16]

In many ritual processes across cultures and certainly within ours, a collective pursuit of the heightened sense of awareness is induced by stimulants and hallucinogens, cast spells and magic, foods of the gods consumed for the production and pleasuring of the gods within us. These gods are called into existence at the hallucinogenic intersections of biology and theater, a temporal suspension spacially experienced as a deeply meaningful staged dance; what they help us reach is an enlivened, dramatic state of crazy narrative consciousness through adulterous bodily rushes and conflicted synaptical overloads, a kind of intoxication understood as a high merger of personal and cultural achievement. On our planet, in our mass-mediated cultures, these stimulants are often simulated through images and sounds, the optical and aural doors of perception mediated by the rock n roll infotainment video tracks of popular culture. The effect is one of speedy hallucinogenic collusion, the mixed but blurring perceptual sense of always moving forward while at the same time standing back, watching, listening, observing, commenting.

TV's not the drug, *politics* is. TV is merely where—and how—we ingest them. This is a medium—an industry—that is all about making addicts of audiences, a tuned-in, turned-on network of dealers and trope-takers, droppers of hits, snorters of lines, deep inhalers of talk about getting higher or lower in the polls. We are communities addicted to continuous copping of drug discourses, and we have to buy into an increasingly larger dosage just to get off. Network news isn't strong enough anymore. Late-night is a better high, at least sometimes. And did you hear about C-SPAN, the purest of the pure, uncut and always available? Blur those boundaries, mix up the possibilities, *accelerate*. Move the black magic wand and eye-graze across the nowhere land of simulated narcotized highs. We are junkies, political junkies, searching the only reality we can deal with for the pleasure-power of news-Xanadu.

Enter the buzzman, hey, the buzzman cometh!

Ross Perot's entry into our living rooms produced the desired effect. The effect was a media-injection of a powerful hallucinogenic drug into the moment-to-moment weirdity of the American infotainment/political scene, a moment of chaotic anti-structural uproar and clarity followed by the grand totality of revolution itself. Jug-eared, plain-speaking, patriotic, proud, and richer than all of you and me put together, his smiling energetic playful seriousness beamed into our shakey, fix-needing, electronic consciousness as an image of ugly necessary salvation—Chariot of the Ross!—the richest of men who would be the greatest of presidents, and who would do so without a party, going directly to the (mediated) People. *Lord of the Deficit*! Defender of traditional 'Merican values! Big Bizness Befriends Big Gov'ment!!! He put the hype back into the hyperdermic needle; Oh give us this day our daily dose of Ross . . .

And like the new drug he was, he represented a heightened sense of awareness, of possibilities, of by-god *damn* good feelings, and of potentially dangerous side effects as yet not fully understood. Seemingly overnight his image rose in the polls until by June he stood numerically eyeball-to-eyeball with Bill Clinton and George Bush. The man without a party had already held his national convention, on television, but he was yet to actually give his acceptance speech.

It has been that kind of year, as the old and new ways of conducting and covering politics in America have collided and merged so that the once familiar outlines of the nation's public discourse now seem completely transformed. Politics 1992-style is a reversal of what is known in physics as the Heisenberg Principle (observing a process alters the process itself); observing this year's political phenomenon—Bill Clinton's titanic tryst with media character cops, for instance, or Perot's self-propulsion over the airwaves—has altered the way the professional observers do their jobs. This has been the year when what is being called 'New News' (infotainment, talk-show politics and pop-culture treatment of breaking stories) has begun to overwhelm the straitlaced coverage and chin-stroking analysis of "Old News."

—*U.S. News and World Report*[17]

. . . high technology has induced a confusion between spacial and temporal boundaries, collapsing the conventions that formerly distinguished fantasy from reality and creating a third, quite polemical cognitive space: that of simulation. . . . In simulation, perception is formulated through media (mainly visual images) that discard all types of categorical distinctions—temporal, geographical, and even physical . . .—leaving signs to look at each other intertextually for signification. Simulation enables us to understand, for instance, how contemporary collective memory is made up of television programs instead of a shared notion of history.

—Celeste Olalquiaga[18]

The secondary structure of subordinate channels is, like everything else that enters into framing, capable of itself being transformed. Channels—subordinate tracks—ostensibly for dealing with one kind of activity, once they are established, may be exploited for other purposes. . . . It is the same kind of transformation which happens with games, where once again, activity pursued for its own sake becomes a *spectacle* for outsiders to watch.

—Tom Burns[19]

Although Ross Perot was often discussed as the "wild card" in the 1992 presidential election, I think his third-party candidacy—a candidacy announced on a cable talk show and supported by his own infomercials—served both to open up the game to new forms of campaigning as well as to deal America a relatively conservative and traditional series of narratives. By contrast, the truer "wild card" was Bill

Clinton, a man who not only initiated the alternative press "town-hall" mediated events during this election year, but furthermore learned how to craft a consistently ambiguous narrative capable of embracing its own inherent contradictions, contradictions and narratives that ultimately suited the alternative forms of media he used so well. So it was that the door metaphorically opened by Ross Perot was precisely the one that Bill Clinton was poised to enter, and to enter triumphantly.

It is unusual to interpret a race for the presidency as a postmodern narrative, perhaps because until 1992 the media and the candidates were content to continue the modernist traditions of campaign speeches, advertisements, and debates as the primary sources of information and discussion. But politics and media—always cautious but friendly bedfellows—were altered in 1992. Perhaps, like comfortable lovers, they were simply bored with campaigns as-is and opted for more variety. Or perhaps they got caught up in the desire to be desired, and market shares dictated the expansion of the campaigning to not-for-prime-time sources. Or perhaps it was just an accident—a collision more than a collusion—of time, characters, opportunity, and the fact that the world reached by the media had changed.

> It is as though there are here two major 'models' for human interrelatedness, juxtaposed and alternating. The first is of a society as a structured, differentiated, and often hierarchical system of politico-legal-economic positions with many types of evaluation, separating men (sic) in terms of 'more' or 'less.' The second, which emerges recognizably in the liminal period, is of society as an unstructured or rudimentarily structured and relatively undifferentiated *communitas*, community, or even communion of equal individuals who submit together to the general authority of the ritual elders. —Victor Turner[20]

He [George Stephanopoulos] and James Carville ran the war room so that different campaign segments worked in harmony.
—Matthew Cooper[21]

So what we have here is a politics of cultural rock n roll read as text about power.

Our national contradictions manifest deep economic and racial divisions when, on television, south central Los Angeles erupts in flames and violence. Is this a *riot* or a *rebellion*? The same images produce different interpretations, spins, stories, and sources of meaning. Major networks cover the events as a riot, underground newspapers and the street talk of gangs discuss it as a rebellion. But as a television show it consumes itself—neutralizes itself—quickly, more of a tragic mini-series than a political and social awakening. Besides, there are other stories circulating, competing, vying for screenage; wilder than the woeful carnage of human perfidity, less depressing than streets and buildings on fire, and more compelling than a metropolitan apocalypse, screenage to capture the imagination.

On 19 May, Vice-President Dan Quayle gives a speech in which he charges that the television show "Murphy Brown," by showing a single mother choosing to have a child, expounds the wrong values for American families.

Several commentators suggest that perhaps Dan Quayle favors abortion after all, if a single mother isn't supposed to . . .

Dan Quayle says that is not what he meant. When he later appears on "Larry King Live," he says if it were his daughter, he would support whatever decision she made. Marilyn Quayle, the next morning, says that isn't what Dan meant.

Addressing a meeting of Jesse Jackson's Rainbow Coalition, Clinton strongly denounces "racist" comments made by rap singer Sister Souljah.

On 3 June, Clinton follows Mandy Grunwald's advice at Hillary's urging and appears on the "Arsenio Hall Show." (Hillary was impressed with Hall's "responsible actions" toward the LA rebellion/riots.) He performs "Heartbreak Hotel" on his saxophone. When asked if he smoked marijuana, he admitted that he did, but that he "didn't inhale."

On 6 June, Clinton appears on MTV to answer questions from host Tabitha Soren and members of the audience. The crowd looks overly cleaned up and Clinton looks overly dressed up, but the occasion is significant. Political narrowcasting follows entertainment narrowcasting and the role of the dominant press is neutralized.

Following the presidential
election, jazz saxophonist
David Sanborn is asked what
he would do to improve Bill
Clinton's musical abilities.
"Inhale," he said. By contrast,
at the MTV Ball, Kenny G
says Clinton is really an excellent saxophone player, a good
man to jam with.

When Bill Clinton appeared on the "Arsenio Hall Show" and played the sax in dark shades, the song he chose was classic rock n roll, Elvis Presley's "Heartbreak Hotel." The words he didn't have to sing, at least two generations of Americans knew them by heart. But this song, as it was played that night, was not about lyrics. It was about politics, rock n roll style.

Music is what happens in the spaces between the notes, and perhaps this too is true of American politics. By the end of his careful solo, an ironic moment given the words to the song he played rather than crooned, he had made a powerful symbolic gesture straight from his heart, unscripted, an interplay of creativity dispersed across a field of constraints, a plea to those of us who heard its call, his call, for a new nation to rise up,

a rock n roll nation,

a nation capable of embracing, celebrating, its own internal contradictions.

If there hadn't been the Los Angeles riots/rebellion, and if Arsenio Hall hadn't impressed Hillary Clinton with his talk about responsibil-ity in the time of the disaster, and if Mandy Grunwald (Clinton's advertising consultant) hadn't pushed the whole deal, and maybe if he had chosen some other song . . . well, it's hard to say, isn't it? What we can say is this: In a world made out of images and sounds,

an imagined nation,

sounds and images count.

So it is that rock n roll operates fully upon an imagined stage, a video soundstage fantastic, and it is there on that stage that a profound public identity can be fashioned and resources for mass audience identification can be found. Its beauty, its truth, is *not* the articulation of one particular image of beauty nor one Olympian truth, but instead is rock n roll's native ability to connect vastly disperate particulars to an imagined sense of a universal: not one voice, but the voices of many understood as one; not one image, but the collective, often unconscious resources of multiple images layered and stacked on some perceived sense of the here and now.

LET'S PARTY! THE DEMOCRATIC CONVENTION

> The position of the senior or paramount chief among the Ndembu, as in many other African societies, is a paradoxical one, for he represents both the apex of the structured politico-legal hierarchy and the total community as an unstructured unit. He is, symbolically, also the tribal territory itself and all its resources.
> —Victor Turner[22]

> Human beings respond equally well to the real and to the imagined.
> —Sigmund Freud[23]

> . . . explanation comes to be regarded as a matter of connecting action to its sense rather than behavior to its determinants.
> —Clifford Geertz[24]

The Democratic National Convention had to work perfectly and be stylishly entertaining. In a media-nation where virtual reality and perfect simulation coalesce to produce masterpieces of staging and graphic fun, the party with the best convention is equated with the party that can bring off the running of the country. What we see, after all, is what we will get. A political convention, then, must be a theater of—and for—the public imagination.

An image, especially one produced and reproduced by the media, is no longer tied to experienced reality or the reality of everyday life.

It becomes an independent reality unto itself: "the media provides the public with the illusion of reality and actuality.

—Denzin[26]

Images and impressions substitute for personal experience. As a *simulacrum* or image, a signifier or expression without a signified or content, is widely reproduced and reified, especially by the mass media, it becomes a commodity.

The reality to which the imagery refers is the reality created by the imagery (other images) and the hyperreality (signs about signs taken as objective or universalized opinion or truth) it produces and reproduces.

Thus does imagery embed communication. Communication arrives both in abstract and general categories and immediate experiences that may be in contradiction.

—Baudrillard, 1988[25]

Night after night Americans watched a made-for-TV production of images, sounds, values, a version of history and a vision for the future that was—at that time—the most singularly unparalleled celebration of itself, at least in my political memory. What we were exposed to was a series of orchestrated talking pictures that revealed a widely diverse, multicultural and multiracial, cross-gendered and age-inclusive, mostly middle-class and newly poor *audience* of lively, talkative participants.

The podium speaker will be mentioning mothers and children in just a few moments. "Find me a pregnant woman," the NBC director orders his cameramen from his deep-freeze control trailer.

A reference to cultural diversity is coming up shortly. "Find me that Gandhi guy again on the floor."

Bob Squier, a Clinton media advisor: "You elect the coverage you want to watch."

Bill Clinton appears on the cover of *People* magazine. Score another hit for Mandy Grunwald.

A young woman stands near MTV's convention space. Does she work for this hot New News network? "Nope," she says. "I work at CBS. But I'm trying to get a job at MTV."

The show was an on-time display of leadership and management, of the uptempo and the politically correct, of the new domination of boom-generation values, attitudes, style, color, and music that demonstrated the ability *to do a good thing well and to do it because it is the right thing.* Woodstock Nation, cleaned-up and finally out of the woods after all these years, appears before us *as* us, and this time—regardless of our ages—to proclaim not only the need to love and trust everyone (not just those under thirty) but first and foremost, *to fix the economy.* That we could be *trusted* to fix the economy and *not* just proclaim love for everyone.

> *Ross Perot calls a news conference and bows out of the race. Calls it off. Says he is impressed by what he has seen this week on television. Tells his supporters that he loves them. Asks them not to forget why they got into this thing.*

'Bye Ross!

Here's that trust thing again. Mediated trust. Trust-Love. Trust to fix the economy. A lot of good people, smart people, even rich and democratic people trusted Ross Perot and looked what he just did! So what does this teach us? Do you trust The Man, or do you trust The Relationship? Can you have The Relationship unless you *first* trust The

Man? What kind of relationship can you have with the man if you don't? This is about What The Man Is. Who He Is. What He Stands For. This trust thing gets complicated. Everything about it gets capitalized. Complicated because trust is media capital, and because through the Media it gets Capitalized. Complicated because it is Mediated Capitalization *and* therefore Heavily Politicized.

Street level: I mean, how do we "do" Trust? We don't ever really "know" these people. Come on. All we got is what we see on TV.

'Bye Ross . . .

Now, how can we *trust* Bill Clinton? And can we really *know* Hillary? This is on TV. To become president—and First Lady—is to gain wide acceptance for nuances more persuasive than the principles of proposed economic policies, it is to vote approval for one's image of self, for one's images of family and upbringing, for one's images of who and what one can become. For a nation more visually literate than politically wise, for a nation instantly bored with anything less than state-of-the-art graphics and scripting, the conveyance of a candidate's life story to audiences of sophisticated life story consumers requires visual poetry, compelling dramatic action, and a social construction of identity derived from a representative sample of reliable narrators.

'Bye Ross

The task of portraying the candidates of the people as real persons on television fell to Linda Bloodworth-Thomason, long-time friend of the Clintons and producer of prime-time smash hits "Designing Women" and "Evening Shade." What resulted was a picture-perfect video dubbed

"A Place Called Hope"

that weaves the romance of Bill and Hillary's real-life stories with deeply symbolic, almost spiritual, definitely poetic footage of President John F. Kennedy shaking hands with the young Bill Clinton at the White House.

"A torch is passed to a New Generation of Americans . . ."

"A torch is passed to a New Generation of Americans . . ."

At the convention, when this
image beamed across the floor,
a wellspring of passion emerged
spontaneously; voices cried out;
there was reverent applause,
there probably wasn't a dry eye
in the house.

Interspersed with these dominant images and themes are excerpts from interviews with family members and friends, a subtle subtext of real-people values and beliefs swelling to a crescendo of hope spelled Clinton. Witnesses to what we imagine as the inside story of their outward public lives, we are moved by Bill's standing up to his alcoholic stepfather, by his tenderness at the birth of his daughter, Chelsea, by the love he has for his brother, and for the loss he still feels for the father he never met.

But Bill's story is not a solo song, but a many-storied story, an ensemble of voices, an expanding collage of shots, images, and angles. Centermost in many of these scenes is a recurring image of Hillary Rodham Clinton in a back-porch country setting, loose and casual like never before, recounting her story-book romance at Yale and later in Arkansas with the man-who-would-be-president. In these scenes she is smiling, girlish, awash in light, happy in the open air, and very pretty. The words she speaks are sweet-smart, partly drawn from schoolgirl nostalgia but tempered now with an adult sense of complexity. What she says seems somehow less important than the event of saying it *this* way, in *this* setting, in this *voice*. Hers is the voice of a lover and a wife, a mother and a lawyer, a reader of great literatures and a watcher, maybe, of some trash. What she combines is what she must combine if her husband is to be successful: She combines *opposites*, and they find in her voice, her presence—on screen—a sense of *unity in their contrasts*. Through these mediated images and sounds, Hillary Clinton is hereby transformed. She becomes what we make of her, but what we make of her is shaped by a script most of us never knew existed. We knew her as smart and sassy—a kind of a Joan Jett to the lawyer set—but here she plays more like a Sweet Melissa to Bill Clinton's gypsy ways.

The video is wrapped from beginning shot to ending moment with an old black-and-white photograph of downtown Hope, Arkansas.

The sign on the store says, simply:

Hope

What does this sign signify? Is it just a four-letter word to mark a small place, back there somewhere in time? Or is it, played to the warmer keys of the public imagination, a kind of symbolic birthplace? Not just Bill Clinton's birthplace, but a birthplace of the imagination that resides within us?

The connection of beginnings and endings in HOPE-FUL images further supports the theme of spiritual connections, of the useful commingling of the new and the old, of the unlikely intersections ultimately responsible for launching great destinations. Against that last shot we hear Bill's still-youthful, most-heartfelt, ultimately sincerest voice proclaiming that "I still believe in a place called Hope . . . ."

"I still believe in a place called Hope." The words scrolled across the Tele-PrompTer and thundered across America. . . . as autumn nears, the campaign knows its political salvation will come not in the minutiae of tax policy but in the elaboration of biography.
—*U.S. News and World Report*[27]

Memo from George Bush. Message: I Care.

Virtual politics is born over the weekend of July 18th, when a cadre of media analysts, entertainment industry producers, directors, and writers gather at a California Chateau. "Their plan: to combine Clinton's Arsenio Hall success with the 'Murphy Brown' controversy. They will, in other words, address the audience/electorate in both its roles simultaneously."
—Charles Paul Freund[28]

Ironically, prime-time network coverage of the convention was severely curtailed. Because the events were totally staged for prime-time audiences, network execs now found them unworthy of much airtime. In this gesture was a meaning far more profound than irony can account for. The old politics of insider-trading and institutional formations was being replaced by what Charles Paul Freund called "the new political TV, in which (the audience/electorate) is the center of the drama."

Viewed this way, the successful production of diversity, infotainment disguised as political partying, and a pastiche economics of style induced—or at least encouraged—the audience/electorate to identify their selves, their lives, and their values with those depicted on TV.

Even when they clashed.

Images that "clash" and stories that reveal "contradictions" can add up to a imagined sum, a bottom-line of the American *democratic* imagination called "balance."

Even when they were sufficiently complex to contain contradictions.

Albert Gore,

Senator from Tennessee,

now vice-presidential candidate,

was the man chosen for the nomination for what the mainstream and alternative media described as "balance." Born in the same generation but into vastly different social and political surroundings, he was a wealthy son who contradicted his father and had voluntarily chosen to serve in Vietnam, his Harvard education complemented Bill's Yale, as a senator he had developed significant foreign-policy expertise where Bill had mastered the fine art of statecraft, he was perceived as a moderate conservative on most economic issues, was a visionary leader in matters of high technology, and at the same time was widely regarded as a radically liberal advocate on behalf of the environment. And there was Tipper, who, alongside Hillary, was similarly educated, socially situated, and dedicated to children's issues, but was a full-time mom not a big-time lawyer, and when it came down to the everyday politics of home and family came down rather hard on the Divine Right of Motherhood side of moral issues, particularly when those issues were related to rock n roll lyrics and images.

The American public imagination is a mediated *communication* environment.

> *Communication is the moment-to-moment working out of the tensions between our need to maintain order (constraint) and the need to promote change (creativity). As such, communication is the material manifestation of consciousness.*
> —Eric M. Eisenberg and H. L. Goodall Jr.[29]

It is a territory made for symbolic play and interplays of words, sounds, and images, an everywhere space that exists nowhere, really, an imagined rock concert arena that welcomes information and contextualizes interpretation, makes somethings out of nothings and vice-versa, contra-versa, hyper-versa, it is the homeplace starship and galaxy of every virtual reality.

What these four individuals carved out in the simulated mindscape of the American public imagination was a precious image of balance, a possible new forum for democratic communication, a

center for dialogue

among respectful, but often contradictory, political positions, personal values, and life experiences. Within their overtly scrutinized public and private lives, each of them represented the best and worst of their American generation (an image that begs the audience to fill-in-the-blanks on what constitutes which), the best and worst of being women and men, the best and worst of the rights and wrongs that simulated our well-imagined media-nation. And this: Clinton's presidential text was already open to multiple, conflicting interpretations, but the addition of Al and Tipper Gore to the ticket *exponentially increased the available narrative space,* intertextual referents and confusions, resources for meanings capable of endlessly diverse interpretations.

And yet, within all of this calculus of wonder, within all this new physics of American politics, surrounding it, too, was now an

image of a center that could indeed
H O L D

because it could, indeed, *be imagined as holding.*
It was theoretical center, like some mysterious quark, that itself was

created of a chaotic, seemingly random openness somehow deeply at peace with the vast, first-cast spell of infinity. This was *cosmic* rock n roll.

MADISON SQUARE GARDEN, THE CONVENTION CENTER, APPEARING LIVE AND IN CONCERT TONIGHT FOR THE VERY FIRST TIME IN THE IMAGINED HISTORY OF AMERICAN POLITICS . . . A MAN WITH A PLAN, A MAN WHO CAN JAM, A MAN WHO CAME BACK FROM THE DEAD TO LEAD US TO A MORE LIBERAL PROMISED LAND . . . YOU KNOW WHO I MEAN . . . LADIES AND GENTLEMEN, CITIZENS OF THIS GREAT DEMOCRATIC REPUBLIC, DENIZENS OF THIS MEDIATED NARRATIVE SPACE . . . BEFORE I INTRODUCE THAT MAN AS OUR FEATURED MAIN EVENT, I AM PROUD TO GIVE YOU HIS HAND-PICKED OPENING ACT, THE DISTINGUISHED LEADER OF THE SENATE BRAT PACK, OUR VICE-HERO, THE NEXT VICE-PREZ'DENT OF THESE UNITED STATES OF AMERICA . . .

FROM THE GREAT STATE OF TENNESSEE!!!

albert gore jr.!!!!!

I have waited for this moment my whole life . . . to appear here in Madison Square Garden as the warm-up act for Elvis.
— Vice-Presidential nominee Al Gore

He was, indeed, the warm-up act. For Elvis. Eloquent without over-shadowing the featured speaker, prosaic rather than fully poetic, sincere and inspirational without spelling out, exactly, the course of the nation's salvation, vice-presidential candidate Albert Gore Jr. of Tennessee performed admirably. The audience was warm. The stage was set.

A presidential nomination speech is a rhetorical rite of passage in American politics. As a party ritual, it must unify the previously opposing camps, but its larger ritual function for the media-nation is to speak a dream into consciousness, to word a series of hopes and promises that satisfy our deep national longing for political, social, and, ultimately, *democratic* fulfillment.

The speech is, analogically, also a song. This year, an American rock n roll song. It evokes an *evolution* of *all* American rock n roll songs. Spiritual inspiration arises from the mystery of the Delta blues, a basic musical form capable of accommodating and developing stylish jazzy solos rendered in the overall tempo of pop. There are a series of calls and responses that add up musically to one grand call and response. Rhythms are spoken rhythmically to remind us of the Sermon on the Mount delivered—sung—secularly in slow pulsating couplets, in quick, poignant prose licks, a chorus of sound bites, a kind of steady electric Whitmanesque celebration of its all-inclusive wide poetic self, evidence by harmonics, proof in the singing from sea to shining sea.

If you are a Democrat living at this vanishing end of the twentieth century, these sounds offer true salvation, a salvation that itself has always been part and parcel of the party song, and you hear in them the purposeful evocation—the mythic presence—of

FDR   JFK   LBJ

and Jimmy Carter. Charismatic lyrics carry the solemnity of every soulful teenage love song, and its message, like the classic teenage love lyric, is always one of revolution. Personal revolution. Social revolution. Our revolution. An American revolution.

An American Democratic Revolution.

Get it?
I said:

Do You Get It?

Hey, you *know* what I mean. Yeah, *that*. And *that* too.

Those who didn't "get it," who didn't hear the music in the words and understand them as *only* rock n roll can be understood, well, those people remain Republicans. They still don't get it.

Even when they do.

Presidential nominee Bill Clinton spoke
very close to a full hour, but this time,
this time, to rounds of wildly
enthusiastic

applause
! ! !

"Don't Stop Thinkin' About Tomorrow . . ."

On stage the family of Clinton, the family of Gore, the family of extended families of all

Democratic families are dancin'.

DANCIN'

for God's Sake!

Tipper and Hillary hug and hold hands

Rock n Roll!

Al does the best he can

Rock n Roll!!

Bill sings the real words and sways while he dances

This is, indeed, Rock n Roll!!!

Lester Bangs, famous rock critic and dead man,
said the central message of rock n roll
was to keep the party goin'

To keep the Party goin'

At the end of this rite of passage, this televised symbolic rite of passage, this dance of celebration and hope, something happened to the shape of things to come. The known boundaries that had once so confidently defined the acceptable mainstreams of the dominant American political culture were irrevocably redrawn by resistance influences, redefined by multiple narrative penetrations, removed by a generation reared on revolution and now rich and resourceful enough to reassert itself.

In a way, all this gospel truth telling and orchestrated symbolic dancing could be just a big-screen advertisement for the rhetorical reinvention of a generational self in the image of Bill Clinton. After all, baby boomers are good at this stuff: We are good at making identifications with self the point of all social interactions, good at peak experience partying, good at "doing" television as a substitute for living outside our living rooms and dens.

We like ourselves well enough to watch ourselves—and hear ourselves—being ourselves on *television* whenever we can. We of the home video and home recording studio, we of the funniest home videos and MTV. We of the great car stereos, hot stars in fast cars everywhere digging our own cool music. We of the owned image of mediated intimacy: think here *personal* stereos, *personal* televisions, *personal* VCRs, *personal* home computers, even *personal* software for the *personal* hardware that increasingly expands our virtual realities. We—those of us who still read—of the *personal* columns. We—those of us who access our souls mainly through the necessary sweat of our bodies—of the *personal* home gym, the *personal* workouts, the *personal* trainer. In this kind of personally mediated nation— this kind of personally imagined, rhetorically identified audio and video culture—why would we not respond to the images of a candidate—to two candidates and their wives and families and sentiments—that correspond to our *personal* own?

Hey, look, like this: We first trust each other's images, then maybe we trust each other; then, possibly, we listen carefully to what each other happen to be saying; then, mostly, we learn how to tolerate our differences. This is how we make politics personal. This is how we live.

Down even lower, into our personal media zones, like this: What we do in the privacy of our own homes, our own cars, our own offices, is to observe ourselves and each other being ourselves for each other, often wisely. Thereby we *experience* ourselves, mediated by our evaluation of the worth, the value, of personal images. There is nothing new in this. Nothing. What is new is that we are so seldom satisfied with the images we find there, that we create, that we live within. So, what this generation has learned to do, in the privacy of our living rooms (how much "living" actually goes on there? Or is "living" increasingly what flickers on the dominant screens and filters through the speakers, while we comment on it?) and dens (is this a metaphor for mediated "camping out," something that used to be done out-of-doors?), is to engage in constant *personal therapies of self-improvement* in order to sell images of who we might be to our selves and each other because we long, always, for the deep experiencing of something beyond the surfaces we know we covet and become.

Therefore:

A candidate's image—his narrative representation—in sum, must strive to evoke by parallel what we, ourselves— our personal selves—are trying to become. More important, that candidate must be *similarly life-situated.* Historied. *Similarly pained.* Scarred. *Similarly conflicted.*

It helps, obviously, if he listens to the same music. And jogs. And eats at McDonald's. It helps most if he does all of these things publicly in images and narratives that constantly revisit his pasts in light of the futures he has articulated. For a *polysemic nation*—a nation made up of many voices—perhaps only a *multiphrenic personality*—a personality dispersed across many mediated roles, images, and surfaces—will do. For a nation involved in personal therapies, perhaps only a candidate delivering what Mimi White calls "Tele-Advising" will do. Listen, friends, to what Dr. White says about this:

. . . no one really expects advertisements to deliver on their purported promises. Consumer fulfillment has less to do with any single product and its local effects than with the narrative fantasy it instigates.

Indeed the value of advertising is that it sells these fantasies as much as it sells specific products; it provides a context in which buying products in general is associated with the lifestyle images and values that advertisements project.

Moreover, this version of the therapeutic ethos, whose ability to generate narrative extends beyond advertising (which nonetheless remains the paradigmatic text of consumer culture), pervades almost all modes of mass mediated culture that include a significant narrative or interpersonal discourse.[31]

Do you get it, yet?

So it was that politics—American media style, rock n roll spectacle, therapy of the self generation, life as TV—became intensely personal in the presidential election of 1992. Viewed from the Democratic majority, this meant the party was over and the real work or organizing the vote remained to be done.

Viewed from the still unsettled but largely confident perspective of the Republican regime, what had transpired at the Democratic National Convention was cause for jokes about Bill and Hillary (Bill and Hill are approached by the Devil, who tells them he can make them the best Prez and First Woman in history. Bill says, "Yeah, big red one, but what's the catch?" Devil smiles, "It will cost you your souls . . . ." Hillary looks at Bill and both of them say, "So what's the catch?") and a need to go on a fishing/working vacation (yeah, right) in the white people's paradise of upper Wyoming.

Imagine the talk:

Who could believe these guys, huh? I mean, really, who in their right mind could take these young dope-smoking,   draft-dodging,

seriously? Get Real!

Crazy music, more tax and spend, gaw, I mean, jeez, isn't this about *character*? About *'xperience*? About, heh, heh—hey Jim, eh Bar—*money*?

The failure to take seriously the challenge posed by the other side, the outright blatant sneering rich egocentric elitist domination patronizing gall of ignoring them, was portrayed as "confidence" by Repubs, but was interpreted widely as further evidence that the president just wasn't in touch with the country. He just didn't get it. Maybe he didn't want to—or have to.

The cover of *Esquire* magazine used an Alfred E. Neuman characterization of the president and featured an article called "How George Bush Went Crazy in the White House." The article detailed how a man who smoothly made his way up from rich white man's son to the top of the rich white people's administration on the strengths of being "nice" and making "friends" and speaking in clichés suddenly discovered that the world was not entirely made up of people who responded well to those virtues. *And this surprised him.* Not only did it surprise him, it personally defeated him. Rendered him blank-minded and kind of spacey. He moved through the White House as a White Person who increasingly felt the presence of ghosts because he felt like maybe he was turning into one. From one "working vacation" to the next he increasingly spoke only to his closest friends, white people who could reassure him that the old values, the old virtues, the old clichés, still worked. Hey, we're having fun, aren't we?

Rolling Stone magazine featured a very confident Bill Clinton on its cover with the White House within his reach, and ran an in-depth interview by top-gun investigative journalists, including that notorious conservative Republican prose slinger P. J. O'Rourke and the equally notorious radical gonzo Hunter S. Thompson, with Jan Wenner, and William Greider serving here as ironic economic and social-centering strategies. Although all the journalists expressed some doubts about Clinton and/or his programs, all of them came away from the experience with respect for his mind, his vision, and his ability to take heat up-close and personally. Maybe, *just maybe,* they all seemed to be hinting. *Rolling Stone* magazine endorsed his candidacy, enthusiastically.

No matter what I read, what I watched, what I overheard, what I overtly heard, this election was clearly coming down to a generational and cultural clash. A clash of values. Of visions. Of histories. Of herstories. Of power. The lines were indelibly etched into every conversation, every cartoon, every editorial. It was the sixties again, lived here in the nineties. And like the sixties, it was messy. Very messy.

This would be close.

In August

Republicans met

in Houston!

On TV it was a

gathering of mostly

White People

angry White People,

complicit with the Regime,

old and with obvious money.

(The entire contents—including the racist, sexist ravings—of the Republican National Convention mercifully deleted here . . .)

To save space, or maybe just

to marginalize it,

certainly to use irreverently

the virtual image and poetics of

the Christian Cross it claims to bear

whose dull nails are, all too clearly,

put there by the rest of us.

Do you get it yet?

HYPERREALITY, ROCK THE VOTE, MURPHY'S BABY, AND THE MAGIC BUS

So it was that politics—always taken personally in America—became personal in the campaign of 1992. The lines were drawn: "We are America," Richard N. Bond, GOP chairman, gushed about his

Republicans. "Those other people are not America." Those "other people"—the images of "other people"—were, of course, Democrats. And so the issues became clear. *Not* just the economy, stupid; *that* issue was the concern of the prime-time cast and editorial crew. But for the marginalized families, the dispossessed un- and underemployed, the simply hungry, the increasingly poor, the people of color, many of the women, many of the young, most of the rock n rollers, the gays and lesbians, the liberal Yuppies, and the rest of the blurred genres of those disconnected "other people," this election was finally about *power*, the power to define an image capable of uniting the states of enchantment *and* of difference, the possible America of our singularly collective unconscious dreams.

The Clinton-Gore campaign deepened the personal touch with the rockstar-like tour on the Magic Bus, an image—for those of us who lived through the sixties—straight out of a Who tune carrying the cultural baggage of serious fun, playful utilities, and an adventurous quest toward the ultimate personal goal of freedom of choice. Choice of lifestyle, choice of life, choice of music.

MTV deepened the personal touch while subtly reinforcing the key "alternative" message of the Clinton-Gore ticket with the spectacularly successful media campaign "Rock the Vote." While not advocating any particular candidate or party, the MTV visual artists ambiguously but strategically placed the word "Choice" in their slogan: "It's your choice; it's your future." Because the Democrats were running the only "choice" campaign, and because the "future" they portrayed certainly included the MTVers, this vehicle served, perhaps, to remind MTV audiences of the importance of "choice" in—and to—their lives.

On 17 September, a new episode—the revenge episode—of "Murphy Brown" aired. Murphy's baby is eased into a peaceful sleep by the sax chorus from "Heartbreak Hotel," and Murphy sez, "Pretty cool, huh?" If ever there was an image of the future-as-television, this was it. The future—represented by the Unknown Fathers and Choosing Mothers that produce Our Children—can sleep peacefully, safely, with the channel locked onto the presidential candidate who knows how to close a set watching over the rock n roll Republic all thru the nite.

Somewhere in mid-September, somewhere between the airing of revenge episodes and the rock touring of buses and the new Republican commercials featuring big trucks, cowboy boots, and country music, our mainstream media-nation merged fully into the high-velocity lanes of hyperreality. What was only months before considered alternative media—the talk shows, the music channels, the popular magazines—became virtually indistinguishable from any other form of commercial—or communicative—appeal.

(We interupt this program to bring you an important message from our theoretical—read: corporate—sponsor):

To say that politics is personal is like saying talk between people is digital.

But talk between people is *both* digital *and* analogic; it is about facts and fantasies, the blurring and merging of language and image worlds into simpler sentences that only barely contain them.

(Now back to our regularly scheduled program . . .)

Politics is, therefore, analogic too. Like talk, politics is mediated—which is to say that it is saturated with images and languages—which is to say that the digital acquires meaning, conceptual framing, from the analogic.

Just when the election seemed simple enough, when the choice seemed clear enough, Ross Perot reentered the campaign. His single issue would be the economy, with special emphasis on reducing the federal deficit; he would pay for his own campaign; he would use television infomercials to take his case to the American people; and he would expect to be invited to participate in the televised debates. And yes, he was in this thing to win!

FROM THE LEFT, STREET-LEVEL: Why did he do it? Why did he do it, now? Why did he drop out in the first place? Was this just an ego trip for a short man with big money?

FROM THE MAIN-STREAM MEDIA PUNDITS: How would the Perot vote influence the election? Did his clear focus on the economy draw closer attention to the details of Clinton's plan or Bush's absence of one?

FROM THE RIGHT, STREET-LEVEL: Go Ross Go! Run Ross Run! Win Ross Win! You are right about all of it, wrong about none of it, and the only man in this chicken fight who will change shit in Warshin'tun.

FROM ROSS: I got out of this race because there were people who would have ruined my daughter's wedding. I'm waiting for George Bush to apologize to me, personally, for this.

FROM THE LEFT, STREET-LEVEL: Is this guy paranoid, or what? There were *what*? Viet Cong in his front yard and only he could see them? Yeah, right. This man is more dangerous than we thought. Crazy.

FROM THE MAINSTREAM MEDIA PUNDITS: Is this a plausible account? Where are the facts to support his allegations? Can we believe this private investigator he hired? And wouldn't one of the richest men in the world be able to provide his own security for his own daughter's wedding?

FROM THE RIGHT, STREET-LEVEL: I knew there was a reason, goddammit! Ross wouldn't lie to us. If he says Bush had dirty tricks goin' on, then you know he did. It was his daughter's weddin', for god's sake.

Facts, perceptions, framing, imagination, lived experiences, and the realities we make out of words and lives—that's all we have because this is what we are. Beliefs and passions, images and sounds, infinite framing. There is a current Magnavox commercial on, with John Cleese playing the trusted truth-teller/sensemaker/spokesmodel, in which larger and larger televisions are advertised in shorter and shorter time frames, and the speech about them simply becomes faster and more meaningless to cope with the senselessness of the actions called for by the script. At framing's end, we are left with Cleese trying too hard to smile and a screen captured by the corporate logo. Is this a metaphor? Isn't everything these days a metaphor?

Some metaphors are better than others. On the campaign trail, President Bush refers to Clinton and Gore as "those Bozos" and repeatedly trashes Gore as "The Ozone Man" in reference to Gore's environmental advocacy. Neither of these metaphors seems to inspire the sort of public response hoped for by Republicans.

And some metaphors seem like the last aural drift from a distant echo. Remember the "Morning in America" or "There is a Bear in these woods" ad campaigns for Reagan-Bush?

DEBATES

The American media operate in self-interested ways—they will present only those images most likely to attract an audience and thus to make money. They are also self-serving, conservative critics argue; they report only news critical to the administration, with which they have an adversarial relationship.

Radical critics argue the opposite, that the news media disseminate only those opinions that maintain and serve the status quo.

In either case, the issue is the power of media accounts to substitute for reality. The fear is that their accounting of the world will not provide the appropriate basis for sound public opinion.

—Joli Jensen[34]

True political debating would not be a media-controlled misnomer, nor would it be a carnival, nor a spectacle. Candidates would simply argue the issues, respond to each other directly, probably become passionate in defense of themselves and their ideas, and perhaps in the end the electorate would be better served because we would have a more rational basis upon which to base voting decisions about the good of the country. At least this is how debates are fantasized, usually by debate coaches and media pundits.

But is the infrastructure in place to support such a reality? I don't think so. The world has changed, and with it the whole notion of what constitutes political campaigning and debating has irrevocably altered. Some basic issues: What is "rational" in a postmodern society? What are the "issues"? Do people vote because of what is "best for the country"? Have they ever behaved this way?

Add to these infrastructure concerns the special, intimate relationship between media and candidates. Prime-time coverage is a commercial enterprise, not a democratic one. The interests that get articulated in the form of questions raised, positions taken, even insults traded, are vested interests. MTV gets invited to the debates, but cannot sponsor them. And this year's prize format for one debate—real people asking real questions for which the candidates may or may not really be prepared—may indeed **"flatten the hierarchy" between candidates and voters,** but it seems to do so in precisely the same way that flattening the hierarchy in a classroom does: Mainstreaming produces *democratic mediocrity*, not excellence.

Aside from Perot's caustic humor, the only memorable sequence is when a woman asks President Bush how the recession has affected him, personally.

Although effective in demonstrating how little he has in common with most Americans and how out of touch with middle-class concerns he is, it's a bit too much like the sort of questioning that occurs on *Donahue* or *Oprah*.

And let's not talk too much about the vice-presidential square-off, okay? An old admiral, obviously addled and brutally honest about the frankly mundane, gets in a few words edgewise in an otherwise scripted presentation by an amateur golfer who has been told to appear assertive and a fellow who has obviously confused this opportunity to smile and crack wise with the need to speak rationally about policies and issues.

Bill Clinton's debate points were mostly won on the strength of his conversational style, his ability to move about and maintain eye contact with the audience when speaking, and his consistent need to demonstrate that he has a plan with numbered subheadings. Contrasted with George Bush's "I'm not very good on details . . . I stand for principles and values" approach, and Perot's feisty "look here, there are plans to solve our problems all over Warshin'tun, we've paid for them, and I will put together the best minds on these things as soon as I'm elected Pres'dent," the media choice was like voting for a four-year contract on a television program that would pit an excruciatingly well-researched documentary against a series of near-fifties reruns and an amusing but potentially dangerous sitcom about the foibles of a capital city narrated by a short man with large ears and too much money for our own good.

Who won and who lost the debates seem like the wrong questions here. It would be like asking the same questions about commercials for new shows, or cars, or detergents. Postmodern rationality asserts a popular appreciation for surface appeals that also values the singular ability to switch "satisficers" (Herbert Simon's term for non-optimal decision possibilities)[33] from vunerable nostalgia to commercially sanctioned products to the info-news with the speed of a practiced thumb stroke on the remote. Viewed this way, the infrastructure is built upon the skip of the electronic fantastic, a series of moves around the screen that asks not what your country can do for you, or what you can do for your country, but instead what do we want to watch tonight, honey, for the next four years?

Viewed this way, it is *not* alternative media but media alternatives that guide the remote. I mean, what *isn't* a talk show any more, exactly? Or this way: The surfaces of media—television, magazines, newspapers, music, radio (and yes, even scholarly essays and books)—can be reframed as both the *resources of* and the *therapeutic alternatives to* our various postmodern conditions. If this were physics, the big picture of these mediated interactions would be like some sort of expanding/collapsing universe made up of electronic blips that traverse the virtual space, call them "nomadic symbolic discourse communities" that are themselves formed—sucked in by some irresistible impulse, some quark—and then at the precise moment of their most precious joining, understanding, sharing, are inexplicably exploded back apart, tossed out into that dark weightless electronic night, fragmentary and disconnected, with only vague rapidly disappearing memories of any meaningful experience. We are the postmodern mediated America of the free-floating signifiers, the nomadic "we" who are always waiting, anticipating, bad-mouthing, and yet searching desperately for the chance inevitability of being sucked in again on another channel of desiring and dissatisfaction.

But this isn't physics, even if the metaphor survives a kind of cyborg-neurotic surface appeal. This is politics. This is the secret inside the surprise that lies beneath the discursive surfaces of postmodern sense making. And because this is politics . . . *Shhhhhhhh*! Listen: This is what we have made up, what we have brought into existence through the commercial interface of our human/technological forming, a virtual democracy where what we see is never what we get because it can't be, because the difference between us and it isn't distinct anymore, and our vote—that singular expression of judgment, of value, of understanding, of hope—is more of an overdetermined purchase based on images than it is a rational decision based on facts. What we are buying is not a candidate, nor a platform, nor even a half-hearted belief in promises; what we are buying is stock in the overall show, which is to say stock in many mediated corporations and their spokesmodels, and what we are buying into is a future in which commercial organizations, not nations—*images of organizations*, not national characters—chart our collective course.

Now do you get it? Don't tell anyone. This is *our* secret.

DECISION '92: VIEWS FROM THE MARGINS

For communitas has an existential quality; it involves the whole man in his relation to other whole men.

Structure, on the other hand, has cognitive quality; as Levi-Straus has perceived, it is essentially a set of classifications, a model for thinking about culture and nature and ordering one's public life.

Communitas has also an aspect of potentiality; it is often in the subjunctive mood. Relations between total beings are generative of symbols and metaphors and comparisons; art and religion are their products rather than legal and political structures.

—Victor Turner[34]

So who do you believe in? What artform appeals to you? What kind of music do you listen to, blend the lyrics of your lifestyle into? Which video representation tells the story that validates and maybe uplifts your life? Whose words—what ju-ju—make the magic happen—at least a little bit—for you?

Today, 3 November 1992, you choose. By tonight it will all be over. Tomorrow morning it will be a memory. And by tomorrow night you will be more concerned with Murphy Brown again, or the new release by a Seattle grunge band/St. Louis rap artist/Tampa country group, or Rush Plegmbaugh's latest dangerous mind-sult. Just more of the same thing. Might as well buy a new car, refinance the old house, change allegiances from Wal-Mart to K-Mart, at least for awhile.

The week of the election one of my most favorite—and certainly the wisest, deepest, best-writing, and overall most provocative— marginalized journalists, Michael Ventura, writes this in the *Los Angeles Weekly*:

> Oh, I wish I could vote for Bill Clinton. I wish I could go into that little booth and fucking punch the fucking card for fucking Bill. Wouldn't I feel righteous, wouldn't I have done the right thing, with right people, at the right time, at last? Anyway, it should be easy for me: I'm one of the few people I know who genuinely like Bill Clinton!
>
> What many call 'slick' I see as disciplined. It took a heroic discipline to face the most vicious scrutiny day after day without flinching or fading. George Bush is only good in a crisis and then only when he has the numbers on his side; Ross Perot retreated even with $2 billion on his side; Bill Clinton was good when nothing was on his side. What Bush does poorly, Clinton does well: I'm talking about the mix of equivocation, obfuscation, outright lies, shadowy maneuvers and smarmy style with which politicians survive. Clinton has proved his mastery of fundamental political craft as practiced by Jefferson, Jackson, Lincoln, both Roosevelts, Eisenhower, and Johnson—our most effective presidents.
>
> Blessed are the slick, for they shall get things done.
>
> The Clinton quality that people call 'wonk' (as in 'policy wonk') I see as a mechanical yet wide-ranging intelligence capable of retaining enormous amounts of seemingly disparate facts and melding them into a whole: a vision. He may try to Bubba it up, but Clinton's intellect is in range of Nixon's, Johnson's and Kennedy's—men who explained things to others, rather than needing others to explain things to them. A guy who understands the banking system *and* can play a pretty mean sax—that's the kind of president I've been waiting for all my life.
>
> As for Clinton's escapades, draft evasion and assorted character flaws—as a draft evader with a messy sex life and character flaws bordering on the schizophrenic, I have no complaints. We've had rapists, philanderers and, to put it delicately, out-of-the-way sexual preferences in the White House from the start. We've had killers, slavers, crooks, alcoholics, gamblers—addicts of every description. (When President Kennedy was asked by a friend why he allowed his lust to endanger the security of the nation, he replied: 'I can't help it.') We've had crack-ups: Woodrow Wilson, Lyndon Johnson and Richard Nixon were in states of severe mental collapse during the last months of their

presidencies. The White House is a dark place. Clinton will bring to it no darkness that hasn't been there before.

The worst thing I've heard said of Bill Clinton and Al Gore is 'They're the boys from student government.' The class presidents who always raised their hand and had it right. The dorks who did all their homework, so anxious to please, so without their own standards that they had to live up to everyone else's—eager both to fit in and to shine, smoothing over the paradox that to fit in is to be dull while to shine is not to fit in. Isn't voting for such people an admission that they were *right?*

Still, all they want to do is govern—an activity in which originality is suspect and imagination is downright dangerous. Given their limits, they have chosen the proper profession. For they don't appear, at least, to be haunted—as Kennedy, Johnson and Nixon clearly were haunted, spooked by spirits with almost Shakespearean auras: Kennedy as Prince Hal, Johnson as King Lear, Nixon as Richard III. That is what 'greatness' means in practice rather than theory: a sense of mission spiced with a secret longing for catastrophe. Clinton and Gore seem, as yet, free of any hint of greatness. . . .

If the polls are right and we elect Bill Clinton, it won't be because of neighborhood banking or college programs or even health care. (Most of the 37 million Americans without health care are in demographic groups that usually don't vote.) Americans will elect Bill Clinton because they don't think they are making enough money—and they are afraid they'll be making even less money in the future. Bill Clinton knows this, they say, and he's going to try to fix it so more people make more money. Period. End of issues. . . .

The difference between a liberal and a radical is this: a liberal wants American civilization to continue at least at its present level, no matter what the cost to the rest of the world. (That's the practice, despite the liberal's rhetoric.) A radical doesn't. A radical can't vote for Bill Clinton.

As for me . . . part of me is a mushy equivocating liberal . . . [a]nd part of me is a stone cold radical. The liberal in me shudders when Clinton goes down a point in the polls—I worry, I find myself rooting for him, hoping for him—while the radical knows Bush will destroy America faster than Clinton, so Bush is better for the planet, in the long run, than Clinton.

No, I can't vote for Bush. I'm not *that* radical. And a vote for Perot just helps elect Bush. But can I vote for Clinton? . . .

Either way, we are every one of us caught in a merciless history that has a long way to go before it's done humiliating us with the necessity for such decisions.[35]

This expresses, I think, the prevalent rock n roll attitude on election day. Shaded, perspectival, deeply cynical. It expresses a desire to resist domination—domination defined globally and locally as the capital rule of corporate politics, resistance defined operationally as singing the blues about the life you see and lead, while doing the work that allows it to go on, complaining, ultimately, about your very own lack of funds.

Viewed this way, a vote for Bill and Al is a political compromise in a life made up, increasingly, of political compromises. It is rock n roll justified, because, in part, at least these guys know what the blues are, where they came from, and why they are sung, and in part because they have worked very hard to beat the very system that sought to silence them. It is liberally justified because the plan they propose will fundamentally change—in albeit guilty but necessary ways—the fundamental organization of three cornerstones of American civilization—in health care, in education, and in banking—IF, and *only* IF, what they now have on paper does not get further compromised in the House and Senate, which, undoubtedly, it will. And it is media justified, finally, simply because the other alternative candidates aren't. Bush and Perot—chief contenders among the thoroughly marginalized, under-capitalized seven other mostly nameless candidates on ballots in many states—simply don't have the perceived show quality of that BIG IT that Clinton-Gore's media machine at least recognized and, on their best nights, allowed to glow.

Experience in corporations has taught me that in times of intense conflict those losing the battle expand the perimeters of the warfare while those winning the battle struggle mostly to contain it. So as I drive my family back to South Carolina after spending a weekend in Alabama, we listen to the radio—all channels—and when we get home watch television—all channels—on the day of the final vote. From scan and seek to seek and scan, ultimately from remote to remote, I move nomadically across the verbal and visual mindscape of political America.

Rude Rush Limbaugh has decided to hate Bush, make tasteless jokes about Hillary and Chelsea, and predicts, again, that Bill and Al will survive this day only to go on and ruin the country. All the while, he angrily rattles invisible papers and, obviously frustrated that his inflated sense of self-worth hasn't had the desired effect on the electorate, pounds soft fists on some hard desk.	Local AM and FM call-in shows in Huntsville, Chattanooga, Atlanta, and Greenville verbalize a neck-and-neck struggle between Bush and Clinton supporters, with Perot voters proud and sure as ever.	Television news reporters on all stations predict a Clinton victory, a record turnout, and disagree only about the margin for Perot.

Thus, all-channel television wins; local radio call-in shows give voice to diversity; and Limbaugh, Inc., is losing major ground, fast. Surely the end is near. And with it, a beginning.

I walk into the voting booth in Six Mile, South Carolina, and quietly vote my conscience. A kindly elderly poll-worker politely asks me to cover my Clinton-Gore T-shirt because political advertising is not allowed in the polling area on election day. I politely agree. We smile at each other, she is a known Democrat too. In this county we will both vote for the loser, who, in a matter of brief mediated hours, will be declared the national winner. My wife, who is the local Clinton-Gore organizer, emerges from her voting booth and gives us all a victory sign.

Election night we held a local victory party in our home, a party dominated by a television set as the results beamed in. The moment of victory came quickly and just as quickly passed. We won! Nobody knew exactly what to do. Mostly we hugged and laughed, then reached for the remote. Winning was jubilant, but almost anticlimactic, and was now, suddenly, gone. The dominant metaphor was: "I still don't believe it," even after all of the channels agreed to say it was true.

For a campaign that had largely been waged on television, there didn't seem to be anything else to do except continue watching the television. So after all the infocasters got in their licks, we got back to basics, tuned in to C-SPAN coverage of the mainstream Little Rock street scene, which is where it was really happening. These images and sounds made a deeply moving communal statement about a new deal, a new frontier, a great society, and, this one time, an emotional place in the heart called hope that was this late night being joyfully resurrected—talked about, danced to, storied—all across a widely diverse, singing, cojoined, deeply imagined, *better* public America. Around midnight, the gospel choir led us all in what struck me as a summary in an old song sung anew:

> America, America, God shed His Grace on thee,
> And crown thy good,
> With brotherhood,
> From sea to shining sea . . . .

CONCLUSION: BEYOND THE SHOW

Communitas breaks in through the interstices of structure, in liminality; at the edges of structure, in marginality; and from beneath structure, in inferiority.
—Victor Turner[36]

Bill Clinton promised that his campaign would be about change. I took him seriously. My attention was, from the outset, focused not on the issues per se, but on the dialogic acts of issuing and interpreting; hence, my analytical focus was on *the campaign as an agent of change*. Rather than isolating the language of Clinton's plan for change, I instead chose to focus on the language of the media framing—in this case, the alternative media framing—that would ultimately define and shape social interpretations of this ritual process. Because this national election was likely to be the most heavily scripted media performance in the history of politics, and because any regularly repeated national event that has the power to transform the society producing it counts as a ritual process, these choices seemed entirely pragmatic.

As luck would have it, my interest in alternative media turned out to be publicly validated: The campaign for change became ideologically and strategically identified with the use of alternative media as an agent of change. At first this tactic was used to simply take Clinton's message directly to the people through televised town-hall meetings, but these events were so successful that Clinton's media advisors and strategists incorporated them to handle crises, develop rapport with the candidate, attract new voters, and, ultimately, to provide the visual and aural architecture of the appeal.

Similarly, Bill Clinton's successful campaign for change contributed to a significant perceptual and symbolic alterations in the traditional ritual process used to elect the president of the United States. Examined pragmatically, this alteration could be summed up as his campaign's unique ability to combine alternative formats of mass media (e.g., talk shows, televised town meetings) with alternative symbolic forms of persuasion (e.g., rock n roll music, autobiographical video) designed to reach out and speak directly to potential voters. Viewed this way, what changed was the *defining site of cultural and narrative power* in this ritual process: Previously marginalized formats of television shows found themselves center stage, and traditionally powerful news shows, investigative journalists, and well-known pundits were effectively removed from orchestrating the major events of the campaign. It was, in a real sense, an election year in which the well-ordered mediated political world as we knew it was suddenly and strategically turned upside-down by forces of popular culture.

But these rather obvious claims having been made, what I have tried to do in this chapter is to examine the changes in this ritual process as indicative of a more fundamental change in American political culture, a change that positions the mediated upside-down popular culture world as narratively coequal to its well-ordered high culture counterpart. Narratively, we are a rock n roll culture, where *rock n roll can be understood as form of social and political life* that organizes power through the framing of aural and visual space, while rendering lyrically and thematically sensible the diverse, often-contradictory mindscape of American public imagination. I have suggested here that this rock n roll repositioning produces the ritual convergence of structure and anti-structure, a convergence itself indicative of the conflicted yet complicit tensions between modernist and postmodernist forms of organizing meaning and dealing with power.

This rock n roll-as-social-and-political-life conceptual framework shapes—in the interplay of the microevents, imagined relationships, and observed practices of the election ritual—the symbolic and cultural resources useful in assessing one critical dimension of Bill Clinton's political victory: *the struggle for meanings within mediated communities.* For a culture that values the choice of music, costume, style, and attitude as symbolically important to other routinely performed ritual processes—marriages, holiday parties, birthdays, et cetera—a meaningful analog to political rituals does not require much of a stretch. And for a culture that, as Zelda Fitzgerald once expressed it, "lives life by the philosophy of popular songs,"[37] using the narrative power of rock n roll to help shape identification with struggles for meaning evidenced by a candidate, a social movement, or as a political revolution seems entirely fitting. As cultural critic George Lipsitz[38] points out, "struggles for meanings" in popular culture should be assessed as "struggles for resources"; in turn, I believe those resourceful meanings provide dialogic interpretive frameworks capable of securing or negating votes.

A political campaign is a social act, specifically, the social act of organizing. As with any act of organizing, the everyday tensions that define and shape cultural meanings are best understood as the material resources of broader cultural/subcultural/counter-cultural dialogues. Voices are raised as much—and as often—in resistance to, as in harmony with, dominant forms and expressions of sense making. Hence, the interplays of order and anti-order are ever-present but are seldom balanced and, at least until this election campaign, never coequal. In assessing the role of social-as-political organizing in this campaign, strategically deployed forces of mainstream news coverage actually became balanced and were eventually coequal with various tactical uses of alternative media. And from this new blending of voices something else happened to the idea of organizing: the forces of domination and the forces of resistance *merged* and became virtually indistinguishable. *By campaign's end, all media was infomedia; all entertainment was infotainment.*

The winner was not democratic balance, nor coequality of voices, but instead the deeper *incorporation* of the struggle by the interests that do, indeed, control the narrative and cultural resources and sites of the political struggle: corporate media. The frame became large enough to accommodate the marketing of those conservative, middling, liberal, and even third-party interests that supported the idea of differences as long as those differences could be incorporated—organized—as meaningful resources for the grander productions and consumptions—advertisements, slogans, products, services—supporting capitalism. This is because capitalism tolerates—even promotes—any form of cultural and political expression that can be converted into capital itself; what it will *not* tolerate is any form of cultural and political expression that threatens the very foundations upon which its power depends. As Michael Ventura suggests, it is the radical who is disenfranchised from voting for Bill Clinton, not the conservative or liberal or mushy middler.

In this campaign—Bill Clinton's "radical" campaign for and about change—ironically, it was the voice of the radical that was effectively—corporately—silenced. In the end, the winner was a mainstream campaign that produced and spent the most money, that garnered the broadest popular appeal by promoting dialogues that were media sanctioned, often simply by being media covered, that remained symbolically and strategically ambiguous in its endless somnambulent detailing of subnumbered plans, and that put on the best and longest-running media show to the widest possible collectivity of nomadic audiences. What this campaign for change organized—and organized successfully—were cultural resources in the spirit of capitalism for the political moving of our wills.

What the uses of alternative media accomplished was the shaping—

the conceptual and pragmatic framing—of America's public imagination. This name for a really nameless thing—"the American public imagination"—is actually a discursive surface that acts—or maybe just wants to be treated like—a series of deep structures. Where it exists is in the blurred boundaries between and among persons and media; what it traffics in is the currency of symbolic expressions. The American public imagination is, therefore, a kind of vast, contested, dialogic territory where symbolic meanings are read into symbolic gestures, a no-place that exists precisely nowhere but is treated, in virtual realities, as if it is everywhere and maybe all there is.

Imagination is a blending of disparate elements or ideas. It may be biology and art, or physics and drugs, or even rock n roll and politics. Regardless of origin, to capture the American public imagination at the end of the twentieth century is necessarily to become a media star; to become a really big media star—a superstar—is to serve as a gravitational force capable of pulling together diverse cultural resources to fill the quark of large public addictions; to become a major resource for large cultural addictions through media superstardom is to end up as either a rock idol, a professional athlete, a movie icon, a best-selling author, a talk-show host, a utility celebrity, or president of the United States. Considered from this vantage, perhaps the last category—at least in this election—required at least mediated participation in all the other categories as well: Clinton as Elvis, Clinton as jogger, Clinton as "The Man from Hope," Clinton as author of his paperback plan, Clinton as host to town-hall meetings and guest on all the daytime, afternoon, evening, and late-night talk shows; ultimately Bill Clinton, president-elect of the United States of America.

My analysis necessarily implicated my writing method. I organized this interpretive assessment as a highly personalized rock n roll text of cultural and media fragments I perceived as significant in the 1992 presidential election process. My focus was on uses of alternative media in the campaign defined *intertextually* to include the circulation of images, sounds, words, silences, and imagination in popular culture and everyday speech. I arranged theoretical statements as the textually mediated equivalent of political/corporate advertisements—the conceptual frameworks that both sponsor and inform our viewing, our listening, our reading—that shape and refine popular (and scholarly) cultural tastes and habits.

Throughout this presentation of events and interpretation, I combined traditional and nontraditional writing with textual design strategies; the inclusion of quotations, excerpts, lyrics, and ambiguity were attempts to create purposefully intertextual voices for the evocation of cultural and narrative complexities inherent to my analysis. To deconstruct infotainment is to approach it, to evoke it, out of its own terms. As rhetorical critic Michael McGee argues, the first task of a rhetorical critic of postmodern culture is to *invent* a text worthy of criticism out of the fragments of the culture being experienced and observed.[39] The point of textual invention is not to claim representative coverage of events or "reality"—or even to suggest that the events, moments, gestures, and practices I pointed to as significant "really" were—but instead to evoke, provoke, and otherwise engage readers in an evolving, complex dialogue about possible ways in which formations of cultural resources converge, divide, haunt, and align in the cultural production and consumption of media in this presidential campaign.

Which brings me back, finally, to my choice of title. "Living in the Rock n Roll Campaign" may strike some readers as misleading; after all, I did not "live" in the War Room during the campaign. For me, the experiential boundaries of mediated life do not begin with the known borders of physical contexts, but with their interplays in symbolic ones. As Kenneth Gergen notes, in a postmodern culture we are "saturated" with mediated symbols and surrounds,[40] an argument that ups the ante considerably on Kenneth Burke's phrase about humans being "the symbol-using (and abusing) animals," although Burke himself told me once that the most ignored important concept in the corpus of his work was the idea that symbols also use (and abuse) us.[41]

Either way, to define humans as symbolic constructors and constructions is to reframe the idea of context in ways that call into question traditional notions of "beginnings and endings" of talk and actions. Privileging the merely physical seems to miss the point of the symbolics of communication, as well as to deny the inherent social (read: dialogic) construction of realities. So I won't do that. Put simply, postmodern surfaces are infinitely permeable and definitively punctuated by mediated selves.

So it is that I "lived" in the rock n roll mystery of this mediated campaign. From it I take away a new sense of the media/politics/corporate interests formulation, as well as a different perspective on the role of popular media in political rituals. From the writing of this essay I take away a renewed appreciation for the old General Semantics idea that "the map is not the territory," which should be read here as "this essay is not this campaign." What I have done, and what I think the Clinton campaign did, was to create a series of permeable surfaces that punctuated opportunities for personal interpretation. This essay, therefore, about "reframing" is analogically similar to Bill Clinton's campaign for "change." To accomplish this essay as worthy of a place in a presidential book—or the events of a campaign as being worthy of a presidential victory—means to incorporate the lyrical sentiments and images of seemingly disparate, mostly nomadic users of symbolic cultural resources into the overall narrative rhythms of a popular song.

NOTES

1. Jean Baudrillard, *Seduction* (New York: St. Martin's Press, 1990), 174.

2. Bill Clinton campaign slogan.

3. Victor Turner, *The Ritual Process* (Ithaca, N.Y.: Cornell University Press, 1966), 95.

4. Jean Baudrillard, *The Ecstacy of Communication* (New York: Semiotext[e], 1988).

5. Kenneth Burke, *Symbols in Society*, ed. Joseph Gusfield (Chicago: University of Chicago Press, 1989), 49.

6. Kenneth Gergen, *The Saturated Self* (New York: Basic Books, 1991), 84.

7. Walt Whitman, *Leaves of Grass*, ed. S. Bradley and H. Blodgett (New York: Norton, 1973).

8. Talcott Parsons and Edward Shils, *Working Papers in the Theory of Action* (New York: Free Press, 1953), 179.

9. James Hillman and Michael Ventura, *We've Had One Hundred Years of Psychotherapy and the World Is Getting Worse* (San Francisco: HarperSanFrancisco), 17.

10. Sigmund Freud, cited in ibid.,17.

11. Morris Zapp, quoted in David Lodge, *Small World* (London: Secker and Warburg, 1984), 29.

12. Gergen, *The Saturated Self*, 173.

13. Sami Ma'ari, cited in ibid., 174.

14. Avital Ronell, *Crack Wars: Literature, Addiction, Mania* (Lincoln: University of Nebraska Press, 1992), 78.

15. Paul Virilio, cited in Celeste Olalquiaga, *Megalopolis: Contemporary Cultural Sensibilities* (Minneapolis: University of Minnesota Press, 1992), 1.

16. Jacques Derria, "Rhetorique de la drogue," quoted in Ronell, *Crack Wars*, 78.

17. *U.S. News and World Report*, 27 July 1992, 34, 38.

18. Olalquiaga, *Megalopolis*, xix.

19. Tom Burns, *Erving Goffman* (New York: Routledge, 1992), 272.

20. Turner, *The Ritual Process*, 96.

21. Matthew Cooper, *U.S. News and World Report*, 7 December 1992, 38.

22. Turner, *The Ritual Process*, 96.

23. Sigmund Freud, cited in H. L. Goodall Jr., *Living in the Rock n Roll Mystery: Reading Context, Self, and Others as Clues* (Carbondale: Southern Illinois University Press, 1991), 53.

24. Clifford Geetz, *Local Knowledge* (New York: Basic Books, 1983), 34.

25. Baudrillard, *The Ecstasy of Communication*, 122.

26. Norman Denzin, *Interpretive Interactionism* (Newbury Park, Calif.: Sage, 1986), 196.

27. *U.S. News and World Report*, 27 July 1992, 4.

28. Charles Paul Freund, "Virtual Politics," *Outlook*, August 1992.

29. Eric M. Eisenberg and H. L. Goodall Jr., *Organizational Communication: Balancing Creativity and Constraint* (New York: St. Martin's Press, 1993), 32.

30. Al Gore, speech to the Democratic National Convention, New York City, July 1992.

31. Mimi White, *Tele-Advising: Therapeutic Discourse in American Television* (Chapel Hill: University of North Carolina Press, 1992), 13.

32. Joli Jensen, *Redeeming Modernity* (Newbury Park, Calif.: Sage, 1990), 77.

33. Discussed in Eisenberg and Goodall, *Organizational Communication*, chapter 4.

34. Turner, *The Ritual Process*, 128.

35. Michael Ventura, "Blessed Are the Slick," *Los Angeles Weekly*, 30 October–5 November 1992, 10.

36. Turner, *The Ritual Process*, 128.

37. H. L. Goodall Jr., *Courtship as a Rhetorical Form: The Interpersonal Communication of F. Scott and Zelda Fitzgerald* (dissertation, Pennsylvania State University, 1980), 143.

38. George Lipsitz, *Time Passages: Collective Memory and American Popular Culture* (Minneapolis: University of Minnesota Press, 1990).

39. Michael McGee, "Text, Context, and the Fragmentation of Contemporary Culture," *Western Journal of Speech Communication* 54 (1990): 274–89.

40. Gergen, *The Saturated Self*, 7.

41. Kenneth Burke, "Definition of Man," in Gusfield, *Symbols in Society*.